Learning and Teaching
in the Elementary School

Learning and Teaching
in the Elementary School

KENNETH H. HOOVER
Arizona State University

PAUL M. HOLLINGSWORTH
University of Nevada

Allyn and Bacon, Inc.   **Boston, Mass.**

Library of Congress Card Number: 70–89868

Printed in the United States of America

Table of Contents

Chapter 1 • **The Elementary School Child: His Unique Self** 1
The Child Grows Up, 2. Needs and Tasks of
the Elementary School Child, 8. Summary, 15.
Questions for Study and Discussion, 15. Selected
Bibliography, 16.

Chapter 2 • **Modifying Behavior: The Learning Process** 17
Basic Considerations for Learning, 18. Factors
Affecting Learning, 22. Summary, 30. Ques-
tions for Study and Discussion, 30. Selected
Bibliography, 31.

Chapter 3 • **Gaining the Concept: Analytical and Intuitive
Thought** 32
Concept Formation, 33. Processes of Concept
Formation, 39. Summary, 47. Questions for
Study and Discussion, 48. Selected Bibliography,
48.

UNIT ONE • **SETTING THE STAGE FOR INSTRUCTION** 49

Chapter 4 • **Establishing Instructional Direction: Aims and
Purposes** 51
The Nature of Instructional Goals, 53. Functional Goal Relationships, 58. Goal Formulation, 63. Problems and Principles Associated

with Instructional Goals, 67. Summary, 72.
Questions for Study and Discussion, 72. Selected
Bibliography, 73.

Chapter 5 • The Framework for Instruction: Long- and Short-
Range Planning   74
The Teaching Unit, 76. The Lesson Plan, 89.
General Problems and Principles in Planning, 92.
Summary, 93. Questions for Study and Discus-
sion, 94. Selected Bibliography, 95.

Chapter 6 • Activating the Desire to Learn: Encouraging Self-
Motivation   96

Bases of Motivation, 97. General Problems and
Principles in Motivation, 111. Summary, 116.
Questions for Study and Discussion, 117. Se-
lected Bibliography, 118.

UNIT TWO • EFFECTIVE GROUP METHODS   119

Chapter 7 • Encouraging Reflective Thought: Discussion Activities   121
Guided Class Discussion, 122. Panel Discussion,
135. Problems and Principles in Discussion, 147.
Summary, 149. Questions for Study and Discussion, 149. Selected Bibliography, 150.

Chapter 8 • Improving Social Relationships: Sociometry, Dramatic Play, and Role Playing   151
Sociometry, 152. The Dramatic Play Experience,
160. Problems and Principles Associated with
Improving Social Relationships, 172. Summary,
179. Questions for Study and Discussion, 179.
Selected Bibliography, 180.

Chapter 9 • The Cooperative Experience: Teacher-Pupil Planning   181
Democratic Foundations of Cooperative Learn-
ing, 182. An Illustrated Model of Cooperative
Learning, 190. General Problems and Principles
in Teacher-Pupil Planning, 197. Summary, 202.

Questions for Study and Discussion, 202. Selected Bibliography, 203.

Chapter 10 • **Personalizing Instruction: The Challenge of Individual Differences**   **204**
Assessing and Analyzing Individual Differences, 205. A Suggested Model for Classroom Grouping, 213. Creative Differences in Children, 222. Problems and Principles in Meeting Individual Differences, 226. Summary, 228. Questions for Study and Discussion, 229. Selected Bibliography, 230.

UNIT THREE • **SOME EMERGENT INSTRUCTIONAL PATTERNS**   **231**

Chapter 11 • **Individualizing Instruction: Programmed Learning and Self-Instructional Devices**   **234**
Programmed Learning, 236. Self-Instructional Devices, 247. Problems and Principles Involved in Programmed Learning and Self-Instructional Devices, 250. Summary, 256. Questions for Study and Discussion, 257. Selected Bibliography, 257.

Chapter 12 • **Changing School Organization: The Ungraded School**   **259**
Ungraded School, 260. Suggested Model for an Ungraded Primary, 265. Problems and Principles in an Ungraded School, 273. Summary, 275. Questions for Study and Discussion, 276. Selected Bibliography, 277.

UNIT FOUR • **COPING WITH PERSISTENT INSTRUCTIONAL PROBLEMS**   **279**

Chapter 13 • **Assessing Learning Experiences: Measuring Instruments, Evaluation and Reporting Procedures** **282**
Techniques of Measurement and Evaluation, 283. Use of Report Cards, 301. Functions and Principles of an Effective Program, 304. Summary, 307. Questions for Study and Discussion, 308. Selected Bibliography, 308.

Chapter 14 • **Maintaining Effective Class Control: Discipline
                  Problems**   **310**
                  Discipline Problems, 311. Problems and Prin-
                  ciples in Handling Discipline, 327. Summary,
                  329. Questions for Study and Discussion, 330.
                  Selected Bibliography, 331.

Chapter 15 • **Directing Study: Assignments, Guided Study, and
                  Homework**   **332**
                  The Assignment, 333. Guided Study Activities,
                  339. Homework, 344. General Principles Asso-
                  ciated with Study Activities, 347. Summary, 349.
                  Questions for Study and Discussion, 349. Se-
                  lected Bibliography, 350.

Chapter 16 • **Enhancing Learning: Audio-Visual Materials and
                  Resources**   **351**
                  The Need for Audio-Visual Materials and Re-
                  sources, 351. Uses and Problems Associated with
                  Certain Audio-Visual Materials and Resources,
                  358. Some Sources of Audio-Visual Materials,
                  370. General Principles and Functions in Using
                  Audio-Visual Materials and Resources, 373. Sum-
                  mary, 375. Questions for Study and Discussion,
                  376. Selected Bibliography, 377.

Index   • **378**

Preface

EDUCATION in an era of mechanization and space exploration is being challenged as never before. No longer can the school remain complacent, relying on historical precedent alone. The school must equip the child to direct his own learning. Above all, the school must help the child *learn how to learn*. This book is designed to assist the teacher as he guides the learning experiences of elementary school pupils. It is based on the premise that thinking is the key to educational method. What, then, is the proper role of the teacher? His function is to work with pupils in the appropriate selection, organization, and evaluation of those classroom experiences which will facilitate sound thinking. His function is to help the learner grow and develop.

For many decades there has been a controversy over subject matter preparation versus methods of teaching. Some teachers maintain that if one knows his subject matter he can teach it. Others feel that almost any educational feat can be accomplished if one is well grounded in teaching techniques. The argument becomes purely academic when learning is viewed as a process of cognitive thinking, as opposed to the older notion of learning as a process of knowledge acquisition. If one is to teach, he must teach *something*. Adequate subject matter background in itself, however, offers no guarantee of effective teaching. Just as the child needs guidance in his problem-solving experiences, so does the teacher—who is also a learner—need guidance in the establishment of a proper environment for learning. Learning is enhanced when certain psychological principles of learning are applied appropriately. Their application, however, varies from one situation to the next. In this book the application of such principles is called *methods* and/or *techniques of teaching*.

Chapters 1, 2, and 3 treat the foundations of learning. In Chapter 1 attention is directed toward the elementary school pupil. The elementary school child is in transition from home to school. The child at this age has certain basic needs that must be satisfied and developmental tasks that he must accomplish if future teaching techniques are to be effective. Chapter 2 describes the learning process and certain psychological principles that aid the learning process. The goals of instruction and the thought processes involved in attaining those goals are discussed in Chapter 3.

The remaining thirteen chapters are divided into four major units: Setting the Stage for Instruction; Effective Group Methods; Some Emergent Instructional Patterns; and Coping with Persistent Instructional Problems.

A good teacher *plans* for teaching. After weighing all the known factors associated with his particular pupils, he decides a plan of approach which, in his judgment, will be most effective in accomplishing the goals of instruction. Although children themselves frequently will become involved in the planning of their own learning experiences, the teacher will want to plan for this and other experiences *in advance*. Establishing instructional direction, long- and short-range planning techniques, and techniques of motivation are treated in Unit One.

Units Two and Three deal with various methods and techniques used in classroom instruction. Chapters 7 through 12 (Units Two and Three) offer systematized approaches to the use of ten different teaching methods.

Unit Four treats a number of persistent problems associated with instructional procedures. Assessing learning experiences, handling discipline problems, directing study activities, and using instructional materials and resources all are interwoven with instructional technique. The person who is unable to cope with these problems can hardly become an effective teacher. Consequently, they have been singled out for intensive investigation.

Each chapter is divided into two or three parts: 1) a theoretical and psychological basis for the method or technique (when appropriate); 2) an explicit description of the method(s) and/or techniques involved; and 3) an analysis of general problems and principles involved. Thus the book is designed to be used in classes which combine curriculum and instructional practices. It should also serve as a supplementary text in curriculum classes.

The methods and techniques described in this book are based on classroom research. The preparation of the book is an outgrowth of the authors' experience at the elementary, junior high, senior high, and college levels of instruction. Several hundred college students have read the manuscript; observed and participated in demonstrations; applied the methods and techniques in simulated teaching situations; and, finally, have successfully used the methods and techniques in their own classrooms. To these students the writers wish to express their gratitude and appreciation.

To the many professional colleagues who have rendered indirect assistance for this volume we are grateful. Recognition must be given to Helene Perry Hoover and Colleen Black Hollingsworth, the authors' wives, who have contributed their professional guidance in the preparation of this book.

Kenneth H. Hoover
Paul M. Hollingsworth

The Elementary School Child:
His Unique Self

THE classroom was buzzing with children's chatter in anticipation of the day's activities, as Miss Bale entered the classroom. In these few minutes prior to the routine of opening exercises for the school day, Miss Bale enjoyed observing the children in her first grade. She was reminded how different and unique each of her pupils was and yet how similar they were in general aspects of growth and development.

In anticipating the day's activities Miss Bale wondered, "Will each child fully respond and enjoy the learning activities today? Have I made ample plans to meet the needs of each child?" Her thoughts were interrupted by the loudspeaker signalling the beginning of the formal school day.

Miss Bale's experience could be multiplied by as many teachers as exist in the elementary school classrooms throughout the country. She is an excellent teacher who enjoys her responsibility of guiding children in a wide variety of learning activities. Her enthusiasm and indeed the enthusiasm of each child generates the spark and excitement of learning and teaching in the elementary school.

This book is written to aid the teacher to develop the proper relationship between learning and teaching in the elementary school. Before one can teach well, he must understand the child he may teach. Indeed, all instructional methods and techniques begin and end with the child. A basic premise of this book is that successful instructional practices are dependent upon perceptions of the learner *at the time of their applications*. None of the methods and techniques to be described will work at all times under *all* conditions. Indeed, no one method is likely to be equally effective in all classes for each child. The uncontrolled variable is always the child. Not only is he changing from moment to moment, but he is continually interacting with his peers.

THE CHILD GROWS UP

The child does not enter the elementary school at age five or six with a blank mind to have stamped into it appropriate modes of behavior. He comes to school with a wide array of preschool experiences. The diverse facets of his environment during the preschool years should have prepared him for the rigors of school life. The teacher must capitalize upon these previous learnings as a basis for elementary instruction.

From the moment of birth until maturity is reached, the child is growing and changing. Growth is a process of transformations. It is sequential, orderly and progressive. Nevertheless, each child has his own unique pattern of growth.

What growth pattern is evident during the preschool years?

To the pre-school child, his affectional family relationships are of primary importance in promoting his sense of security and in forming his self-concept. Only when he is made to feel that he is a valuable and desired member of the family group can he learn to have self-respect and to feel worthy. If he has an adequate home environment, the child becomes confident, outgoing, and begins to form a positive, strong image of himself. During these early years, the two most important factors contributing to the formation of an optimum personality in the developing child are the *love* of a key affectionate adult and the *time* devoted to the child by this adult.

When the child joins a neighborhood group, he takes a step away from the restricted family circle. The pre-school child learns a great deal through such peer relationships. He gains more certainty of his own worth and at the same time gains a better realization of the rights of others. For the first time his authority-dominated culture is replaced by the social code of the peer group. Playing with other children sets the foundation of social togetherness that will aid the child later in life as he enters larger social groups, especially the school. During this early childhood period, the young child responds increasingly to the impact of cultural influences.

The intellectual growth of the pre-school child is manifested in the various mental activities in which he is involved. His vocabulary is increasing rapidly as words become instruments for designating concepts, ideas, and relationships. Increases in vocabulary size or the length of sentences are only one basis for assessing the child's capacity and ability to communicate. During this period of growth, he not only acquires more words, but he learns to use them in a more efficient and flexible way.

The environment in which the child is raised is a most significant factor in the growth and development of intelligence. The growth of intelligence is dependent upon a stimulating environment and a creative relationship with the child's parents. The child must be encouraged to make choices, become independent in his thinking, to solve his own problems, and to ask questions. Intelligence will not develop without opportunity in the environment. The pre-school child does not learn to be verbal nor to think if he has no opportunity to be among people who do these things. His numerous and varied questions reflect a desire to clear up confusion and to order experiences.

An important function of the developing child during pre-school years is to establish readiness for learning by perfecting basic skills, enlarging social experience, and becoming aware of himself as one person among others. The desire to become an independent personality or self begins early in life and apparently never ceases.

What are the developments of growth during the middle childhood years?

The five- to eight-year-old experiences three basic developmental thrusts: 1) a physical thrust into a world of games which requires new skills; 2) a social thrust from the home into the peer group; 3) a mental thrust into a world full of adult concepts.

The middle childhood years are characterized by several basic needs. The child needs adults who will give him direction and regulation and a clear-cut understanding of appropriate behavior. He has a strong need for security. Knowing what is expected of him contributes to his feeling of security. The teacher must let him assume an appropriate amount of responsibility in accordance with mental, physical, and social maturity. It is also important that key adults help him to identify with the appropriate sex role. These adults must treat the child in such a manner that he feels respected and liked for what he is. It is important for him to have play space and materials, since play is the work of children. It is through play that the child learns about society and the various roles expected of him. Since this is the age of early formal education, the child should receive an introduction to education which will not arouse hostility. Thus, teachers and parents should exemplify a love for learning and enjoyment for a task from which something is learned. The three most important elements which teachers should give to these children are love, understanding and intellectual stimulation.

By age five, handedness is usually well-established and the teacher can tell which hand the child favors for writing. The child approaches tasks with his dominant hand. He does not readily transfer a pencil to the free hand. Handedness should not be changed by the teacher.

At the beginning of this period of growth, the child is almost continuously active, whether he is standing or sitting. Toward the end of the period, however, movements of the eight-year-old have become fluid and graceful. He has developed poise. In fact, he is continually on the go; jumping, running, chasing, or wrestling. There is an increase of speed and smoothness in fine motor movements. He approaches objects rapidly and smoothly, and releases them with sure abandon.

Love is one of the basic emotional needs of a child. He gets this love first through home and family. In the middle childhood years the child leaves the home to enter the new world of school and friends. He will be better prepared for this adjustment if he has had love and security at home. During the years from five to eight the child must learn to make friends. One who has had love at home will be able to make friends easier than one who has had little or no love at home.

Each year, as the child grows older, he is given more opportunities in school, church, and different community organizations for contacts with other people, especially children of his own age and level of ability. As a result, there is a gradual increase in social participation throughout the middle childhood years. As he gains more social experiences at school and with peers, his friends become an influential factor in child development and will have a marked impact on later personality development. One of the most important peer group influences is independence from parents as he becomes an individual in his own right. Through associations with peers, the child learns to think independently, to make his own decisions, to accept points of views and values not shared with his family, and to learn forms of behavior approved by the group to which he belongs.

During the middle childhood years, some children dislike experiencing new situations by themselves. They may be afraid of school work because they do not always know how to start. They may be shy and afraid their peers may laugh at them or at their mistakes. Group work for these children is most beneficial.

During the primary grades most children learn to read, to write, and to do simple arithmetic. The child begins to understand the idea of symbolization, to differentiate between reality and the symbol, to develop categories, and to recognize likenesses as well as differences. There is a rapid rate of intellectual development but it is by no means steady.

At this age, interest in cause-and-effect relationships is high. The child is interested in natural phenomena like thunder, lightning and wind. He is beginning to understand the concepts of space and distance. He is interested in size and shapes. He seeks to add to knowledge previously acquired, and in so doing gradually develops knowledge which is organized and integrated.

At five all avenues of sensory reception are active media for discovery. Opportunities to try out all the sensory equipment in a vast variety of situations are essential. The child should be surrounded with all kinds of materials so that his experiences are rich and varied.

At the age of six, he "brings to the task of writing the same concentration and dedication of purpose that he brought to walking at an earlier age—if he is the one who initiates the writing." [1] He seeks to write his own name and works with his whole body. The six-year-old is extremely curious and eager to learn.

The seventh year reveals a trend toward realism, characterized by questions which have perspective and consistency. The child chooses to draw subjects from real life, and he dictates stories which are concerned with events recently experienced. He does not lose originality through such realistic endeavors, however, for he weaves a thread of emotional release and expression into the reconstructions of real life experiences.

At eight the child has built up a firm body of experience and increasingly is able to give as well as to receive information. He shows increased initiative and spontaneity in interacting with his environment.

In middle childhood years, the child becomes capable of reasoning about concrete objects. He begins to establish intellectually some major logical rules of size and shape. Also during these years the child's intellectual growth is reflected in his language development; however, his language does exhibit rather accurately the quality of language spoken in the home. The teacher must create an environment which will aid in continual intellectual growth for his pupils. This environment should be one in which the teacher exemplifies a love of learning, thereby stimulating his pupils to want to learn.

It is seen then that children from five to eight years of age need intellectually challenging experiences at their level of development. They also need intellectually successful and satisfying experiences. They

[1] Howard Lane and Mary Beauchamp, *Understanding Human Development* (Englewood Cliffs, N.J.: Prentice-Hall, Inc., 1959), p. 251.

need the opportunity to participate in creative experiences and in solving problems, as opposed to mere conformity to prescribed conditions and rules.

Many essentials are involved in the proper development of a child. During the middle childhood years, the child must overcome the social thrust of leaving home to go out into a world of peers, the physical thrust into a world of games and work requiring neuromuscular skills, and the mental thrust into the world of adult concepts, logic, symbolism, and communication. Because these years are a big adjustment, children need a firm foundation and continual guidance from the teacher.

How do children grow and develop during the later childhood years?

There are many definitions and descriptions of the later childhood years. This period has been called the "pre-adolescent" period of growth. It has also been referred to as a "stretch of no-man's land in child study work," [2] called "a strange state in which the child is neither fish nor fowl," [3] referred to as a "prelude to instability or reorganization" [4]; but all admit that it seems to be a bewildering stage of development. It is a period of transition from patterns of childhood to new interests and challenge.

A glance at children of this age group reveals one factor that stands out above all others! Children of this age vary widely. The group may be about the same age, even in the same grade, but there the similarities end. They vary widely in their size, interests, activities, and abilities, and these differences, in turn, influence every aspect of the child's development. The child himself, other children, parents, and teachers should realize that these differences are quite normal. Such an attitude minimizes many anxieties, problems, and misunderstandings, and contributes substantially to normal growth and development of personality.

This is a period of slow, steady physical growth until the time of the pre-adolescent spurt. Then the child seems to literally "shoot" upward. For boys the peak is usually at about age twelve or thirteen, but girls may reach their height a year or more earlier. The taller child seems to grow even faster during this phase. Girls are typically taller and heavier

---

[2] Morris Haimowitz and Natalie Haimowitz, *Human Development—Selected Readings*, 2nd Ed. (New York: Thomas Y. Crowell Co., 1966), p. 619.

[3] Helene S. Arnstein, "When and How to Let Go of Your Child," *Family Circle* (June, 1964), pp. 40–41.

[4] Ruth Strang, *An Introduction to Child Study* (New York: The Macmillan Company, 1959), pp. 371–414.

than boys; they are about a year ahead in physical development. This age group has good muscular control, general increase in strength, is particularly sturdy, keenly interested in sports, and acquires the skills for games readily. Watching them at play, one often wonders if they ever get tired. They actually have a lot of stamina. Arms grow longer, hands and feet bigger, the girls' hips and breasts enlarge, as the chest and shoulders develop in boys. Children at this stage are often clumsy and awkward, due to the uneven growth of the different body parts.

To be liked and accepted by his peer group is of vital importance to the pre-teen child. If he is accepted, every aspect of his development is simplified. The child who has known love from his earliest years will have little trouble giving affection and, in so doing, becoming accepted by his peers. This age is characterized by a sex cleavage; a real or apparent dislike of the opposite sex. Toward the end of the pre-adolescent years, however, the sexes are beginning to become conscious of, and more attracted to each other.

Intellectual development during the later childhood years is characterized by the tendency of the child to seek fuller information on matters in which he is less intensely involved than at an earlier time when he was asking questions about his own body structure and functioning and about the persons close to him. The child is curious about many things; he constantly wants information. He asks questions and wants answers that are truthful and make logical sense to him.[5] The pre-adolescent is a collector of facts as well as objects. The wise teacher will help him seek his own answers from whatever material is available. He can be encouraged in independent activities such as furthering his interests in science through experiments and invention. The skills in reading should allow the child to become less dependent upon adults for understanding his environment. This is a searching and inquiring time.

During the later childhood years, intellectual growth is characterized by the ability of the child to reason about hypotheses and to make conclusions without the aid of concrete objects. The pre-adolescent is able to combine mentally many rules, procedures, or steps in solving a problem. In the later childhood years his intellectual growth has reached a level at which he may reason and solve many problems mentally.

It takes an understanding teacher to cope with these children; they can present problems but they can be enjoyable too. He must praise them for individual improvements, set realistic goals, and provide opportunities for developing social skills through group participation. To a teacher,

[5] Harold W. Bernard, *Human Development in Western Culture* (Boston: Allyn and Bacon, Inc., 1966), p. 272.

these years are challenging, rewarding, and sometimes frustrating. They are deeply satisfying, however.

NEEDS AND TASKS OF THE ELEMENTARY SCHOOL CHILD

The elementary school child has various needs. He must continually adjust to an expanding environment. Adjustments to this environment will be necessary if he is to enjoy these years of learning. Many needs also will require satisfaction if he is to be a happy child and if he is to become a well-adjusted adult.

What are the basic needs of elementary school children?

The basic physiological and psychological needs of man have long been emphasized. They are common to all people in all societies. The avenues through which needs may be fulfilled, however, vary from one society to the next. Maslow [6] offers a thorough analysis of basic psychological needs which seems especially apropos to a study of children. He classifies four basic types of needs:

1. Safety needs

2. Belongingness and love needs

3. Esteem needs

4. Self-actualizing needs

Maslow believes that there is a hierarchy of need satisfaction. This he calls a prepotency of need fulfillment. Thus each physiological need (water, food, protection, sex, etc.) is satisfied systematically and in order of prepotency. One must, for example, satisfy his thirst before he can enjoy eating; likewise, protection is relatively unimportant to an extremely hungry person. In a similar manner, Maslow sees a prepotency of the psychological needs which emerges when the physiological needs are satisfied.

Safety needs are almost as prepotent as are the physiological needs

[6] Based on Abraham H. Maslow, *Motivation and Personality* (New York: Harper & Row, 1954), pp. 80–106.

and, for most individuals at least, are first satisfied at an early age. They include freedom from particularly threatening situations, such as falling. One strives for security and protection from life's major hazards. An indication of a child's need for safety is his preference for some kind of undisturbed routine. Maslow points out that young children seem to thrive better under a system of "permissiveness within limits" rather than the extremes of control or absence of control.

The belongingness and love needs, which emerge after the safety needs have been fairly well gratified, include the desire for affection, love, and a feeling of belonging. The family is suited to the fulfillment of these needs. According to Maslow, the thwarting of these needs is the most common source of maladjustment in our society.

The esteem needs in our society are represented by a person's desire for a "stable, firmly based, usually high evaluation" of himself. He needs *self-respect.* He needs to *achieve,* to feel *adequate* or competent, to have confidence enough to "face the world." At the same time the young child desires a favorable *status* or reputation to be bestowed upon him by others. Satisfaction of the self-esteem needs leads to feelings of personal worth, of adequacy, of being useful or necessary in the world.

The need for self-actualization, according to Maslow, is the highest of all the need groups. Even when all other needs are reasonably well fulfilled, a person is discontented and restless unless he is doing that for which he is best fitted. This desire for self-fulfillment, in essence, is the need to become what one is capable of becoming. This need may take many forms. In one child, for example, it may be the desire to become an ideal mother; in another it may be the desire to play ball.

Maslow cautions the reader against assuming that each set of needs must be completely gratified before the next emerges. As a matter of fact, most children are partially satisfied and partially unsatisfied in all their basic needs at the same time. However, a certain degree of fulfillment of the "lower" needs is essential before the individual can effectively concentrate upon the "higher" needs. Furthermore, a need cannot be fulfilled once and for all. A suitable environment for constant "recharging" is essential. It also is apparent that a number of needs often can be gratified in a single act.

How can the teacher help her pupils meet their basic needs?

The theory of need prepotency appears to be a very useful concept in understanding the elementary school child. The child who suddenly finds himself thrust into a new environment, from the home to the school, must now learn a new role. Thus he is disrupted from established routines of living. His *safety needs* are disrupted. He may become apprehensive about school life and changes from grade to grade as he moves through the primary, middle, and upper grades of the elementary school. In this new environment the family is no longer able to fully satisfy his *belonging and love needs*. He is eager to establish himself in the school setting with his teacher and peer group. Rejection by either his teacher or peer group may cause him to lose self-confidence and self-esteem. Failure in school in any one of his subjects may also cause him to lose self-respect or self-esteem. And of course, as he is growing up through the elementary school years he is seeking and making efforts toward *self-actualization*.

Juan was a good natured child in my fifth grade class. However, during lunch period he was not as hospitable as one might expect. He would slump down in his cafeteria seat and eat from his paper bag in such a way that not many of his classmates could see. I observed him carefully and noted that for lunch he had a raw potato and a dry slice of bread in his bag. After further checking, I learned that Juan's parents left early in the morning to pick fruit and he had to get his own breakfast and pack a lunch from whatever he could find in the house.

I mentioned my problem to the school nurse. Through the efforts of the school nurse, principal, and cafeteria manager, we were able to get a noon lunch job in the school cafeteria which made it possible for him to earn his lunch.

As the foregoing illustration suggests, a teacher must direct attention to even the most basic physiological need an individual possesses. A casual observation of a child's lunch or knowledge of what the child does during the lunch period will give clues to his nourishment needs. Likewise, a child may not be getting enough rest or sleep.

Safety needs also may be aided by a competent classroom teacher. If the teacher sets limits and regulations that are fair for each child and if he is consistent in administering these rules, then the child will feel comfortable and safe within the confines of the classroom. Consistency and fairness, however, are necessary. Threats, ridicule, and other such techniques will undermine the safety needs of the child.

Belonging and love needs may be achieved by helping the child become a wanted member of his peer group. The use of sociometric devices (described in Chapter 8) will give the teacher an understanding of the social structure of the class. With thoughtful grouping the teacher will be able to help the child cope with these particular needs. In analyzing individual needs of belonging and love, the teacher should check his own attitudes toward the isolated or neglected child. Many times a child's rejection by the teacher is felt by the child's peers. They, in turn, reflect the teacher's attitudes in peer group relations. Indeed, the teacher should check his attitude manifestations toward all of his pupils.

Once the child gains acceptance among the peer group, he begins to have self-respect and feel confident and adequate in attacking new problems. A teacher can help greatly in this area by teaching the child at his level of achievement, thereby assisting the child to achieve success in schoolwork. The esteem needs are then filled as the child develops feelings of self-worth, adequacy and of being able to succeed. Love and understanding are vital and necessary ingredients for good teaching and proper learning.

What are the developmental tasks of the elementary school child?

As an individual grows and matures he passes through certain physical and psychological stages of living. He must adapt to numerous body changes, for example. Physical growth, in turn, brings about certain society-imposed expectations, such as learning to read and to write. Along with these forces is the evolution of personal values and aspirations—one's emerging personality. Personality development, then, reflects the unique interaction of physical and psychological forces. The school plays a very important part in setting the stage for the development of a healthy personality.

An extremely useful approach to the desirable growth patterns of children has been developed by Havighurst. His "developmental tasks of life" are tasks which Havighurst believes an individual must learn if he is to be judged and to judge himself as a reasonably happy and successful person.

A developmental task is a task which arises at or about a certain period in [the] life of the individual, successful achievement of which leads to his happiness and to success with later tasks, while failure leads to unhappiness in the individual, disapproval by the society, and difficulty with later tasks.[7]

The developmental tasks of the elementary school child are:

1. Learning physical skills necessary for ordinary games.

---

[7] Robert J. Havighurst, *Developmental Tasks and Education* (New York: David McKay Co., Inc., 1962), p. 2.

2. Building wholesome attitudes toward oneself as a growing organism.

3. Learning to get along with age-mates.

4. Learning an appropriate masculine or feminine social role.

5. Developing fundamental skills in reading, writing, and calculating.

6. Developing concepts necessary for everyday living.

7. Developing conscience, morality, and a scale of values.

8. Achieving personal independence.

9. Developing attitudes toward social groups and institutions.[8]

It is evident that developmental tasks of the elementary school child are not only complicated but important. They might be considered the basic dimensions around which all the child's behavior revolves. Developmental tasks, then, are factors which greatly affect the basic need structure of the individual.

How does the teacher help children achieve developmental tasks?

Through play activities at recess, noon, or during class time, a teacher can help children become more proficient in skills for ordinary games. "The acquisition of physical skills needed in ordinary games involves much more than physical maturation. It is a matter intimately tied to social adjustment." [9] A child who is socially comfortable with other children will try and try until he can participate without ridicule from others. The teacher needs to help the child feel socially comfortable in the area of games. This developmental task is actually enhanced when facilities, equipment, and play space are made available for children. The modern concept in school planning does provide space and many facilities for this purpose. In fact, in school plant planning, the ground areas for play become a very important area for the architect's drawing board.

In the achievement of the second developmental task, the teacher becomes a key individual in helping a child build a wholesome attitude toward himself. The teacher may help the child in developing this attitude when he helps the child feel he is a worthy member in the classroom. This can be done by giving each child responsibility at his level

---

[8] *Ibid.*, pp. 15–28.
[9] Bernard, *op. cit.*, p. 254.

of development. This can also be enhanced when the teacher instructs the child at his level of achievement; thus insuring success and accomplishment for the child.

Learning to get along with age-mates is an aspect of socialization which should occur in the classroom, at school and in neighborhood groups. Social groups based upon sociometric techniques discussed in Chapter 8 will help. However, the teacher must help the child with various daily routines and problems of adjustment to other children in his classroom. The classroom teacher can help by affording many opportunities for social contacts in and out of the classroom.

The developmental task of learning an appropriate masculine or feminine social role implies that the child will identify with peers of the same sex. The school can do much to aid children in this task. Schools should provide teachers, male or female, who will encourage male and female development through activities and books. Boys need more stories and books about heroism, courage, and sports. Their teachers need to be less afraid of dirt, frogs, snakes, and tools, such as hammers and saws. The school must also avoid pressuring the child into social relationships. Social dancing in the upper grades, for example, may pressure children into social relationships which the children may not desire at this particular time.

Developing fundamental skills in reading, writing, and computation is another important developmental task that can be aided greatly in the schoolroom. In this particular task physical readiness is very important. The teacher must be sure the child's muscles and nerves have developed sufficiently to be ready for writing; also, the eyes must be sufficiently coordinated to achieve the skill of sweeping over lines of print. In addition, mental growth sufficient for success in reading is essential.[10] Individual differences are very important considerations. All too often, early introduction into reading, writing and computations, along with pressures to conform to adult expectations and pressure to keep up with the rate of development of other children, has resulted in frustrated children. A significant way to help children is to work at their level of development and achievement, moving the child along at his own speed and rate for learning. Good school programs will gear instruction to individual capacities, by providing for writing and listening opportunities, by class discussions, by reading together as well as separately for one's own enjoyment, by supplementing the textbook with field trips, educational TV, resource people, and dramatic play activities. It is also important to realize that girls are usually more fully developed

[10] *Ibid.*, p. 260.

than boys of the same age. For example, the fact that the girls' small muscles are more developed than boys' could make them better writers and readers and aid in other school activities.

Concepts necessary for everyday living can be developed each day in the classroom. Through social studies many concepts for living can be formed. Also, througout the school day, the children, living together in social groups, will develop concepts for social living, such as getting along with one another, learning to take turns, and other social graces. Group roles and responsibilities are important academic aspects of social functioning which can be developed within the classroom.

The development of a conscience, morality, and a scale of values is certainly not restricted to the elementary school years. It begins in infancy and continues into adult life. The teacher needs to help the child realize that he does a certain task or acts a certain way because he ought to do it rather than because he must do the task. If the child is helped to feel worthy and establishes a desirable self-image, then moral codes will be internalized, thus becoming his conscience. Adequate love, affection, and understanding by the teacher will greatly influence the child in achieving morality and values.

In achieving personal independence the teacher may assist the child by minimizing adult supervision and organization on the school grounds. A child also may achieve personal independence through such activities as swimming instruction, music lessons, and scouting activities. In assisting the child in this developmental task, Bernard points out: "It is a fine line of balance which the key adult must maintain—some freedom, some direction, and some authority." [11] The teacher as a key adult figure will still need to direct some of the child's activities, yet also give the child an opportunity to function on his own.

Relating oneself to social groups and institutions is a developmental task common to children in all age groups. The child's attitudes toward these groups and institutions is greatly affected by the attitudes that the child's parents, teachers and peer group have toward these same groups and institutions. Proper attitudes may be developed by keeping the lines of communication open between teacher and child. Such communication can foster clearer understanding of social groups and institutions.

Through the efforts of an elementary school teacher, a child may successfully achieve the developmental tasks for his age group. If the child succeeds in this achievement he will be a happy, developing child in the classroom. If he is unsuccessful, the child will feel failure and

[11] *Ibid.*, p. 279.

disapproval by his peers and society in general. If a child is to learn well in his elementary school years, the teacher must not only be aware of the developmental task, but he will need to assist the child in many ways in the classroom, on the playground, and in social relationships generally.

SUMMARY

In building a foundation for instructional practices attention is directed toward the child. A teacher must understand children, their growth and development as well as their needs and tasks before he can teach well. Each child is unique and progresses individually through the developmental tasks.

Every child is faced with various problems as he grows and develops. An understanding and interested teacher is able to assist the child with his specific needs and his achievement of specific developmental tasks. Developmental tasks and basic needs can be promoted in school by recognizing differences in ability and motivation for each child in the classroom and providing activities for the stimulation of growth in each area.

QUESTIONS FOR STUDY AND DISCUSSION

1. What are some problems of elementary school pupils which influence instructional practices? How would the need for teacher approval influence instructional procedures? Why must the elementary school teacher consider the purposes of formal education *as viewed by the pupils*?

2. Why is it important to study general growth patterns of children if each one is unique and different? What information should each teacher have concerning the children he will teach in school?

3. Visit a classroom and observe one child for a period of time. What basic needs are being met for this child in the classroom? What developmental tasks does he seem to have mastered? How might you as his teacher aid him with basic needs and tasks during the short time you observed?

4. Reread the basic needs. What other ways may a teacher in the classroom help the child meet his needs?

5. Review the developmental tasks. What other methods are available to the teacher in helping the child with these tasks?

SELECTED BIBLIOGRAPHY

Bernard, Harold W., *Human Development in Western Culture*, 2nd Ed. (Boston: Allyn and Bacon, Inc., 1966).

Department of Elementary School Principals, *Those First School Years* (Washington, D.C.: National Education Association, 1963).

Dinkmeyer, Don C., *Child Development: The Emerging Self* (Englewood Cliffs, N.J.: Prentice-Hall, Inc., 1965).

Haimowitz, Morris and Natalie Haimowitz, *Human Development—Selected Readings*, 2nd Ed. (New York: Thomas Y. Crowell Co., 1966).

Havighurst, Robert J., *Developmental Tasks and Education* (New York: David McKay Co., Inc., 1962).

Lane, Howard and Mary Beauchamp, *Understanding Human Development* (Englewood Cliffs, N.J.: Prentice-Hall, Inc., 1959).

Maslow, Abraham H., *Motivation and Personality* (New York: Harper & Row, Publishers, 1954).

Sears, Pauline S. and Vivian S. Sherman, *In Pursuit of Self-Esteem* (California: Wadsworth Publishing Co., 1964).

Strang, Ruth, *An Introduction to Child Study* (New York: The Macmillan Co., 1959).

Modifying Behavior:
The Learning Process

Mrs. Trump had reminded Billy for the sixth time that he was not to ride double on his bike. She had explained to him the chances for an accident. She had appealed to his concern for his bike by mentioning the possibility of overloading the bike with two riders. She had even told him he might ruin the tires on his bike. Not only did all this discussion take place, but Mrs. Trump had also required Billy to write down from memory the safety rules for riding bikes.

All this seemed to fall on deaf ears. As Mrs. Trump looked out her schoolroom window there were Billy and Kenneth riding double on Billy's bike again!!

What learning if any had taken place? Did Billy understand the safety rules? Why did Billy fail to abide by the rules Mrs. Trump had patiently given him? If Billy knew the bike safety rules, had learning taken place?

The teacher and the school are not the only influences upon the life of a child. Learning is not limited to the classroom. Children learn from peers, other adults, other institutions, and other experiences. The classroom teacher is responsible for helping the child adapt or change his behavior. Learning is reflected in a modification of behavior resulting from the interaction of a child with his environment. Knowing a rule is no guarantee that the child will obey the rule. However, when a person moves from not knowing a rule to knowing it, behavior has changed, his thought processes have been modified, and thinking is behaving.

BASIC CONSIDERATIONS FOR LEARNING

What actually happens when an individual learns? This question has been asked in many different ways for hundreds of years. Presumably, there is a restructuring of brain and nerve cells in such a way as to influence future behavior. This, then, gives rise to a subsequent question: What can be expected as a consequence of learning? This question is more meaningful, since behavior can be observed. In a democratic society the basic aim of education is the development of self-direction. It is hoped that the learner will become progressively more able to direct his own affairs.

Within such a framework *processes* of learning and thinking are emphasized. Although facts are basic to thinking, they do not guarantee productive or reflective thought. Pupils who solve problems possess the required facts and information. Not all possessors of factual materials, however, are able to arrive at the most appropriate solution to a problem. Rather than ends in themselves, facts become tools for the solution or decision demanded by the situation. The quality of problem solving, however, is somewhat determined by the starting point employed.

Basic to the thinking process are certain psychological processes which make learning possible. These processes, in a sense, provide a broad framework for instructional processes. When the results of an instructional procedure are disappointing, the source of the difficulty is usually traceable to misapplication of basic psychological principles. Although it is the rare teacher who can apply all the important psychological principles to his teaching situation, certain principles are essential if classroom experiences are to be worthwhile.

What is the nature of the learning process?

When facts are presented first the learning process often ceases; whereas, if problems are presented first, facts or information will be learned because of their applications to the problem. Thus, facts or content materials tend to become goal-directed or purposeful and the acquisition of these facts tends to serve as reinforcement for further learning. A textbook then becomes one of many sources of information, rather than the only source. Goal-directed learning tends to focus attention upon the learning *processes* along with *products* of learning. This type of learning generally has been described in terms of six major steps.

1. Formulation of the problem
2. Gathering relevant data (facts) and applying past experience
3. Synthesis and evaluation of the data
4. Formulation of the hypotheses
5. Examining the validity of each hypothesis
6. Reaching a decision
7. Verification of the validity of the decision.

While it is likely that most of these steps are involved in some way in meeting difficulties, this represents a logical arrangement rather than a psychological one. In all probability, problem solving begins, perhaps unconsciously, even before the problem is stated. The process may begin at any point in the so-called problem solving or cognitive sequence Indeed, a number of smaller problems often must be solved before a larger problem can be.

Some teachers tend to emphasize the mechanical processes of problem solving without involving pupils in the necessary cognitive processes. For instance, a teacher himself may formulate the problem; he may determine the methods or techniques to be followed; he may even go so far as to indicate the answer that is expected. The following anecdote is suggestive of some concomitants of such procedures.

As the pupils took their places in their class they found a problem sheet with complete directions for an activity. The purpose of the problem was stated, along with the procedure to be followed. In large letters across the bottom of the sheet was a detailed description of the expected results. Mayra was tired. Although she attempted to follow the printed directions her problem did not come out as expected. She quickly disposed of her materials, however, and made a record of the results—not as they actually were but as they "should have been." She saw no need to try to do the problem over again.

While few would question the need for development of problem solving techniques, there is sometimes a tendency to identify such an exercise as the equivalent of problem solving. Tyler [1] has suggested that

[1] Ralph W. Tyler, "Human Behavior," *National Education Association Journal*, October, 1955, pp. 426–429.

many teachers think of problem solving as merely the acquisition of answers to questions. When a question arises the pupil merely consults the authority or his writings for the answer. The teacher makes an assignment and the pupils do the problem by looking up the answers in books. Problem *doing* is described as dealing with routine, contrived situations, the solutions of which are foreordained. Instead of *concept seeking*, the problem *doing* type of activity involves mere *concept confirming*. It would seem as if the *creative act* of *resolving* issues would apply equally to all areas of investigation.

As a result of the deliberative (problem-solving) process the problem often comes as a sudden insight. For example, an individual may filter his observations, rearrange his facts, evaluate and re-evaluate the data before his problem suddenly becomes clear to him. The same applies to a solution of the problem. It may not be resolved until hours or even days after the completion of all formal activities.

In describing the central purpose of the school, the Educational Policies Commission recently clarified the importance of critical thinking as a basis for instruction when they said:

> The purpose which runs through and strengthens all other educational purposes—the common thread of education—is the development of the ability to think. This is the central purpose to which the school must be newly accentuated by recent changes in the world. To say that it is central is not to say that it is the sole purpose or in all circumstances the most important purpose, but that it must be a pervasive concern in the work of the school. Many agencies contribute to achieving educational objectives, but this particular objective will not be generally attained unless the school focuses on it. In this context, therefore, the development of every student's rational powers must be recognized as centrally important.[2]

The critical thinking (problem solving) processes then provide a fundamental basis for teaching. Accordingly, the various instructional procedures, techniques, and strategies developed in this book will be conceived within this framework.

How does readiness contribute to the learning process?

To every learning situation the pupil brings a variety of potential responses, concepts, opinions, and motives. These represent his repertoire of past experiences. To this must also be added his physical maturation. A pupil's readiness, then, is a combination of growth development

[2] Educational Policies Commission, *The Central Purpose of American Education* (Washington, D.C.: National Education Association, 1961), p. 12.

and experiences which prepares him to acquire a skill or understanding with economy.[3] Although learning readiness changes with each learning situation there are a number of factors which bear directly upon the problem. Among the more important are: [4]

1. *Physical and mental maturity and capacity.* One important aspect of readiness is physical in nature. Psychologists and teachers have long recognized the need for maturation if training is to be most productive. The development of skills by the elementary school child in motor skills, language, handwriting, reading skills, and in social skills depends upon readiness. In other areas of the curriculum as well, a child must have the readiness necessary before he can take the next step forward in effective learning.

Capacity for learning is a factor deserving utmost attention. In a typical elementary school classroom, scholastic aptitude will vary from the dull-normal to the intellectually gifted. While the majority will fall within an "average" range, it must be remembered that even small differences can have a tremendous impact upon a given learning situation. A teacher cannot expect all pupils to perform the same tasks in the same way. There are many experiences which, if adapted to the average, will be too difficult for the dull and not challenging, or even boring, to the bright pupils in class.

The utilization of class activities, then, must be adapted to a child's learning capacity. Research reading, for instance, is an especially useful method for the bright. Pupils that have the capacity usually enjoy searching out data, organizing, and analyzing it. Frequently they like to report these experiences verbally or in written form. Likewise, the assignment of topics for reports must be adapted to the individual. While all pupils can profit from a class discussion experience, the practice of asking the same type of question for all pupils in the class is questionable.

2. *Experiential background of the learner.* Each person brings his past experiences to bear upon the learning situation. His particular word meanings, study skills and habits, feelings of adequacy, a variety of specific needs, and so on have an important bearing upon his learning readiness. Thus the adequacy of past learning, to a great extent, will bear upon each new experience.

---

[3] Harold W. Bernard, *Human Development in Western Culture*, 2nd Ed. (Boston: Allyn and Bacon, Inc., 1966), p. 503.

[4] Lee J. Cronbach, *Educational Psychology*, 2nd Ed. (New York: Harcourt, Brace & World, Inc., 1963), Chapter 4.

Some teachers utilize pre-tests as a guide in assessing a child's experiential background. In this manner they attempt to identify those experiences which facilitate learning at the pupil's present stage of development. Pupils who have had little experience in directing their own learning experiences often have greater difficulty in following test directions than those who have had a more meaningful background in directing their own learnings. Pre-testing also might reveal such limitations as reading deficiency and comprehension, careless work habits, and mental malfunctions (blocks), all of which relate to one's experiential background. These and other such factors of readiness frequently demand careful, individual attention. Occasionally it may be necessary to refer such problems to the school psychologist or other qualified personnel.

3. *Motivation.* The word motivation is defined as an act or process of attaining an incentive or inducement to action. A vitally important psychological concept of readiness may be stated as follows: A *child learns only when he is motivated to learn.*[5] An experience must have personal meaning to the individual involved if learning is to occur. The teacher who would motivate pupils must consider the factors of readiness described in the foregoing, *in addition to* the particular needs and interests of those involved. As indicated earlier the motives of a child spring from the peer group, from home and school standards, from his desire to learn and to become independent of adults and from other things, such as the physical self. He is concerned with life—life as he is experiencing it. Likewise, formal education is concerned with life. The first task of the teacher is to help the child relate the two, thus establishing learning readiness.

FACTORS AFFECTING LEARNING

Factors that are related to the learning process are: reward, reinforcement, transfer, whole or part learning, knowledge of results, and repetition. Instructional methods and techniques contribute to learning as long as the methods and techniques are consistent psychological processes of learning. The specific aspects of each method or technique should be designed to provide direction for the most appropriate application

[5] Reprinted with permission of the publisher from Percival M. Symonds, *What Education Has to Learn from Psychology* (New York: Teachers College Press, copyright 1958, Teachers College, Columbia University), p. 1.

of various principles of learning. The psychological concepts which follow will influence the method or technique to be selected.

How does reward or reinforcement contribute to learning?

One of the most important conditions of learning is that of reward or reinforcement. According to many psychologists, *learning occurs* only when an act is reinforced or rewarded. Thorndike, in the early years of the present century, came close to the problem in his well known *law of effect:* "Of several responses made to the same situation, those which are accompanied or closely followed by satisfaction . . . will . . . be more . . . likely to recur. . . ." [6] Later psychologists showed that Thorndike's law of effect, in itself, was inadequate and must be supplemented by *purposeful* behavior.

It is believed that much school activity is wasteful and uneconomical because reinforcement or reward is not used effectively. To be effective, reinforcement must come within a few seconds, or a few minutes at most, after a response has been made; and the learning must be broken into steps which permit reinforcement of each stage of learning. Thus it tends to build a self-concept which is conducive to future learning. Reward is a feeling, a satisfying state of affairs. Rewards may be extrinsic or intrinsic. Although certain extrinsic rewards (grades, honor stickers, and the like) are effective, they are not as effective or lasting as such intrinsic rewards as the feeling of acceptance and approval. The ultimate aim, of course, is the learner's formation of his own reasonable standards of attainment—making reinforcement and reward an internal mechanism. The effective teacher will be quick to encourage and praise pupils as they progress toward goals.

The various teaching methods suggested in this book, to be most effective, must be consistent with the concept of reward or reinforcement. In some instances detailed suggestions are presented for this specific purpose. In the guided class discussion, emphasis is placed upon *approval* of correct answers and *acceptance* of all answers which pertain to the problem. In the approach to purely group-centered learning, emphasis is placed upon pupil *acceptance* of all ideas, whether one agrees with another's point of view or not. To illustrate: "I understand your idea, Jack, but I feel that. . . ." These and other such details are essentials if adequate reinforcement is to be supplied.

[6] E. L. Thorndike, *The Principles of Teaching* (New York: A. G. Seiler, 1906), p. 224.

A second aspect of reinforcement emphasizes the necessity of pupil reaction in learning. It is generally agreed that one learns what one does. In other words, one learns the acts which are performed, or the thoughts or feelings which are experienced.[7] Only by participating actively in the classroom activities can a pupil meet this requirement for learning. Basically learning is a process of reorganizing experience, i.e., solving problems, or engaging in reflective thought. Hearing the words of a teacher or "learning" the words in a book may not result in the reorganization of ideas or reflective thought necessary for learning. Pupil involvement is essential. Pupils must themselves personalize the educational experience. "Telling" or lecturing situations always run the risk of having little or no effect upon the pupil. The effect of the telling experience upon the learner is related to the communication skill of the teller, and the degree to which the listener is actively involved in conjuring up mental pictures and testing the ideas expressed by the speaker.

How do teaching techniques contribute to transfer of learning?

Concepts learned in the classroom must be applied to related out-of-school situations or other classroom situations. Frequently, however, the amount and kind of such application is disappointing. The classroom is a contrived situation designed to illustrate one (or at most, a few) applications. What type of classroom activities may contribute most to worthwhile applications of that which is learned? There have been at least three theories which warrant brief examination:

1. *The formal discipline theory.* This theory indicates that memory, attitudes, judgments, imagination can be strengthened through academic exercise. Thus such projects as memorization of verses or speeches were once defended for their contributions in training one's reasoning faculties. From a multitude of studies it has been established that it is not possible to strengthen one's power of critical thinking, memory, perception, and the like, through such academic exercise.[8]

2. *The identical elements theory.* Experimental investigation consistently has revealed that the more two activities or situations are similar, the more training in one is likely to affect performance in the other. In many instances educators today emphasize a set pattern of responses which one should expect to apply in real life situations. Psychologists,

---

[7] Symonds, *op. cit.*, p. 37.
[8] *Ibid.*, pp. 75–81.

however, now place greater emphasis upon the learner's perception of the identical or similar elements rather than someone else's perception of these.

3. *The generalization theory.* A revision of the identical elements theory has been developed. This theory re-emphasizes the complexities of that which is learned. It is recognized that an internalization of broad understandings, skills, attitudes, and values may influence one's behavior in an infinite number of ways. As a result, concept formation can be related to other experiences in many ways, beyond the mere recognition of similar or identical elements.

In general, it seems that the skill type of learning is most likely to be applied to new situations when: a) the initial responses are well learned, b) the learning situation closely resembles the potential out-of-school situation, and c) the learner is able to perceive the range of situations for which his learning is applicable. For other types of learning, transfer to related situations is enhanced when the pupil encounters concepts, principles, theories, values, and attitudes in a variety of ways, and when he actively seeks applications for the learning under consideration.

How does whole versus part learning apply to methods of teaching?

There is, at present, some disagreement as to how an individual learns most effectively. Does he acquire a concept by building up to it through its related parts? Or does he learn best by first perceiving the totality of a situation and then filling in the gaps or parts?

For the classroom teacher it seems desirable to consider these two as merely different ways of viewing the same event. The "parts" advocates stress the importance of goal-directed or purposeful activity. To those who think in terms of "wholes," this would be tantamount to perception or Gestalt of the whole problem. They see a learning of the parts as smaller "wholes" or conceptual patterns.

Purposeful or goal-directed behavior is to be emphasized. The need for reinforcing the learning of each concept is necessary. In this context emphasis is on the making of worthwhile applications—actually a part of the original goals.

What effect does knowledge of results have upon learning?

Knowledge of results, in the sense it will be used here, means the effect of the learner's awareness of the extent of his progress from time to time during the learning process. Various studies have reported the effect knowledge of results has had upon learning. These studies support the findings that "any learning procedure that provides prompt and complete knowledge of one's progress has a facilitating effect upon learning." [9] Knowledge of results gives a child the information necessary for him to check the accuracy or errors of his work immediately. If the child knows what is right or what is wrong in the learning situation, he will be able to redirect his efforts if wrong or continue along the path he is already pursuing if he is right. These studies also indicated that knowledge of results is motivating as well.

Mr. Smith asked his seventh grade pupils to do enormous amounts of homework in arithmetic. Each morning he checked to see that the papers were properly filled in with the child's name and page number of arithmetic work. Each evening after the pupils had left, Mr. Smith dumped the completed papers in the waste basket, explaining that since the work had been completed, the necessary learning had occurred. No papers were checked or returned to the children.

It is imperative that the teacher make *evaluation* an essential part of the teaching situation. Not only did Mr. Smith not give his pupils the information necessary for learning, but he also failed to use the knowledge-of-results principle for motivation. The children had no need to better their performance because they did not know how well they were performing. Furthermore, lack of learner knowledge of process errors may well imbed error-laden learning, and increase the problem of achieving correct processes. Keeping various papers that each child turns in to the teacher so that previous work done by each child may be compared with his own paper done at a later time, or making charts and graphs to show individual progress are effective instructional procedures.

What is the effect of repetition upon learning?

As Miss Hall opened her spelling book she directed her fourth grade children to open their spelling books to lesson five. She quickly read the list of spelling words for lesson five, pronouncing each word distinctly.

"Now children," Miss Hall said, "I want each of you to write each word ten times." Mark asked, "Oh, do we have to?" "Yes," Miss Hall answered, "in this way you will learn how to spell the words for our test on Friday."

"Practice makes perfect" is a common phrase that one hears so often; however, research studies have indicated that repetition may or may not

---

[9] James M. Sawrey and Charles W. Telford, *Educational Psychology*, 2nd Ed. (Boston: Allyn and Bacon, Inc., 1964), p. 186.

result in effective learning.[10] One highly motivated repetition may be as effective as ten poorly motivated exercises. It is quite clear that writing the spelling words ten times without the intent to learn may not produce mastery as the teacher expected. "The significant variable in learning is not the number of repetitions but the accompaniments and consequences of the repetition." [11] This means that repetition in itself is not the only variable associated with the principle. Repetition, then, may enhance learning if appropriate rewards are made available to the child who is repeating the act. Such rewards may be intrinsic, especially if purposes are clearly defined. Another factor involved in repetition is that of pleasantness or unpleasantness of the task. Most generally human beings tend to behave in ways that will produce a pleasant activity; if repetition is pleasant learning will be enhanced.

Evidence indicates that repetition, spaced over a period of time, is more beneficial to learning than is mass repetition at one particular time. Material learned by the massed repetition technique (sometimes colloquially called "cramming") is forgotten much more rapidly than material that is repeated over a period of several weeks.[12]

How is retention maintained after learning?

Retention refers to the amount of learning present after a period of time has passed. One way to improve retention was mentioned in the previous section. Thus if practice is scheduled over an extended period of time (as opposed to concentrated massed practice) retention will be enhanced.

Another technique useful in counteracting forgetting is overlearning. Overlearning is defined as learning beyond the point of bare mastery. A child who has just read a new word, for example, will remember it longer if he has an opportunity to use this new word over and over again in many different contextual situations. After he has mastered the word, then the continual use of the word in reading activities will strengthen retention of the word.

Meaningful material is retained longer than material that does not have any specific meaning. This means that a poem would be easier to remember than a list of nonsense syllables. However, this could also apply to material that may be meaningful to the teacher and his organizational scheme, but is meaningless to the child who fails to grasp the full meaning of the experience. When material is designated "meaningful" it must be determined in what context and for whom. In working

[10] *Ibid.*, p. 197.
[11] *Ibid.*, p. 197.
[12] *Ibid.*, p. 189.

with pupils, the teacher will need to spend sufficient time at the beginning of an assignment to make sure it is meaningful to them.

The learner's intention to learn also affects retention. If the child's intention is to learn the material for a test tomorrow, he may not retain the learning much beyond tomorrow. If the child repeats selected spelling words without the intent to learn them, he certainly will not retain them as well as a child who intends to learn the spelling words. Expectancy or intention of the learner also influences the permanence of learning.

How do instructional methods and techniques contribute to learning?

Now that we have gained some notion of how the elementary school pupil learns, it seems appropriate to take an overall look at the tools available for guiding his learning experiences. It will be recalled that basically there is an orderly process of learning. This process has been variously described as reflective thinking, cognitive processes, and problem solving. The pupil must himself personalize the educative experience in such a way as to reorganize or restructure his ideas and feelings. The process is continuous. Concepts gained from one learning experience are used as data for future learning experiences. A teacher cannot make a child learn; he can only establish a desirable environment for learning. This, then, is the role of instructional methods and techniques. As used in this book *a teaching method is a systematized approach designed to facilitate the orderly processes of critical thinking.*

Teaching methods cannot be tightly structured like a blueprint. There is a need for a basic framework within which the teacher must operate. The basic framework offered for each of the numerous teaching methods is consistent with the psychology of the child. It is worth repeating that the "failure" of any of the described methods cannot be attributed to the method itself. Whenever a teaching method does not produce the desired results the difficulty is associated with the implementation of the psychological principles involved. Teaching is a *personal invention*, dependent upon the numerous circumstances and conditions prevailing at the time of application. This explains why "identical" techniques used with "identical" groups of pupils seldom work with equal effectiveness. When dealing with elementary school children, especially, conditions are *never* identical.

The teacher is urged to profit from the experiences of *many* and *utilize* the several teaching methods herein described *within the framework established*. He is further urged to introduce innovations and adaptations of his own, again within the basic framework suggested.

The relationship between teaching methods and the ends sought is one of the most useful guides now available for method selection. Generally, there is no *one* method which is definitely indicated; but there are usually a number of methods which can be eliminated. In some cases the relationship is vague and indistinct. This is because the different outcomes (e.g., understandings, skills, and attitudes) are themselves overlapping and indistinct. Nevertheless, there *is* a relationship.

There are a number of environmental factors which have a bearing upon learning. Such factors as class size, physical facilities, time limitations, and maturity of pupils must be given due consideration. There also are many principles or generalizations which are common to all learning. Some of these have been reviewed earlier in this chapter as psychological processes of learning. For example, all learning must be goal-directed; it is dependent on readiness to learn; the learner must be actively involved. *It is also possible to identify principles which apply more appropriately to a particular type of learning.* The reader will recall that teacher-made goals of instruction are classifiable into understandings, skills, attitudes, and appreciations. When achieved, these goals become the products or outcomes of learning. They frequently are identified as *concepts*.

There are at least five factors which seem basic to selection of learning experiences.

1. A pupil must have an opportunity to practice the kind of behavior needed for gaining the concept.

2. Learning experiences must be satisfying to the learner.

3. Desired reactions must be possible for those involved.

4. There are many particular experiences possible for the attainment of the same educational objectives.

5. The same learning experience will usually bring about several outcomes.

The fact that one learning experience may bring about a number of changes of behavior provides a challenge to maximize desirable and minimize undesirable outcomes. It is suggested that pupils can acquire facts just as readily under an assign-study-recite procedure as under a teacher-pupil planned operation. The latter, however, affords various opportunities for development of democratic attitudes, group skills, and the like which would not be possible in a chapter-by-chapter type of procedure. A chapter-by-chapter type of procedure is organized by the teacher. He starts the children in the book with the first chapter and has the children continue chapter by chapter through the book. The teaching technique would be one in which the teacher would assign a chapter to be read or studied by the children. The children would study the chapter and answer questions concerning the reading assignment. The teacher would discuss the chapter contents with the children and then the children would recite back to the teacher information read in the chapter.

SUMMARY

In modifying behavior the teacher must remember that he is not the only influence that is affecting the child. The child is reacting to his total environment; therefore, learning is not limited to the classroom.

Emphasis was placed upon the role of the school in developing thinking individuals. Basic to developing thinking individuals is the problem-solving approach in which learning is goal-directed.

Various factors were seen as affecting the learning process. Reward or reinforcement was seen as a very important condition for learning. Thus concepts learned in the classroom must be applied to other activities in the child's life if effective learning is to take place. This transfer of learning contributes to making worthwhile application of what is learned. Both reward or reinforcement and transfer of learning are important factors in the learning process.

The merits of whole and part learning were discussed. Advocates of part learning stress the importance of goal-directed or purposeful activity; advocates of whole learning see parts as smaller wholes. A combination of both ideas seems to be most helpful in the classroom.

Knowledge by the child concerning the results of his efforts also was treated as a basic facilitator of learning. Meaningful spaced repetition is useful for retention.

QUESTIONS FOR STUDY AND DISCUSSION

1. How does a child learn? How does a teacher know when learning has occurred? What is the relationship between learning and readiness? Why is motivation part of learning readiness?

2. How may a teacher contribute to transfer of learning? Is it possible for a teacher to teach for transfer? If so, how could this be accomplished in the classroom?

3. The knowledge-of-results technique is incorporated into teaching machines. How could you use a textbook in applying similar techniques?

4. What is the relationship between psychological principles and instructional practices? How do contrasting psychological theories of learning influence instructional procedures?

5. Scholars have repeatedly asserted that teaching is a "personal invention." If so, what function can a book of instructional practices serve? What relationships, if any, exist between instructional method and learning outcomes desired? What are some possible advantages and limitations associated with "systematized approaches to learning?"

SELECTED BIBLIOGRAPHY

Bernard, Harold W., *Human Development in Western Culture*, 2nd Ed. (Boston: Allyn and Bacon, Inc., 1966).

Cronbach, Lee J., *Educational Psychology*, 2nd Ed. (New York: Harcourt, Brace & World, Inc., 1963).

Educational Policies Commission, *The Central Purpose of American Education* (Washington, D.C.: National Education Association, 1961).

Sawrey, James M. and Charles W. Telford, *Educational Psychology*, 2nd Ed. (Boston: Allyn and Bacon, Inc., 1964).

Seagoe, May V., *A Teacher's Guide to the Learning Process*, 2nd Ed. (Dubuque, Iowa: Wm. C. Brown Co., Publishers, 1961).

Symonds, Percival M., *What Education Has to Learn from Psychology* (New York: Bureau of Publications, Teachers College, Columbia University, 1958).

Tyler, Ralph W., "Human Behavior," *National Education Association Journal*, 426–429 (October, 1955).

Watson, Goodwin, "What Psychology Can We Trust?" *Teachers College Record*, 61, No. 5, 253–257 (February, 1960).

3

Gaining the Concept: Analytical and Intuitive Thought

THERE are two basic dimensions of teaching and learning: processes and outcomes. While this book basically is concerned with the former, the outcomes or products sought have an important bearing on the processes employed. Indeed, the evidence suggests that effectiveness of any instructional approach is dependent on the desired outcomes.

The ultimate objective of the learning experience is its application to future experiences. The outcomes of learning may be applied or *transferred* to future experience in two ways. One is through *specific* applicability to tasks which are highly similar to original ones. This phenomenon is referred to by psychologists as *specific transfer of training*. In essence, it seems to be merely an extension of habits and associations. Specific transfer seems to be limited to skill learnings. Another way that earlier learning renders later learnings more efficient is through the transfer of principles or attitudes. This is often referred to as *nonspecific transfer*. Initially one learns not a skill but a general idea which can be used as a basis for solving subsequent problems. This type of transfer, according to Bruner, ". . . is at the heart of the educational process. . . . The more fundamental or basic is the idea . . . the greater will be its breadth of applicability to new problems." [1] Principles, attitudes, and generalizations are often called *concepts*. They are treated in the first section of this chapter.

Processes involved in concept formation are the concern of the second section. When an individual "stops to think," a definite process seems to be involved. First, he encounters something which raises a doubt or

[1] Jerome S. Bruner, *The Process of Education* (Cambridge, Mass.: Harvard University Press, 1960), pp. 17–18.

snarl which he feels must be resolved before he can continue with his normal activities. Second, he makes sure what the difficulty is and evolves an idea which will correct the situation. Third, he checks out his idea against such facts as are available. Fourth, he draws conclusions which seem to be supported by his inquiry. Finally, he checks them against reality to see if they work. The reader must not infer that the steps of thinking follow an ordered sequence at all times; this is a logical arrangement only. Sometimes, for example, the problem is stated last. Furthermore, within any act of thought the differing steps may be taken many times. Moreover, the unit characteristic of each testing step must be emphasized. Thus it is probably more realistic to speak of prediction-*and*-verification.

The thought process, described in the foregoing, is *basic* for all pupils. It is given various labels, some of which are: problem solving, cognitive processes, reflective or analytical thinking, and scientific method. The teacher, however, should not make his class conform to the steps of the thought process. Rather, he should conduct his classes so that pupils learn to take the steps as the normal way of learning. Thus many of the *teaching methods* described throughout this book are based upon such an approach. It should not be inferred, however, that all worthwhile learning involves problem solving or reflective thought. Indeed, some of the most useful learning comes in a flash of insight. According to Bruner [2] this *intuitive thinking* does not follow such a pattern. It is also recognized that man, like lower animals, acquires many learnings through processes of conditioning.

CONCEPT FORMATION

Instructional practices for what? A teacher must not only know *how* to teach; he must clearly understand the *ends* of instruction. Problem solving is not the center of method; concept formation is. Problem solving is a means of attaining concepts. A *concept may be conceived as a reduction of related experiences or events to a basic idea or pattern.* As a concept gains meaning from subsequent experiences, it is usually accompanied with feelings. Concepts help us classify or analyze; they help us associate or combine as well. McDonald and Nelson identify a number of ingredients of science which are concomitants of the concept-seeking approach.

[2] *Ibid.*, p. 13.

By pursuing this scientific method, children gradually gain scientific attitudes. These attitudes can be applied to all phases of their daily living. They learn not to jump to conclusions without a thorough investigation. They learn to withhold judgment until all of the evidence is in. They are able to distinguish facts from opinions, and thus gain freedom from prejudice.[3]

Concepts then make up the *fundamental structure* of school subjects. They exist at many different levels of abstraction.

A conceptual scheme involves many concepts. We have a concept when we recognize a group of situations which have a resemblance or common element. ". . . general concept may apply to a great variety of problems." [4]

It is believed that teachers must consciously attempt to develop subject matter areas around the major conceptual schemes, while daily lessons should be built around concepts underlying these conceptual schemes. Woodruff [5] attempts to describe different conceptual levels by listing *major* and *supporting* concepts. He contends that each lesson should be constructed around one important concept.

What are the essential properties of concepts?

Concepts or ideas differ in at least two basic dimensions: types and levels. Each will be treated separately.

A concept *type* is a product of the specific experiences which have entered into its formation. The most common type of concept is *classificational*. It is based upon the classification of facts into organized schemes or patterns. In science, for example, a classificational concept may be stated as: An insect is an animal with six legs and three body cavities. Thus certain facts or observations are organized to *describe* certain phenomena in the world of reality.

A second concept type is *correlational* in nature. It is derived from *relating* specific events or observations; it consists of prediction. According to Pella,[6] this type of concept essentially consists of the formulation of general principles. To illustrate in the area of science: If limestone is placed under great heat and pressure, it becomes a harder rock called

---

[3] Blanche McDonald and Leslie W. Nelson, *Methods that Teach* (Dubuque, Iowa: Wm. C. Brown Company, 1958), p. 188.

[4] Lee J. Cronbach, *Educational Psychology* (New York: Harcourt, Brace and Company, 1954), pp. 255, 281.

[5] Asahel D. Woodruff, *Basic Concepts of Teaching* (San Francisco: Chandler Publishing Co., 1961).

[6] Milton O. Pella, "Concept Learning in Science," *The Science Teacher*, 33, No. 9: 31–34 (December, 1966).

marble. It will be noted that the concept consists of an *if . . . then* dimension. Involved is the *relationship* between two variables.

A third concept type may be viewed as *theoretical*. It facilitates the explanation of data or events into organized systems. It involves the process of advancing from the known to the unknown. Example: Everything on earth is changing all the time. Even rocks must be changing. A theoretical concept goes beyond facts, but nevertheless is consistent with the known facts.

Concepts also differ with respect to *level*.[7] The most basic of these have been identified as *concrete concepts*. Such concepts are derived from firsthand sensory experiences of our daily existence. Examples include such common objects as chairs, tables, books, birds, and animals.

Generalized concepts are derived from the mental pictures formed from concrete experiences. They possess common characteristics and serve to *extend meaning* of concrete concepts. Thus chairs are used for sitting, books are read, birds fly, animals walk.

Generalized concepts lead, in turn, to *abstract concepts*. The generalized idea may be held *independently* of its referent. For example, after the learner has generalized that some animals make good pets, that certain plants and animals provide good food, and that certain chairs make one comfortable, he gains an abstract concept of *goodness*. As such, it ceases to have a specific referent.

At the highest levels of conceptualization are *analysis and synthesis*. Analysis is usually associated with mental disassembly or pulling apart various conceptual notions. It involves reevaluation. This, in turn, is usually followed with synthesis—a restructuring of basic ideas or concepts. The *abstract* concept of goodness, for example, must be tempered with conditions.

Conceptual *levels* exist, to some degree, within each of the three concept *types*. By referring to the description of the cognitive domain of educational objectives (treated in the next chapter), the reader will perceive a close relationship between concept and cognition levels.

What functions do concepts play in the affairs of man?

It has been demonstrated repeatedly that specific facts which are not used are quickly and easily forgotten. Concepts provide us with a relatively stable and permanent system of knowledge. The concept or idea, along with a number of relevant facts, is easily recalled. Thus concepts

[7] Woodruff, *op. cit.*, p. 125.

facilitate the sorting out and grouping of knowledge in a systematic manner.

A concept is a generalization—an abstraction gained from experience. Thus when used in future experience it provides a sound basis for analysis, reflection, and discrimination. The process seems to proceed from specific to general and back to specific again as one grapples with real problems. Concept learning enables the individual to supplement his knowledge through drawing on the total connotation of the concept.

Although man's ability to generalize from experience is probably his most distinctive asset, it is not without hazards. There is a tendency to generalize or conceptualize on the basis of inadequate experience and to treat concepts as fixed or final. The process of discrimination and generalization is continual. Concepts are altered, extended, or clarified through analysis and reflection.

Another major function of the concept is its value in providing a framework for thinking. As new data are discovered they are related to existing data for the purpose of extending knowledge. If the data do not fit existing concepts, they must be refined and the new data rechecked. As a case in point, anthropologists for some time have been searching for the "missing link" in the evolution of man. As new data are processed, the continued absence of this missing link eventually would bring about a revision of the concept. Likewise, other conceptual schemes which for centuries have provided useful guideposts for thinking must come under careful scrutiny. In the social studies field nationalism could be cited as an example. With the realistic prediction of a supersonic plane which can make the trip from New York to London in two and one-half hours, along with other equally dramatic developments, existing concepts of nationalism must be carefully re-examined.

Concepts as guideposts for thinking produce order in our daily existence. Some of these everyday values (based on concepts) are: honesty, loyalty, cooperation, freedom, fair play, common good, and so on. Inadequate concepts have led to most of the ills associated with man's existence. Examples are: superior race, caste system, manifest destiny, slavery, and socialism. People act on the basis of concepts they carry around in their heads, but their actions take place in a real, objective world. When one's concepts do not correspond with objective reality, serious and often fatal clashes occur. Such misconceptions, called prejudices and stereotypes, maintain a tremendous power over thinking. A current situation in modern America is reflected in outmoded stereotypes of "the peace of the black in society." Although such concepts may have been quite realistic at one time, they do not fit the demands of reality today.

What general instructional approaches contribute to concept formation?

Pupils form concepts in the natural course of events. Unfortunately, however, they are just as likely to form misconceptions as they are to form correct ones. A few simple techniques are useful, regardless of the type of class activity involved.

In the first place, the learner must be encouraged to organize his facts or data around a concept or conceptual scheme. Woodruff [8] contends that our present curriculum is organized around topics. Topics can be pursued in many different directions, often exposing pupils to far more information than can be learned adequately. Too often the pupil is permitted to "get lost" in the facts without ever deriving significant meaning and relationships from them. Woodruff offers an interesting comparison of topic-centered teaching versus concept-centered teaching.

Centered on Topics	*Centered on Concepts*
Tends to go in several directions	Tends to concentrate on one vital idea
Produces vague impressions of many things	Produces sharp mental pictures of one thing
Obscures the necessary experience	Sharply indicates the required learning experience
Is indefinite as to teaching materials	Identifies the essential teaching materials
Encourages talking *about* many facts	*Selects* and *organizes* facts into a significant idea
Fails to highlight important generalizations	Aims everything at an important generalization
May have a vague relationship to an objective	Makes the *concept itself* the objective [9]

Another useful technique for "teaching for the concept" involves the Socratic technique of questioning. As Hullfish and Smith point out, "When the student *utters*, the teacher should invite him to *speak* by asking a further question." [10] They contend that a ". . . lively imagination, an interest in playing with ideas, and courage enough to step forth

[8] *Ibid.*, p. 102.
[9] *Ibid.*, p. 185.
[10] H. Gordon Hullfish and Philip G. Smith, *Reflective Thinking: The Method of Education* (New York: Dodd, Mead & Co., 1961), p. 197.

without knowing exactly where the course of questioning will lead," will guide the learner to critical analysis and appropriate conceptualization. Teachers should recognize that the initial answer of a pupil is but the starting point in a process. The "right answer," according to Hullfish and Smith, has no greater educative value than a wrong one. What the teacher does after getting an answer will determine its educative function.

Concept formation is enhanced when the learning environment is as realistic as possible. Pupils should be provided with as many different activities and situations as possible. Direct experiences, supplemented with rich vicarious experiences by means of pictures, words, films, dramatizations, and the like, are essential.

Learners should be encouraged to express their concepts in their own words, always relating them to their own level of understanding. Concepts which cannot be verbalized should be expressed in some other manner, as in a dramatization or picture.

Finally, learners should be taught to evaluate their own concepts by tracing the process of their development. They can be expected to present arguments in support of and arguments against conflicting concepts.

It would seem that the basic approach to teaching, then, would be to direct each activity towards the gaining of the concept. Nothing should be left to chance. Pupils need assistance in organizing and sorting data around the main idea. Each lesson should be aimed at building up to the concept from as many different angles as possible. In general, a lesson will end with searching questions to determine if all pupils can state the concept in their own words. Pupils also must be given time to ask questions arising out of the new relationships formed.

What teaching techniques may impede appropriate concept formation?

One of the most serious weaknesses encountered among teachers is the assumption that an ability to recall facts is tantamount to learning. Likewise, some teachers assume that a mere telling or stating of the concepts creates understanding. Such a view is reflected in curriculum guides which begin with statements of principles or concepts in the field. Concepts are sought and discovered, not merely accepted. The learner searches, relates, tries out as he builds the concept. A teacher cannot "give" him the concept; he can only establish a favorable environment for its attainment.

Another problem associated with concept formation is the tendency to crowd learning. A common complaint is that "there is so much to teach in so short a time." Thus the temptation is to cover ground faster, expecting pupils to comprehend faster. A concept cannot be crowded in the manner of verbal memorization. It is worth repeating that the number of facts studied is important only as they provide a repertoire of data from which the learner can sort, organize, and relate these data into meaningful wholes. A wise selection of concepts will prove the time necessary for learning them worthwhile.

A third major error in teaching for adequate concept formation is failure to complete the process. Many times well-meaning teachers provide a favorable environment for learning but they get bogged down with specifics. Pupils may discuss many interesting points but they are not stimulated to generalize from their experience. The basic concepts remain submerged. Concept formation takes time! The culmination of the experience cannot be deleted or rushed without the very real danger of reducing the experience to mere *verbalisms*. A verbalism has been defined as a statement without meaning. When substituted for concepts, verbalisms can actually prevent true concepts from emerging.

PROCESSES OF CONCEPT FORMATION

Development of methods and techniques of guiding pupils in the formation of concepts is one purpose of this book. It seems necessary at this point to lay a foundation for the various teaching methods to be introduced in subsequent chapters. As indicated earlier, there seem to be certain cognitive processes which are normally employed when an individual thinks. In the next five sub-sections, each step of the analytical thought process is described. Although the steps will not always be followed in the order presented nor all steps necessarily employed on each occasion, the classroom teacher should be aware of the sequence as a basis for preparation of classroom experiences. The remaining topics deal with intuitive processes and the relationship of teaching methods to the thought processes described.

How is the problem stated and clarified?

A problem arises when an individual encounters a difficulty in his regular activities. He recognizes that the concepts at hand somehow do not fit the observed events. This may produce a vague feeling of dissatisfaction with things as they are—unhappiness with a definite snarl in the progress of events, or mere curiosity. In any event, this is when the problem should be stated in as precise a manner as possible.

Once a problem has been stated, the terms must be clarified. In the process of defining the problem, the pupil describes the factors or conditions which are blocking progress and even looks beyond to the kind of answer which should emerge. As McDonald and Nelson suggest, "After considering various possible solutions, explanations, or courses of action, select the one which appears to be the most promising." [11] Key assumptions should be identified, and key words defined in the process of problem clarification. The problem may or may not be put in the form of a question, depending upon the nature of exploration anticipated.

Too often intellectual curiosity has been minimized by various elements of society. The teacher must cultivate a questing attitude by initiating specific activities for raising problems and then being sympathetic with pupil questions and inquiries. He can cultivate such an attitude by re-directing questions to children and insisting on precision. Above all, pupils need practice in formulating and clarifying their own questions. Sometimes teachers mistakenly assume that it is their private responsibility to formulate the problems for study and analysis. While this may be necessary on occasion, pupils need ample opportunity to formulate and clarify their own problems.

How are hypotheses developed?

Once the problem has been stated and clarified, the individual has already moved into the next step in the analytical thought process. At this point he develops some hypotheses—bold guesses or hunches with respect to his problem. For the untrained individual, there may be a tendency to accept the first guess (hypothesis) as correct. Thus further thinking is blocked. The trained individual delays reaction and deliberately casts about for several possible solutions. *It is important to remember that hypotheses are necessary as a guide in the acquisition of facts.* Hypotheses, of course, are based upon the facts in the original situation from which the problem grew.

Hypotheses cannot be guaranteed or controlled; they just appear. There are techniques, however, for minimizing ordinary inhibitions built up from past experience. One of these (brainstorming), for example, is discussed in Chapter 6. Dewey [12] suggests that a re-examination of the original situation may contribute to the emergence of hypotheses. An-

---

[11] McDonald and Nelson, *op. cit.*, p. 188.

[12] John Dewey, *How We Think*, Rev. Ed. (Boston: D. C. Heath & Company, 1933), p. 85.

other technique involves taking a careful look at one's own assumptions, biases, or prejudices. The closeness of a situation tends to cause one to overlook the obvious. Thus it is sometimes appropriate temporarily to abandon a problem. In other contexts this has been called an *incubation period.*

How are facts sorted and analyzed?

Obtaining and analyzing facts remains the most basic analytical thought process. In the absence of facts and data the entire educative process becomes meaningless. Facts are present in all stages of any inquiry. Contrary to popular opinion, facts are not fixed and unchangeable. Furthermore, they are subject to many interpretations. Pupils are prone to confuse personal opinion with facts and to confuse their opinions about facts with facts. They also tend to jump to conclusions on the basis of limited evidence. Children, as well as most adults, tend to seek facts which will support a given point of view. Data on all sides of a question must be perused in the interest of intellectual honesty.

When an individual uses facts to support a point of view, he is *theorizing.* In actual practice *theory* and facts cannot be separated. A theory may be defined as a statement of principles which underlie and explain a set of facts and predict a chain of events. Actually a hypothesis is a tentative theory. A theory emerges when facts become more and more numerous, necessitating unification. As Burton, Kimball, and Wing point out, "Theories are subject to change as new facts and principles are discovered. A theory supplies a guide to further study, to policy making and to action." [13] We have a cultural tradition of being a nation of practical people, looking at the facts, while disregarding theory. This fallacy is adequately summed up as follows:

He who will not go beyond the facts rarely ever gets as far as the facts. Thinking without a theory can only be chaotic and incoherent thinking. Thinking (or theory making) without facts is likely to result in fantasy. Activities mental or overt (beyond the trivial and the routine) cannot take place without a theory of some sort.[14]

One of the most crucial aspects of the instructional process is the task of guiding pupils in their selection and analysis of facts. A common misuse of textbooks has contributed to an attitude that the text is the final answer. This also contributes to reliance upon the teacher as a final source of authority. It must be remembered that concept seeking

[13] William H. Burton, Ronald B. Kimball, and Richard L. Wing, *Education for Effective Thinking* (New York: Appleton-Century-Crofts, Inc., 1960), p. 102.
[14] *Ibid.*

is a searching, an inquiring process. Therefore, the teacher must encourage pupils to seek widely for facts or data; he must guide children deliberately to uncover facts which will contribute to widely differing points of view. In discussion of the facts, pupils need to listen, to actively pursue contrasting hypotheses, and to trace their ideas to their conclusion (if this—what then). As indicated in later chapters, buzz groups contribute to such an analysis. Pupils must be assisted in keeping to the problem and supporting their contentions with evidence. Whenever possible, the pupil should compare conclusions based on personal experience with those drawn from the evidence. Above all, *concepts* must be developed from an investigation of the facts. These are tools for developing inferences—for making tentative conclusions. One of the most critical aspects of teaching is helping pupils analyze personal knowledge in light of objective data.

What is the role of inference in analytical thought?

From an analysis of facts, the individual formulates tentative conclusions. His ideas may be in the form of possible explanations to account for a chain of events or they may represent several possible courses of action. An *inference* is a leap from the known to the unknown. This *movement* from present facts to possible (but not present) facts represents the heart of the thinking process. Each individual is continually making inferences as he grapples with large and small difficulties of his daily existence. Since the process is so commonplace, there is a tendency to jump to unwarranted conclusions. It is the function of the instructional process to guide pupils in making *tested* inferences. As Dewey says, ". . . we must discriminate between beliefs that rest upon tested evidence and those that do not, and be accordingly on our guard as to the kind and degree of assent or belief that is justified." [15]

Although inferences cannot be controlled directly, systematic logic has been developed to assist in the process. When ideas preceding an inference are analyzed and expressed in verbal form, we have a system of logic. First, there is the system of deduction which starts with a major, general premise (high abstraction), proceeds to a minor premise, and then follows with a statement about a specific case within the category. For example:

Indians have dark skin.

Susie is an Indian.

Therefore, Susie has dark skin.

[15] Dewey, *op. cit.*, p. 97.

Implied in the major premise is that all Indians have dark skin. While *allness* statements often can be applied, they do not necessarily hold for a particular individual.

Another system of logic is known as *induction*. It involves building up generalizations (concepts) from specific facts. The danger here is the tendency to generalize on too limited evidence. Both deductive and inductive reasoning processes normally are used problem-solving experiences.

Assumptions are involved in the process of making inferences. An *assumption* is anything taken for granted—anything assumed to be self-evident. A teacher may offer considerable assistance by requesting pupils to state their implicit assumptions. In this way pupils become aware of what their implicit assumptions are.

How are conclusions tested?

The resolution of any difficulty rests with a conclusion that works in reality. In many school situations, however, it is not practical to put the conclusion to an adequate test. Actually, the nature of proof depends on the nature of the problem. Mathematical and scientific proof usually can be obtained relatively easily. Proof in the social studies area, however, is another matter.

In any case, there are certain guidelines which may be useful. Reasoning should be checked for consistency. Thus conclusions are checked against known facts and accepted principles. As indicated above, it is useful for the pupil to be made aware of his implicit assumptions, beliefs, biases, and the like. The teacher also can slow down pupils in their process of generalizing so as to minimize premature judgments. Especially in social studies, he should discourage pupils from making their conclusions too final. In many instances pupils will be grappling with controversial problems. While it is appropriate that they should be made aware of such difficulties, it is rather inappropriate to presume that within the confines of a classroom they could or should reach final decisions on such matters. Perhaps they will never reach a point beyond which they will conclude, "On the basis of our limited investigation this seems to be a worthwhile course of action to consider."

What is the role of intuitive thinking in concept formation?

Any treatment of the processes of concept formation would not be complete without some attention to those thought processes which do not seem to follow the scheme outlined on the preceding pages. It has long been recognized that many of the really great contributions to human knowledge have come in sudden flashes of insight. Frequently after an individual has labored over a problem for hours, days, or even weeks the idea suddenly meshes. This very often occurs after the problem has been put aside. It was Archimedes who supposedly jumped from the bathtub shouting *"Eureka!"* at his sudden discovery. Jerome Bruner describes the process as *intuitive thinking*.

Whether intuitive thinking follows a definite pattern or not is not known. Most writers, however, suggest that too much emphasis on the formal structure of analytical thinking processes is detrimental to intuitive thought. Routinized activities of any sort seem to be detrimental to the process. Bruner, however, stresses the complementary nature of the two when he says:

Through intuitive thinking the individual may often arrive at solutions to problems which he would not achieve at all, or at best more slowly, through analytic thinking. Once achieved by intuitive methods, they should, if possible, be checked by analytic methods, while at the same time being respected as worthy hypotheses for such checking. Indeed, the intuitive thinker may even invent or discover problems that the analyst would not. But it may be the analyst who gives these problems the proper formalism.[16]

Accounts of thought-in-progress by individuals who have made singular intuitive leaps are beginning to accumulate. From this evidence a few characteristics of the process are beginning to emerge.

1. The idea comes as a sudden flash—a *Eureka*.

2. It usually comes after the problem has been put aside, often when least expected. Thus an incubation period is necessary.

3. The *Eureka* does not seem to follow any logical sequence of steps.

4. It seems to be built upon a broad understanding of the field of knowledge involved.

5. Individuals using this process seem to be characterized by bold guessing. They seem to have the ability to cut through the conventional, the mundane, the expected.

6. They seem to be willing to abandon false hypotheses no matter how well they are liked.

In discussing the conditions for creativity Bruner [17] suggests the

---

[16] Bruner, *op. cit.*, p. 58.

[17] Jerome S. Bruner, *On Knowing* (Cambridge, Mass.: Harvard University Press, 1962), pp. 23–30.

existence of conditions of paradox and antinomy. First, he sees *detachment and commitment* as essential. One must be willing to divorce himself from the obvious as a prerequisite for the fresh combination which is to produce the "flash." Still, he must be committed to a resolution of the problem. Next, he sees *passion and decorum* as a requirement for creativity. Thus the individual must "have a passion for his work," yet must also have order or decorum. A third requirement for creativity, according to Bruner, is *deferral and immediacy*. As he states in another context, one must have "freedom to be dominated by the object"; still, he desires to defer completion—to take delayed reaction.

The separation of analytical and intuitive thinking may be an artificial one. By cultivating analytical thought—but not too rigidly—there is room for the element of curiosity needed for creativity. McDonald and Nelson state: "Participation in science activities can and will stimulate curiosity to the point where children will seek additional activities and experiences." [18] With the elements of curiosity and creativity, concept formation may come with the *Eureka*, the sudden flash, recognizing that concepts are big and little and that a flash to one child will not necessarily be a flash to another. This seems to be a reasonable position to take, as indicated in a further development to be described next.

How do teaching methods relate to analytical and intuitive thought processes?

It is important to understand that the preceding analysis of how we think has not been presented to suggest a formal outline to follow during the instructional process. A general, flexible scheme is not only possible but necessary. It means that teachers should conduct their classes so that pupils learn to take the steps as the normal way of going about learning, without self-consciousness. In an atmosphere that is reflective in quality, thinking may be expected to break out at any moment. As Burton, Kimball, and Wing so ably express the point, "The mind, contrary to widespread belief, has natural tendencies to generalize, to draw inferences, to be critical, to accept and reject conclusions on evidence." [19] The pupil learns to think through thinking. He needs guidance in perfecting this ability to select and clarify problems, to hypothesize, to secure and analyze facts, to make inferences from data, and to reach valid conclusions. "The task of the school is to provide ample opportunity to exercise the process of thinking, to the end that the natural

[18] McDonald and Nelson, *op. cit.*, p. 187.
[19] Burton, Kimball, and Wing, *op. cit.*, p. 292.

tendencies to reflect and to draw inferences will be transformed into attitudes and habits of systematic inquiry." [20]

A final word of caution is in order, however. To ask teachers to emphasize thinking is not to suggest that they keep pupils so occupied at all times. As is indicated throughout this book, there is a valid place for drill, for lecture, and even for recitation at times. The point is made, however, that whatever is done in the classroom should occur in a pervasive atmosphere of reflective behavior.

Imago Photograph

Concept formation is enhanced when the learning environment
is as realistic as possible.

[20] *Ibid.*, p. 293.

In the development of the various instructional approaches in this book, the reflective or problem-solving process has been used as a guiding theory for teaching. To suggest that such a theory is complete, however, would amount to gross over-simplification. Instructional approaches should be viewed as avenues which follow the normal processes of inquiry. The patterns are flexible and offer ample leeway for each teacher to bring his own personal creativity and *Eurekas* into the picture. Classroom instruction for too long has been a haphazard venture into techniques which seem to work. Some systematization, some unifying structure is needed. This is seen as the natural cognitive processes of thought.

SUMMARY

The purpose of the foregoing chapter was to provide a foundation for the instructional methods and techniques which follow. The chapter, divided into two sections, first sought to describe the desired end of the instructional process. The second section provided an overview of the normal thought processes.

The end—indeed, the content—of instruction was described as the *concept*. Concepts exist at various levels of abstraction. They were described as representing the basic structure of learning which enables the pupil to group and categorize learning for future use. Certain general instructional techniques were offered to aid the pupil to grasp the concept.

Processes of concept formation, the primary concern of the classroom teacher, were described in some detail. In addition, attention was given to *intuitive thought*—the sudden flashes of insight which for so long have baffled the most diligent scholars. An understanding of the natural processes of thought was described as a necessary foundation for the various instructional methods and techniques. The basic structure of most of the instructional methods in the chapters which follow is derived from processes of analytical and intuitive thought described in this chapter.

The chapters which follow represent organized approaches to learning. They are not to be applied blindly but are suggestive only. Each teacher will want to modify, revise, or reconstruct as needed in his particular situation. Classroom methodology, however, does not just happen. Careful organization is essential if effective classroom learning is to be achieved. The chapters which follow are designed to provide this basis.

QUESTIONS FOR STUDY AND DISCUSSION

1. What is the nature of the concept? Distinguish between a verbalism and a concept. What distinction, if any, do you see between labels, principles, generalizations, and concepts?

2. How are concepts formed? Why do some authorities criticize the practice of first identifying the important concept and then working toward full understanding of it? What is the relationship between an objective and the lesson concept?

3. What are the steps of analytical thought? Why is the teacher discouraged from teaching these steps as a formal procedure for learning? If there are potential dangers in such a procedure, why bother with studying about them in the first place?

4. What relationship, if any, do you see between analytical and intuitive thought? What class conditions do you see as being most conducive to intuitive thought? Can a dullard experience intuitive learning? If so, would his sudden flashes of insight likely come as often as for the bright child? Why or why not?

SELECTED BIBLIOGRAPHY

Bruner, Jerome S., *On Knowing* (Cambridge, Mass.: Harvard University Press, 1962).

————, *The Process of Education* (Cambridge, Mass.: Harvard University Press, 1960).

Burton, William H., Ronald B. Kimball, and Richard L. Wing, *Education for Effective Thinking* (New York: Appleton-Century-Crofts, Inc., 1960).

Dewey, John, *How We Think*, Rev. Ed. (Boston: D. C. Heath & Company, 1933).

Hullfish, H. Gordon and Philip G. Smith, *Reflective Thinking: The Method of Education* (New York: Dodd, Mead & Co., 1961).

Pella, Milton O., "Concept Learning in Science," *The Science Teacher*, 33, No. 9: 31–34 (December, 1966).

Woodruff, Asahel D., *Basic Concepts of Teaching* (San Francisco: Chandler Publishing Co., 1961).

UNIT ONE

Setting the Stage
for Instruction

EFFECTIVE teaching represents the culmination of a series of preparatory activities. Long hours of careful preparation often go into one lesson. In setting the stage for effective instruction the teacher must be a skillful predictor of events. Knowledge of pupils and a thorough knowledge of the curriculum areas are necessary prerequisites to instructional excellence. Yet, of themselves, they are inadequate. The professional competence of a teacher, ultimately, rests upon his ability to anticipate pupil needs and behaviors *in advance* of the actual experience. Instructional preparation, then, involves applied imagination in planning for the experience. Above all, it demands a thorough understanding of those forces which tend to activate within the pupil a desire to profit from the learning experience. Such is the subject of this unit.

The cornerstone of all classroom instruction is an educational aim or purpose. The teacher, in establishing educational direction, focuses upon course, unit, and lesson aims or goals. Once purpose has been determined, the rest of the instructional process begins to take shape. The key to effective planning and to effective teaching is the formulation of goals in behavioral terms. Attention also must be given to a variety of goal types and levels. Three basic taxonomies of objectives have been recognized: cognitive, affective, and psychomotor. These techniques are treated in Chapter 4.

Long- and short-range planning, described in Chapter 5, remains a controversial issue associated with instruction. The issue is not whether or not one should plan; rather, it is the nature and extent of planning necessary. There are effective teachers who prefer an unstructured classroom experience just as there are those who insist on a highly structured classroom experience. Both extremes can be beneficial in certain situations, depending upon the particular objectives involved. When lesson planning is viewed as a problem-solving experience the dilemma becomes much less ambiguous. Each person must resolve *his* problems in *his* own way. Planning needs will vary with each teacher and with each learning experience. Aside from the lesson objective involved, some teachers will need the psychological security of thoroughly developed lesson plans; other teachers will feel limited or boxed in with detailed lesson plans.

In an effort to provide a basis for the extreme needs associated with lesson planning, detailed long- and short-range planning techniques are offered. Every teacher needs some experience in detailed unit and lesson planning. Just as a beginning lawyer relies heavily upon his debate brief, so does a beginning teacher need the benefit of elaborate planning. As the lawyer gains experience he tends to carry an increasing amount of his debate brief in his head. The same holds for experienced teachers. The precise amount of written planning necessary must be decided by each teacher *in each teaching situation.* In the final analysis, the essential function of planning is to set the stage for learning. In a sense it is a dress rehearsal for the real thing. Even the best laid plans go awry. Nevertheless, the mere act of planning can prepare one for the unexpected!

Even the most careful planning cannot produce beneficial results unless the pupil himself feels a need for learning. Pupils are continually solving problems of immediate concern. Activating a desire to learn in a particular area, however, is another matter. As indicated in Chapter 6, motivation cannot be *taught*—rather, it has to be *caught.* Capitalizing on the basic needs and curiosities of pupils is an art which sets the stage for learning. Like all other dimensions of instruction, children differ in the desire to learn. Accordingly, motivational techniques must vary with the needs of those involved. Chapter 6 suggests how to provide such a basis for learning.

Establishing Instructional Direction: Aims and Purposes

THE mere mention of educational aims and objectives often conveys a touch of nostalgia to experienced teachers. Although most teachers will quickly acknowledge the theoretical importance of goals or purposes in providing instructional direction, many fail to see practical applications. The words of one experienced classroom teacher are not at all uncommon: "My goal for the next six weeks is to teach phonics. Why bother to make an issue of the matter?" More basic questions, however, might be: "Are the pupils learning phonic generalizations?" "Do they know how to utilize phonic generalizations?"

The general functions of education have been phrased and rephrased in many ways. Typical statements have been summarized in this chapter. Despite the usefulness of such statements in providing general direction, they have not been very useful to the classroom teacher. Accordingly, the purpose of this chapter is to assist the teacher to translate general goal statements into practical, specific classroom applications.

The following excerpts are indicative of numerous statements relative to the basic functions of the school. They provide clues into the nature of the task before us.

The world we live in demands self-starting, self-directing citizens capable of independent action. The world is changing so fast that we cannot hope to teach each person what he will need to know in twenty years. Our only hope to meet the demands of the future is the production of intelligent, independent people. . . . The efficiency of learning must be measured in behavior change: Whether students *behave differently* as a consequence of their learning experience. This requires active participation by the student. So learning itself is dependent upon the capacity for self-direction.

Arthur W. Combs [1]

. . . Knowing *what* to learn, how to learn, how deeply to learn, how to use what is learned, and what not to learn—these are the enduring and never-ending challenges of the human race. . . . (the learner) stands in need of profound help, as always, in deciding how to apply the power (to learn).

Ivor Kraft [2]

We must provide (students) with the opportunity to learn how to think; to learn how to be interested in learning; and how to keep on learning. . . . And yet we must never forget that our central purpose is an intellectual one, and that we provide other than intellectual school experiences primarily to make our intellectual goals more attainable and more effective. . . . We try to make life in the schoolroom more interesting and exciting—not to amuse students, but to stimulate them to further their intellectual activities.

Lee A. DuBridge [3]

We believe the following values underlie science:

1. Longing to know and to understand
2. Questioning of all things
3. Search for data and their meaning
4. Demand for verification
5. Respect for logic
6. Consideration of premises
7. Consideration of consequences

. . . these values . . . are part and parcel of any true education. These are characteristic of what not only is commonly called science but, more importantly, of rational thought—and that applies not only to science, but in every area of life . . . .

. . . To communicate the spirit of science and to develop people's capability to use its values should therefore be among the principal goals of education in our country and every other country.

Educational Policies Commission [4]

[1] Arthur W. Combs, "Fostering Self-Direction," *Educational Leadership,* 23, No. 5: 373–376 (February, 1966).

[2] Ivor Kraft, "Learning How to Learn: Myth or Reality?" *Journal of Negro Education,* 33, No. 4: 390–395 (Fall, 1964).

[3] Lee A. DuBridge, "Unity and Variety in Education," *Virginia Journal of Education,* 59, No. 4: 9–11 (December, 1965).

[4] *Education and the Spirit of Science* (Washington, D.C.: National Education Association, 1966), pp. 15, 27.

Although each of the preceding statements seems to focus on the role of the school in a slightly different way, a great deal of commonality is apparent. These commonalities provide a useful basis for the formulation of instructional objectives.

1. The ultimate aim of the school is a self-directed individual.

2. Goal attainment is dependent upon thinking, feeling, and doing.

3. Rational behavior is the essence of the educated man.

4. The ultimate test of learning is reflected in terms of pupil behavior.

THE NATURE OF INSTRUCTIONAL GOALS

An instructional goal is a destination. It spans a distance to be traveled. It raises questions relative to the recognizable characteristics of destination attainment. Moreover, it provides a basis for choosing means (activities) of achieving the desired destination. Indeed goals or purposes constitute the hub around which all other instructional activities revolve.

Goals vary from simple to complex, from mere knowledge and simple habit formation to the attainment of complex value orientations. Some can be reached in one class period; others are slowly attained over a period of several years. The classifications of goals into cognitive, affective, and psychomotor domains are offered for the purpose of providing a point of emphasis. They cannot be conceived as mutually exclusive; the attainment of one, however, does not guarantee the attainment of another.

What are the properties of cognitive goals?

Traditionally, the most common educational objective has been the acquisition of knowledge or information. Thus, successful completion of a course, a unit of work, or a lesson has been judged by how well certain facts are remembered. In many cases, knowledge acquisition has been the primary, if not the only, objective sought. Under such a system it is assumed that the knowledge will be useful in those areas represented. Recognizing the discrepancy between knowing and doing, some teachers have not been satisfied with a demonstration of knowledge retention, however. They have sought to set up realistic situations demanding *knowledge application*. Cognitive objectives vary, then, from simple recall of facts to highly original and creative ways of combining and synthesizing new ideas and materials.

For many years teachers have used the expressions of, "to know," "to understand," "to comprehend," as a means of denoting cognitive or intellectual goals of learning. Such categories, however, do not denote sharp distinctions between cognitive levels. Fortunately a useful taxonomy of cognitive objectives has been developed.[5] The classifications of the taxonomy range from the simple to the more complex behaviors and from the concrete or tangible to the abstract or intangible. The six cognitive levels are as follows:

1. *Knowledge.* This involves the lowest level of learning including recall and memory. At this level the learner is expected to recall specifics with concrete referents. They include terminology, specific facts such as dates, events, persons, places. Also included is *recall* of basic principles and generalizations.

2. *Comprehension.* This represents the lowest level of understanding. The individual is able to make use of the materials or idea without relating it to other materials. For example, he is able to paraphrase or even interpret something he has gained from reading or listening. At the highest level of this category the learner may be able to *extend* his thinking beyond the data by making simple inferences. Thus, in science class he is able to draw conclusions from a simple demonstration or experiment.

3. *Application.* This intellectual skill entails the *use* of information in specific situations. The information may be in the form of general ideas or concepts, principles, or theories which must be remembered and applied. The science student, for example, who draws conclusions from a particular experiment at the comprehension level is now able to *apply* the basic principle(s) to *related* experiments or scientific phenomena.

4. *Analysis.* This involves taking apart the information and making relationships. The purpose is to clarify by discovering hidden meaning and basic structure. The pupil is able to "read between the lines"; to distinguish between fact and opinion; to assess degree of consistency or inconsistency. Thus, our science pupil is able to distinguish between relevant and extraneous materials or events. Likewise, in social studies the pupil is able to detect unstated assumptions.

[5] Benjamin S. Bloom, Ed., *Taxonomy of Educational Objectives, Handbook I; Cognitive Domain* (New York: David McKay Co., 1956). This section is based upon Bloom's taxonomy.

5. *Synthesis.* At this level the learner is able to reassemble the component parts for new meaning. This recombining process permits the emergence of a new pattern or structure not previously apparent. Thus, the learner may develop new or creative ideas from the process. While a certain amount of combining is involved at the lower levels, at this level the process is more complete. He draws upon elements from many sources *in addition to* the particular problem under consideration. In the science class the pupil, for instance, may propose a unique plan (to him at least) for testing an hypothesis. In the mathematics class the pupil may make a discovery or generalization which is not evident from the given communication.

6. *Evaluation.* This highest level of cognition involves making judgments on the materials, information, or method for specific purposes. This represents the end process of cognition, involving distinct criteria as a basis for such decisions. When conceived in relation to the problem-solving or cognitive process it involves selecting one of the proposed alternatives over all the rest.

It is seen from Bloom's taxonomy that intellectual or cognitive learnings vary from the simple to the complex. *Attainment of the highest cognitive levels is dependent upon satisfactory progress at the lower levels of cognition.* If, for example, the teacher desired to develop proficiency in analysis, the lower levels of knowledge, comprehension, and application become very much involved. Implicit in the taxonomy is the process of "critical thinking," "reflective thinking," or "problem solving." Bloom and his colleagues use the term "intellectual abilities and skills."

It should be noted that an abundance of goal illustrations and illustrative test items at each of the cognitive levels is provided in Bloom's taxonomy.

What are the properties of affective goals?

Along with the attainment of intellectual or cognitive objectives, teachers have emphasized emotional or affective purposes. The goal designations of "interests," "attitudes," and "appreciations" are common. This classification scheme, however, also leaves much to be desired. Each term has many meanings, often preventing a sharp delineation of what is expected in terms of behavior. "Attitude," for example, may be used to denote a positive feeling about something, or it may imply going out of the way to express a given feeling. As Krathwohl points out, a teacher needs to provide a range of emotion from neutrality through mild to strong emotion, and possibly of a positive as well as a negative kind.[6] He has developed such a taxonomy. As with the cognitive domain, the affective taxonomy ranges from the simple to the complex. This is described in terms of relative degrees of *internalization*. By internalization one means a process through which there is first an incomplete and tentative adoption of the desired emotion to a more complete adoption of the feeling in the latter stages of learning. The five levels of the affective domain follow.

1. *Receiving (attending)*. At this level the learner merely becomes aware of an idea, process, or thing. Thus he is willing to listen or to attend to a given communication. From a purely passive role of a captive receiver he may advance to the active roll of directing his attention to the communication, despite competing or distracting stimuli. For example, he listens for rhythm in poetry or prose read aloud.

2. *Responding*. This level involves doing something with or about the phenomenon other than merely perceiving it. At this low level of commitment, the pupil has not yet bestowed a value upon the phenomenon. To use a common expression of teachers, "He displays an *interest* in the phenomenon." From obedient participation, the pupil may advance to voluntary response, and finally to a *pleasurable feeling* or *satisfaction* which accompanies his behavior. This feeling may be expressed by the goal, "reads poetry for personal pleasure."

3. *Valuing*. As the term implies, at this level an object, phenomenon, or behavior has worth. Behavior at this level reflects a belief or an attitude. Thus it might be said that he "holds the value." This level is characterized by motivated behavior in which the individual's commitment guides his behavior. At the lower end of the continuum, the learner might be said to hold the belief somewhat tentatively; at the other end, his value becomes one of conviction—certainly "beyond the shadow of a doubt." Indeed at the upper end of the continuum he is likely to try to persuade others to his way of thinking.

4. *Organization*. Here the individual has established a conscious basis for choice-making. He has organized his values into a system—a

---

[6] From David R. Krathwohl, "Stating Objectives Appropriatively for Program, for Curriculum, and for Instructional Materials Development," *The Journal of Teacher Education*, 16, No. 1: 83–92 (March, 1965). This section is based upon this taxonomy.

set of criteria—for guiding his behavior. Accordingly, he will be able to defend his choices and will be aware of the basis of his attitudes.

5. *Characterization.* At this level the internalization process is complete. Values are *integrated* into some kind of internally consistent system. Thus the person is described as having certain controlling tendencies. He has a recognized "philosophy of life."

The affective taxonomy has clarified a dimension of teaching that teachers have long recognized as important. In an area where both feelings and thoughts interact, evaluation of pupil progress is extremely difficult. Nevertheless, it *can* be accomplished; each level is amply illustrated with test items in this article [7] on affective taxonomy.

What are the properties of psychomotor goals?

A third major instructional domain is in the area of mental or motor skills. Teachers have long recognized that as a result of certain instructional activities, pupils should be able to perform certain motor skills, as in playing certain games. Sometimes the skill will be primarily of a mental nature, as in spelling and writing sequences; other skills will be neuromuscular as in writing or operating a machine. Frequently the development of certain habits is emphasized, as in science laboratory techniques.

Goals in this realm traditionally have been designated as "skills," or "habits." The shortcomings of such designations also have been noted, on the grounds that they are not definite enough to sufficiently cover the entire range. Accordingly, the term "psychomotor" is recommended by some of those responsible for developing taxonomies in the cognitive and the affective domains.[8] Although the third taxonomy is being prepared it has not yet been published. Fortunately, however, certain aspects of a skills taxonomy can be extrapolated from established methodology, sometimes called "drill techniques." The four levels which follow must be regarded as much more tentative than the preceding taxonomies.

1. *Observing.* At this level the learner observes a more experienced person in his performance of the activity. He is usually asked to observe sequences and relationships and to pay particular attention to the finished product. Sometimes the reading of directions substitutes for this experience. Frequently, however, reading is *supplemented* by direct

[7] *Ibid.*
[8] *Ibid.*

observation. Thus, the beginning marble player may read about playing marbles and then watch an older pupil demonstrate certain techniques.

2. **Imitating.** By the time the learner has advanced to this level he has begun to acquire the basic rudiments of the desired behavior. He follows directions and sequences under close supervision. The total act is not important, nor is timing or coordination emphasized. He is conscious of deliberate effort to imitate the model. The marble player, for example, may practice a prescribed way of holding the marble.

3. **Practicing.** The entire sequence is performed repeatedly at this level. All aspects of the act are performed in sequence. Conscious effort is no longer necessary as the performance becomes more or less habitual in nature. At this level we might reasonably say that the person has acquired the skill.

4. **Adapting.** The terminal level is often referred to as "perfection of the skill." Although a few individuals develop much greater skill in certain areas than do most individuals, there is nearly always room for "greater perfection." The process involves adapting "minor" details which, in turn, influence the total performance. Such modifications may be initiated by the learner or by his teacher. This is the process a player goes through, for example, when a "good" player becomes a better player.

It is obvious that the psychomotor domain also involves a graded sequence from simple to complex. By deciding upon the degree of skill development needed, the instructor is able to more efficiently plan his instructional activities. Likewise, evaluational techniques will vary considerably with the different levels.

FUNCTIONAL GOAL RELATIONSHIPS

The derivation of taxonomies of educational objectives has called attention to areas of neglect in teaching. Moreover, it has pin pointed a need for greater specificity of goal formulation. At the same time it has raised a number of questions relative to important goal relationships. Before the practitioner can most effectively implement instructional developments, he must perceive how they can be integrated into the total instructional framework. Accordingly, this section treats relationships among the three goal taxonomies; relationships between goals and instructional procedures; relationships between broad and specific goals; relationhips between goals and concepts. Each is treated as a separate problem.

How are cognitive, affective, and psychomotor goals related?

In both the congnitive and psychomotor domains the major concern is that the learner gains proficiency. Thus, he must acquire proficiency in problem solving; he must develop skill in a given area. In the affective domain, however, the concern relates to what the individual does with this knowledge or skill. Although *evaluation* of goal achievement has emphasized the *can do* dimension, it is the *does do* dimension that every teacher seeks.

It has been generally assumed that achievement of cognitive goals automatically insures achievement of affective goals. Certainly it must be recognized that the three domains are not mutually exclusive. Emotion is an essential aspect of intellectual processes. Likewise, motor and mental skills are accompanied with an affective dimension. Nevertheless, the three areas of emphasis seem to serve useful purposes. It is recognized, for example, that some behaviors are more intellectual than emotional, whereas other acts are more emotional than intellectual. Still other action requires more mental and/or physical dexterity than anything else.

Despite the fact that there is a definite relationship among the three domains, it is recognized that *negative emotions* may accompany intellectual learnings. A classroom teacher, for example, may instill a knowledge of good literature in pupils while producing an aversion, or at least a reduced interest, in the subject. Although the objective, "reads good poetry *with pleasure*," is seldom stated, it is nevertheless implied. After reviewing the evidence, Krathwohl, Bloom, and Masia conclude: "The evidence suggests that affective behaviors develop when appropriate learning experiences are provided for pupils much the same as cognitive behaviors develop from appropriate learning experiences." [9] Thus, it would seem that, primarily, instructional goals and procedures must be consistent with the major domain involved. *At the same time, one must be mindful of essential aspects of the other domains which are always present.*

Many goals in a given domain are reached through the avenue of another domain. For example, every good teacher attempts to develop

[9] *Ibid.*

interest (affective goal) in an area so the pupil will learn it (cognitive goal). At other times he provides a pupil with information as one means of bringing about an attitude change. The really outstanding teacher has likely achieved such a status as a result of his intuitive ability to reach cognitive goals through the affective domain. The most liked and respected teachers, for example, are often described by pupils as those who take a deep interest in each pupil, those who challenge pupils, those who understand the anxieties of pupils, those who respect opinions and do not embarrass pupils, those who maintain high interest, those who instill a love of the subject.[10] It should be noted that each of these attributes is affective in nature.

What is the relationship between goals and instructional procedures?

Formulation of instructional goal or purpose is the very first step in instructional technique. Once this task has been completed, one proceeds to select the learning experiences which seem most appropriate for reaching the destination (goal). Finally, he develops evaluational techniques for determining how well the goal has been reached.

In the *cognitive domain,* the lowest level (knowledge objectives) can be reached by a great variety of learning experiences. The basic requirement is merely an attentive and well motivated learner and the presentation of accurate information. For the more complex and higher categories of this domain, however, more involved learning experiences are required. Much more *activity and pupil participation* is essential if the learner is to gain insight into his own thinking processes. As he advances through the entire sequence of critical thinking (which characterizes the hierarchical structure of the cognitive domain) group processes take on added significance. It should be observed that the lower levels of cognition are necessarily reached *in the process of achieving the higher levels.* The reverse, however, does not follow. Achievement of knowledge objectives does *not* insure achievement of the higher levels of cognition. If the higher levels of cognition are deemed essential objectives of a given course, the more complex learning experiences should become the basic instructional theme. These include various techniques of discussion, various simulated techniques, and project work of all kinds. Lectures *as a basis for* more involved goals also may be included.

[10] Ardelle Llewellyn and David Cahoon, "Teaching for Affective Learning," *Educational Leadership,* 22, No. 7: 460–472 (April, 1965).

It is believed that similar principles apply to the *affective domain.* At the lowest level the pupil merely receives and attends to new materials. It seems likely that little more than an effective presentation is all that is necessary. The conditions of interest, free from distraction, seem essential. As one moves into the next level (responding), however, far more complex instructional arrangements are more essential than are usually provided in the classroom. Krathwohl, Bloom, and Masia believe that if the higher affective objectives are to be reached considerable time and effort must be expended. Some objectives may take several years for attainment. Coordinated curriculum planning is essential under such circumstances.

Research evidence indicates that the more complex affective goals are not easily achieved by mere exhortations. Neither can much significant change be expected through debate techniques (except for the actual participants who debate the side in opposition to their feelings). What is needed, it seems, is an opportunity for the learner to examine his feelings in the open so that they can be compared with the feelings and views of others. This enables him to move from an intellectual awareness of his position to an actual commitment to the new value.

Values may be affected when the learner sees the need—when the problem is *his own.* But if he has developed strong convictions to the contrary he needs more than activities involving listening *or* practice. He must *identify* with someone whose behavior is consistent with his own concept of himself. This means, then, that he must want to pattern his behavior after another with whom he can *identify.* For younger elementary pupils this may be the teacher himself (who tends to replace the parent ideal). The older elementary pupil, however, tends to identify more readily with the *peer group.* Thus, the upper-grade elementary teacher must rely heavily upon group processes in the area. Teacher-pupil planning, group processes, and dramatic play are more effective in changing attitudes. Dramatic play especially has been effective in processes of *identification.* A realistic problem is essential, however, if this identification is to come about.

Psychomotor learning seems to parallel cognitive and affective learnings. At the lowest (observing) level the learner may profit from any number of techniques designed to provide him with basic information. As he moves to the higher, more complex levels, however, active involvement must be of an individualized nature. Even in team motor skills much individual practice is necessary prior to, and along with, the final phases of skill development. Drill techniques have been severely criticized as a result of group practice of mental skills.

How are broad and specific goals related?

Instructional aims and objectives vary considerably in degrees of abstraction. It has been noted that the higher level goals are more complex and abstract than the lower level goals.

Teachers sometimes wonder if achievement of the lower level goals, in a more or less piecemeal manner, will not indirectly lead to acquisition of the more complex ones. To illustrate: Will not the attainment of the cognition levels of knowledge, comprehension, application and so on eventually increase the learner's capacity to utilize the whole cognitive process? It is quite likely that this process does occur to a limited degree. It is extremely important, nevertheless, that the learner experience all levels of the cognitive process in an integrated sequence as often as possible. This seems to be implied from studies in field psychology. Thus, the learner must develop a mental picture or pattern for most efficient learning. It is for this reason that learning as a process of problem solving is emphasized throughout this book. The concept is also supported through unit-teaching procedures.

In the affective domain the problem is even more complex. It has been observed that interests, attitudes, and other personality characteristics develop relatively slowly, sometimes over a period of several months or years. If this is so, are affective objectives the responsibility of any one teacher? While *some* interests, attitudes, and values *may* evolve over a long period of time, there is mounting evidence that indicates some of these feelings may be altered rather suddenly. The impact of some dramatic or traumatic experience, for example, is well known. It seems quite likely that *some* objectives in the affective domain and *some* objectives in the cognitive domain may be attained quickly, while others in both domains may be developed only over a long period of time. Similar principles probably apply to the psychomotor domain.

Implied from the foregoing discussion is the importance of broad planning of educational objectives. Certain teachers must work together rather closely if related goals are to be sufficiently integrated for the attainment of certain long range objectives. This is one definite advantage of recent developments in the best team-teaching arrangements.

What is the relationship between goals and concepts?

As indicated in the preceding chapter, concepts are the outcomes or products of learning. Many cognitive goals, when achieved, can be stated as generalizations or concepts. A cognitive goal at the analysis level, for example, might be stated as a pupil behavior in the following manner: "Possesses ability to detect logical fallacies in advertisements." As an attained concept the idea may be stated as, "Advertisements often contain logical fallacies." One authority even goes so far as to suggest that the lesson goal may be stated in the form of a concept and presented to pupils as the lesson begins.[11] Thus, pupils are given an opportunity to clearly visualize the end result expected as they begin to work toward it. Most authorities, however, prefer to guide the learner, inductively, toward the concept.

Goals in the affective and psychomotor domains, however, can be translated into concepts only in the cognitive sense. An affective goal at the valuing level, for example, may be stated as follows: "The learner possesses increased appetite and taste for what is good in literature." As an end product the new concept may be stated as, "Good literature consists of plot, style, and movement." Thus, it is seen that the affective goal when stated as a concept loses its affective dimension. Likewise, psychomotor goals, when expressed as concepts, appear in the cognitive sense.

GOAL FORMULATION

Goal achievement, to a marked degree, is dependent upon the way goals are formulated. For many years teachers have been stating worthwhile goals. Unfortunately, however, goals often have been stated so vaguely as to hold little real meaning. The almost inevitable consequence is an unimaginative, memoritor-type of experience, commonly known as textbook teaching. When this situation exists, there is a tendency to emphasize textbook facts as ends in themselves. Accordingly, relatively little transfer or application to related life problems can be expected. This part of the chapter provides a structure which can do much to correct the difficulties usually encountered in the area.

How are goals stated?

A great deal of confusion exists today as to what constitutes a worthy goal. Some teachers, for instance, have contended that specific assignments are tantamount to goals. To illustrate: "After this class the

---

[11] Ashel D. Woodruff, *Basic Concepts of Teaching* (San Francisco: Chandler Publishing Co., 1961), Chapter 10.

pupil should know the date Columbus Day is celebrated, as evidenced by the pupil's ability to give this date at the end of the lesson." This is not a goal but merely a job to be done which may have no apparent purpose for the pupil. A *practical, real life application is either stated or implied in a worthy goal.* By answering the question "why" to the above "goal" the teacher is able to approach more clearly the worth of the exercise.

The verb "to know," as used in the English language, is probably responsible for much of the confusion which exists. It can mean "to recognize or become aware of," or it may mean "to understand or comprehend." Most languages utilize two different verbs for these two distinctly different meanings. Teachers should aim for the latter meaning—*understanding.* In actual practice some teachers apparently have assumed that the first of these meanings is sufficient. Therefore, emphasis has been placed upon rote memorization of facts. It is recommended that teachers use the word *understand,* instead of *know,* when stating cognitive goals. Techniques of referring to the three domains of educational objectives are offered.

1. *Understandings.* The initial step in concept-seeking is that of assembling the relevant facts. Although they are necessary, facts are of little value unless they are combined into related ideas. A *group of related ideas forms an understanding.* Evidence of an understanding usually is in the form of an activity that a child performs. While the term, *understanding,* has been criticized because of its many meanings, it seems to be a useful term when making reference to cognitive goals. The specific behaviors will be phrased in terms of one or more of the six cognitive levels.

2. *Interests, Attitudes, and Appreciations.* These are terms which almost defy definition. Indeed, they are frequently used interchangeably. Interest is a feeling, wanting to know, see, do, own, share or take part in something. Many psychologists suggest that an *attitude* represents a state of *readiness* or predisposition to respond in a certain manner. An *appreciation,* on the other hand, represents more generally *emotionalized* controls. The teacher hopes the child will learn to enjoy or obtain satisfaction from certain experiences. Such labels, of course, are used merely to alert the teacher to the particular domain to be emphasized. Specific pupil outcomes (stated as behaviors) will be made in reference to one or more of the five levels of the affective domain. It should be noted that the two higher levels of the affective domain (organization and characterization) are seldom stated as a subject area goal; they are never included as a unit or lesson goal.

3. *Skills and Habits.* In most subject areas there are basic skills which are needed. These, too, have a practical life application. Evidence of achievement of a general skill usually will be indicated by a number of lesser skills. For example, a goal in a social studies class might be the acquisition of skill in the use of reference materials. This general skill would involve skills in indexing, using a table of contents, dictionary alphabetizing, and the like. In reality, these skills are little different from understandings, except that the emphasis throughout is on the process of doing.

How are pupil behaviors incorporated into instructional goals?

The ultimate goal of the educative experience is to produce persons whose behaviors have been changed in such ways as to make them better able to cope with the problems of modern-day living. As Bloom points out, "Educational objectives are statements of desired changes in the thoughts, actions, or feelings of students that a particular course or educational program should bring about." Thus, it seems to follow that the most effective way to state lesson or unit goals is to describe a type of behavior which may be expected as a result of the experience. This means, then, that specific goals or outcomes should be described in terms of *pupil behaviors.* The emphasis immediately shifts from the concern of the teacher to that of the pupil.

One's goal as a teacher, then, is to bring about a changed behavior. By stating specific behaviors expected by the end of the unit or lesson, one has not only stated realistic goals (outcomes) but has provided a clue to worthwhile class activities and pupil appraisal. Some teachers find it desirable to begin a goal with the introductory phrase, "After this class (unit or lesson) the student should. . . ." This tends to keep the center of attention upon youngsters. To illustrate: "After this unit in reading the pupil should further understand 'tall tale' stories." Many teachers would agree that this is a worthy goal, but what does it mean? It involves an intellectual process only. The next question is *how* this understanding is to be developed. The answer bears directly upon *methods* of teaching. Finally the teacher somehow must determine how well the goal has been accomplished, i.e., he must measure and evaluate.

The goal becomes much more meaningful if expected specific behavioral outcomes are incorporated within the goal framework. For example: "After this unit in reading, the pupil should further *understand* the 'tall tale' stories, as evidenced by: 1) his response in a class discussion comparing tall tale stories with other fictional materials; 2) his ability to write his own tall tale story; 3) his skill in discriminating between tall tale paragraphs and real life situation paragraphs." Such statements offer definite clues to *methods* and activities which might produce the anticipated outcomes. The teacher now has a basis for answering the question: "How can I help Johnny learn to develop his writing abilities?"

The specific behaviors are, of course, not goals at all but actually *outcomes* of goals. Instead of stopping with a statement of a goal the teacher and pupils have gone one step further and identified probable *results* of goal accomplishment. Thus, the first part of a lesson goal is *intellectual*, whereas the latter part is *behavioral*. At this point there is no way of knowing when or if the value has been attained.

The goal becomes much more meaningful if expected specific behavioral outcomes are incorporated within the goal framework. If the goal falls within the *affective* domain, one would seek to elicit specific behaviors from selected levels of this taxonomy. For example, "After reading the story about an immigrant family, the pupil should further appreciate the social inequalities resulting from a social class structure, as evidenced by: 1) his realistic *responses* in a class discussion on the problem: What should be the United States' policy with respect to immigrant people?; 2) his willingness to examine feeling reactions resulting from a dramatic play designed to portray feelings in a specified social situation; 3) his greater cooperation in class and school with children that dress differently or speak with an accent." It should be noted that Outcome One relates to Level Two of the affective domain (responding), while Outcomes Two and Three suggest different levels of Number Three (valuing) of this domain. Such statements offer definite clues to *methods* and activities which might produce the anticipated outcomes. The foregoing behaviors are selected (from among many other possible behaviors) as most appropriate under a given set of conditions. Furthermore, some of them are *not* conceived as terminal behaviors. Rather, they are seen as intermediate behaviors which might be elicited as *means to goal achievement*. Outcome Three is a terminal behavior but one which may not be measurable under normal school conditions. Its usefulness may be primarily to the teacher as a reminder of the ultimate objective being sought.

In *evaluating* goal achievement, the teacher must direct attention to *terminal* behaviors. This usually demands even more specific statements of outcomes. Esbensen [12] suggests that, in addition to indicating specific behaviors, the teacher also must specify under what *conditions*

---

[12] Thorwald Esbensen, "Writing Instructional Objectives," *Phi Delta Kappan*, 48, No. 5: 246–247 (January, 1967).

and to what *extent or level* a kind of pupil performance can be expected to take place. Outcomes One and Two of our illustration do specify conditions but they are seldom appropriate for evaluational purposes. (If they were used, the teacher would have to set up a special discussion situation with a *different problem* at the culmination of the unit. He also would have to develop an acceptable measuring instrument.) The illustrated outcomes do not specify the extent or levels necessary. As indicated in the next chapter, some teachers like to indicate *terminal (test) conditions* by inserting a special note following each *unit* outcome. (Refer to the illustrated teaching unit in the next chapter.) Extent or level of terminal performance is sometimes determined by using a modified normal curve of probability. If individual performance is to be evaluated, an acceptable level must be established.

What are the implications for teaching?

By rereading the excerpts of basic educational functions, cited at the beginning of this chapter, the reader can gain an added perspective on teaching. As suggested by the four definitive statements, pupil activity is necessary. It is apparent from the description of the three taxonomies that active pupil participation in the learning process is indeed essential if the higher, more complex goals are to be attained. The lowest level of each domain contributes relatively little toward pupil independence and self-direction.

It has been noted that the development of basic intellectual abilities and skills is, to a substantial degree, dependent upon the creation of class problem-solving situations. Likewise, substantial affective goals are often appropriately realized through the avenue of open, problem-solving discussion. Psychomotor learnings also demand critical analysis, the major difference being individual, as opposed to group, analysis. Although some class activities need *not* involve all phases of the critical thinking process, the evidence does suggest the need for an overall conceptual orientation along these lines.

PROBLEMS AND PRINCIPLES ASSOCIATED WITH INSTRUCTIONAL GOALS

The formulation and effective use of instructional aims and objectives is one of the most difficult tasks faced by the teacher. A casual perusal of the literature will reveal gross differences in points of view with respect to this problem. Although the writers have presented one defensible approach to the problem, there are others which are equally acceptable.[13] The experienced teacher can usually profit most from a review of basic questions and problems in the area, supplemented with an analysis of basic principles involved. This section is designed to fulfill such a function.

What ethical limits, if any, should be imposed in the affective realm?

What attitudes and values should be taught and which ones should be left alone? This is a basic question faced by every teacher? It is an especially critical one in the social studies area and certainly comes up in all areas.

Whereas in the cognitive and psychomotor domains achievement and productivity are considered public matters, one's beliefs, attitudes, values, and personality characteristics are more likely to be viewed as private matters. An individual's attitude toward religion, politics, and family, for example, is usually respected as a private, personal affair. "Every man's home is his castle" is a cliché indicating the strength of this position.

On the other hand, the schools have long been charged with the responsibility for teaching values. Acts of delinquency and other deviant behaviors are often linked with criticism of the schools. Some religious leaders literally make the school a "whipping boy" for not teaching "moral and spiritual values."

These contrasting views have left the teacher in a state of confusion. Sometimes basic affective goals have been neglected as a result of this uncertainty. There is a definite need for clarification of the issue.

For purposes of analysis, values might be considered in three broad categories: behavioral, procedural, and substantive.[14] The first of these concerns classroom procedures. Certain standards of behavior are expected and enforced. A teacher cannot tolerate unnecessary interruption when he is talking, for example. Neither can he tolerate other disruptive behavior. Such behaviors are classified under the heading of discipline. Compliance is expected. Without it, there can be no effective teaching!

[13] For a different approach to the problem the reader is referred to Robert M. Gagne, *Conditions of Learning* (New York: Holt, Rinehart and Winston, Inc., 1965).

[14] This analysis is based on Edwin Fenton's "Teaching About Values in the Public Schools," from Edwin Fenton, *Teaching the New Social Studies in Secondary Schools: an Inductive Approach* (New York: Holt, Rinehart and Winston, Inc., 1966), pp. 40–45.

H. *Armstrong Roberts*

Activity and pupil participation are essential
if the learner is to gain insight into his own thinking processes.

The second broad value category, according to Fenton, is procedural in nature. In describing this value he says: "Critical thinking is better than uncritical thinking; this canon underlies the entire scholarly world. If a pupil insists that his prejudices should not be challenged and defends them with an emotional appeal, he should be *forced* to subject them to the test of evidence and to defend them in the face of the full array of scholarly argument." Thus, the processes of critical thinking itself are seen as a value—one that the teacher has the right to emphasize.

The third category consists of a broad range of substantive values. Such values represent the "goods" and "bads," the "rights" and "wrongs" of our society. This category gives rise to some of society's greatest controversies. Some of these values have been codified into law; others are commonly accepted as moral law. This domain of substantive values, according to Fenton, is what cements and unifies our society. Thus, they must be taught. Beyond this point, however, substantive values must be left for the learner to decide. To illustrate: Religion is a good thing. Therefore, young people should attend church. The family is the basis of society, so divorce ought not to be permitted. Young people ought to go along with the crowd rather than pursue an independent course. These statements illustrate values that may be taught, but the outcome of the learning should be decided by the learner.

Although "unsettled" substantive values should not be taught, according to Fenton, *the teacher does have the right and responsibility to teach about such values.* By this he means raising questions for discussion and analysis. In short, he would support treating such issues *through the avenue of procedural values,* i.e., through critical thinking processes. In such situations, however, the teacher must not indoctrinate by reaching decisions *for* pupils. To illustrate: "Should we teach students to conform, or to be leaders, or to contribute to charity?" As Fenton says, "I do not want teachers to make such statements to my children, even if I agree with them. On the other hand, I do want teachers to raise these issues for discussion, always keeping the discussion under the control of evidence within a framework of critical thinking."

What problems are frequently encountered?

The most common problem in writing instructional objectives is associated with phraseology. There is a definite tendency to develop an orientation of "what I want to teach," as opposed to "what pupils ought to learn." As a means of counteracting this tendency, it is preferable to begin every goal with the clause, "After this lesson (unit) the pupil should . . . ." Then each goal should be supplemented with the phrase, "as evidenced by: . . . ." Such a procedure offers a practical means of connecting teacher goals with pupil outcomes.

The problem of specificity of pupil outcomes is associated with phraseology. Instructional outcomes are very often fuzzy. Such goals as "the pupil should become a good citizen," for example, give no indication of what behaviors are recognizable as attributes of a good citizen. Specific behaviors are overt manifestation of goal achievement.

A third problem relates to number and kind of pupil outcomes sought. Any number of behaviors could be selected as indicative of progress toward the goal. In preplanning activities, the teacher lists as many as seem appropriate and then selects those which seem most appropriate for his particular teaching situation. He then modifies these plans after pupils become involved in the process, recognizing that other methods may be equally effective.

A fourth problem concerns the difference between those behaviors which are sought *during* the learning experience and those sought as *terminal* behaviors. One's first concern must be with those behaviors which are likely to contribute to growth toward goals. Eventually, however, he must direct attention toward final goal achievement. The latter behaviors must be much more specific than the former.

A fifth problem deals with affective goals. When stated in terms of pupil behavior the affective dimension is often lost. An individual can sham an attitude or value, for example, to impress the teacher.

A sixth, related problem is that of evaluation. It is relatively easy to measure congnitive goals through paper-and-pencil tests. Likewise, psychomotor outcomes can be readily assessed. In the affective domain, however, evaluation is often difficult. As indicated in the preceding problem, substantive values cannot be left to chance. Yet, final value determination must be considered a private matter. How can such processes be evaluated? While the problem has not been fully solved, substantial progress is being made, as indicated in the chapter on measurement and evaluation.

What principles apply?

Continued teacher growth is a product of experience. The guiding forces of teacher experience are principles. Specific techniques, then, are of minimum value unless they are consistent with basic principles in the area. The principles which follow should serve as useful guidelines for those who desire to improve their instructional aims and objectives.

1. Instructional goals provide the hub around which all other instructional activities revolve. Once goals have been stated, it is relatively easy to select learning experiences and to employ appropriate evaluational techniques.

2. Goals exist in at least three overlapping domains: cognitive, affective, and psychomotor. Attainment of some goals in all three domains is essential in all areas of the curriculum. In some areas, however, greater *emphasis* may be placed in one or more domains.

3. The key to effective goal formulation is specific pupil behaviors, stated as

outcomes. Attention to the various levels of each taxonomy can assist in this process.

4. Higher level goals in each domain are more abstract and complex than those at the lower levels. Thus, achievement of these levels results in achievement of the lower levels as well. The reverse does not as readily apply, however.

5. Achievement of the higher, more complex goals in each domain essentially entails processes of critical thinking. The affective dimension of this process involves the human interaction processes essential to open exchange of ideas.

6. Some complex goals cannot be attained as a result of completing a single subject matter area. Thus, teachers should work together as a team for attainment of such goals. This is especially important if the more complex affective goals are to be achieved.

7. Evaluation of goal attainment is based upon as many different pupil behaviors as possible.

SUMMARY

Instructional goals, in this chapter, were seen as necessary bases for effective teaching. Specific goal levels in three instructional domains were described. These domains—cognitive, affective, and psychomotor—were seen as representing points of emphasis sought in the learning process.

Relationships of the three domains were viewed, along with relationships of broad and specific goals. The close relationship between goals and concepts was treated in some detail.

Since teacher goals are often not specific enough for effective use, a definite procedure was recommended for goal formulation. This essentially involved a process of connecting broad goal statements with specific pupil behaviors. Finally, attention was given to problems and principles associated with instructional aims and objectives.

QUESTIONS FOR STUDY AND DISCUSSION

1. How are the three taxonomies of educational objectives related? How do they differ? What values do such taxonomies serve? What problems are raised?

2. What are the advantages of stating goals in terms of pupil behavior? Should those pupil outcomes which cannot be measured in the confines of a classroom be stated? Why or why not?

3. If substantive values are private and personal, why emphasize them through construction of an affective domain? What values, if any, should not be subjected to critical analysis?

4. Should a teacher indoctrinate when discussing our democratic system? What dangers and advantages are apparent?

5. It has been stated that the higher, more complex levels of educational objectives also include the lower, less complex objectives. Explain. Why is the reverse not necessarily true? What are the implications for teaching?

SELECTED BIBLIOGRAPHY

Bloom, Benjamin S., Ed., *Taxonomy of Educational Objectives, Handbook I: Cognitive Domain* (New York: David McKay Co., 1956).

Educational Leadership, 23, No. 7 (February, 1966). Several articles dealing with the affective domain are treated in this issue.

Esbensen, Thorwald, "Writing Instructional Objectives," *Phi Delta Kappan*, 48, No. 5: 246–247 (January, 1967).

Gagne, Robert M., *Conditions of Learning* (New York: Holt, Rinehart and Winston, Inc., 1965).

Krathwohl, David R., "Stating Objectives Appropriately for Program, for Curriculum, and for Instructional Materials Development," *Journal of Teacher Education* 16, No. 1: 83–92 (March, 1965).

Krathwohl, David R., Benjamin S. Bloom, and Bertram S. Masia, *Taxonomy of Educational Objectives, Handbook II: Affective Domain* (New York: David McKay Co., 1964).

Llewellyn, Ardelle and David Cahoon, "Teaching for Affective Learning," *Educational Leadership*, 22, No. 7: 460–472 (April, 1965).

Mager, Robert F., *Preparing Instructional Objectives* (Palo Alto, Calif.: Fearon Publishers, 1962).

Thomas, R. Murray, *Judging Student Progress*, Rev. Ed. (New York: David McKay Co., Inc., 1962).

Woodruff, Ashel D., *Basic Concepts of Teaching* (San Francisco: Chandler Publishing Co., 1961), Chapter 10.

The Framework for Instruction:
Long- and Short-Range Planning

A group of elementary education students was required during their observation-participation class to determine the actual nature and extent of planning activities utilized by the school teachers whom they observed. After observing these teachers for a period of time, each student was to report on the planning situation briefly. As indicated below, their generalizations appeared to be conflicting and confusing.

Some teachers made absolutely no use of any kind of plan. Such teachers said, "We have our plans in our heads." Others emphatically contended that preplanned lessons were unnecessary.

A few teachers relied heavily on written lesson plans, frequently reading from prepared materials. One teacher had an elaborate planning board about the size of her desk. Most of this group tended to cut off pupil questions which were not closely related to the preplanned lessons.

Other teachers occasionally referred to plans ranging from a few scribbled notes to detailed, elaborate plans. Some relied on a predetermined time schedule, while others placed greater emphasis on preplanned objectives.

In a subjective evaluation of the quality of instruction involved, the students decided that some planning seemed to contribute to the effectiveness of teaching. It was noted that too little or, in a few cases, too much planning seemed to be associated with undesirable teaching situations. There were exceptions, however. In two or three instances those who planned the least and those who planned the most seemed to be very effective teachers.

Although its limitations must be recognized, such an assignment does disclose an important concept with respect to teaching and planning for teaching. *Planning, like teaching, is a personal invention.* The amount and nature of planning is dependent on a variety of factors. Among these are the particular nature of the lesson or topic under consideration, the number of years one has been teaching, the particular type of learning experience involved, and the personality and special skills of the teacher involved.

The purpose of this chapter is to offer some guidelines for planning that teachers generally have found useful. They should be used by the beginning teacher *as a basis* for determining his own personal needs and preferences in the area. Experienced teachers generally agree that some planning is essential. While some teachers may verbally deny the need for planning, if pressed they usually will admit some efforts in this direction. Just as the lawyer prepares his legal brief, so must the teacher organize his thinking with respect to teaching. The lawyer, like the teacher, is unable to predetermine his entire strategy, but his pre-planned activities can be very useful in providing an organized framework consistent with his purposes.

The beginning teacher sometimes is confused by the kinds, types, and levels of planning. These levels have been identified as: 1) curriculum guides, 2) subject area planning guides, 3) units, both resource and teaching, and 4) lessons. *Curriculum guides* are often worked out in states, counties, or cities by teachers in cooperation with curriculum consultants, administrators, and lay citizens. The guide may cover the whole school experience from kindergarten to twelfth grade. Usually it includes sample units for each grade level. Some school systems develop subject area planning guides. These may include many or all of the subjects to be taught at a grade level or in a total school. Subject area planning guides are similar to curriculum guides except that they usually are more comprehensive. Both are useful to the teacher in the overall planning of a year's or a semester's work. *Resource units* can be prepared by one or several persons. They usually are made available to other teachers as resources for planning classroom experiences. The sample units which often are a part of curriculum guides or subject area planning guides are resource units. Resource units are designed to provide a teacher with a variety of *resources* when planning a teaching unit. The *teaching unit* differs from a resource unit in that it contains only those resources which a teacher expects to utilize during the unit. The *lesson plan* contains the specific activities for each day of the time allotted to the unit; it is the means by which the unit is taught.

According to Crow and Crow: "Subject area planning includes program scheduling, long-range or unit planning, and short-range or daily lesson planning." [1] The classroom teacher, then, is directly responsible for both unit and lesson planning. This chapter is designed to offer specific assistance to teachers in these areas.

THE TEACHING UNIT

Unit organization first received prominent recognition in the early part of the twentieth century. One of the early leaders in the development of the unit plan defined the unit plan very well. A *unit*, according to Beauchamp, is a "means of organizing a series of studies or activities around some central theme or problem." [2] By definition, then, a unit covers an aspect of some activity or event which is large enough to be comprehensive. Teaching units are not confined to subject matter alone; they may include other possible learning areas such as the pupil's conduct, or environment. Michaelis wrote, "The content of the unit may be drawn from geography, history, science, art, music, and other subject-matter fields as needed to contribute to social learning." [3]

The unit plan of organizing a subject area has contributed immeasurably to the elimination of the traditional assign-recite-test formula for teaching. In so doing it has helped teachers break away from mere textbook teaching with its inherent ground-to-be-covered procedures. Its primary contribution seems to be that of providing positive motivation and directing attention to individual differences. Motivation is provided by breaking the year's work into sections small enough for pupils to grasp during a brief overview. The unit, which is concerned with both content and method, provides a basis for recognition of individual differences, discussed in Chapter 10.

What characterizes a unit of work?

Unit planning is designed to center the work of the classroom around meaningful wholes or patterns and to make the work of different days focus on a central theme until some degree of unified learning is attained. Such a unit concept approaches what Jerome Bruner has termed

[1] Lester D. Crow and Alice Crow, *The Student Teacher in the Elementary School* (New York: David McKay Co., Inc., 1965), p. 161.

[2] George A. Beauchamp, *Basic Dimensions of Elementary Method*, 2nd Ed. (Boston: Allyn and Bacon, Inc., 1965), p. 153.

[3] John V. Michaelis, *Social Studies for Children in a Democracy* (Englewood Cliffs, N. J.: Prentice-Hall, Inc., 1956), p. 129.

the basic structure of knowledge.[4] It embodies the notion of critical thinking or problem solving as its base. A unit is usually planned in three different phases: *initiating* activities; *developing* activities; *culminating* activities. Thus, a teaching unit has a structure of its own. It is neither a block of subject matter nor a series of independent lessons. While it is true that various adjectives have been applied to a unit (e.g., subject matter and experience), teachers are coming to recognize these as indicating differences in emphasis only. Some writers also refer to appreciation units, process units, and other special-purpose units; these, likewise, merely call attention to a certain type of learning product to be desired.

In planning a unit of work the teacher must concern himself with a number of important questions. If these questions can be answered in the affirmative the characteristics of a unit exist.

1. Is there a central theme or problem about which various activities may be organized?
2. Is the range of materials and experiences sufficiently wide to interest all pupils?
3. Is it possible for the more capable pupils to extend their experiences beyond the limits suggested?
4. Does the unit contain a variety of direct applications to the immediate lives of the pupils?
5. Does the unit anticipate some of the future needs of pupils?
6. Can the unit be completed within a reasonable length of time?
7. Can the unit be integrated with past and future learnings of the pupils?
8. Does the unit permit social interaction and growth in problem solving?

In planning units of work it is appropriate for a teacher to think in terms of *weeks* of the school year rather than in terms of daily lessons. Units will vary in length, depending on the emphasis and the nature of the work to be done. In most elementary classes units will range in length from two to six weeks. If in preliminary planning one conceives a unit of less than two weeks it is likely that the unit theme or problem can be integrated with another of the problems proposed. Likewise, problems which demand more than six weeks for their development can usually be divided into two parts. If the time span is excessive the integrated theme or pattern can become lost or distorted. With younger

[4] Jerome Bruner, *The Process of Education* (Cambridge, Mass.: Harvard University Press, 1961), pp. 17–18.

children the unit may be for a shorter duration; however, interesting units may be longer and as effective even with young children. The interest and maturity of the children in the class must be planned for in advance.

What are the stages in planning?

Classroom planning normally will fall into three stages or steps: planning the subject area as a whole; planning each unit of the subject area; and planning the specific activities for each topic and sub-topic. Unit planning must be preceded with adequate subject area planning. This involves a broad look at the subject area with a view to identifying the major themes to be emphasized. Relative emphasis is usually designated by an indication of time blocks for each unit. Lesson planning, in turn, follows unit planning.

The recommended procedure for subject area and unit planning is as follows:

Part I: The Subject Area Layout

1. a. List the few most important *subject area goals* which are to determine the nature and direction of the subject area as a whole. A subject area goal should suggest practical applications.
   b. Incorporate these into a *subject area introduction* addressed to pupils. The subject area introduction permits class members and the teacher to see clearly the values to be gained from the work that is to follow. Essentially it is designed to answer the following question: "Of what value can this subject be to me as a pupil?"

2. With the goals of the subject clearly in mind, block out the *major units* which should make up the subject area. Arrange in the order which can be learned best.

3. Develop *titles* for the selected units which will give some indication of the basic theme of the units.

4. Establish *time* needed for each unit. (Write in the margin after each unit title.)
   Note: Interest and maturity of the children will determine the length of the unit in weeks.

Part II: The Unit Plan

1. a. List the *unit goals*. They will relate to the subject area goals listed in Part I. The number of unit goals will be small, usually five to eight in number. Group unit goals under the following general categories: Understandings; Skills and Habits; Attitudes and Appreciations. (Usually there will be goals in each of the three categories.)
   Following the unit goals list *specific outcomes in terms of actual pupil behavior which may be indicative of progress toward the goal.* Leave

three or four spaces below each pupil outcome for an indication of means by which you can evaluate progress toward that outcome.
Note: A unit goal should indicate a real-life application. The specific outcomes should indicate how they fit into the unit. For example, instead of just "class discussion," indicate class discussion on a particular problem.

  b. Incorporate the goals into a *unit introduction* addressed to pupils. (See #1 of subject area layout.) The introduction (overview) may be in the form of a class discussion or some other technique. An adequate unit introduction probably will need at least two or three typewritten pages for its development.

2. *Outline* briefly the subject matter to be used or emphasized in the unit. Explain briefly each facet of the outline.

3. Make a list of the *major concepts* which you expect pupils to acquire during the unit. (Such concepts are broad. Example from a fifth grade health class: Although some bacteria are harmful to man, the vast majority are beneficial to his survival.)

4. a. List the *pupil experiences* (activities) which will insure that pupils reach the desired goals. These will include assignments, exercises, readings, problems, projects, films, trips, laboratory exercises, papers to write, diagrams and/or maps, oral reports, and the like. *This is the crucial stage in planning.* Generally it is desirable to include more things to do than can be done within the time limits, thus making a reservoir of potential activities. Some of these activities might be suggested in resource units and programs of study.

  b. Provide for *individual differences.* One way is to group exercises required of all and those which are optional. Teacher may implement by simple marginal notes.

  c. Check the proposed pupil experiences (activities) in terms of *consistency* with the unit goals.

5. a. State the means you will use in *evaluating progress* toward unit goals. *Note:* Place these in the space following statement of goals. (See #1A.)

  b. Construct situational test items, rating scales by teacher, check lists, observational forms, and so on which seem appropriate measures of stated goals.

Part III: Specific Lesson Plans

Construct lesson plans in those areas which demand further expansion. Some lesson plans will cover two or three or more days of class work. Be certain that your plans cover a logically complete block of work.

How does a teacher develop a subject area layout?

The most obvious *aid* in laying out a subject area is the selected textbook. Also needed is a collection of other textbooks and subject area planning guides in the area. The teacher then makes a preliminary list of seemingly desirable units in the form of ideas, topics, or problems. Next he arranges the proposed unit titles into a tentative order. Finally the direction of emphasis is indicated by establishing appropriate titles for each unit as suggested in the foregoing outline. The preliminary subject area layout usually will contain more proposed units than is permitted within the time limits. At this point one is obliged to alter, combine, eliminate, or otherwise adjust to the local school situation and problems involved. The amount of emphasis for each unit usually is determined by the particular values of the individual teacher involved.

Although subject area layouts frequently are prepared by each individual teacher, increasing emphasis is being given to joint participation of all members within a grade level. Each teacher, however, should be left to determine varying degrees of emphasis between units, the nature and types of experiences desired for achieving the broad goals, and so on.

A subject area layout follows:

SUBJECT AREA LAYOUT

Subject Area Goals

1. After this school year in social studies, the pupil should have furthered his understanding of people and nations beyond the American continents, including information about their cultures, the work they do, and the standards of living they have attained.

2. After this school year in social studies, the pupil should have developed an appreciation of the contributions of people from countries other than those in the Americas.

3. After this school year in social studies, the pupil should be able to pick out the many likenesses and differences among nations and their people, as well as see relationships among nations in the same region and in different regions of the world.

4. After this school year in social studies, the pupil should become acquainted with the influences that geographical location has upon historical events and upon the cultures of peoples.

Subject Area Introduction

As we study these people this year, we will learn that their way of life is made up of many things. Their way of life is the language they speak and the way they write it. It is their homes and places of worship, their schools, libraries, museums, hospitals, theatres, and parks. Their way of life is their farms and ranches, mines and forests, mills and factories. Their way of life is also made up of their villages, towns, and cities, and their transportation and communication networks. It is the foods they eat, and even how they eat them. Their way of life is also the work they do and how they spend their leisure time. It is also their heritage of ideals and values that guide their daily living, the freedoms they cherish, and the laws they have. Their way of life—their culture—is all this and more. In social studies this year we will have an opportunity to examine these wonderful people and learn of cultures that are similar and different from ours.

This year you will learn how people are living in regions of nations beyond the Americas. You will discover that people live in different ways in various places. But you will also find that there are many similarities among people the world over.

Major Units

I.	Viewing the world	3 weeks
II.	In Europe	6 weeks
III.	In the Soviet Union	4 weeks
IV.	In the Middle East and North Africa	2 weeks
V.	In Africa South of the Sahara	2 weeks
VI.	In Japan and Korea	3 weeks
VII.	In China	3 weeks
VIII.	In South Asia	3 weeks
IX.	In Southeast Asia	2 weeks
X.	In the Island World	3 weeks
XI.	Working Together	4 weeks

How is a teaching unit planned?

The first steps in planning a teaching unit are similar to the first steps in planning a subject area layout. The steps in the preparation of a teaching unit are necessarily more restricted and specific than those of the subject area layout. In all cases, however, they must be consistent with and fit into the overall framework established in the subject area layout.

Unit goals. As indicated in the preceding chapter (see pages 63–64) goals should be stated in behavioral terms. It is often useful to break down the proposed learnings into types: Understandings; Skills and Habits; Attitudes and Appreciations. Although such a classification of learning types must be somewhat arbitrary, the processes of learning involved do differ to a degree. For example, the activities essential for *understanding* are not usually sufficient for the development of a *skill* or *attitude*. Although most unit plans normally include all *types* of learning, there may be instances when the plan does *not* include all types.

As indicated in the sample unit plan illustrated on pages 84–89, it seems desirable to begin a goal with the clause, "After this unit the pupil should . . . ." This serves as a constant reminder that emphasis should be on what the pupil may accomplish. Then, when the goal has been stated, a number of *anticipated outcomes* are listed. As indicated in the sample unit plan, anticipated outcomes offer direction for activities essential for goal fulfillment. Furthermore a sound basis is provided for measurement and evaluation. It may be desirable to indicate, at the outset, anticipated techniques of evaluation. This enables the teacher to construct at least some of the necessary devices in advance of the experience. Appropriate statement of unit goals provides a sound basis for the remainder of the unit operation.

Unit introduction. The unit introduction, like a subject area introduction, is designed to develop interest. It will incorporate the proposed goals or objectives in a language which pupils can understand and to which they will respond favorably. Not only will the process of expressing goals or objectives to pupils help the teacher clarify his own thinking, but it also will help in establishing the work of the unit at the maturity levels of the pupils. Although the illustration presented on pages 85–86 is essentially a short, informal lecture, the subject area introduction may be just as effectively developed through a motivation-type discussion. In addition to the illustrated unit introduction any number of other motivational experiences can be included. These can include films, resource speakers, short pupil reports, and demonstrations. Sometimes, however, teachers defeat their own purpose by employing lengthy discussion periods in an attempt to persuade pupils that the unit will be interesting and meaningful. One or possibly two hours should be fully adequate for the initiating activities of a unit and for primary children, the introduction may be much shorter.

Subject-matter outline. Development of a teaching unit is dependent on a body of content upon which activities of the unit rest. One cannot learn without learning something. Whatever is learned is subject matter or becomes subject matter. The subject-matter outline serves to identify the content material which is needed and the problem of relative emphasis. The subject-matter outline must be complete enough to guide the teacher in planning specific activities.

Major concepts. It has been established that individuals tend to conceptualize learnings. Concepts are among the most important products of learning which are applied to out-of-school situations. Transfer, however, may be expected to occur only to the degree that pupils are taught to transfer. Therefore, it seems desirable that the teacher identify for himself, in advance of the learning experience, some of the important concepts which should be developed. This serves as an additional guide in establishing activities which have functional value to pupils.

Learning experiences. This is the crucial stage of planning. Learning experiences must be set up which will enable pupils to achieve the unit goals. They will usually include a variety of activities which employ many of the methods and techniques of teaching such as assignments, movies, discussions, dramatic plays, short talks, written reports, demonstrations, experiments, field trips, and resource speakers. What the pupils do will determine what they learn. The activities, however, should be specifically related to unit goals. For this reason it is essential to identify a goal with each planned activity. Furthermore, each proposed experience should be related to some specific part of the content outline.

The act of preplanning some of the activities does not mean that the teacher must assume the role of taskmaster. Pupils may actively participate in the planning of class activities, but this does not replace the need for a certain number of preplanned activities *suggested* by the teacher. As in the sample unit, different pupils often will be involved in different activities; thus provision for individual differences may become a reality. For both beginning and experienced teachers it may be necessary to make a special point of this in the unit plan.

Unit evaluation. A unit plan is incomplete without some forecast of progress toward unit goals. Unit plans may be rendered ineffective if pupils anticipate being asked to recall specific facts only, from the textbook. Measurement and evaluation should be made consistent with the goals and the originally outlined subject matter of the unit. It is for this reason that provision was made in the Suggested Unit Outline for an indication of measurement and evaluation techniques immediately following the stated goals.

The unit plan illustration is preceded by a subject area layout. It is followed with a description of lesson planning (illustrated in the various methods chapters throughout the book). The illustrated unit plan is not necessarily the best approach to planning; rather it represents *one* approach to the problem.

What does a well-planned unit look like? The unit which follows was developed by a beginning teacher. While the reader may recognize certain weaknesses, the example should be useful in illustrating how the Suggested Unit Outline can be applied.

UNIT PLAN

Subject: **Social Studies**
Unit: In the Soviet Union [5]

Unit Goals

1. After this unit the pupil should have furthered his understanding concerning the world's largest country, as evidenced by:
   A. His location of the U.S.S.R. on maps and globes. (Evaluation: Test items)
   B. His measurement of the air distances across Russia and relation of this to time and distance study which involves problem solving. (Evaluation: Test items)
   C. His construction of the U.S.S.R. map and superimposition of the 50 states of America over the Russian map. (Evaluation: Rating scale by teacher)

2. After this unit the pupil should have furthered his understanding concerning the Russian people and culture, as evidenced by:
   A. His correspondence with various agencies for information concerning the Russian people. (Evaluation: Research paper)
   B. His collection of magazine articles and pictures that portray the Russian people and culture. (Evaluation: Oral report)
   C. His collection of actual Russian objects to display for the class. (Evaluation: Rating scale by teacher and test items)
   D. His ability to write a short article about the Russian people. (Evaluation: Written report)
   E. His participation in tasting caviar and other Russian foods to understand different foods in Russia. (Evaluation: Check list)
   F. His participation in class discussion after watching movies on Russian people. (Evaluation: Rating scale by teacher and test items)
   G. His participation in listening to Russian music for comparison with U. S. music and identification of musical scores. (Evaluation: Check list and test items)
   H. His ability to figure the cost of consumer goods (cars, clothes, etc.) in terms of days or hours worked as compared with costs in U.S.A. (Evaluation: Test items)

3. After this unit the pupil should have developed a familiarization with the climate, resources, geography, and industry of Russia, as evidenced by:
   A. His location of the five geographic divisions of the U.S.S.R. (Evaluation: Rating scale by teacher and test items)
   B. His maintenance of a record of local temperatures related to U.S.S.R. temperatures. (Evaluation: Analysis report)
   C. His report about one type of industry within the U.S.S.R. (Evaluation: Written report)

---

[5] The writers are indebted to Jerry W. Miller for his permission to reproduce portions of his unit constructed in a course at the University of Nevada.

D. His ability to fill in natural resources by symbols on a map of Russia. (Evaluation: Check list)

4. After this unit the pupil should be familiar with the type of government and the historical events that brought about this type of government, as evidenced by:
   A. His ability to relate the revolt in Russia to the Communist Party. (Evaluation: Reading analysis report and test items)
   B. His review of the factors and causes of the communist revolt with Czarist Russia. (Evaluation: Test items)
   C. His participation on a panel discussion: "What should the policy of the United States be toward the communist countries?" (Evaluation: Check list)
   D. His ability to compare the democratic system of government to the Russian system. (Evaluation: Written report)

Unit Introduction

The Soviet Union is the largest country in the world. Its population exceeds 200 million people, most of whom live in western Russia. The U.S.S.R. has many resources which include timber, farmland, iron, coal, and oil. The people are attempting to develop these resources to their fullest.

Its people have traditionally settled along its rivers which run north and south and have for centuries provided the only means of transportation. Even the Viking traders used these rivers. They traveled into this great primitive country to trade and some of them stayed as protectors and eventually became the rulers and noblemen. They were called "Russ," hence the name Russia.

Russia has had a long history of oppression. The Mongolians overran most of Asia, including Russia, in the 13th century. For about 240 years their cruel rule existed. Finally, in 1480, some strong Russian leaders emerged—beginning with Ivan III—and overthrew these conquerors.

The first Czar was Ivan IV (The Terrible). His rule began in 1533, and in 1547 he declared himself Czar. Ivan IV was followed by others, each taking "Czar" as title, including Peter the Great who reigned from 1689 to 1725. He was responsible for bringing western culture to Russia. He was the first ruler to leave the homeland and he traveled in Europe studying ship-building and navigation and absorbing the culture of the countries he visited. Upon his return he began construction of Russia's new capital on the Baltic Sea, St. Petersburg (now Leningrad). After Peter's death, Moscow became Russia's capital city.

The long reign of the Romanov family began in 1613 with Michael and ended in 1917 with Nicholas II, the last Czar. Nicholas was removed by open revolt which led to a period of trouble and confusion. During this period of trouble and confusion the Communist Party, under the leadership of Lenin, seized control of the government and forcefully instituted their own reforms. Sweeping changes began to take place almost immediately— they seized industry, they collectivized farming, and they set up controls upon education.

In spite of all the promises and predictions by the small group of Communist Party members, the Russian people weren't any better off than they were under the reign of the Czars.

World War II saw Russia unprepared and in need of help as Nazi Germany overran parts of the large country. Eventually, with the massive assistance of the United States, the intruders were pushed back out of Russia as the Soviets continued to get stronger. As war ended additional troubles developed between the "Communist Bloc" countries and the western powers. These problems continued, even growing, until Stalin's death, at which time the tensions began to ease. Since then tension has generally continued to decrease.

Subject Matter (Content) Outline

While discussing this unit we will try to understand this largest country, its people and culture. We will try to familiarize ourselves with information concerning the climate, resources, geography, and industry in the U.S.S.R. We will try to see the differences between our way of life and the Russian way of life.

   I. From Baltic to Pacific
      A. Reading the maps
      B. Exploring Asiatic U.S.S.R.
      C. European U.S.S.R.
      D. Moscow—the capital

  II. Living Under the Communist Rulers
      A. Past history and revolt
      B. Farming the collective way
      C. Pre-collective farming
      D. Day to day in the city
      E. Longing for freedom

Important Concepts

1. Our form of government in the U.S.A. is different from the Russian form of government.

2. We, as Americans, have many personal freedoms.

3. The type of government we have is designed to preserve our freedoms.

4. Human rights, human dignity, and the need to preserve these, at whatever cost, are very important to human beings.

5. Many changes were brought about by modern transportation in Russia.

6. Progress is important, but only with consideration for human resources.

Student Activities

   1. Letter Writing
         In advance of the actual beginning of this unit on the Soviet Union, the proper form for a letter will be exhibited on the chalkboard. The

class will then jointly compose a letter, or letters, to agencies that can furnish information on the U.S.S.R.
(Goal 2: The pupil should have furthered his understanding concerning the Russian people.)

2. Oral Reports
Each pupil will collect magazine articles and pictures that portray the Russian people and culture. Each pupil will have an opportunity to orally report on these items as well as any object of Russian origin. These items to be placed on display in order to generate class interest—taken one by one the items can be used to evaluate present class knowledge on subject as well as giving opportunity to open areas of study.
(Goal 2: See above)

3. Collateral Readings
The pupil is expected to read at least 25 pages from any one or more of the following books. The purpose of the assignment is to supplement the material in the textbook.
(Goal 2: See above)
Dawson, Grace S., *Your World and Mine.*
Dolch, Edward W. and Marguerite P., *Stories from Old Russia*
Geis, Darlene, *Let's Travel in the Soviet Union*
Parker, Dr. Fan, *The Russian Alphabet Book*
Ponsot, Marie (translater), ill. by Benvenuti, *Russian Fairy Tales*
Thayer, Charles W. and the Editors of *Life*, Life-World Library, *Russia*

4. Written Reports
Each pupil is required to prepare a short article about the Russian people. The purpose is to give the pupil experience in expressing himself in a clear, precise, and understandable manner.
(Goal 2: See above)
Each pupil is to write letters to various travel agencies and ask for materials which he will then use to prepare a research paper.
(Goal 2: See above)
Each pupil will write a short report on a particular industry within the U.S.S.R.
(Goal 3: The pupil should develop a familiarization with the climate, resources, geography, and *industry* of Russia.)
Each pupil will make a comparison of the democratic system of government with the Russian government.
(Goal 4: The pupil should be familiar with the type of government and the historical events that brought about this type of government.)

5. Films
The purpose of showing films is to stimulate interest on the part of the pupils and permit them to associate what they have learned in class with real-life situations.
(Goal 1: The student should have furthered his understanding of the world's largest country; Goal 3: The pupil should develop a familiarization with the climate, resources, geography, and industry of Russia; Goal 4: See above.)
A. Show film entitled, "Russia"

    B. Show film entitled, "Russian Life Today—Inside the Soviet Union"
    C. Show film entitled, "Russia and the World Today"

6. Recordings
    The purpose of playing the records is to give each pupil an opportunity to listen to Russian music for comparison with music here in the United States and to be able to identify certain Russian musical scores. (Goal 2: See above)
    A. Peter Ilyich Tchaikowsky's *1812 Overture*
    B. Standard School Broadcast, Program 24, *St. Peterburg*, 1960–61
    C. #FH5420, *History of the Soviet Union in Ballad and Song* (Russian Lang.)

7. Class Discussion
    This activity will be the mainstay of classroom activities throughout this unit. This method of teaching may help pupils search for answers and topics to be discussed in the class. A good topic for classroom discussion is: "How can we better communicate to the Russian people details of our way of life?"
    (Goal 2: See above)

8. Panel Discussion
    The purpose is to stimulate each one's thinking and improve one's ability to express himself before a group. The panel will discuss: "What should be the trade policy of the United States toward the communist countries?"
    (Goal 4: See above)

9. Assignments
    A. Construct a map of U.S.S.R. and superimpose the 50 states of the United States over the Russian map.
    (Goal 1: See above)
    B. Bring to class articles and pictures that portray the Russian people.
    (Goal 2: See above)
    C. Bring to class objects of Russian origin to display for the class.
    (Goal 2: See above)
    D. Construct a map showing the five geographic divisions of Russia.
    (Goal 3: See above)
    E. Construct a map of Russia showing the location of natural resources in this country.
    (Goal 3: See above)

10. Informal Lectures
    Informal lectures will be used throughout the unit to clarify concepts which are not adequately developed in the textbook or supplementary materials. Example: "The Major Revolt in Russia."
    (Goal 4: See above)

Provision for Individual Differences

    The teacher is conscious of the fact that there are individual differences so he will expect all pupils to do the following projects only:

1. Participate in classroom discussion.

2. Complete written and oral reports.

3. Read textbook assignments.

4. Do workbook assignments.

5. Participate in class projects.

Those desiring to do additional or different work will be asked to read collateral readings and report orally or in writing on an historical development of Russia that is of particular interest to them.

THE LESSON PLAN

There is perhaps today as much confusion and difference of opinion with respect to lesson planning as in any other area of teaching. Since the advent of the unit plan some teachers, and indeed many textbook writers, have minimized its usefulness. Other writers and most administrators stress the need for at least some informal lesson notes. In a sense the de-emphasis on lesson planning may represent a reaction against the type of daily planning which was in vogue prior to the appearance of the unit plan. Although the unit plan did have a marked impact upon the preparation of lesson plans it *did not replace* the need for lesson planning. The description which follows presupposes adequate unit planning.

What is the relationship between unit and lesson planning?

A lesson plan is an expanded portion of a unit plan. It represents a more or less detailed analysis of a particular *activity* described in the unit plan. For example, one of the unit outcomes anticipated in the sample Social Studies unit was ". . . the pupil's reaction during class discussion." While the problem title was stated in the unit plan, no indication was given as to *how* the problem would be developed. In discussing a *problem of policy*, as described in Chapter 7, careful planning is essential. The lesson plan serves such a purpose.

Instead of a *daily* lesson plan (a different plan for each day), as was common prior to development of the teaching unit, the same plan frequently serves for two or three or more days. For example, a thorough discussion of the problem, "What preparations would be necessary if we planned to tour the Soviet Union?" would in all probability demand more than the daily schedule would allow. Likewise, a panel discussion and its follow-through discussion may require parts of two days. Sometimes, however, the nature of an activity does render a formal lesson plan unnecessary. Usually one does not need to prepare a special plan, for example, when the day's schedule calls for hearing oral reports, studying reference materials, or engaging in collateral reading activities. Here the unit plan may be fully adequate. The type and length of a lesson plan will depend on such factors as the particular teacher involved, the nature of the activity, and administrative policy.

How is a lesson plan prepared?

The essentials of a lesson plan are somewhat similar to the important elements of a unit plan. Although forms and styles differ markedly from one teacher to another, a lesson plan usually contains a goal, lesson introduction (approach), lesson development, and a lesson summary. Depending on the nature of the lesson it also may include a list of materials needed, provision for individual differences, and an assignment.

The common elements of lesson planning erroneously suggest a more or less standard routine. While it is true that most plans will be structured around the common elements described, significant differences will be observed within this framework. Different teaching methods often are designed for different instructional purposes; they involve different sequences. Thus, lesson plans must be modified accordingly. Sample lesson plans, prepared for the purposes of illustrating each of the major teaching methods, appear in the respective methods chapters. A comparison of some of these plans is recommended. The particular style of lesson planning illustrated in this book is suggestive only.

As indicated in the illustrated lesson plans the *goals*, with their accompanying behavioral outcomes, are more specific than unit goals. As a matter of fact, two or more lesson goals often are necessary for the achievement of one unit goal. The outcomes are those which might be reasonably anticipated as a result of the particular lesson involved.

The *lesson approach* is usually short. It is designed to develop immediate interest in the lesson. In a discussion-type lesson the transition between the lesson approach and lesson development may be indistinct. The lesson approach is comparable to the initiating experiences of a unit plan.

The heart of a lesson is the *lesson development*. This section of the lesson contains an outline of the major activities included in the learning experiences. In case of a demonstration, procedures may be planned to the greatest detail. In class discussion lessons a few key questions only

National Education Association

A teaching unit with live animals.

may be indicated. These may not be asked if the discussion renders them unnecessary at the time. They merely serve the purpose of suggesting to the teacher the type of question which might be appropriate. The beginning teacher frequently finds it convenient to write out answers to key questions.

The sequence of key questions (or events) is extremely important in achieving lesson objectives. Essentially, questions serve a dual role. They focus on the content of what is being discussed and on the cognitive processes as well. Instructional processes which foster critical thinking must be sequenced. As illustrated in the discussion lesson plan (pages 128–129) the first sequence of questions pertains to analysis of the problem. These, in turn, are followed with key questions which pertain to the higher levels of cognition, analysis, and synthesis of hypotheses or proposed solutions. Finally, some attention is given to the highest level of cognition (evaluation).

If questions at the higher levels of cognition are raised too early in the discussion, the processes of analysis break down. Usually the discussion must again revert to the lower cognitive levels until pupils are prepared for the higher levels of thinking.

An important aspect of teaching which is *not* usually shown in a lesson plan is that of pacing. When are pupils ready to move to the next level of thinking? What evidence suggests the need for further expansion of a point? This is something that cannot be predicted in advance. Rather, by careful observation one develops a feeling for the type of question needed. Questions may fulfill functions of focusing, refocusing, change of focus, deviating from focus, extending thought on the same level, lifting thought, and controlling thought.[6] Another aspect of teaching *not shown* in the lesson plan includes those questions and statements which are psychological and managerial in nature. These include comments or nonverbal expressions of approval, disapproval, and the like. They too constitute key aspects of the teaching process.

A lesson summary is usually short, but its importance cannot be over-emphasized. This is the portion of a lesson which enables the pupil to "put the loose ends into place." The summary affords an excellent opportunity for the pupil to formulate major concepts—to generalize his learnings. For the most part it is these generalizations or concepts which are transferred to related life problems. A summary may be included at the end of a lesson and/or at the beginning of a new lesson. In a discussion-type lesson the summary may incorporate the final decision or solution to the problem being discussed.

GENERAL PROBLEMS AND PRINCIPLES
IN PLANNING

Planning, like any other aspect of teaching, can be improperly applied. Unfortunately, most of us have observed the teacher who allows

[6] Hilda Taba, "The Teaching of Thinking," *Elementary English*, 42, No. 5: 34–42 (May, 1965).

his planning activities to place both himself and his pupils in a strait jacket. This is the individual who will not deviate from his plan under any conditions. Pupils who may be stimulated to voice original ideas pertaining to the lesson are quickly brought back into line. Unexpected events which *could* be used as a means of developing keen interest in an area are disregarded in preference to preplanned activities. One's best laid plans, whether they be inside or outside the classroom, sometimes go awry. Unexpected circumstances sometimes may make it necessary to alter one's plans in the midst of an activity. On the other hand, a lack of adequate planning can lead to disorganization and chaos.

A number of important guidelines should be useful to the teacher who would make most efficient use of unit and lesson planning:

1. Plans serve as useful guides or blueprints for teaching. They must be flexible enough to permit modification or revision as the occasion may demand.

2. Pupils appropriately play a part in planning classroom experiences. This does not imply that the teacher waits until he enters the classroom before he begins to plan. The prepared teacher has set up general goals, some definite activities, and some specific sources of materials which *may* be used.

3. Unit planning is designed to emphasize important patterns or relationships. Such an arrangement facilitates transfer of training to out-of-school situations.

4. Through adequate planning the teacher's attention tends to be directed to important problems of motivation and individual differences.

5. The lesson plan provides a handy reference to important statistics, illustrations, difficult words, special procedures, and the like.

6. Planning increases the teacher's own understanding of the problems involved.

7. Planning brings into proper balance and focus goals, subject matter, activities, and evaluation.

8. Adequate planning provides a basis for future teaching experiences. By making use of marginal notes the teacher easily can make substantial improvements in succeeding years.

9. Unit and lesson plans may be used more than once. It makes good sense to capitalize the next year on a highly successful experience. A word of caution is in order here, however. The responsible teacher does not permit his teaching to become staid—going through the same motions year after year. Prior to each experience he asks himself what improvements, changes, or substitutions might be in order. Continuous experimentation provides a basis for improved teaching.

10. Planning is a personal invention. The thoroughness and nature of unit and lesson planning will depend on the needs of each individual teacher involved.

SUMMARY

In this chapter emphasis has been placed on functions and techniques of planning. Relationships between different levels of planning, such as the teaching unit and lesson planning, have been considered.

Goals, when stated in behavioral terms, may serve as a basis for other planning activities. In addition to goals the unit consists of three important parts: subject-matter outline, activities, and evaluation. Each of these can be readily developed from appropriately stated goals.

The lesson plan is designed to make a unit plan come alive. It is an expanded portion of a unit, including the specific activities of a particular lesson. The basic essentials of a lesson plan are goals, motivation activities, developing activities, and summarizing activities. Lesson plans should correspond to important concepts rather than one scheduled lesson. In other words, they may extend through one, two, or even more class days. One may or may not need a lesson plan for each day's work, depending upon the nature of the activity.

Finally, some important problems and principles for planning were offered. Emphasis throughout this chapter has been placed on planning as an individual matter, depending upon the felt needs of each teacher. Beginning teachers usually need more detailed plans than do experienced teachers. All teachers, however, can profit from some planning. Indeed, without adequate planning teaching is usually ineffective.

QUESTIONS FOR STUDY AND DISCUSSION

1. What is the relationship among curriculum guides, subject area planning guides, resource and teaching units, and lesson plans? Refer to those sections in Chapter 2 which deal with the psychology of learning. Which theory seems most closely associated with subject area and unit planning? Why?

2. What are the distinctive features of a unit plan? Why is the subject area layout considered essential? How do subject area goals differ from unit goals? What is the basic difference between the subject-matter outline and a list of major concepts? How do learning experiences relate to unit goals? What are the advantages of planning units well in advance of actual instruction? What are the potential disadvantages? Why do the authors

recommend some indication of measurement and evaluation techniques immediately following a statement of unit goals?

3. What is the specific relationship between lesson and unit planning? Instead of a *daily* lesson plan, the authors suggest that a lesson plan sometimes may serve for three or more days. Why? If a lesson plan can sometimes serve for three or more days, why not rely exclusively on the unit plan? How does current lesson planning differ from the day-by-day planning recommended prior to development of the teaching unit? What advantages are associated with detailed lesson planning? Disadvantages?

4. What are the minimum essentials of a lesson plan? How are lesson goals integrated with unit goals? What basic differences, if any, do you see in lesson planning in the various curriculum areas? What areas would most likely demand most elaborate planning? Why? Under what conditions might a teacher function adequately without a formal lesson plan? What dangers are associated with little or no formal lesson planning? It has been demonstrated repeatedly that experienced teachers are more likely to omit lesson goals than any other segment from written lesson plans. Why? Why is a statement of lesson goals considered the most basic and essential element of lesson planning? Why is it impractical to prepare lesson plans more than two or three days in advance of actual instruction? Should lesson plans be re-used? What are the advantages and disadvantages of such a practice?

SELECTED BIBLIOGRAPHY

Beauchamp, George A., *Basic Dimensions of Elementary Method*, 2nd Ed. (Boston: Allyn and Bacon, Inc., 1965).

Bellack, Arno A., *The Language of the Classroom, Part II* (New York: Institute of Psychological Research, Teachers College, 1963).

Bruner, Jerome, *The Process of Education* (Cambridge, Mass.: Harvard University Press, 1961).

Crow, Lester D. and Alice, *The Student Teacher in the Elementary School* (New York: David McKay Co., Inc., 1965).

Grant, Dorothy A., "A Refocus on Lesson Planning," *Teachers College Record*, 63, No. 6: 503–508 (March, 1967).

Michaelis, John V., *Social Studies for Children in a Democracy* (Englewood Cliffs, N.J.: Prentice-Hall, Inc., 1956).

Taba, Hilda, "The Teaching of Thinking," *Elementary English*, 42, No. 5: 34–42 (May, 1965).

Wagner, Guy, "What Schools are Doing: Unit Teaching in the Elementary Schools," *Education*, 443–445 (March, 1965).

Activating the Desire to Learn:
Encouraging Self-Motivation

HISTORY is filled with accounts of eminent men and women, unquestionably gifted, who did not achieve very well during certain periods of their school careers. At least they did not learn what their teachers tried to teach them. Albert Einstein, President Franklin Roosevelt, President John F. Kennedy, and Sir Winston Churchill are examples of men who at times appeared to be unmotivated to learn what their schools offered and made "C's." Wernher von Braun, our famous space scientist, failed his high school courses in mathematics and physics. Of course, after he became enthusiastic about rocketry, he excelled in mathematics and physics. Thomas Edison's teacher thought that Tom was mentally "addled" and his mother withdrew him from school and taught him herself. Edison was motivated to continue to learn throughout his life and contributed numerous inventions even after he was eighty years old. Goertzel and Goertzel (1962) reported that 60 percent of the 400 eminent people in their study had serious school problems. They would have been classified as unmotivated.[1]

The foregoing excerpt suggests the seriousness of a problem which confronts every teacher. Some children apparently possess little desire to learn. Why? What are the mainsprings of human behavior? What can the teacher do to make pupils want to learn?

Creating, developing, or otherwise activating a desire to learn is not a problem with some children; with others it may be the most difficult aspect of teaching. An individual can be forced to attend class, but he *cannot* be forced to learn. Yet, teachers must somehow provide an environment which sparks the will to learn. The basic prompters of human behavior are examined in this chapter in terms of their influences on classroom methodology.

[1] E. Paul Torrance, "Motivating Children with School Problems," in E. Paul Torrance and Robert D. Strom, Eds., *Mental Health and Achievement* (New York: John Wiley & Sons, Inc., 1965), p. 339.

BASES OF MOTIVATING

Perhaps there has been a general tendency to oversimplify the problem of motivation by including all motivating factors under the heading of interest. Beauchamp has stated: "We have long recognized the significance of both interest and need as motivating factors for boys and girls in learning situations." [2] Interest is the expression of a felt need. Individuals may display similar interests as a result of quite different needs. One girl, for example, will indicate an interest in painting a frieze because of the close association with certain other children the experience provides. Another pupil will display an interest in the same project because she recognizes a rare opportunity to excel. As needs change, interests change. Because any given need may be expressed as interest in several ways it is extremely difficult to make accurate predictions of interest. Many needs, however, are so common to *all* children that a teacher can anticipate them without knowing pupils very well as individuals. Of course there are some needs which are peculiar to or at least acute with certain individuals, making thorough acquaintance with those who hold them particularly desirable. Thus interest in this chapter is approached both from the standpoint of the entire class group as well as from the standpoint of certain individuals within the group.

Motivation is defined as that part of the self which impels a person to learn—to work toward a goal. It is thought to represent a basic aspect of personality structure. Accordingly, motivation is a fairly stable characteristic. Yet one's motivational structure may be altered over a period of a few months or years. The teacher has the responsibility for encouraging and cultivating desirable motivational patterns. Alteration of existing patterns, however, is an involved process related to basic personality changes. It is usually approached indirectly through the avenue of interests.

Can pupils be motivated?

Traditionally, teachers have concerned themselves with motivating pupils to do good work. They have sought to help children see the fundamental values and purposes of education, of a particular class, or of a particular unit within a class subject. All too often, however, those pupils

[2] George A. Beauchamp, *Basic Dimensions of Elementary Method*, 2nd Edition (Boston: Allyn and Bacon, Inc., 1965), pp. 69–70.

who seem highly motivated at the outset continue to exhibit such behaviors, while those who appear to lack this quality seldom change their
behaviors very dramatically. Every teacher is aware of those pupils who
have self-sustaining motivation qualities. They need relatively little motivation. They already have an abundance of it! Other children tend to
have little motivation to achieve in any subject.

Such observations have led investigators to examine the personality
determinants of motivation.[3] Mounting evidence suggests that motivation is an aspect of personality; *that motivation is something a child
already possesses*. It is *not* something which a teacher does to pupils
directly.

From extensive research in the area Frymier[4] contends that there
are at least three crucial aspects of personality which influence motivation: self-concept and the concept of others; values; and openness to
experience.

Highly motivated pupils tend to have a positive picture of *themselves*. They feel competent to handle the problems of their everyday
existence. They feel accepted and respected. Being free of their own
problems they tend to have a positive concept of others, as evidenced by
a willingness to trust and rely upon the integrity of others.

On the other hand, children with low motivation tend to have a
low self-esteem. They feel that they are not liked and respected; that
they are not worthy, not important. Accordingly, they feel that other
people cannot be trusted, that others will take advantage of them if
possible.

The *values* associated with motivation seem to be related specifically
to the time dimension. As Frymier points out, "Highly motivated students tend to have an awareness of the future, a consciousness of the
present, and a realistic appraisal of the past." The low-motivated pupil,
in contrast, tends to be fearful or to ignore the future; he is obsessed with
the past or is completely preoccupied with the present. He seems to
become fixated on one segment of time.

In terms of *openness to experience*, the highly motivated child tends
to accept education as a challenge, feeling that he can cope with school
and class situations and problems. He seems to view specific problems
within a broad perspective. Conversely, the low-motivated child tends to
feel threatened by specific school or class experiences. He tends to build

---

[3] Some of the foremost work in this area has been done by Jack R. Frymier. His
work was recently synthesized in his book *The Nature of Educational Method*
(Columbus, Ohio: Charles E. Merrill, Inc., 1965).

[4] Jack R. Frymier, "Strategies to Reinforce Learning," *Bulletin of the National
Association of Secondary School Principals*, 10, No. 314: 69–92 (December, 1966).

the task up to a point that is out of proportion with the other aspects of his environment.

After studying the motivational patterns of several thousand students, Frymier concluded that low-motivated students are basically different from other students. In establishing a profile of such individuals, five basic personality characteristics have been identified: they are unhappy and afraid; they lack confidence in themselves; they resist change and new ideas; they are unduly concerned with the objective and the materialistic; they dislike school intensely.[5]

Based upon the foregoing analysis, then, it appears that motivation as an aspect of personality changes slowly as personality changes; that a teacher must start with pupils as they tend to be; that his initial task is to understand the fears and frustrations of such individuals and to help them alter their feelings toward themselves and others. In short, he must develop the mental health approach to learning. Although motivational patterns can be expected to change, this will come about over an extended period of time. Instead of trying to motivate pupils, he will try to *interest* them. Interests, as opposed to motivation, are immediate and of a relatively short duration. Sustained interest over a period of time, however, can lead to motivational changes.

What is the nature of motives?

Miss Smith noticed that her pupils in the classroom were restless and inattentive during the lesson. A change was needed. She said, "All right, children, I want to teach you a new song." She sang a little song by herself and at the same time went through the actions. "I'm a little teapot short and stout. Here is my handle. Here is my spout." In only a few minutes the children were all singing and going through the actions. The pupils' restlessness seemed to disappear and all of the children were alert and singing. The pupils' attention was with the teacher and everyone was involved in the activity.

Needless to say, interest was almost universal during this activity. Even those pupils who usually displayed little interest in class functions participated freely in this activity. Now, why was interest high under these conditions? The answer is obvious—all these children possess a *need* for personal involvement and physical activity. Other needs common to all individuals include the desire for affection, security, self-esteem, and a reasonable degree of success. In many instances teachers are able to capitalize on these needs. The basic instructional problem is to devise techniques of relating these needs to the values associated with the class involved.

[5] Frymier, *The Nature of Educational Method, op. cit.*, p. 116.

Closely associated with basic needs is the element of *curiosity*. All individuals are curious. From the small child who asks "Why?" a thousand times a day to the elderly person who rushes to the scene of a fire or accident, individuals display a compelling urge to "know." Mr. Sample, a fourth grade teacher, capitalized on this natural urge when he set off a volcano eruption which literally exploded and threw ash all over the model. "What happened? Why? How? What caused it?"— such questions came from all corners of the room. The problem was no longer one of interest, but one of directing the enthusiasm displayed.

For many years teachers have attempted to capitalize on the *individual interests* of children as an avenue for developing interest in class instruction. While it is true that interests offer clues to certain needs of the individual, superficial inspection of a special interest may fail to disclose the particular need(s) being met. There is a tendency, however, for an individual to generalize in the area of special interests to *all* aspects of the interest involved. Thus, the need fulfillment of satisfaction coming from one aspect of a special interest tends to *predispose* an individual to view other aspects of his special interest in a favorable light. For instance, a girl may have an interest in doll collecting because it enables her to enjoy many hours of solitude made necessary because of her particular home environment. If the interest is strong enough she will continue the activity long after the home environment has been altered. In other words, the activity began to fulfill other basic needs, such as gaining prestige from the collection, realizing a certain amount of success in the area, and the like.

The classroom teacher, then, can be reasonably certain that an individual's special interest (especially if it is noticeably high) is intimately associated with the fulfillment of a number of basic needs. His major task is to help the pupil relate the needs and values associated with his special interest to the needs and values associated with the class values. Almost any special interest *can* be related to class values *provided* the teacher allows himself to think creatively about the issue. The illustration which follows is designed to suggest ways a special interest can be related to different subject fields.

Mary indicated an interest in collecting dolls. She frequently showed her rather large collection to friends and neighbors.

In *history*, the teacher can capitalize on this interest by encouraging Mary to make a study of the historical events related to certain dolls.

In *mathematics*, the teacher can help Mary develop a graph depicting the relative size of the dolls in a measurement unit.

In *geography*, the teacher might use Mary's doll collection to illustrate the clothes and costumes from many different countries.

In *English*, the teacher can develop Mary's interest in writing about her doll collection.

Likewise, such an interest can be related in some way to almost any content field. It rests upon the teacher to channel the existing interest to fit the problems at hand.

Capitalizing upon a special individual interest involves two important teaching problems in addition to that of associating special interests with class values, described in the foregoing.

First is the problem of discovering special interests. Some teachers conduct simple interest surveys in their classes. These sometimes take the form of queries concerning what pupils do. For example: "Things I prefer to do when I have time on my hands." Sometimes, however, verbal expressions of interests are inconsistent with actual interests. Actual observation of pupil behavior may be very effective in discovering pupil interests, especially if the observation includes out-of-class activities. Likewise, the pupil's cumulative school record offers valuable clues as to interest trends.

Next is the exploration of subject values. The teacher must be keenly aware of the human values inherent in what he teaches. The clues of such values are to be found in what children do rather than what they may say about things. Thus, the teacher looks into the world outside of school to see what people are doing with what he is attempting to teach. He will want to seek answers to many questions. Where do people use arithmetic? How do people use arithmetic? What kinds of problems do people in general have which lend themselves to arithmetic processes? What do people do with history? What current problems might be better solved by an understanding of United States history? What type of material do people read during their spare time?

In order to effectively guide pupils into life applications the teacher, of course, must be well read. Indeed, he must be constantly in tune with changes and developments which affect the subjects taught in the elementary school.

Incentives or extrinsic instructional devices have been included among classroom activities for many years. Some of the better known of these are threat of failure, emphasis upon grades, honor roll lists, stars, labels, or other marks upon their papers or classroom charts.

Although extrinsic pressure *may* spur some pupils to greater effort, it is not without serious hazards. Motivation for high grades usually has a favorable impact on only those individuals who have a chance to win!

In most class situations this will be a very small percentage of the group. Moreover, those who are most likely to be motivated by competition usually need it least. They are the individuals who are self-motivated to do high quality work, with or without special motivational activities.

The impact of keen competition for marks on the less able pupil is likely to be quite unhealthy. Having failed before, he tends to be overly anxious at the outset of the learning experience. Added pressure tends to result in *less* effort in academic areas and a turning to other, less desirable avenues of fulfilling his needs for success.

Extrinsic devices *can* be effective if the learner has a fair chance of success *as he sees it*. Some teachers, for example, have devised ways of permitting a pupil to compete with *his own past record*. For instance, in a reading class a pupil can attempt to improve his speed and comprehension as measured by past performances; in a spelling class one may keep a list of his own spelling errors from unit to unit.

How are motives integrated for effective teaching?

The effective teacher, of course, makes use of all the motives described in the foregoing. He integrates basic needs, curiosity, special interests, and incentives into a pattern which he hopes will be effective for all pupils. Yet too often in today's schools one can observe too many children whose needs are not being met. In almost every class one can readily spot pupils who display little or no interest in the legitimate class activities. Why is this? There is certainly no pat answer which can be given! A few general guidelines, however, are disclosed from the foregoing analysis of motives.

1. Since *all* children have certain *basic needs and a basic curiosity*, the teacher might focus his attention *first* upon these areas. Thus, if the unit or lesson approach were effectively executed *most* of the pupils might respond. One might reasonably expect a *few* pupils to show relatively little response, simply because their most urgent current needs are little affected by the motivational device(s).

2. The teacher's second line of attack might be in the area of *special interests*. While this might be just as desirable as the first, it is not likely to be as economical of time and effort. If, however, the desire to learn can be effectively activated in *most* pupils through basic needs or through the element of curiosity, the teacher can afford the time needed to work through the area of special interests.

3. As a last resort, the teacher can hold out *incentives* to pupils who have not yet responded to previous efforts at motivation. For example, he *may* find it necessary to warn one or two children that failure

to do the work now will most certainly mean failure to move on to a different type of activity later on. A great deal of discretion is needed, however, in terms of the individual involved. Sometimes an incentive or threat will provide the stimulus needed for development of interest. In the overwhelming majority of cases, however, incentives and threats can do more harm than good to those pupils who are in greatest need of motivation. Far too many teachers rely almost exclusively on the use of incentives as an approach to motivation.

How do pupils differ in motivation?

One spring morning a group of prospective teachers observed a veteran teacher at work. Instead of concentrating on what the teacher did, they made notes, as instructed, of pupil behaviors pertaining to the problem of motivation. The lesson basically was one of supervised reading and writing exercises. A summary of the observations was as follows:

Six pupils displayed enthusiasm by asking questions, volunteering information, and the like.

Three children might have been classified as "clinkers." For all observable intent and purposes they were simply occupying space within the classroom; none of them were at all actively involved in the class situation. The psychologist would call them withdrawn.

Three or four individuals apparently were responsible for 90 percent of the class disturbances. They seemed to hold no interest in the legitimate class activities, but interest was obviously high in a variety of nonacceptable activities.

One child appeared detached from the rest of the group. He was reading a book. When the teacher inquired what he was reading the fellow gave the name of another text in the subject area. Upon the suggestion that he study the assigned text the boy claimed to have already completed the assignment. He was allowed to continue his individual study.

Several pupils appeared to make some effort to concentrate on the class activities. Although most of them seemed to need help from time to time, they displayed a reasonable degree of motivation. This attention did seem to wander from the immediate problem when the teacher failed to pass by their desks every few minutes.

The pupil behaviors indicated in the foregoing are not unlike those in many elementary school classrooms. The ability range, as in many classes today, was from dull normal to the bright and even gifted. The teacher had planned instruction around some definite motivational activities. This was evidenced by a ten-minute introduction in which he attempted to direct the pupils' attention to the subject under consideration. Reference was made to a resource speaker who had visited the class the first day of the unit. At this point in the lesson interest *was* apparently moderate to high with most children. Why, then, was interest of a transitory nature with several members of the class? This was a question the teacher asked of the observing group after the class. He admitted an inability to answer the question satisfactorily. Although the answer is far from clear, fairly recent research suggests that individual differences may be as important in the area of motivation as in any other area of instruction. Traditionally, teachers have attempted to develop instructional interest in the same manner with *all* pupils. Evidence indicates that the type of motivation which appeals to those who have found school a reasonably satisfactory experience is *not* appropriate for those who have found school a highly frustrating experience.

What is the relationship between leadership strategies and motivational patterns?

The teacher's role in minimizing a threatening situation is of paramount importance. To a substantial degree, the learning experience will be influenced by how a teacher structures the situation. Six different structural strategies are described.

Manipulative. This strategy is characterized by an *apparent equalitarian* relationship between teacher and pupil. In the final analysis, however, the teacher always gets his way. Through skillful maneuvering, the teacher's predetermined ends are followed, regardless of the desires of the group. Pupils are moved in a predetermined direction, despite the fact that they are led to believe that they themselves are involved in the decision-making process. Not only is the strategy undemocratic, but it is dishonest as well.

Directive. In this situation the leader openly directs the learner. He prescribes class activities and expects children to follow. His methods are primarily teacher-centered, e.g., lecture and recitation. His purpose is to bring the group to a predetermined end. In contrast to the manipulative strategy, the directive approach is openly a superior-inferior relationship. Pupils know where they stand. Under appropriate conditions it is fully legitimate in a democracy.

Persuasive. This type of leadership emphasizes the equalitarian role of the teacher. Along with the ideas of others he offers his own ideas for consideration. He urges the adoption of his views on the basis of merit. As Frymier says, he is ". . . effective in a pulling sort of way." The position, in many ways, resembles that of manipulation, except that the teacher does not insist upon his own way when group consensus is against him.

Discussive. This position embodies the true discussion spirit, described in the next chapter. Here the leader pools his ideas along with the rest of the group. Each idea, regardless of its source, is considered for its own merit. The usual result is the evolution of new ideas, new avenues of thought.

Supportive. This instructional strategy features the child "in the driver's seat." Children set direction—map out areas of concern—and then proceed with the support of the teacher. The teacher's role is merely to offer guidance and assistance as needed.

Nondirective. A final strategy is called *nondirective*, since it permits pupils to do just as they please. The teacher does not provide any sort of direction, except as an individual may ask for it. It is completely open-ended. This strategy, according to Frymier, is not appropriate for elementary school use. He suggests it is a form of educational anarchy, since pupils have no walls to press against.

When motivation is viewed as an aspect of personality, four distinct combinations emerge: high motivation–adequate personality; high motivation–inadequate personality; low motivation–adequate personality; low motivation–inadequate personality. Frymier contends that the type of instructional strategy employed should be determined by the motivational structure present. As a general principle, he believes, greater structure should accompany greater motivation.[6] To illustrate:

High motivation–adequate personality. This sort of individual would probably respond best to a *supportive* instructional strategy. Here the pupil creates his own structure.

High motivation–inadequate personality. The insecurity and apprehensiveness of such a child calls for an abundance of teacher structuring, characteristic of the *directive* approach.

Low motivation–adequate personality. Such an individual does not want to learn. Thus, he probably responds best to some kind of *discussive* strategy. According to Frymier, such a child is encouraged by the extensive involvement and participation made necessary.

Low motivation–inadequate personality. This most difficult child to

[6] *Ibid.*, p. 206.

work with needs a strong leader. He needs someone to tell him what to do and to attract him to the learning task. Thus the *persuasive* strategy is favored.

Although Frymier's analysis seems to presuppose an ideal situation in which pupils with like motivation are grouped together, the implications for accommodating individual differences within the classroom are many. In Chapter 10, for example, an instructional model for classroom grouping is offered. Although this model is based upon academic achievement, it is entirely possible that such an arrangement could be based upon differing motivational patterns. The legitimate leadership strategies introduced here are more fully developed as instructional methods in various chapters of this book.

What techniques seem best for low-motivated pupils?

Prior to an analysis of teaching techniques that seem appropriate for pupils who find school a frustrating experience, it is important to know something about the common characteristics of such individuals. As reported on page 99 in this book, Frymier described a low-motivated pupil as follows: [7]

. . . they are unhappy and afraid, they lack confidence in themselves, they resist change and new ideas, they are unduly concerned with the objective and the materialistic, and they dislike school intensely. Most of the group fall into the category of *slow* learners. This slowness may be directly related to a lack of ability, low motivation, or both. They have lost interest in school, in the teachers, and especially in themselves. These pupils typically seem to have a narrow range of interests, short interest spans, limited powers of self-direction; they learn slowly and forget quickly and generally lack "social intelligence." In guiding the learning activities of such children, the following techniques are often effective:

1. Teach only a few basic elements at a time, capitalizing upon special interests. Although such youngsters tend to have a narrow range of interests, they respond to activities of immediate concern.

2. Utilize short, simple question techniques which are consistent with their short interest spans.

3. Closely supervise self-directed activities, offering constant guidance and encouragement. This approach demands elaborate advance planning of the most minute details of an experience.

4. Constant repetition, extensive practice in specific skills, and detailed initial learning activities are essential. Such children learn slowly and forget quickly.

[7] *Ibid.*, p. 116.

5. Emphasize qualities of social living and correct habit formation. These youngsters are usually deficient in the social sensitivity expected of their age mates.

6. Joint teacher-pupil planning of class activities is an exceedingly useful technique. These activities tend to develop self-confidence in planning one's own work and tends to carry over to after-school years.

7. The presentation of new activities should be developed as a step-by-step sequence involving immediate repetition when needed. The use of practical illustrations seems a desirable adjunct to the introduction of new materials.

8. Supervised study should be broken into periods of 15 minutes or less. Whenever possible, initial motivating activities should precede reading. Reading sessions may be effective only when purpose has been carefully developed with these children. Immediately following short reading sessions a few simple content questions are definitely in order for clarifying concepts. Generally, activities for children who have been frustrated by their school experience should be short and varied. Such pupils need a reverse order of teaching: activity, reading, discussing, and writing. Each of these activities in turn, tends to reinforce the next activity through a necessary sequence.

What factors are associated with self-motivated pupils?

Creativity, according to Torrance,[8] is important from the standpoint of personality development and mental health. He believes that creative thinking contributes to the acquisition of information and is essential in the application of knowledge. Perhaps most important is the value of the child's talent to society. Civilization ultimately depends upon the quality of creative imagination of each succeeding generation.

The individual who possesses a high potential for originality and creativity must have an opportunity to be "original" and to "create" at his own level. This demands both time and motivation within an encouraging school atmosphere.

Before any systematic attempt can be made in the realm of cultivating high creative potential it is important to recognize factors which seem to be associated with such potential. Although it is quite difficult to identify *all* factors essential for high creative potential, Dinkmeyer [9] has offered a few clues to characterize behavior of such children:

1. *Daring and Courageous.* The creative child is one who is daring and courageous in his thinking.

[8] E. Paul Torrance, "Exploration in Creative Thinking," *Education*, 81: 216–220 (December, 1960).

[9] Don C. Dinkmeyer, *Child Development, The Emerging Self* (Englewood Cliffs, N.J.: Prentice-Hall, Inc., © 1965), pp. 247–248. By permission.

2. *Originality*. He is able to break away from conformity and is open to new experiences.

3. *Transition*. He is quick to grasp sequences of events.

4. *Innovator*. He is curious, imaginative, and inventive.

Such an individual tends to be a high achiever who produces in depth and scope, who displays an unusual degree of originality, invention, and innovation; one who holds a high degree of tolerance for uncertainty, resisting early and simple solutions to complex situations. He may be almost ruthless with himself and others when involved in the pursuit of an intellectual commitment. A good part of his reward is in the activity itself, rather than recognition which it may bring.

How does brainstorming stimulate creative thinking?

Although the foregoing section represents an attempt to describe the self-motivated or the "already creative" child, the reader should not infer that self-motivation or existing creativity is restricted to this group. Indeed each person is creative in his own way! Many educators, however, are beginning to realize the folly of letting the self-motivated, and usually able, pupil get along on his own, centering class time primarily on the normal or slow pupil. The able pupil is of high potential value to his culture. While it is true that he quickly forms concepts, there is no guarantee that he will form correct ones. There is clear evidence that many potentially great individuals are at least partially blocked because they are permitted to develop poor work habits and standards while in school. The teacher must be responsible for cultivating and directing the efforts of the able, self-motivated pupil to ever higher levels of originality.

Brainstorming as a means of idea production is today recognized as an important part of the creative problem-solving process. It usually is effective for all pupils, regardless of age and ability, but can be especially productive for the more able, self-motivated individuals. Even primary grade school children can profit from brainstorming activities. They are an integral part of the act of creative thinking. The teacher will usually be the leader and recorder. As the children become more mature and capable, as in the middle and upper grades, these responsibilities may be given to the pupils. The following description of brainstorming, based upon that of Alex F. Osborn, has served as a guide for many and varied groups.

Brainstorming literally means "using the *brain* to *storm* a problem."

The leader, in essence, calls for ideas for solving a given problem. Four basic rules must be faithfully followed: [10]

1. *Criticism is ruled out.* Adverse judgment of ideas must be withheld until later.

2. *"Free-wheeling" is welcomed.* The wilder the idea the better; it is easier to tame down than to think up.

3. *Quantity is wanted.* The greater the number of ideas, the more the likelihood of useful ideas.

4. *Combination and improvement are sought.* In addition to contributing ideas of their own, participants should suggest how ideas of others can be turned into *better* ideas; or how two or more ideas can be joined into still another idea.

Brainstorming should be kept informal, except for a recorder or two who keeps a written record of all ideas produced. Its function is idea-finding —not to deal with problems which primarily depend upon judgment.

How are the problems and the pupils prepared for brainstorming? In preparation for a brainstorming session the leader (a pupil or the teacher) must select a *specific* as opposed to a general problem. The problem, "How should we behave in school?" is too broad. Perhaps it should be broken into at least four subproblems: 1) behavior on the playground, 2) behavior in committee work, 3) behavior in regular classroom work, and, 4) behavior with special teachers or guests invited into the classroom.

When the problem has been reduced to its lowest common denominator, each subproblem is then phrased as a concise, definite question. Questions of *what, why, where, when, who,* and *how* often serve to stimulate ideation on a problem. For example: Why is it needed? Where should it be done? Who should do it? How should it be done? When should it be done?

What is the proper conduct of the brainstorming leader? In preparation for a brainstorming session the leader can develop his own list of suggested solutions to the problem. They are to be used, however, only for "pump priming," i.e., when the flow of ideas slows down. He should also be prepared to suggest leads by way of new categories which might open up new lines of thought.

[10] Reprinted and adapted with the permission of Charles Scribner's Sons from *Applied Imagination* by Alex Osborn. Copyright 1953, © 1957, 1963 Charles Scribner's Sons.

The setting for brainstorming should be informal and relaxed. Following a short explanation of the problem a list of the four basic rules (indicated in the first part of this section) is made plainly visible. These rules should be carefully reviewed again, especially for the primary grade child. The leader explains that he will give a specified signal when a member violates any of the rules. The pupils are not permitted to read lists of ideas. Only one idea is offered at a time by any individual. If several children desire to speak at once the participants are encouraged to jot down ideas before they are forgotten. Because ideas tend to be contagious and many children often desire to speak at once, groups of about 8–12 are best adapted to the technique. Much larger groups, however, have been effective under the direction of expert leaders.

How are ideas and afterthoughts utilized? Experience has indicated that by contacting each of the participants the following day a number of valuable *afterthoughts* are usually added to the original list of ideas. Frequently these ideas are of a higher quality than the original ones. This is the phase of the creative process which calls for little or no conscious effort, sometimes designated as the *incubation* period. At the close of the brainstorming session the participants are asked to keep the problems in their minds until the next day, when they will be asked for their afterthoughts.

The final processing of ideas actually is one of selecting from numerous alternatives (ideas) the solutions which seem most appropriate under the circumstances. Sometimes the teacher will want to make such decisions, while on other occasions he may want to guide pupils in this process. In any event, however, the teacher is very much involved. At this point the creative, self-motivated pupil can apply his *individual* creative processes in putting the idea into operation. The brainstorming session is fun; if conducted appropriately, interest reaches a very high point. It also starts the process of original, creative thought which tends to continue as ideas are applied to task situations. The technique may be useful in developing a desire to learn among all pupils within the class. It tends to be especially beneficial to the more able pupils who need help in channeling and directing their thinking.

What other devices help activate imagination?

It is estimated that tremendous creative potential is lost by inadequate planning. Although there is no established pattern for activating one's imagination, there are a number of guidelines which many creative persons have found effective.

Waetjen [11] has stated that nothing erodes motivation more than constant exposure to the predictable and familiar situation. All classrooms should have some element of unpredictability, which gently nudges pupils into an "off balance" position that makes it necessary for them to obtain information in order to regain their balance.

Suchman [12] has developed several guidelines to activate imagination. These are:

1. One should not be forced into a rigid pattern.
2. The child needs to have facility and materials.
3. He needs to have a responsive person both as a receiver and as a reflector of ideas.
4. The imaginative child needs an environment that encourages inquiry and the pursuit of meaning.

The classroom teacher must assume responsibility for guiding children into fruitful avenues of creativity. Although originality and creative imagination are private, guidance and training *can* substantially increase one's output, as in any other area of education. Too often the able, self-motivated person is permitted to shift for himself while attention is focused on the less able and less motivated pupil.

GENERAL PROBLEMS AND PRINCIPLES IN MOTIVATION

In the foregoing portion of this chapter, emphasis was placed on techniques of motivation. Teachers must help pupils develop a desire to learn. Learning in today's schools, however, occurs in a social setting. Classrooms are crowded; individuals from all walks of life frequently are thrown together; interests, abilities, and achievement vary tremendously within each classroom. Such factors necessarily create problems of classroom motivation. Thus, the desire to learn must be carefully guided so as to create optimum conditions for all. It is not too difficult to discover and evolve motivation techniques which "work" for the moment; it is more difficult to develop techniques which will result in

[11] Walter B. Waetjen, "The Prevention of Failure," *NEA Journal*, 55: 37–40 (April, 1966).
[12] J. Richard Suchman, "Inquiry: The Motivation to Inquire," *The Instructor*, 65: 26+ (October, 1965).

self-motivation. Nevertheless, this is the aim of effective teaching. Individuals who lack self-motivation tend to become a menace and a liability to society.

This portion of the chapter offers a number of psychological principles which have been established by extensive experimentation. They should be especially useful to teachers who wish to check their own techniques against pertinent research findings.

What are some problems of motivation?

Individuals are different. Some differences can be detected readily; others are subtle but have been established through scientific investigation. Motivation is probably the most subtle and least understood of all individual differences. Teachers tend to assume that those motivating experiences which activate their own interests will be effective experiences for their pupils. It must be rememberd that the factors and conditions which create motivation are directly related to the values one holds. Children from middle-class homes, for instance, tend to accept the teacher and approve of formal education as an instrument for getting ahead. Children from lower-class homes, however, tend to break away from school as soon as possible; they frequently desire to avoid being "taken-in" by the teacher; teacher approval may even pose a threat to acceptance by members of their own social class groups.

While there is a natural tendency to look for a set of rules which works, techniques of motivation must be as variable as the individuals who occupy the classroom. Motivation problems are but manifestations of numerous factors that make a person what he is. The mere process of keeping pupils busy and orderly is not enough; ultimately they will be expected to operate under their own initiative and direction. An important function of the school is to *build* these essential ingredients of good citizenship.

While interest seems to be the best avenue for activating a desire to learn, it is merely a temporary measure and can be quite transitory. If interest is to be sustained it must tap the basic motives of the individual. Basic motives, however, are influenced profoundly by the personality characteristics of each individual. Thus, the mainsprings of motivation will vary from child to child.

In the preceding paragraphs emphasis has been placed on the individual nature of motivation. Yet some *consistency* is essential. A teacher who would normally accept, or at least tolerate, a given act must not suddenly start punishing pupils for such behavior. Both teacher and pupils need clearly defined guidelines.

What are some principles of motivation?

For several decades teachers have attempted to follow acceptable practices of motivating pupils. Often, recommendations have been derived largely from tradition or non-verified experiences of outstanding teachers. During the early years of the American republic, floggings, torture, and all sorts of inhumane treatment were considered quite appropriate as means of motivation and class control. The Constitution was viewed more as a guide to political action than as a way of life. The schools were open only to children who were able to adjust to a predetermined curriculum.

Today, however, the school is for the child—every child. It is viewed as a primary avenue through which democracy can be inculcated into each generation. It is now believed that democracy can best be internalized through democratic teaching processes. Accordingly, a great deal of investigation has attempted to determine what factors and conditions are most conducive to self-motivation and self-discipline. The principles which follow are subject to revision as more research becomes available. In some instances the principles are still little more than professional guesses. Taken collectively, however, they can serve as a very useful approach to classroom practice.

1. *Reward is more effective than punishment.* Having one's errors pointed out is less effective motivation for learning than having his correct responses acknowledged. Stopping or blocking an act does not point the way to more appropriate responses. It only informs one of the inappropriateness of the particular response. However, there is some evidence to suggest that information supplied through reproof is more beneficial to the highly motivated pupil than to the pupil who has little desire to learn.

2. *All pupils have certain basic psychological needs which must be met.* Although these needs have been stated in many different ways they usually are thought to include: acceptance, approval, self-esteem, achievement, and independence. Pupils who are able to meet these needs effectively through the learning activities in the classroom need little specific assistance in motivation and discipline.

3. *Motivation which originates with the individual is more effective than that which is imposed from without.* The basic satisfactions which a teacher can furnish are *acceptance* and *approval*. It is on this basis that the individual acquires and maintains his own standards of attainment. He wants to be accepted and approved by others.

4. *Immediate reinforcement of a desirable response is needed.* En-

couragement enables the learner to determine that his actions are bringing him closer to his goal. To be effective, reinforcement must follow within a few minutes. If the learning experience involves an extended period of time it should be broken into steps so that each stage of learning can be reinforced. Reinforcement need not be an elaborate affair. Such expressions as "right" or a smile may be fully satisfactory to most pupils. Traditionally, teachers have followed the practice of administering tests one day and discussing results the following day. A preferred practice may be to split the test into two parts, allowing adequate time for discussion of each part on the day of its administration.

5. *Motivation is contagious.* A highly interested and enthusiastic teacher tends to produce highly interested and enthusiastic pupils. Often, too, a few enthusiastic pupils can motivate other pupils. The effective teacher must be enthusiastic and excited in the things he does in the classroom and then the pupils will be too. In most areas of the curriculum there is a wealth of interesting materials available to create an exciting atmosphere.

6. *A clear understanding of purposes enhances motivation.* Children normally regulate their actions to achieve desired ends. Imposed tasks that appear to have no greater purpose than merely to keep them busy are avoided whenever possible. Not only should purposes be known, but they should be interpreted in terms of the everyday problems of those involved.

7. *Self-imposed tasks tend to create more interest than do teacher-imposed tasks.* Pupils who are provided opportunities to develop their own problems and techniques of solving them seldom develop serious problems of motivation and discipline.

8. *"External" rewards sometimes are necessary and effective in stimulating initial interest.* Sometimes the effort expended in order to "make the honor roll," become eligible for "a star after his name," or earn a "smiling face" mark on his paper is important in developing initial interest. Soon after the initial efforts the pupils may develop an intrinsic interest in the task. Incentives are motivating, however, only when they lead to approval of others and result in need reduction or a feeling of satisfaction within the learner.

9. *Varied teaching techniques and procedures are effective in maintaining interest.* Most of us like to change our dress or suit of clothes frequently. We like to travel different routes, play different games, associate with different people, and so on. Likewise, variety in teaching prevents once exciting and challenging situations from becoming routine and boring.

10. *It is economical to capitalize on existing interests.* It has been demonstrated that the spark which is generated from such activities as a festive holiday, some special school activity, or a local happening can be effectively transferred to academic work. Likewise, a special interest of a given individual frequently can be related to the particular problem under study.

11. *Activities which may stimulate interest for the less able may be inappropriate for the more able pupil, and vice versa.* One becomes motivated to complete a given task to the degree to which one can personally perceive a satisfactory reward. A reward for one individual frequently will not be a reward for another. This is especially true for pupils who happen to fall at the extremes in ability. To motivate pupils effectively a teacher must be able to project himself into the frame of reference of the learner. Teachers, who are usually above average in ability, often find it easier to empathize with the more able than with the less able pupil.

12. *High anxiety makes learning difficult or impossible.* The more complicated and difficult the problem the more will anxiety interfere with performance. An anxious child tends to deflect attention from the task to the anxiety-producing stimulus. For example, a child who is anxious over his peer relationships will tend to direct his attention from the subject to peer incidents and learning will be less effective. Conversely, an absence of attention is not conducive to learning. A self-satisfied, apathetic pupil is not a motivated one. A good teacher is a problem maker!

13. *Anxiety and frustration in mild form can be beneficial to learning.* As long as the emotion is mild it may act as an energizer. Persistent but mild anxiety actually may result in higher performance on relatively simple tasks.

14. *If the task is too difficult and if assistance is not readily available, frustration quickly leads to demoralization.*

15. *Each pupil has a different level of frustration tolerance.* Many teachers believe that failure or threat of failure serves as an incentive. While this can be effective for pupils who have experienced a lot of success in school, it tends to have a negative influence on the anxious, fear-ridden pupil. The frustration tolerance of a child is dependent upon his emotional stability—the amount of anxiety he brings to the situation.

16. *Peer-group pressure is much more effective in motivation than adult-imposed pressure.* The elementary school child tends to approve that which the group approves; he disapproves that which the group

disapproves. Therefore, if the teacher can guide the *group* in *wanting* to study, individual members of the group tend to value study. The child who fails to value it runs the risk of group rejection or disapproval.

17. *High motivation is closely related to creativity.* Through certain teaching techniques the highly motivated child be led into creative activities. This might involve any technique which would tend to remove artificial blocks to originality, such as criticism, on-the-spot evaluation, excessive school and class rules, and excessively large class groups.

It is important to realize the relationships that do exist between and among the motivation principles listed above. The relationship between approval, acceptance, and achievement is often misunderstood by teachers. A teacher must first *accept* a child, then help him to become more *acceptable* to himself and to others. Often a child's level of peer acceptance is enhanced greatly by increased reading skill or some other skill. A teacher *must* help a child *become.* Mere acceptance is not enough. Lasting acceptance and approval are earned.

SUMMARY

In this chapter emphasis has been placed on motivation (the desire to learn) as basic to all other instructional processes. When all pupils are highly motivated to learn there can be no serious discipline problems. Motivation springs from certain basic physical and psychological urges. The psychological urges (needs) include acceptance, approval, self-esteem, achievement, and independence. Although there is this basic common denominator associated with motivation, one reacts in terms of his past experiences. General encouragement may help some pupils develop interest, but not all. Here an appeal to special, individual interests will be effective. Incentives or extrinsic motivation also may be necessary and effective for some pupils.

Less able and generally discouraged pupils often need the aid of a special approach to teaching. The discouraged, frustrated pupil often has a narrow range of interest, short interest span, limited powers of self-direction, learns slowly and forgets quickly, and lacks social intelligence. These pupils need short periods of study and only a few basic elements taught at a time. Much and constant repetition is needed for these discouraged pupils.

The more able pupils often are self-motivated. Nevertheless, it was pointed out that techniques are available for helping them channel their interests into truly creative activities. Brainstorming was described as an important technique in developing creativity. Brainstorming is a technique designed to release inhibitions and traditional patterns of thought, which often block originality.

Finally, a number of problems and principles were offered. Although many of these apply to the whole instructional process (and to the problem of discipline in particular), they should be useful to the teacher who would activate the pupil's desire to learn.

QUESTIONS FOR STUDY AND DISCUSSION

1. Why is motivation sometimes referred to as a symptom rather than a cause? What justification can be offered for making motivation a specific instructional goal? It has been contended that some pupils have no desire to learn. Defend or refute this statement.

2. How do basic needs relate to classroom motivational activities? Why are basic needs considered more practical avenues to group motivation than individual interests? What are some fallacies commonly associated with incentives as an avenue to effective motivation? In suggesting an integration of motives for effective teaching the authors would use incentives as a "last resort." This is strangely at odds with common practice. What justification do you see for such a recommendation?

3. It was suggested in this chapter that the ineffectiveness of motivation often can be traced to failure to consider individual differences in motivation. Observe a class of elementary school children. What evidences of individual differences in a desire to learn do you find? What solutions would you offer? What motivational responsibilities, if any, does a teacher have for the self-motivated individual? Contrast effective motivational techniques for pupils with a relatively low desire to learn with those who might be classified as self-motivated. Would you consider high motivation more basic than high ability? Why or why not?

4. Why is *brainstorming* considered an important motivational technique? Groups of 8–12 are considered most effective for the purposes of brainstorming. Would you formulate such subgroups on the basis of interest, ability, and/or motivation? Why or why not? Why is criticism or evaluation of ideas considered so detrimental to the processes of brainstorming? What relationship can you see between such criticism and current practices with respect to measurement and evaluation?

5. It was suggested that *all* pupils are creative. Why, then, do teachers generally associate creativeness only with the more able child? What relationship do you see between creativeness and motivation? Setting a time and place for cognitive thought is considered important in activating imagination. What techniques might the teacher employ in such efforts to "lure the muse"?

6. What practical problems might a teacher encounter in implementing Frymier's recommendations with respect to instructional strategy and motivation? Are some children highly motivated in some areas while possessing low motivation in other areas? Relate your answer to Frymier's contention that motivation is an aspect of personality which changes gradually.

SELECTED BIBLIOGRAPHY

Beauchamp, George A., *Basic Dimensions of Elementary Method*, 2nd Ed. (Boston: Allyn and Bacon, Inc., 1965).

Bernard, Haldane, "Focus on Success Instead of Failure," *NEA Journal*, 55: 32 (April, 1966).

Dinkmeyer, Don C., *Child Development, the Emerging Self* (Englewood Cliffs, N.J.: Prentice-Hall, Inc., 1965).

Frymier, Jack R., *The Nature of Educational Method* (Ohio: Charles E. Merrill Books, Inc., 1965).

Harris, Chester W., Ed., *Encyclopedia of Educational Research*, 3rd Ed. New York: The Macmillan Co., 1960).

Marx, M. H., "Motivation," in *Encyclopedia of Educational Research*, 3rd Ed. (New York: The Macmillan Co., 1960).

Osborn, Alex F., *Applied Imagination* (New York: Charles Scribner's Sons, 1963).

Suchman, Richard J., "Inquiry: The Motivation to Inquire," *The Instructor*, 65: 26+ (October, 1965).

Torrance, Paul E., "Exploration in Creative Thinking," *Education*, 81: 216–220 (December, 1960).

———, "Motivating Children with School Problems," in E. Paul Torrance and Robert D. Strom, Eds., *Mental Health and Achievement* (New York: John Wiley & Sons, Inc., 1965).

Waetjen, Walter B., "The Prevention of Failure," *NEA Journal*, 55: 37–40 (April, 1966).

UNIT TWO

Effective Group Methods

EDUCATION for all the people is dependent on effective instructional groups. Pupils universally are assigned to groups, both large and small. While there is indeed some merit in the tutorial relationship, costs involved are prohibitive. Groups, however, are much more than necessary evils. They represent life at its best. Man is a social animal. His very existence is dependent on the cooperative effort of all the people. In today's age of space exploration, traditional boundaries are becoming less important as man finds it necessary to rely more and more upon all the peoples of the world.

The class group does much more than provide a setting for instruction. It lends support and offers direction to those involved. It permits the emergence of leadership, realistic group problem solving, and the application of democratic principles to everyday living.

The instructional methods and techniques described in the four chapters following have one important characteristic: they utilize the class group structure to enhance learning. The organization and sequence of the chapters is a logical one, proceeding from an emphasis on relatively small subgroups to utilization of the class group as a whole. This is not to imply, however, that one will rely wholly on small discussion groups *or* on the larger, purely democratic group approaches. There is also value in the committee or group of *one*, where the child's right to work independently as well as being able to work in larger groups, is possible. As indicated throughout, an integration of instructional procedures is essential if the broad range of pupil needs is to be met.

Chapter 7 offers a systematic approach to two closely related techniques: Guided Class Discussion and Panel Discussion. Perhaps the most widely used instructional approach today is class discussion in some form. The guided class discussion treated in Chapter 7 emphasizes use of the class group in the processes of inquiry. It is known that pupils will indulge in serious reflection only to the extent that the group setting is conducive to such reflection. While groups of 30 to 40 pupils admittedly are not of optimum size for such activities, the technique can be far more effective than it typically is. A much less used but often more effective instructional tool is the closely related technique of panel discussion. Again, the misuse of panel discussion groups frequently has produced disappointing results. In this chapter a systematic approach is offered. Panel discussion, designed to facilitate the problem-solving pursuits of the *entire class group*, is emphasized.

Techniques of sociometry, dramatic play, and role playing, discussed in Chapter 8, emphasize the importance of social relationships in human affairs. By organizing a class and subgroups on the basis of choice preference, through sociometric procedures a teacher can do much to create emotionally supportive classroom conditions. Dramatic play and role playing as a systematic approach to learning are seen as an effective tool for developing empathy. In the final analysis, effective choice-making is dependent upon pupils' reactions to other pupils and the feelings of class members toward each other. Children especially need assistance in the art of human relationships.

Approaches to classroom utilization of democratic processes are described in Chapter 9. Overall problem-solving activities under such conditions are planned and directed by the class group. The teacher, instead of assuming his traditional role of taskmaster, director, and evaluator, works cooperatively with pupils. He assumes joint responsibility with pupils for planning and directing learning activities. Chapter 9 describes instructional processes that put into effect the widely quoted slogan, "Democracy is a way of life."

The final chapter of the unit offers a systematic approach to the problem of providing for individual differences. Pupils, in whatever manner they may be grouped, will vary widely in any number of ways. With the typical class size of 30 to 40 pupils, individualization of instruction can be most difficult unless some systematized approach is employed. Accordingly, a useful technique for subgrouping within the classroom is presented in Chapter 10. Subgrouping on the basis of achievement and/or ability is employed widely in the elementary schools. The function of such an approach, of course, is to facilitate personalization of instruction.

7

Encouraging Reflective Thought:
Discussion Activities

WHEN individuals engage in reflective thought they ponder or meditate; they consider or think carefully. The *discusser* has not made up his mind. He is a searcher, an inquirer. As a rational person he has ideas and preferences with respect to the problem, but such ideas are held tentatively. He uses discussion as an opportunity to inspect and weigh his own ideas along with those of others. Indeed, he expects to modify his own notions if the best interests of the group warrant it.

The basic discussion attitude is *openmindedness*, which renders one receptive to new ideas. One examines or ponders new ideas alongside his own notions, making objective comparisons and contrasts. As Gulley states, "The discusser must cultivate the ability to *look at himself* and his ideas objectively and dispassionately." [1] First of all he seeks to *identify* his own biases and prejudices. He avoids a two-valued orientation, seeking to find the middle ground. This does not mean, of course, that he must change his attitudes. It does suggest, however, that each participant probably will see that his own notions are not quite as good and the ideas of others not quite as bad as he had originally seen them.

Although the spirit and life of a discussion is projected through basic human emotions, objective intellectual processes are emphasized. Ideas advanced by others are accepted on their own merits. The participant realizes that valuable contributions sometimes come from what he considers an unlikely source. Likewise, *unsound* ideas sometimes come from

[1] Halbert E. Gulley, *Discussion, Conference and Group Process* (New York: Holt, Rinehart & Winston, Inc., 1960), p. 120.

121

a person of high prestige or esteem.* Thus one is able to distinguish between ideas and their sources.

This chapter analyzes guided class discussion and panel discussion, and general problems and principles associated with discussion. Efforts are made to distinguish between these related but essentially different teaching techniques under practical classroom conditions.

GUIDED CLASS DISCUSSION

Whenever people associate with each other they usually *discuss*. Individuals often find solutions to their daily problems by talking them over with others. Ask your neighbor what he thinks of the slate of candidates for the school board and he will likely respond, "I don't know; what do you think?" After some *discussion*, it is quite likely that both you and your neighbor will have clarified your views on the problem. This process of interchange of ideas (discussion) is basic to the democratic process. In a democracy human progress is limited by the will of the people. "Experts" often know of efficient ways of solving problems in their specialized fields, but their solutions may be rejected by the people because of a lack of understanding and enthusiasm. Dedication to the value of majority decision demands a well-informed public. One of the chief avenues through which this important goal may be reached is informal *discussion*. How can this method of deliberation best be applied in the classroom?

What is guided class discussion?

Miss Killinger was questioning her science pupils on their assigned readings. Most of the questions dealt with definitions and facts presented. Occasionally a pupil asked a question, which Miss Killinger was only too happy to answer, about important relationships.

Mr. Buell was using the factual materials of an assigned lesson to help pupils see relationships and make conclusions. It soon became obvious that few pupils had read the materials. Their responses, for the most part, consisted of value judgments, many of which were not related to the facts introduced in the assigned reading.

While the above illustrations represent discussion in the broad sense, neither of them characterizes the guided class discussion techniques described in this chapter. The method of teaching, whether it be lecture,

---

* For a thorough treatment of the forces of interaction the reader is referred to the first section of Chapter 3.

demonstration, or something else may be appropriate, but it does not qualify as guided class discussion. Nor does the method of having pupils recite materials from their texts constitute a true class discussion. The rather questionable classroom practice of discussing anything and everything which just happens to evolve—often called "bull sessions" by the participants—certainly does not qualify as a guided discussion. *The guided class discussion is designed to develop group agreement through talk and reflective thinking.* Its aims are to stimulate analysis; encourage interpretations; develop or change attitudes. In other words, the individual is guided in some sort of *reflection* on a problem which involves "weighing" the evidence before a decision or opinion can be reached. Through appropriate leadership, evidence is brought to bear on the crucial issues of a problem; the evidence is analyzed and evaluated *by the group*; and certain generalizations are reached.

In brief, the guided class discussion must satisfy the following conditions:

1. A definite problem is involved.

2. The group must be qualified to solve the problem.

3. Facts or data are used to analyze the problem.

4. Ideas, value judgments, and the like are exchanged and relationships are made more specific.

5. The group seeks to reach some sort of agreement on the issues involved.

What type of problems is involved in problem-solving discussion?

It must have become obvious to the reader by this time that guided class discussion is designed to help the participants reach a consensus on worthwhile problems. It is doubtful if any worthwhile problems can be solved merely by assembling the available facts; nor is it usually profitable to spend time in reciting certain alleged facts that are already accessible to the group. For example, it is important to know the answer to the question, "What is the park and playground policy in the United States?" but it is hardly worthwhile to devote class time to discussing the facts of the situation. Some confusion and/or disagreement is essential to the type of guided discussion described here. Facts or data are essential to class discussion (reflective thinking); indeed, discussion presupposes a working knowledge of them. They therefore become useful tools in forming enlightened opinions. It is little short of ridiculous to expect a pupil to reflect upon data which he does not possess! Facts are not ends in themselves, however.

Discussion often breaks down because of the wording of the discussion problem. Four major types or kinds of problems have been identified. All may become involved during the discussion process. The *policy* problem, however, is basic to the problem-solving type of discussion emphasized in this chapter. It should serve as the major focus for discussion. The four kinds of problems that lend themselves to varying degrees of reflective thinking are described.

Fact. Problems of fact are concerned with the discovery and evaluation of factual information. They are emphasized during the analysis of the problem when facts are introduced and clarified. For example: "What are the rules, if any, concerning walking on the grass?"

Value. Problems of value are concerned with matters relative to value judgments. They call for the application of accepted standards in determining the appropriateness, rightness, or effectiveness of an issue. Example: "How well are our rules being followed?" Questions of value arise frequently during the early phases of a discussion. They are related to the *evaluation* of facts.

Problems of fact and problems of value usually can be identified by the presence of some form of the verb "to be." Indeed they are sometimes referred to as *is* or *are* questions.

Advocacy. Problems of advocacy, as the term implies, focus upon specific solutions. Such a question encourages argument rather than discussion. Advocacy questions most often emerge when hypotheses or tentative solutions to a problem are being evaluated. It is for this reason that establishment of accepted criteria should be developed prior to weighing the alternatives. To illustrate the type of questions: "Should more rules be added about walking on the grass?" The question can be answered by *yes* or *no*. Wording of the question precludes consideration of other alternatives. Such questions usually begin with *should* or *ought*.

Policy. Problems of policy deal with matters necessitating decisions or action. Implied in the problem is the importance of exploring all possible solutions. Policy questions often begin with the words "what," "how," or "why." The words "should" or "ought" are also stated or implied in the question. For example: "What should be the policy about walking on the grass in front of the school building?"

In resolving problems of policy, questions of *fact, value,* and *advocacy* will be involved. The reverse does not follow, however. In formulating problems for discussion, teachers often confuse policy and advocacy questions. Advocacy immediately directs attention to concern for one particular solution. Furthermore, it tends to divide a group into opposing camps.

How should the teacher guide a discussion?

The guided group discussion, like other teaching methods, is designed to assist pupils in solving recognized difficulties. Due to limitations necessarily imposed by a typical class situation, certain steps in the problem-solving process may be circumvented. There are certain minimum steps essential to any discussion, however. These are:

1. Analyzing the problem;
2. Examining the possible solutions;
3. Attempting to arrive at individual enlightenment and group consensus.

How is the problem identified? While it must be recognized that pupils ideally should evolve appropriate discussion problems from existing interests, in practical class situations the teacher often selects and phrases the discussion problems. The basis for such a decision will depend on his ability to stimulate interest in the problem. Thus, problems which are not directly related to current interests of pupils will be developed in a manner that bears upon interests common to most children. Current controversial issues afford a natural basis for class discussion problems.

In tackling the problem, "What should be the United States' policy on public parks and playgrounds?" interest might be gained through some current news item relating to the problem. Through a series of questions or any number of interest-arousing devices pupils are prepared for discussion. Many teachers favor the practice of writing the problem on the board when interest has become evident. Included in the introductory activities are questions which will assist in the definition of certain ambiguous terms, causes and effects of the problem, the urgency for action, and the probable continued seriousness of the problem.

How is the problem analyzed? The first consideration in any discussion is the definition of terms and limitation of the problem for discussion. Until the participants fully understand what is to be considered, little productive effort can be expected.

From a definition of terms the discussion moves into an analysis of the facts and issues germane to the problem. Thus from the "What do we mean?" phase the class asks, "What are the facts and circumstances surrounding the problem?" The essential functions of the analysis stage are to describe, to examine, to gain new insights. Certain basic issues usually need consideration.

1. What evidence indicates the seriousness of the problem? In discussing the question on public parks and playgrounds, cited earlier, the teacher can open the discussion with, "How do we know that this nation's policy on public parks and playgrounds is a problem?"

2. What are some causes of the problem?

3. What are some effects of the present policy? In considering any discussion problem the assumption is that there is some basis for doubting the *status quo*, i.e., the problem is somewhat controversial. The important consideration here, then, becomes one of considering how the present policy has affected the problem. For example, the question, "What effect has our existing policy on public parks and playgrounds had upon our conservation program?" might evoke a great deal of thought.

4. What are the indications that the problem is likely to persist? The pupil turns from the present state of affairs to likely consequences if conditions remain essentially unchanged.

What steps can be taken to solve the discussion problem? In the solution stage of any discussion, participants are ready to answer the question, "What should be done?" or "What plan of action is best?" Through a give-and-take series of questions and comments each proposal, after adequate criteria have been established, is weighed by the group. The procedure can be one in which alternative A is described and its advantages and disadvantages weighed. Then other major alternatives are evaluated in turn. During the entire process the teacher must remain as impartial as possible. If the teacher attempts to guide the contributions in a predetermined direction the process falls short of its objectives. By definition, in a discussion the group must be free to explore whatever avenues the members themselves want to investigate. When all proposals have been carefully weighed group consensus may be achieved. Nevertheless, the teacher must be quick to caution pupils against making hasty decisions on broad policy questions. Such decisions at best are tentative and are based on rather limited data. The processes of reflection are much more important than any immediate pupil solutions which might be derived.

What course of action seems most appropriate? Seldom in an ordinary class situation will a group reach any final solution to a problem, although it usually will reach certain conclusions or generalizations. In the cognitive process this stage is often called the *evaluation step*.

It should be observed at this point that a class discussion, as described here, does not necessarily begin and end in one class period. Indeed, it may extend over a number of days. The amount and kind of consideration devoted to each of the basic steps (analysis of problem, examination of possible courses of action, and the attempt to reach a group consensus) will depend on a variety of factors. There are times when most of the deliberations will be given to possible solutions, especially if the nature of the problem is already common knowledge. The reader also is reminded that in many class discussions possible alternatives to existing conditions often are interjected during analysis of the problem. This is to say that problem solving is actually a process; the steps are not by any means discrete entities.

What preplanning does the teacher do? Guided class discussion often breaks down as a result of inadequate preplanning by the teacher. The preplanned outline is organized around certain basic issues. These issues usually are presented in the form of brief, precise questions. Whenever the group has effectively explored the implications of one issue another one will be brought forth until some sort of consensus is possible.

Some teachers tend to overplan a discussion outline. They develop so many basic questions that the group is rushed from one point to another in a manner that stifles creative thought. The problem, as a consequence, often receives only superficial study. A teacher normally lists more basic questions in his discussion outline than he anticipates will be considered, however. The main point is that the teacher's purpose is to stimulate reflective thought on an important problem. The majority of questions *and* answers will come from the group. Most pupil questions will be redirected to the group for consideration. The teacher clarifies, resolves different points of view, interposes intermittent summaries when needed, and steers the discussion into new areas as the occasion demands.

There also is a tendency for beginning teachers to plan inadequately for class discussion. They are, accordingly, vague as to how the problem is to be analyzed and developed. Their own questions tend to be vague and ambiguous. Vague questions, of course, tend to elicit vague responses. Too often the pupil merely indulges in a game of trying to guess what the teacher has in mind. This soon evolves into a session of verbalizing what the teacher wants. Such a situation is not conducive to the processes of reflection.

A discussion lesson is organized along the lines suggested in the steps of solving the problem. In short, it usually has three major subdivisions: Analyzing the problem; examining possible solutions; attempting to reach group consensus. The following illustrated lesson plan is suggestive only.

DISCUSSION LESSON PLAN

Subject: Social Studies

Unit: The School

Problem: What should be the policy about walking on the grass in front of the school building?

Goals: After this lesson the pupil should have furthered his understanding concerning rules, regulations, and needs concerning the grass, as evidenced by:

1. His contributions and questions posed during the discussion.

2. His ability to draw conclusions during a follow-through discussion of the problem.

3. His making a poster concerning the grass.

Lesson Approach:

Yesterday morning we took a field trip to visit the helpers in our school. We visited our school principal. While talking with our principal, he took us through his office and told us some of the kinds of work he does. On our way back to class, several class members wanted to know why there were large areas in our lawn with no grass growing.

We then discussed why the grass had died. By reading in our science books, we now understand why the grass needs some protection.

Lesson Development:

I. *Analysis of the Problem*

1. What are the reasons for walking on the grass?

2. Why does the grass die at school but not at home when walked on?

3. Why aren't the school sidewalks used?

4. What might happen if we do not stop walking on the grass?

5. What can be done to keep the grass growing?

6. Is it desirable to have grass growing there or not?

II. *Establishing the Hypotheses*

Now in view of our discussion, WHAT SHOULD BE THE POLICY ABOUT WALKING ON THE GRASS IN FRONT OF THE SCHOOL BUILDING?

Possible solutions (suggestions only):

1. Fence the front lawn.

2. Put up signs, "Keep Off the Grass."

3. The principal should talk to other children in school about walking on the grass.

4. Make up rules about walking on the grass.

5. Plant grass seeds in the bare spots.

What might be some advantages and disadvantages of each of these solutions?
Was the group consensus a good one?

Summary:

We have discussed a problem about our own school lawn today. We know that some of these solutions will require help from people outside our class. But we do know that some of the things we can do, such as making posters to tell other children about the grass problem, each one of us using the sidewalk and keeping off the grass.

In our class discussion we have indicated several main ideas, namely. . . . (List on the chalkboard areas that were discussed. This will make a good summary for each child.)

＊　＊　＊　＊　＊　＊　＊　＊　＊

The first portion of the lesson development, analysis of the problem, deals with definition of terms, cause-and-effect relationship, and so on. It is in this phase of the lesson that the basic facts will be introduced and evaluated—in terms of the problem being discussed. Normally some two-thirds or three-fourths of the discussion time will focus upon this phase of the experience.

The latter part of the lesson development, called establishing the hypotheses, focuses directly upon the problem. It is designed to lead the child from the facts of the situation to a plan of action for solving the problem.

Teachers who neglect formal planning all too often omit the hypothesis phase of class discussion. This is particularly unfortunate since, without this phase of the discussion, such an experience is of minimal value. The major class purpose is not reached.

The questions posed in the plan serve as guidelines only. They are asked only if and when they are needed. They also serve to guide the teacher as he moves from one phase of discussion to another. An experienced teacher, of course, will tend to have fewer questions in his plan than will an inexperienced teacher. It is imperative, nevertheless, that all teachers pose at least a few such questions for each of the discussion phases described.

In which subject areas is class discussion most usable?

If the most ideal subject for discussion is one of policy where sincere disagreement exists, it is obvious that social studies offers many appropriate areas for such discussion. It is impossible to escape the social implications in *any* class, however. There are occasions in any class when the guided class discussion would be an appropriate method of teaching. For example, it is important to stimulate interest in a subject just as it is essential to build interest in each unit of that subject.

By changing the so-called motivating discussion into a problem of policy the pupil can gain a glimpse of possible future courses of action. Finally he is encouraged to reflect on the desirability or feasibility of these proposals. At this point the teacher is under no obligation to utilize the resources suggested by pupils. The only objective is to create interest in a unit or area. Most teachers will find, however, that if interest is to be maintained throughout the unit, serious consideration of the wishes and desires of the group is definitely in order.

What principles are essential to effective discussion questions?

The controlling element in resolving issues through class discussion is the type of questions asked. Pupils frequently complain of difficulty in interpreting the meaning of a teacher's questions. Likewise, pupil responses may be vague or otherwise not indicative of intended meanings. Although there is some value in expression as a means of clarifying one's own thoughts, it is essential to know what is being clarified. As indicated earlier, the teacher, in advance of a class discussion, often formulates a few key questions designed to disclose major issues. As each is considered the group comes closer to its purpose until, finally, the purpose has been achieved. Thus the teacher's questions must be broad, yet specific enough to direct group thinking. A number of principles seems to apply.

First, *questions contribute to progress toward the discussion goal.* In the spontaneous interplay of individual reactions to issues a variety of questions tends to emerge. Indeed, when individuals reflect on a problem many remote questions or problems may emerge. The teacher must continually make quick decisions as to the desirability of pursuing given questions. To push the group too forcibly can impede or even block group reflection, while to entertain any and all questions can lead to a myriad of blind alleys, resulting in little or no progress. Sometimes the wise teacher may simply ask the questioner, "Would you clarify for us how your point relates to our problem?" Some teachers practice putting both the problem and the key questions on the board *in advance* of the discussion; this practice tends to keep the issue constantly before the group.

Second, *pupil questions often are redirected to the group.* It can be assumed that the teacher has a fairly good understanding of the discussion problem when the discussion begins. His purpose, then, is to provide an opportunity for the group to develop an understanding by discussing the problem through to a conclusion. The act of answering questions tends to emphasize his role as an "expert." Few individuals do their best thinking when they are constantly reminded that the leader already "knows" the answers. Under such conditions they are inclined merely to let this person think for them. Redirection of pupil questions tends to bring out new relationships and interpretations. If a question is vague, it is sometimes appropriate to redirect it to the person doing the asking. A rephrasing of a question will be in order at other times.

Third, *contributions are accepted whenever possible.* Skillful teachers generally adopt an air of acceptance when dealing with pupil responses to questions. If, however, a response obviously is in error pupils themselves can handle the situation if adequate time for reflection is provided. Inaccurate responses may stimulate further questions and analysis designed to evoke re-appraisal of the issue. Undue pupil embarrassment should be carefully avoided, however, if reflection is to continue. A teacher sometimes accepts an inaccurate response temporarily, simply by calling for other ideas pertaining to the issue. Usually subsequent responses will clarify the inaccuracy. (Occasionally the matter may have to be clarified before the group is permitted to advance to the next point.) In the final analysis, a teacher's reaction to responses sets the "feeling tone" for the entire discussion. Warm acceptance and praise reinforce the participants and lead to full participation.

Fourth, *questions are adapted to the individual differences of children.* Today the ability range of pupils in any given class may vary from dull normal to exceedingly bright. A teacher must consider this factor when directing discussion questions. Yet, in the heat of a spirited discussion, some teachers make the mistake of directing difficult questions to pupils who simply are not capable of adequate responses. Although full participation is desirable the teacher must not put an individual on the spot. A show of hands is one, but by no means the only, clue to a likely respondent. Sometimes a twinkle of the eye or a squaring of the shoulders will indicate a ready response. It is sometimes desirable to ask for a response in the absense of any such clue, if done with caution. For example, an inattentive individual occasionally may be brought back to the group in this manner.

Fifth, *full participation is encouraged.* Pupils may dislike the discussion method because a few members tend to do all the talking. There seems to be a human tendency to rely heavily on those assumed to be best qualified. In the give and take of class discussion the more social individual is usually ready with a response. While some such individuals can be depended upon to contribute to group progress, others can just as consistently impede group progress through their superficial remarks. It behooves the teacher to "see behind" the show of hands. Reliance upon a few individuals can result in those few solving the problem while the majority sit passively through the experience.

Sixth, *clear thinking is encouraged by allowing ample time for responses.* Reflection demands time! The glib person can impede such thinking. The teacher can inadvertently encourage glibness by rushing responses unnecessarily. The pressure of time, especially in large classes, frequently contributes to this problem. As one pupil expressed it, "He doesn't care what you say so long as you say it in a hurry." There are times, however, when through a sudden insight an individual needs to make a quick response. This is usually evidenced by the unusual eagerness of the respondent.

Seventh, *questions are asked in a natural, conversational manner.* This type of approach is especially desirable in class discussion. Most individuals seem to perform better in a relaxed atmosphere. While it is important to follow techniques of good speaking at all times, bookish terminology can have a depressing effect on a discussion group. Even though the teacher may have prepared his key questions well in advance, he usually rewords them to serve better the needs of the moment.

Eighth, *one does not hesitate to say, "I don't know."* Although it is not the primary purpose of the teacher to supply answers during a discussion, he *is* a much needed resource person. There will be some questions which he must answer in order to insure continued progress. If an important answer is needed at once he may be forced to say, "I don't know." If, however, the data are relevant to the discussion purpose he usually follows with, "I will find the answer, however." In such cases it is essential that he follow through with his promise.

Finally, *questions are impartially stated.* It is relatively easy for a biased leader to slant the discussion through his wording of basic key questions. The question, "Why should we be opposed to cutting the redwoods in California?" calls for the immediate assumption that the redwood forest should not be cut. In this case the discussion merely involves supporting a preconceived point of view. In guided class discussion a group should be capable of making its own decisions.

What are the mechanics of appropriate discussion questions?

Many teachers encounter difficulty in developing reflective thought because of the way they phrase their questions. A question which calls for a "yes" or "no" answer usually discourages discussion. For example, the question, "Do you agree with Johnny on his idea concerning the redwood trees?" demands a supplementary, "Why?"

The skillful teacher directs his questions to the entire class, hesitates, and then calls the name of a selected respondent. The longer he hesitates, the more the entire group thinks or ponders over possible responses. Many beginning teachers tend to call a pupil's name first. While such a practice catches the attention of the intended respondent, it tends to impede reflective processes of the other pupils.

It is usually desirable to distribute questions fairly evenly among the members of a group. Another common error is that of repeating answers. Not only is this practice time-consuming, but it encourages respondents to address their remarks solely to the teacher. To avoid unnecessary repetition a teacher frequently will need to ask the pupil to repeat his responses so that all can hear. The teacher who minimizes his repetition of pupil responses encourages pupils to make answers distinct, concise, and to the point. There are times, of course, when repetition is to the best interests of the class.

How can class discussion be evaluated?

The worth of a class discussion or of any other method of teaching ultimately must be measured in terms of its original aims or purposes. Central to aims or goals will be how well the problem has been analyzed and solved. There are other equally important purposes, however, which must be considered. For example, a teacher may have as one of his purposes "helping Johnny, Sue, and Mary feel capable of sharing their ideas with the group." The extreme variety of individual differences and needs represented in most elementary school groups is indeed a complicating factor. The fact that the teacher often is the leader and is preoccupied with matters related to solving the discussion problem is another complicating factor. On the one hand he has the task of evaluating group progress toward the goal, while on the other hand he must be concerned with individual progress. Both dimensions are important.

Braden and Brandenburg [2] suggest that the teacher can evaluate the results of a discussion ". . . by determining any one or any combination of the following:"

1. What action is undertaken as a result of the discussion?
2. Was the group consensus a good one?
3. Did individual members of the group acquire information through the discussion activity?
4. Can attitude tests which measure beliefs and opinions be utilized?
5. Is there evidence that the product of the discussion is something different from what would have resulted from an immediate combination of individual beliefs and reactions?
6. How much interest in the discussed issue seemed to be aroused?
7. What was the nature and extent of participation in the discussions?

As a means of measuring the foregoing a few selected procedures have been suggested.

1. *A short summary.* By summarizing briefly the major points of consensus in terms of the original purposes, a group can become conscious of accomplishments. This technique also can serve to clarify important points. Such summaries usually are more meaningful if made by pupils. Small children may dictate the summary to the teacher.

2. *Participation by many members.* An important criterion of group progress is indicated by the number of individuals who desire to speak simultaneously. While this certainly is a clue to group understanding, it is highly subjective. Interest can be mistaken for progress. Furthermore, reactions of a few members can lead to erroneous impressions of general group interest. A few members of most groups probably could solve the problem *without guided assistance.*

Interest may be carried over to out-of-school class situations. For example, some pupils may continue to seek new evidence on the problem by talking with others, reading books, and the like. Teachers must be on the alert for such indications of progress.

---

[2] Waldo W. Braden and Ernest Brandenburg, *Oral Decision Making: Principles of Discussion and Debate* (New York: Harper & Row, Publishers, 1955), pp. 337–338.

PANEL DISCUSSION

"The panel groups are doing satisfactorily," thought Mrs. Tagert as she observed her social studies class. Yesterday she had asked the class to prepare panel discussions on "some area of conservation." Pupils had almost quit coming to her for help because she had requested that this be *their* project, planned as each panel group thought best. She was a little dubious, but would see the thing through before passing judgment.

Finally the day for the first presentation arrived. The group had selected the topic, "Conservation and the Deer Hunter." Jane opened with a short overview of the topic. Then Mary related the reason for deer in our forests. Bill discussed the rules for deer hunting; Tom then talked about deer seasons; Margaret gave several reasons why deer need to be killed. By way of summary Jane suggested that the evidence indicated that deer hunting was necessary for conservation.

Mrs. Tagert was disappointed. Her feelings were supported by the following observations:

Although the panelists did present a wealth of information, much of it was read or memorized. (She wondered why a series of reports would not have accomplished as much or even more. "Were not these actually a series of reports which were read from a sitting position?") The material, although useful, was covered in the textbook.

The rest of the class soon lost interest. At times it was necessary to correct pupils who were disturbing.

"No," thought Mrs. Tagert, "I know when a worthwhile learning experience is present, and this was not it!"

Mrs. Tagert's experience with the panel is not uncommon. To be sure it did not produce a desirable learning situation, and certainly what she *called* a panel discussion would not be worth repeating. Perhaps a more thorough analysis of the situation will indicate why the experience was disappointing.

The area selected for exploration did include problems. Furthermore, the one group apparently attempted to narrow its subject to specific areas of exploration. The difficulty, however, probably was due to a lack of understanding of the purpose involved. Panel discussions are designed to enlighten or solve problems. A topic represents a general area of investigation, whereas a problem is more specific identification of a situation which the panel wishes to solve.[3] Mrs. Tagert's pupils were presenting facts which served no obvious purpose. The panel group had a topic rather than a problem. A discussion problem, properly stated,

[3] John W. Keltner, *Group Discussion Processes* (New York: Longmans, Green & Co., Inc., 1956), p. 39.

indicates a *purpose* and some *obstacle* to be overcome. Hence, it implies elements of disagreement. In a problem-solving situation facts are needed to support or refute value judgments, which in turn are necessary to resolve difficulties. Many panels do indeed deal with the *status quo*— if and when existing conditions are themselves of a controversial nature.

Moreover, Mrs. Tagert and her pupils seemed to assume that the panel was another technique of presenting information. Information is useful in a panel only to the extent that it bears upon the problems under consideration. As in the formal lecture, a series of oral presentations soon falls upon deaf ears. Elementary school children, as do all human beings, have limited attention spans. Pupils understandably tend to adopt certain techniques for informing others, unless careful guidance is available. Most of them have been conditioned to react in this manner through several years of school experience. Just as any teacher must understand the particular method he wishes to employ, so must the pupil understand those techniques he is to employ.

In this chapter an approach to panel discussion is offered which should enable a teacher to avoid many of the mistakes evident from Mrs. Tagert's experience.

What is a panel discussion?

"Let's have a panel!" These words ring repeatedly from the lips of old and young alike as people "shop around" for a method to re-place the formal lecture. Sometimes individuals are asked to take op-posing sides of an issue, while other times a panel of "experts" is used. Famous television programs utilize "panels of judges." One company recently employed a "panel of salesmen" to "ring doorbells" of pros-pective buyers. Seldom does a prospective teacher experience "panels" which bear more than a remote resemblance from one class to another. It is no wonder that such mass confusion has driven some teachers to avoid panels altogether!

From these conflicting statements one common characteristic is evident, however. A panel consists of a small number of people who "discuss" something. As indicated in the previous section, the term *dis-cussion* may refer to almost any form of verbal discourse. As used here, though, discussion aims at developing group agreement through re-flective thinking. *The panel discussion involves a group of five to eight children who are seeking agreement on a problem of concern to them-selves and to an audience.* A panel discussion (like the guided class dis-cussion) usually is built around a problem of policy which, as yet, has not been settled to the satisfaction of the group. The chief instrument at the disposal of the participants is an exchange of ideas and the weighing of evidence and proposals made by the members.

How does panel discussion differ from guided class discussion?

Upon casual inspection one might assume that an understanding of the technique of guided class discussion can be readily applied to panel discussion. While it is true that the objectives are basically the same, the approaches are vastly different. As a matter of fact, the purposes of most teaching methods described in this book are concerned with problem solving as an avenue to learning—only the approaches differ. Some of the features which distinguish the panel from guided class discussion are listed below.

1. The *teacher* directs the entire class in guided class discussion, whereas a panel of pupils has control of the panel operation.

2. Preparation for guided class discussion is controlled to a large degree by the teacher, while the panel members plan and prepare for their discussion.

3. Guided class discussion, when used appropriately, involves the whole process of solving a problem; the panel group can discuss one major issue of the problem only.

4. A class discussion leader is nearly always a dominant, central figure. The panel chairman, at his best, is the quietest person on the panel.

5. Even in a balanced class discussion the amount of actual participation is limited, whereas all panel members have ample opportunity to participate in their discussion.

6. Class discussion is controlled and directed by an authority figure who, by pupil standards, can be considered an expert. The panel, on the other hand, is led by one of the peer group who is neither an authority nor an expert.

What place do panel groups have in classrooms?

The panel discussion method has been applied in a wide variety of classroom situations. About the only requirement is that the problem involve an unsettled issue that is of vital importance to pupils. It should be one involving the use of facts which can be evaluated in resolving a difficulty. The problem should be limited enough for the panel group to explore in the time available.

Discussion, involving whole class groups, frequently does not flow as readily or as easily as might be expected. Fear of the audience or of the teacher may stifle free interchange of ideas. Sometimes there is a tendency for pupils to rely on the more outspoken individuals to carry the discussion. Consequently, educators have attempted to develop discussion techniques that will dispel fear and promote full participation. The panel has proven to be most effective in giving people a feeling of actual and active participation. Panel groups are usually characterized by a free, uninhibited exchange of ideas which bear upon the discussion problem. Thus, as each child has ample opportunity to participate on a panel, complete participation is virtually assured. Panel discussions are especially effective in paving the way for later class discussions.

What are the steps in development of a panel discussion?

Panel groups may originate in any number of ways. Many times the preliminary discussion (overview) of a unit will reveal a number of significant social problems which need to be considered. The diversified interests of pupils tend to make the formation of panel groups an easy matter. In any event, the success of the operation is directly dependent on the procedures followed. Teachers who have been most successful with the approach generally have directed attention to the following:

1. Selection and statement of discussion problem

2. Selection of panel group

3. Organization of panel group

4. Preparation for the panel presentation

5. Preparation of the leader for directing the discussion

6. Preparation of panel members for the presentation

7. Preparation of audience for the panel presentation

8. Panel presentation

9. Question period which follows the discussion

How is the discussion topic selected and stated?

The selection of a topic for panel discussion is extremely important. The problem frequently grows out of ongoing class activities which reveal a need to explore a topic further.

Mrs. Wilson's third grade class was reviewing the section from their science book concerning the taming of birds for pets. Some pupils thought the idea that it is often against the law to keep most wild birds as pets was unfair. One or two children actually suggested ideas as to how this situation could be improved, only to be reminded of the immediate disadvantages.

Mrs. Wilson, recognizing the keen interest shown by some of the children, asked, "Would some of you like to study this problem further? You could then recommend changes which might be helpful." Ten children indicated an immediate interest.

The need for panel groups in Mrs. Wilson's class evolved from a class review. The children involved, however, were guided into a problem area of immediate concern to them.

Sometimes use of panel discussion is anticipated and preplanned somewhat by the teacher. It may be that the preliminary overview discussion of a unit will be designed to develop interest in appropriate panel topics. While this procedure has many advantages, it is essential that the pupils involved feel the need for such an experience before the activity gets underway.

Mrs. Wilson was making advance preparation for her third grade science class. The unit, "Keeping a Pet," was planned. She decided that the goals of the unit could be well achieved through the utilization of various pupil activities, one of which might well be the formation of panel groups. As most of the children in her class had pets of one kind or another, she thought that they would be interested in discovering why children are not allowed to tame wild birds for pets.

After a brief discussion of pets children have, Mrs. Wilson began asking the children why they didn't have wild birds as pets. Very quickly the group decided that baby birds would be difficult to take care of and the game warden doesn't want these birds removed from their forest homes. This led to expressions of dissatisfaction.

Mrs. Wilson then suggested that "we might like to divide into panel groups to explore these problems more fully." The children agreed.

The foregoing illustration represents an approach to the panel method favored by many teachers. It has the advantage of providing pupils with ample time and opportunity for preparation. Furthermore, the different panel groups fit into the overall purposes of the unit, which actually are being clarified in the introductory overview.

Once the different problem areas have been established the teacher usually assists pupils in stating the problems. He can review, with the entire class, the essential phases of the deliberative process of coming to grips with an issue. A group may find it necessary to focus attention on the difficulty of keeping baby birds. Another group may consider the laws and rules. A third group may work out the problem of taming grown birds.

If the current policy is common knowledge to the class, it may be appropriate for panelists to focus attention on the desirability of different steps (solutions) which can be taken to solve the problem. Thus, the chairman may briefly summarize the essential requirements of a satisfactory plan and then state the problem as, "What steps might be taken to preserve the diminishing wild birds?" The discussion would evolve around the desirability of the different proposals.

While panel discussion is built around an issue of conflict, which essentially involves disagreement, there is little place for argumentation in such a discussion. The objective is for some sort of *agreement*. Sometimes a discussion on a proposed course of action results in the formation of opposing factions. Another limitation in discussing a proposed course of action is the implicit assumption that the specific solution is preferred to all other solutions. By restricting panel discussions of this sort to proposals of authoritative bodies, the limitation may be avoided.

Once the problem has been selected, the first step in planning for a panel discussion is to determine at what stage the question should come before the group.[4] These steps, as indicated above, may center around the confusing facts of the current situation, alternative steps (proposals) which might be taken, or a single, definite proposal. Sometimes, of course, all phases of the deliberative or problem-solving process will be discussed by the panel group. This is especially likely when the problem is somewhat restricted in scope.

Theoretically, each panel group should decide at which stage the discussion question should come before the class. The teacher should elect to play a major role in stating the discussion problems. This not only saves time but utilizes his more comprehensive understanding of the issues. Each panel problem thus may be clearly defined and stated before the panelists are selected.

How are panel groups organized for action?

After the panelists have been selected they usually need a 10- to 15-minute planning session for selection of a leader and division of labor. The group is instructed to select the most able and tolerant person for its leader. (If the groups have been determined sociometrically the teacher will want to select the leader.) The problem is then subdivided

---

[4] Alan H. Monroe, *Principles and Types of Speech*, 5th Ed. (Chicago: Scott, Foresman & Company, 1962).

into major issues or ideas which are pertinent to the discussion question. The chairman will not be assigned any particular topic, but rather will have more comprehensive responsibilities. He should be better informed than any other panel member. The following subtopics were developed by members of one panel group which was to discuss the problem, "Why does the law protect wild birds?"

1. How are they helpful to farmers?
2. How are they helpful to city people?
3. What would happen if they were not protected?

Although all the foregoing problems may not be of equal importance the division of labor enables each member to become better informed in *one* area than in all areas at once. Under optimum conditions it probably would be desirable for each panelist to study equally in each of the areas indicated. In practical classroom situations, however, this is seldom possible. Each member, however, should do *some* investigation in each area—so that he can at least ask questions intelligently!

Monroe suggests steps that the panelists can take as they prepare for the discussion:

First, review the facts you already know . . . Second, find out what recent changes have occurred affecting the problem. . . . However, keep your decision tentative; be willing to change your mind if additional facts disclosed in the discussion prove you to be wrong. Finally, examine the effect your idea or proposal will have upon the other members of the group.[5]

For most discussion problems, as illustrated in this chapter, pupils will need a short time to prepare for the presentation; however, older elementary children may need about a week. For larger problems some teachers have followed the practice of asking the chairman for a brief progress report each day to insure continued progress.

The day before the panel discussion the group should meet briefly, but only to determine and clarify problems. The discussion should *never* be rehearsed, however. Many teachers limit such prior "discussion" to a period of 15 minutes. The members should be careful to avoid the formulation of specific questions and answers in advance of the exercise.

What are the responsibilities of the panel leader?

The most important member of a panel is the leader. It is his responsibility to direct preplanning activities; to assist any member who

[5] *Ibid.*

is experiencing difficulty; to maintain a liaison between the teacher and panel members. By making the chairman responsible for keeping the group moving along, the teacher is relieved of many routine functions. The leader must play the role of a helpful participant, however, or the panel group will literally fall apart. With younger children, the teacher must also play the role of a helpful participant.

In addition to becoming better prepared generally than any other individual member, the leader builds a discussion outline. This outline usually consists of a series of questions built around the major issues to be emphasized. *Very few of these questions will be asked in a good panel discussion. They serve, instead, to guide thinking so that progress may be assured.* As one can readily see, a teacher with younger elementary children must take an active role in aiding the leader. A sample panel guide has been illustrated.

PUPIL GUIDE FOR PANEL DISCUSSION

Subject: Social Studies

Problem: What should be the policy about walking on the grass in front of the school building? *

    I. Analysis of Problem
       A. Should a policy be established?
       B. Are rules needed to protect the grass?
       C. What are the advantages or disadvantages of having rules to protect the lawn?
       D. Is the lawn likely to become more bare? Why or why not?

    II. NOW IN VIEW OF THE POINTS WE HAVE DISCUSSED, WHAT SHOULD BE THE POLICY ABOUT WALKING ON THE GRASS IN FRONT OF THE SCHOOL BUILDING? Advantages of each proposed solution? Disadvantages?

    III. Which of the proposed solutions best meets our class standards for deciding the issue?

When the panel is about to begin, the chairman will offer a few introductory remarks, state the problem (which can also be written on the board), and ask a question or challenge the group. (This is the one question which is usually prepared in advance; it may be memorized.)

---

* For purposes of comparison, the illustration is the same discussion problem as that used for the sample lesson plan for class discussion.

From this point on, the chairman helps the group move toward the ultimate solution of the problem. The following guidelines should be of service to the panel leader.

First, he is the quietest person on the panel, allowing a free flow of ideas from the participants. He steers, nudges, clarifies, summarizes, and the like, in an unobtrusive manner.

An inexperienced leader sometimes erroneously assumes that he should be *the* central figure of the group, and that it is his responsibility to ask questions which the panel members will answer. Nothing can be more inimical to the reflective efforts of the group.

Second, the leader is ever mindful of his duty to control the remarks of the vociferous person, while encouraging the more timid or shy individuals.

He may find it necessary to cut off the verbose person as unobtrusively as possible. He can say, "Bill, will you briefly get to the point?" Then, when the point has been briefly restated he quickly says, "Thank you. Would someone else like to speak on that point?" Another approach would be, "Wait just a minute, Bill. Let's see if someone else would like to speak on that point?" At other times it may be sufficient merely to use prudence in calling on this type of participant.

The quiet person usually poses a more difficult problem. Sometimes he can be drawn out by a skillful question. To avoid possible embarrassment, however, the question usually should be of a general nature— for example, "Joe, do you agree or disagree with Bill's comment?" or "How would Bill's idea help solve the problem, Joe?"

Third, the discussion is kept as reasonable and informative as possible. Here the leader's preplanned outline will be useful. What is the evidence? Is the speaker's conclusion warranted by the facts? Such comments as the following can do much to aid the group:

"You have heard Bill's point. Does anyone have any information which may support it?"

"Bill, why do you hold that opinion?" (This may remind Bill that he was actually voicing a value judgment.)

"Bill has reached a conclusion. Do you go along with him?"

"Bill seems to be accepting the assumption that . . . . Is this assumption possible?"

"The speaker used Mr. Jones as his source of authority. Is Mr. Jones qualified on this subject?"

Fourth, the chairman summarizes intermittently. This can take the form of a brief restatement of points or an emphasis on areas of agreement. Whenever he believes it time to move to another point a short summary can provide a ready transition, especially if he ends with, "Are there any other points to this problem which we need to discuss now?"

Fifth, he keeps the discussion on the topic. This is sometimes a difficult function to perform, as the relationship may be clear to the participant but not clear to the leader. He can tactfully handle the situation by asking, "How does your point relate to our problem?"

Sixth, the leader provides smooth transitions from one aspect of the problem to another. Frequently a comment from some member can be used to bring up another aspect of the problem. For example, "John has just mentioned. . . . Perhaps we can discuss his point now." Intermittent summaries, described above, can be used to provide appropriate transitions. The leader usually avoids such remarks as, "Johnny, what did you find on the topic?" or "Jack, would you like to begin our discussion with your topic?" At no time should the audience be conscious of the specific aspect of the problem which a certain individual has explored. While one will probably make more specific points when his area of investigation is under consideration, the other panelists will be asking questions, reacting to statements, proposals, and the like.

Seventh, the final summary is often made by the discussion leader. This will not be a restatement of points made, but a reminder of what the group has accomplished. Points of agreement will be stressed. The final summary is usually very brief—often not more than two or three comments.

Finally, he directs the question session which follows the panel presentation. Questions are addressed directly to him, and these in turn are redirected to some member of the panel.

What are the responsibilities of panel members?

After selecting an aspect of the problem for exploration, each panelist will need to give some attention to the entire discussion problem before he examines that aspect to which he has been assigned. Such a preliminary examination is essential if the problem is new to the group. Sometimes a textbook reference will provide the necessary overview of the problem; at other times the teacher will need to suggest one or two general reference readings.

As a panelist studies a particular aspect of the discussion problem he must be ever mindful of his purpose: What is the present state of affairs? What weaknesses seem apparent? What step(s) might be taken to improve existing conditions? Why would such action be desirable?

Of course, it is possible that present conditions, as they apply to his particular aspect of the discussion problem, may be quite satisfactory. Then he will attempt to find out why this seems to be the case. His notes will be brief but to the point. References will be noted. Occasionally one's source of authority will have a decided bearing on the final outcome. Some teachers like to have pupils submit their study notes after the discussion is completed. This enables the teacher to diagnose difficulties in the collection and evaluation of data.

During a panel discussion the members actually are exchanging ideas among themselves. *They are doing this, however, for the benefit of the class.* For this reason it seems desirable to have the panelists arranged in a semicircle in front of the class, with the chairman occupying a position near the center of the panel group. The objective is to have the participants partially facing each other, the chairman, and the audience. They will need to speak more loudly than would be necessary under ordinary conditions.

The amount, manner, and quality of participation is of utmost importance. First and foremost, the group must remember that *central to a panel discussion is reflective thinking, which is necessary to solve a problem.* It is the function of the panelists to present information *only insofar as necessary to reflect upon the issues.* Consequently, prepared speeches are not in order. It is essential that pupils thoroughly understand the following responsibilities of panel members:

1. Seldom will it be appropriate for a panelist to make a contribution longer than one minute's duration. Instead, he will bring out enough of an important point to elicit further discussion and/or questions. The whole arrangement is a give-and-take situation.

2. The best panelist develops an inquisitive attitude during the proceedings. This does not mean, however, that he becomes argumentative. Instead, he probes assumptions, asks for clarification, points out hidden weaknesses, and the like. This enables the group to cope with basic issues necessary for the resolution of the problem.

3. He follows the discussion carefully. By listening (and actually hearing what others have to say) his own thoughts are stimulated so that his contributions fit the situation. Some panel discussions are characterized by brief silent periods, which may be indicative of reflective thinking.

   A panelist follows his impulse to speak when an idea prompts him. By hesitating too long he may find himself playing the role of a listener entirely. Thus, he becomes a liability to the group.

4. The panel participant relates his remarks to what has been said. He can accomplish this by opening his contribution with specific reference to the

point, argument, or idea he wants to explain further, add to, criticize, question, or refute.

"Bill's point relating to the effects of . . . seems to be a good one. Here is another reason why it might be worth our serious consideration. . . ."

"I think your point on the . . . is well taken, Charley, but how would it solve the problem? For instance. . . ."

"The argument that . . . seems a wrong one to me. What would happen if . . . ?"

5. Tact is essential in attempting to reach agreement. Disparaging remarks and uncomplimentary labels tend to divert the discussion from the problem to personalities. One who is the recipient of such remarks, if he is unable to ignore the situation, may direct his response through the chairman. A simple request for an explanation of the assertion may cause one to alter his original statement.

It is also well to avoid dogmatic statements. One should continuously give evidence of "to-me-ness," expressed perhaps as, "As I see it . . . ," "It seems to me . . . ," or "On the basis of this or that evidence . . . ."

6. Flexibility is basic to any sort of agreement. One is ever ready to consider new points of view and alter his views when this is warranted. He is willing to compromise, but does not give ground just for the sake of agreement. If one feels he must stand pat he can strengthen his position by calling for an examination of an obvious weakness in the position of the other person.

How can the audience profit most from the presentation?

The worth of a panel discussion to the active participants is obvious —they experience actual, cooperative problem-solving activities. Practical considerations, however, must be given to the other 25 or more pupils in the classroom. Is the panel presentation a valuable learning experience for the majority of the group? How can members of the audience make the most of their observations?

When the panel presentation is completed the chairman invites members of the class to ask questions. They are instructed to direct their questions to the chairman, indicating whom they wish to respond. The class is advised to make questions brief and to the point. Likewise, the respondent makes his answer short. Nothing is more discouraging than a five-minute discourse when several people have questions to ask. The teacher will need to discourage members of the class who would make contributions rather than ask questions.

Following the question period it may be appropriate to compliment the panel group and offer two or three general suggestions if needed, as a guide for future groups.

PROBLEMS AND PRINCIPLES IN DISCUSSION

By following the procedures outlined in this chapter, a teacher can effectively make the first break from purely teacher-centered methods to procedures which emphasize the group. Although the guided class discussion is teacher-centered and directed, the resolution of issues finally rests with pupils. Then, through panel discussion, a large share of the responsibilities of teacher direction and control passes to the pupils. The teacher's first step in becoming competent in the use of any method is that of developing a *thorough initial understanding* of the process involved. These processes have been described. The next step involves *improving with practice*. By becoming thoroughly acquainted with, and practicing, the general problems and principles described below the teacher may accomplish this. Many sound psychological principles are incorporated in the following suggestions and recommendations.

How can discussion groups be used effectively?

The principles listed below are central to discussion. They can serve as guidelines to both teacher and pupils.

1. The discussion problem usually is stated in question form.

2. There are no formal speeches in discussion. Length of each contribution should seldom exceed one minute.

3. Discussion members should develop an attitude of searching, while avoiding argumentation.

4. Specific questions by panelists are not prepared in advance.

5. Purpose of the experience is reflection through the spirit of inquiry—not presentation of information.

6. Most panel discussions should be followed by a class discussion period. Here points are clarified and expanded; mistakes corrected. At this point the teacher may desire to present additional information that bears upon the problem under consideration. The problem-solving process does not often terminate until completion of the follow-up discussion.

What are some hazards to the effective use of discussion?

Like any other method, discussion can be misused. It is through just such misuse that some teachers have become discouraged with these approaches to teaching. By becoming aware of the hazards involved, the resourceful teacher should be able to place discussion methods in their proper perspective among the different teaching techniques available.

1. Discussion presupposes adequate preparation. It is impossible to reflect effectively upon facts and concepts which are unknown or incompletely understood by the participants. The discussion situation can enable an individual to relax and contribute, at least sporadically. This tends to reduce the immediate urgency for preparation. In other words, one may actually submerge himself "within" the group.

2. The permissive characteristic of discussion tends to encourage digression. In order to minimize this, an expert leader must be at the helm. Not all teachers are as competent as they might be in this respect.

3. The discussion leader may be unable to maintain an "open mind" toward the issues. Ideally the leader is an impartial observer. He represses his own attitudes and biases, while encouraging others to express themselves. At the same time he needs to have a complete general knowledge of the issues involved. This, in effect, calls for preparedness while limiting his freedom to share his knowledge and evaluations. On many occasions teachers are obliged to direct and pass judgment. Sometimes it is difficult to step out of this role. Slow but essential progress may be identified as insufficient and a waste of time.

4. Discussion requires training. As the foregoing should indicate, the guided class discussion is not a simple process. There are many who *talk* class discussion but few who possess the needed training and skill for its appropriate application.

5. Even when carefully organized, class discussion is unpredictable. If a "discussion" were predictable it would not be a discussion in the strict sense at all. It is just this element of chance which limits its desirability for some teachers. The traditionally-oriented teacher, especially, desires more control over the situation.

6. Class discussion is often inappropriate for matters of fact. Teachers who emphasize textbook teaching find little use for this method. One need hardly discuss problems which can be solved by merely perusing certain documents. Likewise, problems of fact are often inappropriate for panel groups. If, however, the facts are of a conflicting or confusing nature such problems might be fully adaptable to discussion.

SUMMARY

In the foregoing chapter, class and panel discussion have been described. The two teaching methods, although distinctly different in many respects, are closely related in others. Each can be concerned with the resolution of policy problems which can be analyzed, in some manner, by the class group.

The guided class discussion, unlike panel procedures, is definitely teacher-centered. The teacher assumes a major share of the planning responsibilities. He guides the group in solving the discussion problem. In the discussion process he decides on the relevancy of pupil questions and points. The degree of guidance, finally, rests with the teacher.

Panel discussion, on the other hand, utilizes the efforts of a group of five to eight pupils who are seeking areas of agreement on some unsettled problem. Through processes of deliberation the participants bring all their resources to bear upon the situation. Although the discussion, technically, is among the panel group, it is commonly performed before an audience—the rest of the class. When the panel deliberations have ended, the audience is given an opportunity to question the panelists. Finally, the teacher leads the class in a review of principles, concepts, and relationships which have emerged during the proceedings. Attention is given to related problems and other parallels which may be made from the experience.

It was noted that formation of panel groups may represent the first break from purely individual-centered teaching procedures. In some respects the panel approach in solving problems enables pupils to perform under conditions closely related to real-life situations. The panel group usually has full responsibility for planning and developing its problem. Instead of having some adult authority in charge, the panel is led by one of its own members. It is the panel leader who guides the group, passes upon the relevancy of points, and reconciles different points of view. He can expect little interference from the teacher.

QUESTIONS FOR STUDY AND DISCUSSION

1. What are the characteristic features of discussion? Why is guided class discussion sometimes referred to as *pseudo* discussion? What precautions are necessary in minimizing this danger? Distinguish between the class

recitation, a "factual"-type discussion, and the problem-type discussion treated in this chapter. What advantages are attributed to the problem-type discussion? What disadvantages seem likely?

2. Distinguish among questions of fact, value, and policy. Explain how a policy question includes questions of fact and value. Formulate three questions of policy in elementary education. What difficulties do you encounter? Why?

3. How does panel discussion differ from guided class discussion? What advantages does panel discussion have over guided class discussion? What disadvantages? What are the major functions of the discussion leader? Above all, the panel participant must display a *searching* attitude. Why?

4. Why is balanced participation desirable? How would you develop this?

5. What end product(s) might be expected from discussion? It has been contended that discussion process is more important than the end product. Why? Suppose a panel discussion group reached a conclusion quite different from your expectations. What would you do? Why?

SELECTED BIBLIOGRAPHY

Braden, Waldo W. and Ernest Brandenburg, *Oral Decision Making: Principles of Discussion and Debate* (New York: Harper & Row, Publishers, 1955).

Gulley, Halbert E., *Discussion, Conference and Group Process* (New York: Holt, Rinehart & Winston, Inc., 1960).

Hoover, K. H., "Effect of Structured Small Groups Upon Attitude Change," *Educational Research*, 9: 233–236 (June, 1967).

Keltner, John W., *Group Discussion Processes* (New York: Longmans, Green & Co., Inc., 1956).

Laughlin, P. R. and M. A. Doherty, "Discussion Versus Memory in Cooperative Group Concept Attainment," *Journal of Educational Psychology*, 58: 123–128 (April, 1967).

Maryanna, Sister, "Small Group Discussion," *The Catholic School Journal*, 66: 43–44 (May, 1966).

Monroe, Alan H., *Principles and Types of Speech*, 5th Ed. (Chicago: Scott, Foresman & Company, 1962).

Suchman, J. R., "Play and Discussion," *The Instructor*, 76: 33+ (February, 1967).

Improving Social Relationships: Sociometry, Dramatic Play, and Role Playing

Mrs. Townsen had observed her pupils for three weeks now. She had permitted her pupils to select their own seats. In her own words, "For the first few weeks a child needs the security of his friends." Now she thought it was time to revise the seating arrangement. She was anxious to separate a few close friends and two or three tight cliques. Mrs. Townsen believed that in this way the apparent "social exclusiveness" could be substantially reduced. This, in turn, should promote the important job of the school: to do the class assignments.

A few days after the new seating arrangement was effected Mrs. Townsen again took stock of the situation. Things were not going as well as she had hoped. The group as a whole seemed to be restless. Someone seemed to be constantly giggling, shoving, or otherwise interrupting. Those who had been separated from close friends seemed to be looking for excuses to work together. Certain people who had formerly been trying to attract attention were still disturbing. In general, class atmosphere seemed to have deteriorated. Few seemed able to do better work, while some were making less progress than formerly.

Mrs. Townsen's difficulties are little different than those encountered by thousands of teachers every year. What are some of the aggravating causes of the problem? What is there about the social structure of a group that may build or destroy a desirable class atmosphere? Can a teacher somehow gain control of the interplay of forces going on in the social group? Fortunately, during the last two decades a great deal has been discovered about the interactions of the peer group. A more systematic approach to the building of good human relationships might have saved Mrs. Townsen a lot of worry and frustration.

This chapter is divided into three parts: Sociometry; Dramatic Play; and Problems and Principles Associated with Improving Social Relationships. Although sociometry and dramatic play are distinctly different techniques, they serve a similar function: both are designed to improve social relationships.

SOCIOMETRY

The foregoing anecdote illustrates how competent, well-meaning teachers may contribute to insecurity in the classroom. Unfortunately, many academically competent teachers are *not* competent in fostering desirable human relationships. An analysis of Mrs. Townsen's experience may suggest some typical problems in the area.

On the positive side, Mrs. Townsen's decision to let children select their own seats for the first few weeks was probably sound. Many pupils were undoubtedly able to gain security through association with a close friend in class. Likewise, after children have become acquainted in a new class situation a reseating arrangement is usually desirable. It is sometimes desirable to break up tight cliques. Mrs. Townsen's efforts, however, were based on her own observations only and on one or two false assumptions.

While observation of pupil interaction patterns is certainly a most valuable aid, it does not reveal preferred associations of many children. Whether a teacher realizes it or not, interpersonal relationships have a tremendous impact on learning. The emphasis on purely independent learning in group situations has many harmful effects. Jennings [1] contends that disciplinary problems arise from the fact that children are taught two lives: one officially in school and the other undercover, to satisfy the social needs forbidden in school. Sociometry tends to "bring these two lives together."

Mrs. Townsen noticed that her attention-seekers continued to play their roles even after her reseating arrangement. This was undoubtedly because their social needs were not being met either before or after the action was taken. Indeed, some teachers have helped pupils feel secure by maintaining a voluntary seating pattern throughout the year. This, however, often does not assist those who need help most. The unpopular pupil seldom has an opportunity to sit by or work with one who may give him needed security. He may find himself alone or with others of his kind. Soon he starts seeking attention through other channels, such

[1] Helen Hall Jennings, *Sociometry in Group Relations*, Rev. Ed. (Washington, D. C.: American Council on Education, 1959), pp. 4–5.

as disturbing others. Sometimes he withdraws from the situation entirely to live in his own dream world. While it is sometimes desirable to break up tight cliques, it must be done with prudence. The security of the individual must be considered.

What is sociometry?

The word *sociometry* is derived from Latin and means literally *social or companion measurement*. The term has become closely identified with the *sociometric test*, originated and popularized by Jacob L. Moreno.[2] Actually it is not a test in the common sense of the word, but a technique or method. *The sociometric test (sometimes referred to as sociometric technique or inventory) is designed to evaluate the feelings of the group on the basis of a given situation.*

Sociometry, then, would include all techniques for determining social status within a given group. Some of these, such as various teacher-observation and pupil-reporting procedures, have long been used in the classroom. The emphasis here, however, will be on more recent sociometric techniques which have contributed to a simple, yet highly satisfactory, approach to the improvement of social relationships.

Sociometry, and especially sociometric testing, are based on the premise that both social and academic learning are accelerated by recognizing and making use of existing friendship patterns and encouraging the development of others. The approach described in the following pages may be applied to classroom seating arrangements and/or group work of all kinds.

What constitutes an appropriate criterion question?

Teachers frequently want to arrange pupils sociometrically for specific purposes, such as traveling companions on a school trip or for temporary buzz groups. Although such specific situations meet the necessary requirement of realism, they are of minimal value for diagnostic purposes. The most stable and generally useful results are obtained from a general criterion question. The above questions can be expanded as follows: What individuals would you prefer to be with while on school trips? Whom would you prefer to work with on committees?

Generally the criterion question must indicate the nature of the activity or situation to be applied. It should be one that is thoroughly familiar and realistic to children. It must be general enough to minimize

[2] Jacob L. Moreno, *Who Shall Survive?* (Washington, D. C.: Nervous and Mental Disease Publishing Co., 1934).

the influence of transitory interests and should provide opportunity for mutual association and interaction.

Research generally has indicated that the main aspects of personal and social relationships are included in the general areas of seating, play, and work. Thus, three criterion questions are needed if the entire range of class interaction is sought. Use of questions demanding psychological analysis should be avoided. For example, the criterion question "Which individuals make you feel most secure?" should *not* be used.

How are sociometric data obtained?

The sociometric test (inventory) is a flexible procedure that can be administered in a matter of minutes. Directions may be oral, or a sociometric form may be constructed. In any event, the directions may be somewhat as follows:

During the next three or four weeks we will be working in groups of five. Each group will have a selected problem to solve. This will involve a number of activities, such as making outlines and plans, reading books, interviewing people, collecting pictures and illustrations, and combining and evaluating the materials. Finally, each group will be responsible for presenting its findings to the rest of the class. These activities will involve a lot of teamwork. Some jobs will be hard, other jobs will be somewhat monotonous. It has occurred to your teacher that we might enjoy this work more and have better cooperation if we were permitted to work with our preferred classmates. What do you think of the idea? (Responses are nearly always enthusiastic.)

Now, let us remember that if we are to accept the privilege of working with our preferred classmates we must also accept the responsibilities which go with it. In other words, each person must do his share in helping his group and the entire class complete its job. This means that we must guard against wasting time discussing nonrelated topics; that we must work quietly enough to allow other groups to do their jobs, too. One who, through his behavior, demonstrates his inability to accept these responsibilities will be deprived of this privilege.

Indicate on a sheet of paper the names of five people with whom you would prefer to work. Indicate the order of preference of your choices. I will make every effort possible to place you with one or more of your choices when groups are formed. It is impossible to give everyone his first choice, but each person will get at least one of his five choices. *Your choices will be kept strictly confidential.*

Now, before you begin, put your own name on the back of your paper.

The foregoing directions indicate a number of essential characteristics of the sociometric inventory:

1. The nature of the activity or situation must be clearly delineated.

2. Research findings indicate that five choices provide the most stable or reliable sociometric results.[3]

3. The use of negative choices (rejections) is usually avoided, as this may make individuals more conscious of their feelings of rejection. In cases of extreme rejection the chooser is likely to reveal his feelings anyhow. Whenever such a rejection is indicated his wishes should be respected.

4. A definite commitment to honor indicated preferences should be made.

5. Pupils are asked to accept sociometric grouping as a privilege, which entails definite responsibilities.

6. The confidential nature of the responses must be stressed.

7. Pupils must have had ample opportunity to become acquainted with each other before the test or technique is administered. This may take three to six weeks.

How may sociometric data be analyzed?

Sociometric test results from a class of 35 or more pupils can discourage the most conscientious teacher unless easy analysis of the data can be developed. Frequently the matrix table is used as the first step in such an analysis. This is merely a twofold table which shows the choices each person has given and received. The teacher who desires to make a thorough evaluation of interpersonal relationships will find the matrix table or some related graphic presentation a valuable tool.

Forms may be prepared and reproduced in quantity. The following steps are useful guidelines.

1. List names of pupils in alphabetical order. Then number consecutively from top to bottom.

2. Number consecutively across the top of the page.

3. Draw a diagonal line from the upper left to lower right corner of paper. This serves as a focal point for identifying mutual choices. It bisects the squares not used.

4. Provide for a "total" column at bottom of page.

Table 1 (page 156) has been completed with the appropriate sociometric data included. Bill chose the following individuals: Clark, Howard, Otis, Mike, Virginia. His choices were recorded by entering, across from his name, number one in column five, indicating Clark. Number one is used in Clark's column because it was his first choice.

---

[3] Norman E. Gronlund, *Sociometry in the Classroom* (New York: Harper & Row, Publishers, 1959), p. 48.

PUPILS CHOSEN

Chooser		1	2	3	4	5	6	7	8	9	10	11	12	13	14	15	16	17	18	19	20	21	22	23	24	25	26	27	28	29
Bill	1				1		2			4					3															5
Ben	2			1	2					4		(3)		5																
Dick	3		5		4	(1)			2	3																				
Chris	4				(2)									(3)	(1)								4					(5)		
Clark	5			(2)	(3)			(1)																5						
Gam	6	5			3				(1)					4		2														
Howard	7								4					1	3					2					5					
Lucky	8				(2)											1	(3)						4		5					
Mack	9			1	4	(5)									3				(2)											
Mike	10			2	1	4									3				5											
Mitchell	11					3	4		2						1				5											
Morris	12		(3)					1							2						4				5					
Mund	13				(1)															(4)		(3)						(2)		
Nagy	14				(3)												4					(2)								(1)
Otis	15			3		1									2								5					4		
Paul	16	3				1									3				2									4		
Porkey	17						(4)								2			3		(1)										
Tommy	18		5	2	4						3									(1)										
Tonky	19								(1)					(2)	3	5		4												
Wes	20				2		4								1								3					5		
Grace	21				3																			(4)		2	(1)		5	
Lucy	22												5	(2)	(3)											(4)		(1)		
Linda	23																						(5)	2		(4)			(1)	(3)
Rana	24	3																					4			2	(5)			(1)
Rachell	25				4																		(1)	O				3		(2)
Sally	26						2																(1)		5	(3)		4		
Sonya	27			(4)										(3)	(2)								(1)	(5)						
Tam	28																						2	(1)				.	3	
Virginia	29																						4	2	(3)	(1)				
TOTAL		3	3	3	12	8	4	2	8	3	4		3	11	7	6	1	3	2	4	2	2	12	7	2	7	2	12	2	3

TABLE 1.   *Matrix Table*

Likewise, number two is used in column seven to indicate Howard as his second choice. Accordingly, the numbers three, four, and five are placed in Otis's, Mike's, and Virginia's columns respectively to indicate his third, fourth, and fifth choices.

After all choices are recorded it becomes apparent that choices given go across the table, whereas choices received go down the table. Mutual choices may be identified and circled. This can be readily accomplished by using the diagonal as a focal point to find the vertical column indicating those who chose a given pupil. Mack, for example, chose Chris, Clark, Gam, Nagy, and Tonky. By following the vertical line of number nine (Mack's number) it is seen that Mack was chosen by Dick, Gam, and Tonky. Two of these individuals, Tonky and Gam, were also chosen by Mack. Thus, mutual choices have been circled in *both* horizontal and vertical columns.

Finally, the choices received are totaled at the bottom of the page. The teacher is now able to determine the sociometric status of individual pupils, but before he can arrange appropriate groups he must make use of a *sociogram* (page 158).

The *sociogram* is designed to portray the indicated group social structure. Originally this consisted of symbols for each member, with a system of arrows to indicate direction of choice. The Northway and Bronfenbrenner refinements of the original sociogram may be most useful to the classroom teacher.[4]

The sociogram, Figure 1., is a blank target. The vertical line through the center of the diagram is to separate the sexes, as there tends to be a sex cleavage at all ages. The numbers along the line below each circle indicate the choice levels for each of the circles. The numbers are based on Bronfenbrenner's fixed frame of reference.*

Pupils receiving one or no choices would be placed in the outer ring of the diagram; those receiving between 1 and 5 would be placed in the next ring and so forth. The sociogram may be plotted easily by beginning with the least chosen pupils and moving toward the most chosen children.

It will be noted that mutual choices only have been indicated. This provides a clear picture of the indicated group social structure with a minimum of effort. When it is desirable to ascertain one-way choices the matrix table may be reviewed. The resourceful teacher usually has a number of blank sociogram "targets" duplicated and ready for use.

Sometimes teachers may desire a simplified method of grouping pupils sociometrically. For the purpose of expediency only, the matrix table may be bypassed. In such cases the papers (indicating pupil choices) may be sorted into groups by casual inspection. In most cases there are three or four ill-defined groups indicated. The next step is to pick out the most highly chosen individuals of each group in preparation for the construction of a sociogram. The sociogram may consist of symbols with lines and arrows to indicate mutual and one-way choices. Three choices can be readily plotted in this manner; this will produce the data needed and can be completed very quickly. After some experience the writers were able to complete such an analysis in about 20 minutes with groups ranging from 35 to 40 in number.

---

[4] N. L. Northway, "A Method for Depicting Social Relationships Obtained by Sociometric Testing," and U. Bronfenbrenner, "The Graphic Presentation of Sociometric Data," from Norman E. Gronlund, *op. cit.*, p. 69.

* Bronfenbrenner developed critical sociometric status scores for varying numbers of choices. Based on five choices, the lower and upper limits of 1 and 9 (as seen in Figure 1) actually represent limits of statistical significance at the .02 and .03 levels. When two and three criteria or sociometric situations are used the upper and lower limits are 4 and 16, 9 and 22, respectively.

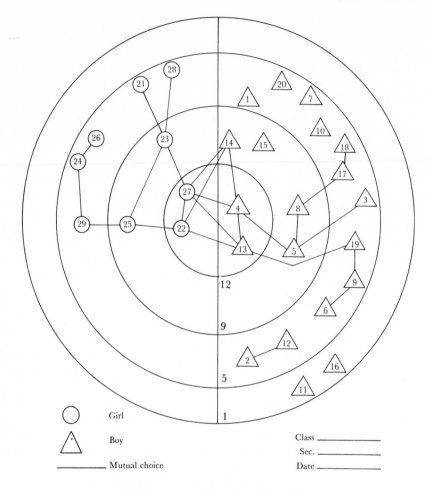

FIGURE 1. *Sociogram-Mutual Choices*

How are sociometric data utilized?

After sociometric data have been analyzed, the first step in improving social relations is that of putting pupil choices into effect. Sociometric information should not be considered the sole basis for the rearrangement of groups but a valuable guide. The teacher attempts to develop more satisfying social relationships as well as a cohesive group structure. The following steps are recommended for sociometric grouping:

1. Decide the size of the groups to be formed. Work groups of five are often satisfactory.

2. Give unchosen children (isolates) their highest choices. Honor their first two choices if possible, but avoid placing two isolates in the same group whenever possible. Never place more than two isolates in a single group.

3. Consider those who received only one choice (neglectees). If the choice was reciprocated put him with the other person involved, regardless of the level of choice.

4. Continue to work from the least chosen to the most chosen individuals. In each case attempt to satisfy mutual choices first.

A number of other considerations should be taken into account when groups are being formed:

1. When more than two choices are possible, attempt to give them to isolates and neglectees.

2. When group cleavages exist it is often desirable to formulate groups with a view of minimizing them. Such cleavages may be socioeconomic, sex, race, rural-urban, and the like. There should be a minimum of two from such subgroups to provide additional security to those involved.

3. Sometimes it is desirable to break up tight cliques. A typical work group, thus formulated, may have one or two isolates or neglectees, one highly chosen individual, and about two pupils of average choice status. Variations can be expected, of course.

This process necessitates careful observation of unpopular pupils. Gronlund [5] offers some guidelines that should prove helpful in analyzing and understanding such pupils:

1. Does the pupil voluntarily withdraw from social interaction or does he attempt to establish social contacts with other pupils?

2. Are there any obvious reasons for the pupil's social isolation (e.g., physical handicap, inadequate attention to cleanliness, lack of social skill)?

3. Does the isolated pupil enjoy constructive, individual activities, or does he appear unhappy in his position of isolation?

4. Does the pupil reflect a need and desire for social acceptance by making excessive efforts to obtain the approval of the teacher?

5. Do any of the class members initiate social interaction with the isolated pupil? How does he react to their efforts?

6. How do the class members react to the isolated pupil's attempts to initiate social interaction with them?

7. What type of social contacts does the isolated pupil seem to have outside the classroom? Does he play alone on the playground? Does he walk home alone? Does he have friends in other classes?

[5] Gronlund, *op. cit.*, pp. 273–274.

8. Is there anything notable in the isolated pupil's social behavior that can be used as a basis for helping him build better social relationships?

Following a period of careful observation, a conference or conferences with pupils becomes essential. The nondirective approach is usually preferred in such cases. The teacher usually desires to find out how the pupil feels about his peers, himself, and his social acceptance. The pupil should not be informed of his low social status. Emphasis is placed on his attitudes and feelings and the degree to which his social aspirations are consistent with his social reality.

Low social status may be a normal phenomenon with the child. Some people, by preference, enjoy pursuing individual interests. If so, little need be done. Other individuals withdraw from social contacts because they lack self-confidence. They are generally unhappy people. Such individuals need social acceptance. There also is the aggressive person who tends to be rejected by his peers. This child needs guidance into more socially acceptable behavior. Finally, there is the cultural isolate. In this case emphasis probably should be placed on altering group attitudes toward cultural and racial differences.

There are any number of additional techniques which may be utilized to help the unpopular pupil gain acceptance. One of the most valuable approaches involves the use of dramatic play, which will be described next. Another approach involves helping such pupils attract favorable recognition from their peers. Many times situations can be arranged which afford an opportunity for one to demonstrate a skill which is highly valued by the group. Collections, special knowledge, and the like also fall into this category.

THE DRAMATIC PLAY EXPERIENCE

An analysis of pupil friendship preferences, made possible through the sociometric inventory, is of limited value until appropriate action is taken to correct existing difficulties. Even sociometric grouping techniques may fail to bring about acceptance of some pupils.

Mary was a lonely child. She received no friendship choices among her class group. Even a casual observer could see that she also was alone outside of class. She frequently was seen standing alone in the halls or walking to and from school by herself.

Mary's sociometric choices were directed toward the most popular pupils in the classroom. Realizing the seriousness of the problem, Miss Jones had placed Mary in a work group with two of her choices. This seemed to please her very much.

After a few days, however, it was obvious that things were not going well. Mary was "of" the group but not "in" the group. She tended to be ignored or given individual jobs. The problem reached a climax at the end of the second meeting of the group operation. Members of the committee remained after class to request that Mary be transferred to another group.

Miss Jones was puzzled. "Why?" The answer was direct and to the point. "Mary won't share with us," said Susie. "And she uses funny language besides," added Joan.

What can a teacher do under such circumstances? Telling a child about such annoyances *is* practically impossible.

The foregoing illustration reveals the need for a teaching technique for making abstract ideas more concrete. Mary needed to become aware of her problems. The other members of her committee needed help in giving her the assistance needed. How can pupils be helped in the *application* of such learnings? A "show me how" approach is needed.

This is only one of the many instances in which a role-playing experience can be helpful in bridging the gap between classroom learnings and real life experiences.

What is the relationship between role playing and dramatic play?

"Play is a natural expression of children." [6] By listening to a group of young children at play one is likely to hear someone say, "Let's pretend we're mommies, daddies, brothers, and sisters, and that we have children." Another may add, "All right, I'll be the mommie and you be the big sister." Likewise, the others are assigned definite roles and the "pretend game" begins. The observer might be surprised to discover that the game is usually built around a series of conflict situations, which are resolved as the children think the real parents would resolve them. Although situations may change every few minutes, the role playing sometimes continues for an hour or more.

People of all ages seem to enjoy projecting themselves into "another's shoes." Elementary school pupils welcome opportunities to act. Indeed, some seem to enjoy playing self-assigned roles in the classroom, as evidenced by the attention-seeker, the apple-polisher, the needler, and the like.

Role playing as a method of teaching is a means of providing practice in ways of behaving in selected situations. Hence, it is often called "real-

[6] Lavone A. Hanna and others, *Unit Teaching in the Elementary School* (New York: Holt, Rinehart & Winston, Inc., 1963), p. 316.

ity practice." The emphasis is upon the *role* played. Was it "true to life"? Did the actor "live" the part assigned to him? Dramatic play is closely related and intertwined with role playing, but it has a broader base. *In dramatic play, role playing is used as the vehicle to portray a situation for study and analysis.* Little emphasis is placed on the roles played, but is on *reactions* to the *situation* thus created. Frequently one needs to rehearse a role if his audience is to learn how to perform in a similar manner. Role playing is a common method in sales training where a given approach is emphasized. In dramatic play, however, role rehearsal is not appropriate. Here the emphasis is on how one would act in an actual situation. Any number of alternative roles may be available and appropriate. The pupil must never play his real life role. Through the *spontaneous* situation which is created the group is able to analyze and critically evaluate reactions. Since role play and dramatic play are so closely connected they are treated together here, with emphasis on the latter.

How is dramatic play related to sociometry?

Through a sociometric inventory the teacher is able to determine friendship preferences of pupils. He can accordingly identify those who have few friends, those who are popular, those who are members of tight cliques, and so forth. Once the social pattern is made clear to him he is in a position to employ other sociometric techniques to help those who are having difficulty making satisfactory adjustments. Dramatic play may be *one* of these techniques. It is one thing to be aware that a boy is not well liked, but quite another to correct the situation.

Role playing reveals a pattern of behavior acceptable to the group. The sociometric inventory can be useful in guiding a teacher in appropriate use of dramatic play. For example, Johnny and Ruth are not participating; in the free time activity they do not appear to have a feeling of belonging. It may be difficult for these two pupils to act out the situation together, but by using the sociometric inventory as a guide, another child and Johnny or Ruth may be able to portray their feelings in such a way that Johnny and Ruth may understand the behavior which is acceptable to the group.

It should be emphasized, however, that dramatic play has other uses, e.g., as a method of bridging the gap between the child and the adult worlds. "This natural desire to play at adult activities has educative value if it is under the guidance of a watchful and discriminating teacher." [7] In general, the enactment should be of real persons reacting to situations

---

[7] *Ibid.*, p. 317.

which in all probaility have been experienced by those in the classroom and which are likely to be experienced again in the near future.

When is the dramatic play method appropriate?

Enacting a real life situation is appropriate whenever it is necessary for one to perceive how others feel. An individual, for example, frequently develops an intellectual understanding of desirable behavior in others, but he may be unable to make his own behavior consistent with this knowledge. In a sense, all human beings are bound by habitual behavior. It takes a great deal of conscious and persistent effort to break a habit. Dramatic play can provide the motivation necessary by dramatically illustrating reactions of others. The unpopular pupil (described in the first part of this chapter) usually knows how to act in a social situation. His actual behavior, however, continues to be unacceptable to others, as illustrated below.

Carol wasn't too happy in her fourth grade classroom this year. She had just moved to this new school. The harder she tried to be friends with the other children the less they seemed to like her. Her mother had told her that to have friends she had to be a friend. Indeed, she thought she was a good friend to others. Her behavior, however, conveyed a different message.

She liked to talk about herself. She exaggerated some stories about her friends in her previous school and how important she was to her previous friends.

Through the efforts of the class in dramatic play of specific situations involving human relations, Carol was able to identify (through actually playing and observing) with roles played by others. Furthermore, the situations could be discussed somewhat objectively, since they were "just pretend." This freed her of emotional involvement, and automatic defenses already established. By reacting herself to one who "does all the talking" she gained insight into her own behavior. The insights gained served to direct her efforts into productive channels.

One of the most difficult problems encountered by the teacher of children is that of transfer of learning. One's learning tends to be subject-centered. Pupils, and sometimes teachers, tend to feel that the understanding of a subject insures immediate transfer to other situations. It has been found, however, that this is not the case. The amount of transfer is directly dependent on the degree to which one can visualize similar elements in other situations. Similar or identical elements may be present in both situations, but unless a person becomes aware of them little transfer can be expected. This means that a teacher must *teach for transfer*. What better classroom method can be found than that of enacting simulated situations involving such transfer? The content of any course is worth no more than its effect upon the lives of those involved. Social studies, for instance, is of little value unless the principles involved have some worthwhile application value.

Thelen [8] likens the role-playing method to that of a laboratory experiment in physics. Both are designed for solving problems. The actors in role playing, however, can be interviewed to get their testimony. This, he suggests, is another kind of evidence to weigh, whereas the weights and pulleys in an experiment remain mute.

Michaelis [9] suggests several ways in which dramatic play may be used in the classroom. Some of the topics suggested are: the home, the food store, the community, the farm, the wholesale market, trains, our state, colonial life, pioneers, westward movement, communication through radio and airport. Dramatic play need not be restricted to social studies, however. It can be applied to any area of investigation where social interaction is involved. Dramatic play may be used in reading, science, health education, and other areas of the curriculum. Even the laboratory scientist must convince others of the worthwhileness of his findings. The Louis Pasteur story offers a dramatic example of the impact of superstition and incorrect assumptions upon scientific findings. Some teachers have found, for example, that the dramatic play technique can be extremely useful in combating superstitions existing among pupils in a science classroom.

How is dramatic play applied?

Like many other methods of teaching, dramatic play is another approach to problem solving. As such, it involves a series of steps stemming from problem solving. It is basically a group-oriented approach concerned with feeling reactions as individuals interact with one another. Consequently, the following two conditions are necessary for implementation: (1) the situations dramatized must be representative of the problems felt by members of the class, and (2) most of the group must want or feel the need for exploring the situation. To facilitate appropriate implementation of the method one should consider the following steps:

1. Defining the problem

8 Herbert A. Thelen, "Role-Playing in the Classroom," in R. M. Cooper, Ed. *Two Ends of the Log* (Minneapolis: University of Minnesota Press, 1958), p. 242.
9 John U. Michaelis, *Social Studies for Children in a Democracy* (Englewood Cliffs, N. J.: Prentice-Hall, Inc., 1956), pp. 374–376.

2. Creating group readiness

3. Establishing the situation

4. Selecting a volunteer cast

5. Briefing and warming-up actors

6. Helping the group observe intelligently

7. Acting out the situation

8. Analyzing and discussing the situation

9. Evaluating

10. Preplanning

How is the problem defined and delineated?

Role playing may arise spontaneously from a problem under consideration. A group can understand the issues involved and know what course of action to take, but it can still wonder if appropriate application is possible. Such remarks as these suggest a need for dramatic play:

I'm confused!
Can you show me how this would work in our school?
How does one know if the idea will work or not?

The teacher can then suggest that the problem might be clarified somewhat by acting it out. Thereupon the group members decide on a problem which might be typical for them.

When the teacher desires to make some of the more formalized content learnings more readily applicable to the lives of his pupils, he can introduce the approach through a series of carefully worded questions. For purposes of illustration, let us suppose the general topic is "In Russia." The immediate problem might be, "How should the United States citizen treat a Communist leader in our country?" After analyzing the problem in a guided class discussion or by some other means, the teacher may want to help the pupil apply the discussion to his own operational level of understanding. He then may proceed as follows:

Do we have any similar problems here in school? (Yes, people who have different ideas or beliefs.)

Do we sometimes try to exclude those who hold beliefs which differ sharply from our own? (Yes, we do.)

How does it make a person feel? (Not very good, I guess.) Perhaps not, but actually it is *only* a guess with some of us. With others it may be only a guess as to how one feels who really wants to do the excluding.

Would you like to help set up a situation which might help us "stand in the other fellow's boots" for a few minutes?

It will be noted that the teacher is careful to enlist the help of pupils in problem selection. This is a most desirable approach, as the value of the experience is directly dependent on its realism for the children.

Once the problem has been defined, the teacher attempts to introduce as much threat reduction as possible. He explains that no participant is to be criticized or judged and that those who play the roles will receive the most benefit from the experience. It is also desirable to emphasize that no one is playing the role for himself, but as he thinks someone else might play it. Role playing is a vehicle only for rendering analysis of the problem.

How is the situation developed and how are the players and class prepared?

For illustrative purposes, let us assume that the group has decided to enact the problem: "How might we help the son of a migrant worker (new to our school) feel accepted among us?" Through careful guidance from the teacher, the group establishes details of the situation. Here are some of the points which probably should be clarified:

Where does the encounter occur? (It is usually desirable to begin with simple situations involving two or three individuals only.) When does it occur? What are the participants doing? How long has the boy been in school? What seems to be his general attitude toward school? Does he particularly enjoy or seem interested in sports or some hobby? How is he dressed?

The situation, fully developed, might produce the following details:

Henry has been in school three weeks. Usually he is poorly dressed but clean. He seems smart enough, but so far has been rather quiet and withdrawn from the group. One day when a few of the fellows were discussing National League baseball scores he corrected one who had misquoted a score. Henry brings his lunch to school, as do some of the other fellows.

On this particular day, Joe (one of the more popular fellows in school) happens to sit by Henry during lunch. They are some distance removed from other pupils. They begin talking. Joe desires to make Henry feel wanted at school. Henry, quite naturally, is a bit suspicious of overtures of friendship, so Joe must be careful.

Thus, the situation is developed in some detail by the group. The individual roles, however, are left to the actors. It is desirable to let class members volunteer for the roles. Otherwise, it may be difficult for one to identify himself adequately with the role to be played. Occasionally pupils are a bit reluctant to "stick their necks out." If the stage has been well set, however, little difficulty may be expected. It is surprising how valuable the integrative pause proves to be in such instances. First, pupils need time to think through the situation. The longer a teacher waits for a response the more ill at ease the members become. Seldom must the pause be extended for longer than a minute or two before somebody volunteers. If the analysis directs attention to the situation (as it should) rather than to the players, selection of a volunteer cast for the next dramatic play is likely to be from among those who offer to help. For some groups it is sometimes advantageous to divide the class into small groups for a role-playing practice session before asking for a volunteer cast to perform before the entire group. This may be necessary for some adult groups, but seldom should be necessary for elementary school children; they like to act and are usually less inhibited than adults.

The players do not use their own names, nor do they mimic real life roles of other members of the group. Similarly, one does not play his own life role so far as it may relate to an identifiable group. A black, for instance, would not play the role of a black in a situation involving racial discrimination.

When the roles have been assigned the participant(s) who is *leading* the situation is asked to leave the room while the class defines more clearly the situation and roles of the other participant(s). The person or persons who remain in the room may be likened somewhat to the interviewee in a counseling situation. In the case cited above, Henry (the migrant worker's son) would remain in the room; Joe would be asked to leave. Henry, like any child of his age, has certain interests, abilities, and problems which are different from those of any other person. These are peculiarities which likely would not be apparent to Joe prior to such a conversation. One class added the following circumstances to the above situation after Joe had left the room:

Henry enjoys softball, although he seldom has an opportunity even to watch the boys practice. He is especially interested in hunting. He has four brothers and two sisters. His parents quarrel continually, partially as a result of his father's drinking habits.

Henry is instructed to begin the conversation with a slightly suspicious attitude, as might reasonably be expected under such circumstances. *From the time of the first two or three remarks he is instructed to react as Joe makes him want to react.* For example, if Joe's behavior or attitude is such as to make him more suspicious or even resentful he is to play that role; if Joe's approach makes him feel like warming up to the situation he reacts accordingly. He drops clues or indications of his special interests and problems only as he wants to do so.

Finally, the leader helps Henry to project himself into his role by asking a few specific questions:

Exactly what time of day is it? Where are you eating lunch? What are you having for lunch today? How did you get to school this morning?

The player who has left the room is likewise made ready for the situation by helping in becoming familiar with the role he will play. The class is also briefed so that they might be able to observe the dramatic play and get the most out of it. For young children to sit quietly may be a hard task, because they will want to react with the players, too. Some pupils may be asked to watch for specific things.

What factors need attention during dramatic play?

Above all, the actors should play their assigned roles without interruption, according to their own feeling reactions at the time.

The teacher normally lets the role-playing scene continue until the purpose has been achieved. It is easy to defeat the cause by letting the scene continue beyond its usefulness. In a simple situation, involving two or three people, the play seldom continues for more than 15 minutes. Five to ten minutes is a more typical length of time.

The action is cut when enough of the scene has been portrayed to enable the class to analyze the problem or when an impasse has been reached. When one of the participants begins repeating himself, or when it becomes obvious that emotional responses are getting out of control, the scene obviously should be stopped.

How is the situation analyzed and discussed?

The guided class discussion which follows the playacting climaxes the experience. It is at this point that many of the meaningful learnings are achieved. The enacted scene provides not only a basis for discussion, but it usually motivates children to talk about it. The players are not criticized. The discussion which follows the playacting places emphasis on the situation rather than the players.

When the scene is completed, the teacher begins by asking the group if such an enactment actually might have happened. Then the interviewee is asked how he felt. At all times role names are used to emphasize the character rather than the actual person involved. Then members of the class can be asked for clues which were or might have been picked up by the interviewee.

Following a thorough analysis of the situation it is important that alternative approaches be discussed. The group may reach some agreement as to *another* approach which may have been more effective. The situation then can be reenacted to illustrate applications of the new insights. The roles may be reversed. This forces the players to put themselves in the other person's place. In any event, emphasis is placed on *other* ways of doing the jobs, questions which *might have been asked*, and so forth. At no time are the recommendations made to imply *better* ways of approaching the situation.

How are results of dramatic play evaluated?

How can a teacher determine if role playing in his particular class was a valuable learning experience or not? Regardless of how much the group may have enjoyed the experience (most groups usually do!), the approach was a waste of time and effort if no new insights were developed. Situational-type test items can be used for determining the extent of such learnings.

Perhaps the best index of the value of such experiences is the degree of change evidenced in social situations that arise in actual classroom and school situations. The eagerness with which a group enters into succeeding role-playing experiences is an indication of a satisfying experience. If the players tend to become defensive during the discussion which follows an enacted scene, the teacher might well do a bit of introspection. "What questions did I ask which made the actors feel they were being criticized personally?"

What preplanning is necessary?

The dramatic play experience demands intricate planning. Since there are so many aspects of the process, the recommended time limits should only be used as a guide.

LESSON PLAN FOR DRAMATIC PLAY

Subject: Social Studies

Unit: In the Soviet Union

Problem: How the Soviet people may feel because they are not permitted to choose candidates for government office.

Goals: After this lesson the pupil should be able to understand how freedoms differ in our government as compared with freedoms allowed by the Soviet people, as evidenced by:

1. His participation in the discussion following the play.

2. His ability to make a comparison sheet for freedoms between these two countries.

Lesson Approach: (8 minutes)

In our earlier class discussions we have been talking about the rights the Soviet people have in theory only. We have also discussed that the guarantees of freedom are interpreted according to the orders of the Communist Party. Even though the Soviet Union has a bill of rights which reads much like the Constitution of the United States, the people do not have these rights as we do.

These freedoms denied the Soviet people could also be denied in our classroom. How would you feel if our classroom election were handled in the way these pupils will play for us?

Lesson Development: (20–25 minutes)

Broad situation: A committee of pupils in the class has decided on a slate of officers for the class. No one from the class will be permitted to nominate anyone for any of the offices. Only one person has been selected for each office. Everyone in the class is required to vote for these people because they are allowed "freedom" to vote.

Details of situation: (Class and committee establish)

Threat reduction: In this type of experience no one is to be criticized on his play-acting ability. There is no right or wrong way of doing this.

Selection of players: Volunteers (One should not be permitted to play his real-life role.)

Send leading characters from the room:

Fill in additional details: (By class)

Help class to observe intelligently:

1. Jot down key words and phrases that seem to affect feelings—either positively or negatively.

2. Note how you would feel under similar circumstances.

3. Note expressions on pupils' faces.

Warm up the players:

1. Who are you?

United Press International

The pupils were permitted to select their own seats.

2. Where are you?

3. What time of the day?

Dramatic play: (Not more than 10 minutes)

Follow-up discussion:

1. How did you feel? (To each of the players in turn)

2. What clues did we get which may have accounted for these feelings?

3. How else might the situation have been played?

4. How might this have changed feelings or reactions?

Replay if desirable:

Summary: (5 minutes)

What other similar situations might also illustrate the lack of freedoms allowed the Soviet people?

What things can we do in the United States to continue to enjoy the freedoms we have?

(Class discussion and summarize by listing several important ideas coming from the pupils.)

* * * * * * * * *

PROBLEMS AND PRINCIPLES ASSOCIATED WITH IMPROVING SOCIAL RELATIONSHIPS

In the preceding portion emphasis was placed on procedures or methods of improving social relationships within the classroom. The approaches have been used in a wide variety of school situations, as evidenced by a wealth of research in the literature, much of which has just recently been integrated and interpreted. Each teacher, however, finally must decide for himself whether or not he will use the approaches suggested. In weighing any set of alternatives one usually seeks satisfactory answers to a number of practical considerations.

Why attempt to improve social relationships?

Sociometry and dramatic play are group processes designed to help individuals develop satisfying social relationships. Sociometry may help the *teacher* assess existing social relationships, while dramatic play is especially useful in helping the *pupil* visualize the impact of his behavior on others. Thus, a close inspection of the processes of social interaction by both teacher and pupil may result in needed corrective measures. Some of the more important functions and values of the social techniques described in this chapter are summarized below.

Sociometry

1. The teachnique may help the teacher identify pupils needing help in social relationships. Further diagnosis and appropriate remedial action is thus made possible.

2. The sociometric test is an excellent means of identifying leadership potential within the classroom. Consequently, the teacher may help the leader(s) develop skills necessary for actual leadership in school situations. Furthermore, leader identification offers a valid basis for classroom management. Even the most rebellious child will usually conform if his actions threaten desired status within the peer group.

3. Sociometric procedures reveal the presence or absence of existing cleavages. These may be social cliques, prejudices toward certain races, religious or cultural minorities, and the like.

4. A basis for organizing class groups and seating arrangements is afforded through sociometric devices.

5. By occasionally permitting an unlimited number of choices, it is possible to gain some understanding of one's desire for social contact. An unpopu-

lar pupil who makes many choices probably needs immediate assistance.

6. Sociometric test results help explain certain discipline cases.

Dramatic play or role playing

1. An individual may project himself into the shoes of another, to experiment with new ways of behaving. He thereby tends to gain greater social sensitivity and insights that may not be acquired through any other teaching procedure.

2. Abstract principles can be rendered more specific than might otherwise be possible. This enables a pupil to transfer learnings to other situations.

3. Role playing eliminates the risks involved in the real life situation, thereby making room for practice. In real life one's behavior cannot be recalled, while role playing can be reenacted at will. Yet, most of the other realities of the situation are present.

4. The method has the advantage of pupil involvement. One learns by doing!

5. The role-playing experience provides individuals an opportunity actually to feel an experience. This is far superior to being told what to say, think, and feel.

6. Through the enactment of a specific situation a teacher is almost certain to gain full participation in the class discussion that follows.

Does teacher judgment render sociometric procedures unnecessary?

There is a tendency among teachers who have not made use of sociometric data to contend that they are already aware of friendship patterns of their pupils. Observational procedures, indeed, do afford valuable assistance in assessing interpersonal conflicts and mutual attractions of pupils. Most teachers, however, are usually surprised to find that certain pupils who appear to be very popular are, in fact, rarely chosen by the group; whereas some children are actually much more accepted by the group than was assumed. It must be remembered that an elementary school group tends to hold a constellation of values that is often quite different from that of an adult group.

A number of investigations of the accuracy of teacher judgments in determining sociometric status of pupils are available. In general, accuracy of teacher judgments has ranged from very low to very high, with an average near .60. Even the best judges can make large errors concerning individual pupils. Neither the size of the group nor the training and experience of the teacher can account for differences in accuracy of judgments. The need for an objective measure of social acceptance is roughly equivalent to the need for an IQ test in the academic area. In a recent study of elementary teachers in the two areas, it was reported that average accuracy in judging students' IQ was represented by a correlation of .73; whereas the average correlational accuracy of judging pupils' sociometric status was .70.[10] Any teacher may check his observational rating by administering a sociometric test.

Are sociometric procedures economical of time and effort?

The answer to this question is to be found in the value system of each individual teacher. Almost any activity can be deemed too difficult and time-consuming if the activity is of little importance to the person involved. It would seem inconceivable, however, that any teacher could reasonably question the worth of assisting his pupils to adjust socially. Since the turn of the century, almost every statement of general purposes of education in a democracy has emphasized the importance of human relationships. Unfortunately, however, there are still human beings in teaching who insist that their responsibilities end when they have "covered a specified amount of arithmetic, social studies, language arts, or science." What these teachers apparently fail to realize is that learning takes place in a social setting, which has a tremendous impact upon the quality of learning.

1. Satisfactory social relationships free one from emotional tensions, permitting him to concentrate on the more formal learning tasks.

2. Peer acceptance increases motivation to learn. Increased social contacts that follow peer acceptance aid and reinforce classroom learning experiences by providing greater opportunity for idea exchange among the members.

3. Improved morale, which accompanies satisfying social relationships, tends to create a favorable attitude toward the learning experience.

Furthermore, the school offers about the only opportunity pupils have for developing wholesome cross-class contacts. Due to the social structure of our society and the tendency of other social institutions to limit contacts with "out-groups," it is left to the school to develop the democratic ideals of cultural pluralism and equal opportunities for all. These

---

[10] N. E. Gronlund and A. P. Whitney, "The Relation Between Teachers' Judgments of Pupils' Sociometric Status and Intelligence," *Elementary School Journal,* 59: 264–268 (1958).

contacts may not occur unless a systematic effort is made to promote their development.

Sociometric procedures are characterized by their simplicity. A teacher with some experience in the area can develop a sociogram for a class of about 35 pupils in about 20 minutes. To analyze the data carefully, he will probably need to construct both a matrix table and a sociogram. This may demand an hour or more of his time. Some teachers have prepared forms in advance for this task, which substantially reduces the effort necessary. It should be reemphasized, however, that the administration, analysis, and regrouping of pupils is only the beginning of sociometry. The sociometric test provides an approach to any number of classroom guidance activities that characterize good teaching.

Is learning improved when individuals work closely with preferred associates?

This is one of the first questions asked by the skeptic. For some time the practitioner had assumed that one of the most favorable conditions of learning was to separate a boy or girl from his friends.

Mrs. Molton was a teacher in the elementary school with many years of experience. Although she was a kindly teacher, she tended to have difficulty within the classroom. The spirit of cooperation was frequently lacking and group morale, at times, became dangerously low.

When Mrs. Metley joined the teaching staff and taught on the same grade level as Mrs. Molton, a difference was noted in Mrs. Metley's room compared to Mrs. Molton's room. Mrs. Molton, who prided herself in being a flexible teacher, asked permission to observe this new teacher.

The observation revealed one outstanding difference between the groups of pupils: a higher class morale or improved group atmosphere was evident in Mrs. Metley's classroom. It was obvious that this factor was having a positive effect on the learning situation. Why?

When Mrs. Molton heard of the sociometric techniques being employed she became enthusiastic. Yes, she had heard of sociometrics but had not understood the techniques very well. When she was told that the procedure was based on the assumption that pupils work better when placed in close proximity to those with whom they prefer to associate, Mrs. Molton became somewhat dubious. Still, she could not forget what she had observed, so finally decided to try it. After a week of sociometric grouping, Mrs. Molton called off the whole thing. In her own words, "I did not think children could concentrate when working with their pals. One more week and they would have run me out of the classroom!"

Mrs. Molton's experience has been repeated many times. A teacher hears of the idea and is persuaded or persuades himself to "give it a try."

From the start he doubts that it will work. A week's "try" is sufficient to convince him for all time of the impractical nature of "some of this new theory." Let us examine some of the prerequisites which indicate the fallacies involved in such an evaluation:

1. A teacher must sincerely believe in such a teaching technique before it is likely to succeed for him.

2. He must be able to differentiate between failure and relative success. It may be too much to expect a first attempt to produce purely positive results. Teaching methods are skills which must be developed.

3. Most groups require an adjustment period before normal classroom reactions are completely restored. Teachers should expect some confusion and inattention during the first week or two of such an operation. After all, the idea is new to the pupils, too! A marked improvement, however, usually becomes apparent by the end of the third week.

4. Sociometric devices must be accompanied by other techniques of building healthy social relationships. One of the best supplementary techniques is a warm, permissive type of teaching personality, which engenders confidence. Few positive results can be expected in an atmosphere of authoritarianism.

There is evidence available which suggests that a social group is most effective when the individuals are placed in close proximity to their best friends.[11] The practitioner may easily set up an experimental situation within his own school groups.

How stable are sociometric preferences among pupils?

The use of sociometrics is based on two important premises: (1) there is some stability in an individual's preferred associations, and (2) existing friendship patterns may be altered through close association. Is there research evidence to support such assumptions? Fortunately, these premises have been quite thoroughly examined.

Gronlund, in reviewing research in the area, concludes that there seems to be substantial agreement concerning the stability of sociometric status among children:

. . . In general, they suggest that stability coefficients of approximately .90 might be expected over time intervals of less than a week. Coefficients in the vicinity of .80 are indicated for time intervals of several weeks, and coefficients of approximately .60 are indicated for time intervals ranging between eight and twenty months.[12]

[11] J. S. Mouton and others, "The Validity of Sociometric Responses," *Sociometry*, 18: 181–206 (1955).
[12] Gronlund, *op. cit.*, p. 129.

Likewise, after 6 to 8 weeks of sociometric grouping one can reasonably expect the number of isolates in a class of 35 to drop from about 5 to 1, while the number of mutual choices will be increased from 25 to 35 or more. It seems as though children are quite capable of widening their circle of friends without dropping the old ones.

Closely related to the foregoing is the ever important question of choice differences when different criteria or choice situations are involved. Several studies have shown a significant relationship between various pairs of criteria. Individuals who are highly chosen for one situation tend to be highly chosen in other situations; the reverse holds for those who are little chosen. It has been concluded by many that such findings point toward the presence of a general social acceptability factor.

What principles govern proper use of dramatic play and related techniques?

Once a teacher thoroughly understands a recommended procedure for dramatic play he needs courage only in putting the method to work. And it does take courage, for one can never be certain of the pattern of events, especially during the dramatization phase. As in the development of any skill, however, practice tends to produce efficiency and security. There are a number of principles which may guide a teacher in developing the needed competencies:

1. Dramatic play is set within the framework of group participation for discussion and analysis.

2. The class should have a cooperative group feeling.

3. The problem should be a real one—one the group is interested in having explored.

4. Pupils should have some knowledge of the situations and persons they represent.

5. The situation should be clear and brief and should involve personalities. A description of the situation should not imply the correctness of certain behaviors.

6. Dramatic play should be conceived as a series of essential steps.

7. Pupils should volunteer for roles.

8. Some principles and conclusions should result from the role-played experience.

9. The teacher must be enthusiastic about the problem to be explored. He guides pupils in reaching their own conclusions and generalizations, rather than making these for them.

What are some limitations associated with techniques for improving social relationships?

Most of the points listed below are associated with the user, rather than with the methods involved. They may be useful, however, as general guidelines to teachers who have met with difficulty or those who desire to try the methods for the first time.

Sociometry

1. The use of improper situations may seriously limit the value of results obtained. The situation must appear realistic to the respondents. The practice of asking pupils to indicate preferences for travel companions to the North Pole would represent a highly unrealistic situation.

2. Validity of pupil choices is dependent on rapport established in the class situation.

3. The sociometric test measures what choice patterns exist but not why they exist.

4. Some isolates may not be "true" isolates. They may have friends in other classes, be new to the school, and the like.

5. A low sociometric rating does not necessarily indicate social difficulties. There are some persons who have developed satisfactory individual pursuits.

6. A highly chosen individual is not necessarily a leader, although this is usually indicative of leadership potential.

7. Sociometric testing is at best only a starting point for furthering human relationships.

Dramatic play or role playing

1. The method is applicable to class situations dealing with social relationships. It can be used in "content" teaching, or it can be used to build healthy social relationships within the classroom group.

2. The entire dramatic play experience often takes a full class period. Indeed, a teacher needs to be mindful of his time schedule if there is to be sufficient time for class discussion of the play. In general, the 15-10-25 formula seems to be appropriate: 15 minutes for preparation; 10 minutes for the play; and 25 minutes for class discussion.

3. Role playing is a means rather than an end in itself. The follow-through discussion is the most important part of the process. It is at this point that principles are evolved and clarified.

4. The technique deals with real problems that are closely related to the lives of those involved. The more remote the situation, the less likely it is that worthwhile results will be obtained.

5. Therapy has no place in the classroom. Guard against this by keeping the analysis off the persons who play the roles. A useful device is to refer to the players throughout the experience by their role names.

6. Arrange the situation in such a manner that the players have several alternatives open to them. In other words, avoid "loading the dice."

7. Guard against a role-playing situation which is used to "put somebody in his place." Also avoid having one play his real life role.

SUMMARY

This chapter has offered the reader an approach to improving social relationships within the classroom. The sociometric test or inventory was suggested as a first step in determining what pattern of friendship preferences exists. When the teacher is made aware of the social situation, he is in a position to make use of a number of classroom guidance techniques. Some of these are teacher observation, teacher counseling techniques, parent conferences, dramatic play, and role playing.

The dramatic play experience is a method of helping pupils gain social sensitivity and insights into their own social problems. Furthermore, it is a useful device for bridging the gap between theory and practice in dealing with the more academic learnings of social nature.

Procedures described in this chapter focus attention on group processes; succeeding chapters will deal with other group-oriented approaches to the teaching-learning process.

QUESTIONS FOR STUDY AND DISCUSSION

1. What basic assumptions are associated with sociometry? How do these differ from traditional assumptions with respect to the learning environment? What dangers and limitations are associated with the use of sociometric procedures?

2. What is the fundamental purpose of dramatic play and role playing? What is the relationship between dramatic play and role playing and sociometry? Most teachers and pupils who have experienced the sociometric approach to teaching have been pleased with the results. Yet, some teachers will not make use of the technique on the grounds that they lack the "courage needed." What factors probably account for this problem? What solutions seem appropriate?

3. The most common instructional difficulty associated with dramatic play is a tendency for the players to feel defensive after the experience has been discussed. What instructional deficiency probably accounts for this feeling? Why is the problem so common? Why are fictitious names and situations essential? Can you think of any problems which might be "too hot to handle"? Why? How could you use the technique to work on such problems *indirectly*?

4. What factors may limit the use of dramatic play and role playing? Suggest appropriate situations for dramatic play in several different teaching areas. What problems did you encounter? Do you accept the premise made in this chapter that there is a "place for dramatic play" in every subject area? Why or why not?

5. What could be possible solutions for Mary's problem cited on pages 160–161 of this chapter? Give reasons for each solution selected.

SELECTED BIBLIOGRAPHY

Amidon, E. and C. B. Hoffman, "Can Teachers Help the Socially Rejected?" *Elementary School Journal*, 66: 149–154 (December, 1965).

Barclay, J. R., "Sociometry: Rationale and Technique for Effecting Behavior Change in Elementary School," *Personnel and Guidance Journal*, 44: 1067–1076 (June, 1966).

Bronfenbrenner, U., "The Graphic Presentation of Sociometric Data," from Norman E. Gronlund, *Sociometry in the Classroom* (New York: Harper & Row, Publishers, 1959).

Cheong, G. S. C., "Relations Among Experimental Attitude, Creativity, School Attitude, and Sociometric Status of Fourth–Sixth-Grade Pupils," *The Journal of Teacher Education*, 18: 186–191 (Summer, 1967).

Gronlund, Norman E., *Sociometry in the Classroom* (New York: Harper & Row, Publishers, 1959).

Gronlund, Norman E. and A. P. Whitney, "The Relation Between Teachers' Judgments of Pupils' Sociometric Status and Intelligence," *Elementary School Journal*, 59: 264–268 (1958).

Thelen, Herbert A., "Role-Playing in the Classroom," in Cooper, R. M., Ed., *Two Ends of the Log* (Minneapolis: University of Minnesota Press, 1958).

Williams, E., "Helping Children Feel Like Someone Else, and Talk Like Someone Else," *Elementary English*, 44: 57–58+ (January, 1967).

The Cooperative Experience:
Teacher-Pupil Planning

No child is too young to sense whether or not he lives in a cooperative relation with the people around him . . . the cooperative atmosphere is one
of involvement. The growing self must feel that it is involved, that it is really
part of what is going on, that in some degree it is helping shape its own
destiny, together with the destiny of all . . . involvement . . . gives a
person a "reason to be." The lack of consultation and involvement is the
cause of the continuing war between parents and their children, between
teachers and learners, between teachers and administrators, employers and
employees, *ad infinitum*. When the person is a part of something, then he
becomes responsible.

Earl C. Kelley

The classroom must become a place where the exciting experience of
exploring and discovering meaning is the central activity . . . Meanings
lie inside of people and cannot be dealt with directly. It follows that the
teacher's role must not be that of a director, a maker, a manipulator, but
he must be a person who assists, helps, aids, ministers to a growing, living,
dynamic organism already in the process of becoming. It means that teaching
must be a process of helping children explore and discover the personal meaning of events for them.[1]

Ideas contained in the foregoing quotes have been expressed many
times in many ways. They pinpoint an urgent need of all peoples everywhere: that of living together harmoniously. Viewing learning as a
process of exploring and discovering personal meaning suggests the need
for jointly planned classroom procedures. How does one begin? What
techniques encourage the development of a cooperative classroom experience?

[1] Association for Supervision and Curriculum Development, *Perceiving, Behaving,
Becoming*, Yearbook (Washington, D. C.: The Association, 1962), p. 90.

Cooperative teacher-pupil planning and direction of learning activities occur in a variety of ways at various levels of abstraction. Indeed, they are utilized to some degree in all group work, as illustrated in the preceding chapters. The present chapter, however, deals with cooperative approaches to teaching which employ democratic processes. Instead of assuming the role of taskmaster in setting goals, selecting procedures, constructing and administering tests, the teacher becomes a participating guide. He leads pupils into *self*-discovery and analysis of problems. This chapter deals with the dynamic forces of groups. In teacher-pupil planning the teacher retains more responsibility for direction and control.

This chapter is divided into three parts. The first of these is designed to acquaint the reader with the democratic foundations of teacher-pupil planning. By establishing a theoretical and practical basis for a cooperative approach to learning, we hope that the classroom teacher will be able to clarify his new role, changed to that of a helper rather than a director. In short, his function is to help the learner identify problems, develop interests, satisfy curiosities, and seek solutions to problems. The second section of this chapter, accordingly, illustrates an approach to democratic problem-solving processes. It is not intended as *the* approach to cooperative teacher-pupil planning; rather, it is designed to open up new vistas to the teacher who is contemplating the approach for the first time. In the *final* analysis, each teacher and his particular group of pupils must *create* their own approaches to "the cooperative experience." The final section of the chapter introduces basic principles and problems that function in democratic teaching processes. The experienced teacher, especially, will find them useful in his efforts to create for himself effective approaches to teaching.

DEMOCRATIC FOUNDATIONS OF COOPERATIVE LEARNING

The cooperative experience, like most other instructional approaches, involves the processes of inquiry. Unlike some other approaches, however, this technique employs as a starting point existing pupil needs and interests rather than organized bodies of subject matter. Once a need has been identified, selected, and defined, a desire to resolve the need produces purpose. A purpose creates the need for a plan of action, involving consideration and evaluation of any number of possible means of accomplishment. In short, the processes of reflective thought are applied by the entire class group. The topics which follow describe the functions and purposes of democratic class procedures in some detail.

What is the cooperative experience?

The cooperative experience is an application of democratic processes applied to group learning. It may be conceived as a series of steps, frequently known as the problem-solving process. The reader will recall from Chapter 3 that the problem-solving process was established as a basis for educational method. In teacher-pupil planning, however, pupils themselves are expected to employ the procedures effectively. The problem-solving process is continuous; the "steps" may occur simultaneously or in a different order from those listed here. The classroom teacher, however, will find the usual sequence most helpful when working with groups.

1. *Problem identification.* One does not attempt to solve a problem until he meets with difficulty. For the most part, force of habit carries us through the day. Much of what we do is a result of habit. When a person gets out of bed each morning he puts on his shoes from habit and he may hardly be conscious of the act. If, however, one of his shoes is missing, a problem arises. Still in a routine sort of way, he may proceed through the elementary steps of solving the problem. If this does not accomplish the goal, he eventually may be forced to do reflective thinking. This is what is meant when we say *problem solving.* The more reflective thinking one is required to do, the better the problem-solving development. In teacher-pupil planning the teacher guides pupils in recognizing a difficulty in a particular area.

2. *Problem clarification and goal setting.* Once the area of difficulty is identified, the person must clarify his thinking in the area. One of the best means of accomplishing this task is to formulate clear, meaningful questions. Indeed, the terminology of a question determines the terminology of the answer one will obtain. The clarification of goals in large measure determines the value of the activities which follow. Pupils need to determine for themselves why they are concerned with the general problem area. To the degree that the difficulty is understood and actually felt by pupils the questions asked will be meaningful and worthwhile.

3. *Plan and development of the learning experience.* When the problem has been clarified through development of meaningful questions, one must direct his observations and activities. He must ask him-

self continually, "If I do this, what is the result likely to be?" He is at this point *hypothesizing* as to the most appropriate method of solving the problem. In a sense he is *evaluating* what would be likely to happen if he chose one of a variety of possibilities open to him. "How feasible is this solution? Is it economical of time and effort?"

When a tentative course of action has been selected, there are a variety of planning decisions to be made. "What do we now know about the problem?" "What other things do we need to know?" "How can we best secure this data?" "*Who* is to assume *what* responsibility?" It is usually appropriate at this point for the teacher to guide pupils in establishing a set of criteria to govern the extent and nature of exploration. Some consideration should be given to possible applications to real life situations. The following criteria were established by one group of pupils which was studying the human body:

1. Findings should be applicable to our own health problems.

2. Sources of information must be readily available.

3. A time schedule should be established and followed.

4. Material which is shared with the rest of the class must be interesting.

5. Research must involve all of our group.

6. Data must be related to body systems which we have studied in class.

7. Findings should be related to current news which comes to us through the press, radio, and television.

When the problem has been somewhat clarified and delineated it often is helpful to direct attention to possible sources of data. Some of these may be books and other reference materials, resource speakers, interviews, and audio-visual materials. The general sources of information deemed appropriate and acceptable to the group will determine somewhat the type of special planning needed. The teacher must help each subgroup make reasonable choices. The younger the children the more help from the teacher will be necessary. This is not meant to suggest, however, that he should make these basic decisions for the group. Rather, he will guide pupils in viewing problems realistically.

4. *Collection of data or research.* Individuals who have planned realistically should experience minimum difficulty in completing needed research. If the teacher has made *prior* arrangements for pupil access to available sources of data, the operation usually proceeds smoothly. If

there are several subgroups a minimum of direction will be possible. For the most part, children who are busy on problems of their choice will be able to progress satisfactorily under their own direction. Occasionally, however, help is needed. If this help is not available *when needed* the whole procedure can quickly disintegrate. As in all teaching situations, the teacher must be on the alert for incipient trouble. His task is to "nip in the bud" distracting elements. The librarian can be of invaluable assistance here.

If the groups have reorganized and regrouped their questions into meaningful wholes, research should be significant. Let us take the example from a health lesson cited earlier. One of the questions asked by the class was, "What causes a cancer?" A simple procedure for determining causes of cancer likely would lead to only superficial understanding of the problem. A *functional understanding* of the question, however, would demand a much broader background. For example, one can assume that the person who asked the question actually was expressing a concern for a much broader problem, i.e., causes, symptoms, treatment, and measures which can reduce the dangers of cancer. By building such an outline the material usually is made more meaningful to all concerned. The teacher who would ensure accuracy will do independent library research so that he can assume the proper role of a resource person when needed.

It is essential that individual subgroup problems be balanced somewhat, in view of the individual differences encountered, availability of resource materials, and time schedules established. There invariably will be a difference in rate of progress between the groups. The problem of providing for group differences offers a real test for the classroom teacher. If motivation is high, however, a group will not stop when its immediate task is completed, but will proceed along the lines of newly developed interests.

5. *Report of findings.* One's ability to communicate with others is the crucial test of the cooperative experience. When a division of labor has been established between subgroups, each group must clarify its findings if the overall pattern or *Gestalt* is to be achieved. This means that methods of reporting become highly significant. Elementary school children often need considerable assistance in techniques of reporting. It behooves the teacher and the entire class to guide each group carefully in developing original patterns of presenting its findings.

Following group reports the teacher can profitably spend one or two days in expanding, clarifying, or drawing out additional concepts that seem warranted.

6. *Evaluation.* One of the best indications of a worthwhile experience is the kind and number of questions that pupils ask when the project is completed. They frequently have more questions than at the outset! Indeed, investigation of a problem usually reveals a host of additional problems worthy of investigation.

As in the preceding steps in teacher-pupil planning, the teacher's major task is to guide the group in *reflection*. Pupils must visualize what has been accomplished in terms of original aims or goals. A variety of specific techniques is suggested in the next section.

Perhaps one of the most frequent inconsistencies encountered in teacher-pupil planning is teacher domination in the realm of evaluation. Due to their traditional roles, many teachers have identified themselves as *the* evaluator. If pupils assist in selecting the problems, setting the goals, and collecting and reporting their findings, they also should be involved in evaluating the worth of the enterprise. It may be that they will delegate some of this responsibility to the teacher, but usually with directions. If the teacher cannot or will not let the class determine the system of evaluation, this limitation must be made known at the outset. In the final analysis, even with young elementary school children the best evaluation is *self*-evaluation, if the child's perceptions are reasonably accurate.

What function does cooperative planning serve?

The essence of good teaching is not to protect the pupil from exposure of inadequacies, learning, and change but to create supportive conditions enabling the individual to undergo the process of learning, to handle his anxieties and concerns, to experiment with new ways of thinking and behaving . . . *the teacher alone cannot supply all of the support necessary for all pupils,* particularly when the classroom climate itself creates more stress for the individual.

Group and individual mental health are interactive. The climate—symptomatic measure of group health—affects the emotional health and development of the individual student as well as his degree of learning.[2]

In the preceding quote, Bradford seems to pinpoint a basic function of the class group. While it is true that class groups were born of necessity when mass education was first introduced, the evidence clearly indicates that the group itself can provide a supportive environment important in learning. Extensive group problem-solving experiences of necessity result in a certain amount of disorganization and insecurity.

[2] Leland P. Bradford, "Developing Potentialities Through Class Groups," *Teachers College Record,* 61: 443–450 (May, 1960).

Creation of a healthy group climate can do much to support and reassure children who, by the nature of the society itself, have been accustomed to "final answers" and traditional modes of behavior.

In discussing the unrealistic nature of education, Earl Kelley contends that teachers have been operating under a number of *false assumptions.* Some of these seem to support the need for more democratic procedures.

1. We assume the answer to a problem is more important than the process.

2. We assume it is more important to measure what has been learned than it is to learn.

3. We assume that the teacher can and should furnish the purpose needed for the acquiring of knowledge.[3]

Kelley suggests that the learning experience must provide for trial and error, recognizing that more is learned from what is done wrong than from what is done right. The teacher must occupy a role between being useless and being authoritarian, helping the group achieve its ends. The evidence suggests that Kelley's criticisms are as valid today as they were some twenty years ago.[4]

Certainly an important function of teacher-pupil planning experiences is the cooperative nature of the approach. There is no better place than the classroom to learn how to contribute and receive assistance from one's peers. It is from the class group that he can secure the emotional gains of acceptance and affection, belonging, and creative expression. Most psychologists believe that competition has been misused and that cooperation must receive much greater emphasis in the schools. They suggest that the school often presents an unrealistic situation that offers relatively little security for most pupils.

Cooperative learning represents an approach to solving problems that represents life at its best in a democracy. It is a known fact that the way human beings tend to interact with each other depends on their own life experiences. The cooperative resolution of difficulties can be effective only to the degree that it has been experienced. The school as an agent of society has the direct responsibility of preparing children for democratic living.

Cooperative learning, of course, embodies many aspects of competition. Both cooperation and competition are important. It is the imbal-

[3] Earl C. Kelley, *Education for What is Real* (New York: Harper & Row, Publishers, 1947), pp. 20–22.
[4] *Association for Supervision and Curriculum Development, op. cit.,* Ch. 3.

ance of one over the other that creates problems. For many years competition was emphasized at all costs. Today, however, as our society becomes progressively more "open," the cooperative educational experience is receiving increased attention.[5]

What are some misconceptions associated with cooperative planning?

Cooperative teacher-pupil planning represents a desirable approach for any elementary school group within the classroom. It may be used on any subject area of the elementary school curriculum. The approach uses pupils as active participants in proposing, planning, working, reporting, and evaluating on a group basis.

The evidence clearly indicates that presently there is relatively little teacher-pupil planning and direction of activities in the elementary schools. Many teachers, however, verbally support and erroneously believe that they are making adequate application of democratic problem-solving procedures because of a number of problem-solving myths. In order to clarify the issue a number of these are discussed.

In the first place, many people have asumed that problem solving is limited to the natural science areas of investigation. This is far from the truth. As has been pointed out, all of us try to solve problems whenever we get into trouble. Our efforts may be misdirected or little better than trial and error, but still we make the effort. The *method* which might be most fruitful to us often will be little different than that of the research chemist. Perhaps the myth of leaving problem solving to the laboratory partially accounts for the present gulf between materialistic advances and progress in the social studies area.

Another misconception is that problem solving is assured in science. In science most of the problem solving *in fact* is done by the teacher or the author of the textbooks used. Let us take the case of an elementary school teacher who has laboratory experiments already set up for pupils to perform. In many instances it is the teacher who identifies the problem; who sets the goals to be accomplished; who plans the learning activities; and who determines *in advance* what the findings will be. There is problem solving going on all right, but it is done by the teacher instead of the pupils! Have you, the reader, ever tried to solve such a problem? In all probability you were told what the results were supposed to be. When these expected results did not materialize you probably

[5] Mario D. Fantini, "Open v. Closed Classrooms," *The Clearing House*, 37, No. 2: 67–72 (October, 1962).

manipulated a few variables to achieve that which was expected. There are times when such an assignment is necessary; nevertheless, it is *not* problem solving as defined in this book. Such *techniques* may be a necessary part of a science program. Frequently, however, science techniques and memorization of certain verbal symbols may constitute the bulk of such classes.

A third danger is that of identifying arithmetic with problem solving. As a matter of fact, central to the language of arithmetic is the term *problem solving*. A teacher may show or illustrate the solution to a new problem and then assign a dozen "problems" which involve similar principles. The *practice* which pupils get from the experience may be essential, but pupils are *not* solving problems as defined in this chapter. They are merely *doing* problems! The "new mathematics" introduced into many schools is endeavoring to focus on problem solving as defined in this chapter, however.

A final misconception is that the process of problem solving is a series of steps which must be logically followed. To be sure, it is convenient to describe the process in a series of steps, but in reality no one phase of the formula can be isolated from the others. For example, the minute one meets with a difficulty he begins evaluating. Furthermore, one frequently begins his research with the solution or results and then proceeds to determine the why, or the causal factors, responsible for the result. In a sense he *is* following logical steps, but in terms of overall difficulty he is not!

Teacher-pupil planning is a *continuous process* which emanates from those with inquiring minds. It evolves from man's contact with his environment and continues as long as he must cope with that environment. The question is not *who* will solve problems, but *how well* one will solve the problems with which he comes in contact. The school environment can assist in the process, but efficiency cannot be assumed from mere chance.

The reader can now see that in actuality much learning involves some type of problem solving, even if it is no more than enduring a boring teacher for a whole school year. As used in this chapter, however, problem solving denotes questing, inquiring, or engaging in reflective thinking.

AN ILLUSTRATED MODEL OF
COOPERATIVE LEARNING

It is an easy matter to accept intellectually the need for democratic planning and execution of instructional activities. The actual process of making a break with tradition, preconceived notions, or past experience is quite another matter, however. Not only does the teacher need the courage of his convictions; he also must be able to *imagine* how such an approach can be applied in *his* classroom. In short, he himself must indulge in some sort of creative problem solving before launching any program of action.

The teacher who would initiate teacher-pupil planning must recognize differences between his world and the world of the child. He asks himself such questions as, "What are the immediate interests of these children?" and "How can these interests be channeled into objectives and subsequent processes of inquiry?" The teacher who would apply democratic procedures will become concerned with larger rather than narrower questions. He will take a somewhat detached look at the entire curriculum area under consideration, looking at "big ideas" or broad concepts rather than isolated facts and details. As opposed to content coverage, he will explore potentials for new relationships, wondering what procedures will contribute most to concept formations and generalizations. He will view his task as one of contriving learning experiences, but not as one of coercing outcomes. A natural desire to cover territory will give way to selection of significant areas for depth analysis.

A basic function of any how-to-do textbook is to provide an acceptable basis for action. To facilitate the process of *imagining* how the teacher-pupil planned approach can work in a situation, an instructional model is offered. This model is based on an actual experience in the second grade. It is not recommended as *the* approach, but is designed to illustrate how many of the elements of democratic procedures *can* be applied. Each teacher will want to develop his own approach to fit his own needs and the needs of his pupils.

How is the problem identified?

In teacher-pupil planning, as here conceived, the teacher identifies the problem *area*. His first problem then is to guide pupils in developing interest in the *area*, in preparation for self-direction. When interest has been sufficiently developed, pupils decide what specific problems will be pursued *within the selected area.*

For purposes of illustration, an example from the social studies book is employed. Let us assume the unit is entitled *Community Helpers.*

The teacher arranged areas of interest in the classroom with boxes, cartons, signs, and toy people. She put a sign on one of the boxes: Police Station; labeled another box: Fire Station. She made a fence with corrugated cardboard and put up a sign: Zoo. The teacher placed open books about community workers on tables and chalkboard ledges. She also arranged a bulletin board display with pictures of community helpers.

The teacher permitted the children to explore the room and encouraged them to use the materials.

This introductory activity may be less than thirty minutes, or it may continue somewhat longer.

How is the problem clarified and the goals set?

After creating interest in community helpers through the classroom environment of materials, the teacher called the group together for discussing and questioning. The teacher guided the children in stating their problems and questions.

The questions were written on the chalkboard by the teacher; later they were transferred to a chart so the pupils could refer to them during the unit. Some of the questions were:

What kind of trucks do firemen have?

What do firemen do at the station?

Who tells policemen what to do?

Who builds fire stations?

Do policemen get paid?

Who feeds the animals in a zoo?

Where do the zoo animals come from?

How are the learning activities planned and developed?

After the questions had been transferred from the chalkboard to a chart, the class was ready to explore means of solving the problems. The teacher approached the problems as follows:

Teacher: Who would like to look for answers to those questions which relate to the firemen? policemen? zoo? etc.

There are times when the teacher may want to organize the groups as indicated in Chapter 8 under *Sociometry.* When subgroups had been formed the pupils and the teacher organized for action. The teacher planned with the committees how to get the facts, to record the facts, and to share the facts. At this time it is important that the teacher review with the children the steps of the problem-solving operation again.

The teacher moves from group to group, to guide and direct as necessary. The teacher may at times find himself fulfilling the following roles:

A *resource person.* There will be frequent inquiries regarding many aspects of the problem. Due to his greater experience, training, and maturity the teacher can render valuable assistance. At the same time, he must be careful not to take the problem solving away from the pupils. In many instances pupil questions will be reflected back to the subgroup from which they came. For example, to the question, "Where can we find materials?" the teacher might parry with, "Well, where do *you* think we might look?" Eventually he might supplement answers with ideas of his own—*not* as requirements to be followed but as a point for consideration.

A *guide.* When pupils are having difficulties in reaching agreement or making choices, the teacher may guide them in important considerations. For example, "What might be a difficulty in bringing in a policeman?" A pupil then might suggest a policeman who has "retired" and can come to the school.

An *authority.* If conflicts or impasses of any sort develop the teacher may need to be directive at times. It is especially important, at first, to be on the alert for distracting elements within the groups; these should be handled as the situation demands. Techniques of class control are treated in Chapter 14.

How can data be collected?

There are few things more frustrating to a child than his inability to follow through with carefully prepared plans. Once he is ready to embark on his problem the teacher needs to guide very carefully. The teacher, well in advance of the need, should have secured key library books for the classroom, and made arrangements for some of the class to go to the library.

In the course of investigating a variety of problems, the groups will have different resource needs. These require careful supervision, a great deal of trust in pupils, and a cooperative attitude on the part of other teachers and administrators. The wise teacher will set the stage carefully. During each work period the teacher might check on the progress made and the plans for the day's activities. The teacher should quickly determine which problems need immediate attention. A short class discussion on how to find information may be in order, especially for younger groups or older groups who are inexperienced in research methods.

How can findings be reported?

Although a group may have accomplished a great deal in planning and research activities, the value to the class group depends on how well findings are shared with others. Somewhere in the process the entire class might profitably set up standards for this phase of the project. Each group can be asked to consider the problem before planning its specific method of reporting. In the actual teaching situation illustrated, the children were encouraged to share their research with the class by using pictures, drawings, small models, actual objects, an oral report to the class, or some other device.

Following each presentation the teacher may lead the class in a general review for the purpose of expanding, clarifying, or correcting important points.

How can learnings be evaluated?

Evaluation actually begins with teacher-pupil planning. When pupils are encouraged to formulate meaningful questions they are asked to evaluate. When a problem is being solved, an individual is continuously evaluating, deciding if this or that procedure would be preferable, whether the sources of information are available, and so on. In real life situations the most important type of evaluation probably occurs as one is experiencing.

Some teachers have used the tape recorder to evaluate group interaction. This technique can be especially valuable when a group contains distracting elements such as the "wise guy," the "giggler," the overly verbose individual, or the silent one. By replaying, pupils usually can evaluate themselves successfully.

Perhaps the most commonly used evaluation technique still is some type of written device. Such evaluations may be more effective if developed by both pupils and teacher. With older children (beyond the second grade) perhaps one of the most valuable written forms would consist of the following:

What references did I read?

What people did I interview?

What materials did I contribute to the project?

What difficulties did I encounter?

Another promising written evaluation instrument for older children is a technique of rating each other. At the end of the project the teacher can make available a list of the class members, divided into the subgroups. Pupils are asked to indicate which person they feel made the greatest individual progress. The same type of evaluation may be applied to the various subgroups on the basis of committee presentations.

If a formal written examination is to be administered to older pupils they should agree to it as to the other devices mentioned. Some teachers have found that each group may desire to construct a specified number (usually two or three) of questions which pertain exclusively to their areas of investigation.

By some sort of arrangement developed jointly between teacher and pupils the various evaluations are combined for the purposes of grading. Above all, pupils should share in determining techniques of evaluation just as they share in the other steps of problem solving.

When the project is completed the teacher asks pupils for suggestions for directing future experiences of this kind. This not only enables him to see himself through the eyes of pupils, but it indicates to pupils a teacher's willingness to seek help. The reader will recognize that, in a sense, the teacher is now doing problem solving of his own. Due to the tendency of older pupils to tell their teacher what they assume he wants to hear, certain precautions are in order if validity is to be achieved. It is suggested that some sort of multiple-choice form be constructed. This enables the pupils to respond by checking their choices. Under such circumstances papers should not be signed. Then, if additional suggestions and comments are desired, they can be written on a separate evaluation form.

What preplanning is necessary?

The steps in planning for the cooperative experience have been fully described in the illustrative model. Experience has indicated, however, that beginning teachers experience considerable difficulty in preplanning such activities. It is hoped that the sample lesson plan will further clarify the technique.

LESSON PLAN FOR TEACHER-PUPIL PLANNING

Subject: Social Studies

Unit: Community Helpers

Problem: Who are our community helpers and how do they help us?

Goals: A. After this experience the pupil should know who our community helpers are and understand what each community helper does, as evidenced by:

    1. His identification of community helpers.

    2. His evaluation of each helper's contribution to the community.

  B. After this experience the pupil should understand that everyone in the community has a responsibility for making it a better place in which to live, as evidenced by:

    1. His understanding of how community helpers are paid through taxes.

    2. His identification of himself as a responsible member of community groups.

    3. His responsibility for keeping the playground clean by picking up paper and trash.

  C. After this experience the pupil should have furthered his skill in independent and semi-independent study, as evidenced by:

    1. His ability to find needed resource materials.

    2. His ability to function effectively in community activities.

Lesson Approach:

Creating Interest. Arrange areas of interest in the classroom with boxes, cartons, signs, and toy people. Put a sign on one of the boxes: Police Station; label another box: Fire Station. Make a fence out of corrugated cardboard and put a sign on it: Zoo. Place open books about community workers on tables and chalkboard ledges. Arrange a bulletin board display with pictures of community helpers.

Discussing and Questioning. What did you see and play with in our new display today, children? What do you want to learn about our community helpers? (Write on the chalkboard the questions raised by the children. These questions will be transferred to chart paper for use during the unit.)

Assignment. Collect pictures of community workers and add these to the classroom picture file box.

Formation of Groups. At this time separate groups will be formed for each identified area. (Ask for volunteers.) Check with each group and ask for other questions and add the new questions to the group concerned. (Divide the chart with questions so each group will have its particular questions.)

Development of Learning Activities:

Committee Groups. Our task is to find the answers to our list of questions and to provide the class with these answers. What are some possible sources of information? (List on chalkboard.) *Examples:*

1. Books

2. Our weekly class magazines

3. Resource people

Collecting Data:

Have books, magazines, and filmstrips available for the children. At the conclusion of each day's committee work, check on progress for that day.

Looking ahead—anticipating reporting techniques. Now that we have had an opportunity to work on our projects, what is the best way to report this information to the other children in the class? What are some possibilities? (List) *Examples:*

1. Oral reports

2. Illustrated reports

3. Playlets

4. Pictures

5. "Filmstrip"—pictures made by children mounted on shelf paper

Organize for reporting:

At this time each group should decide upon a technique for group presentations. Children will discuss plans with the teacher.

Evaluation:

How should the material presented by each group be evaluated? Let us list some possibilities. (List)

Examples:

1. Story written by each child concerning his role in the community.

2. Picture identification of community helper and what he does.

3. Matching test.

Culminating Activity:

Invite another class to the presentation. Present a program demonstrating what the children have learned about community workers. Such a program might include showing pictures of community workers and telling about their work. Dramatizing the community at work and showing the filmstrip are other possibilities.

* * * * * * * * *

The foregoing plan covers an extended period of time. Teacher-pupil planning, however, need not be as extensive as indicated. As a general rule, teacher-pupil planning covers a time period of not more than about three weeks. It seems quite likely that this particular experience encompassed the entire unit (of two weeks).

The goals for the foregoing lesson are comparable to unit goals. The lesson outcomes are not as specific as those for other lessons for two reasons: (1) Unit goals are not ever as specific as lesson goals. (This type of lesson is essentially a unit or subunit activity.) (2) In the cooperative experience the preplanned activities must provide leeway for pupil direction. For example, it would be inappropriate to predict outcomes similar to those provided in the discussion lesson (illustrated in Chapter 7) because *the teacher does not know if pupils will elect to use discussion method or not.*

The reader will note certain differences between the illustrated model and the illustrated lesson plan. This suggests the extreme flexibility of the method. The major requirement is that *pupils are guided into making their own decisions at every step.* Manipulating children toward preconceived decisions is not acceptable. It not only makes a sham of democratic processes but is dishonest as well. Children easily detect such practices and resent them.

GENERAL PROBLEMS AND PRINCIPLES
IN TEACHER-PUPIL PLANNING

There are a number of important considerations to be taken into account when pupils become involved in planning and directing their own learning experiences. These considerations also apply to other methods of teaching, but are particularly essential to the practice of teacher-pupil planning. In this section general guidelines are stated and expanded briefly. Not only will the teacher want to study them, but they can be particularly useful to anyone who needs to *improve* his efforts in the area. The reader will recognize that many of the points are sound psychological principles applied to the teaching-learning process.

What problems may be encountered?

In any classroom method certain problems will arise. Many are functions of the particular group involved. There are some, however, which are general enough to pinpoint here. This is not to imply that such conditions should discourage a teacher from utilizing the method. On the contrary, no set of conditions is sufficient grounds for *not* involving pupils in the problem-solving process; they *are* conditions which might well be considered in preplanning such procedures.

Institutional tradition. There are still a few principals who think of teaching as lesson-hearing. Such individuals are suspicious of anybody who would deviate from purely autocratic methods. Teacher-pupil planning involves activity; activity produces a certain amount of noise and at times a bit of confusion. The teacher owes it to his superior to talk over his plans with him if there is any question of acceptance. In most instances problems will not develop once those who are involved know what is planned.

In some cases it might be feasible to devise a plan aimed at changing a supervisor's viewpoint. For example, most school administrators are willing to have teachers experiment with new methods. If so, the individual might be invited into the classroom to see for himself the results obtained and to offer suggestions. Obviously, most teachers have a great deal of autonomy in their own classrooms.

Difficulty in finding legitimate areas of choice. In every area of investigation some methods of attack are more appropriate than others. It might be inappropriate, for instance, to ask for pupil planning in a purely skills area, such as phonics. It is quite feasible, nevertheless, to involve pupils in planning and directing their own learning experiences in emphasizing the story content from their reader.

Inability of pupils to accept freedom. Pupils who have been told what to do most of their lives may at times resent thinking for themselves. Once again the prudent teacher carefully avoids giving pupils a greater dose of responsibility than they can take. There may occasionally be a child who cannot accept any responsibility; he may have to work in isolation for a few days, but eventually he will want to accept equal responsibility with the others. In a democracy there are both rights and responsibilities. Other pupils have a right to class conditions conducive to effective progress.

Inability of teacher to share with his class the significant areas of self-direction. There are undoubtedly a few teachers who have selected the profession because of their own feelings of inadequacy. Through controlling others they hope to bolster their own egos. Such individuals, it is hoped, gradually will be eliminated from situations which can have an adverse effect on growing children. With better teacher screening systems it is hoped that such persons will be directed into other endeavors.

Overemphasis on competition. The dull, as well as the underprivileged, are now in the public schools, along with the bright and the middle-class children. In too many cases measurement and evaluation policies still are based on individual competition, regardless of one's chances. This type of competition tends to discourage cooperative *group* effort. Although competition is still desirable at times, the emphasis is being shifted. That competition which is retained is more often related to self-improvement or healthy competition between subgroups within the class, rather than to all members of a heterogeneous group.

What principles apply?

A teacher who is considering the involvement of pupils in the problem-solving process must be careful to avoid violating certain basic democratic principles. Elementary school children usually like the idea of active participation in solving their own problems, but may become disillusioned or demoralized quickly if a teacher is inconsistent in his own behavior. The guidelines which follow may assist the teacher in appropriate application of such principles. In discussing 50 principles which "we can feel sure about," Watson mentions at least four (the first four in this list) that seem basic to teacher-pupil planning:

1. Children are more apt to throw themselves wholeheartedly into any project if they themselves have participated in the selection and planning of the enterprise.

2. When groups act for a common goal there is better cooperation and more friendliness than when individuals in the group are engaged in competitive rivalry with one another.

3. If there is a discrepancy between the real *objectives* and the *tests* used to measure achievement, the latter become the main influence upon choice of subject matter and method.

4. The superiority of man over calculating machines is more evident in the formulation of questions than the working out of answers.[6]

5. *Rules in a democracy are used to ensure fair play.* Some groups still operate under the delusion that rules of procedure (whether formal or informal) act to impede the progress of group action. It has been said, "Let us not adopt any rules and just operate democratically." This, of course, enables a leader to adopt his own rules. At times he may allow the group to proceed in a democratic manner, while at other times he may become quite arbitrary in his behavior. If the group has already established certain rules of procedure, behavior is much more likely to be consistent.

6. *Pupils and teacher clearly understand the other's role and areas of responsibility.* How many times has an individual felt insecure or afraid because he did not know what was expected of him? What usually happens under such circumstances is that one tends to resist taking any action until he knows more of the situation. Many teachers have identified such a group attitude as indicative of the group's inability to direct its own learning experiences. The real difficulty, however, usually can be found in the preliminary planning stage of the problem. A great deal of planning is necessary prior to the action stage of problem solving. It may be necessary to devote approximately one week of a three-week project to the preparation phases of the task. Answers to questions become valuable clues for pupils in determining their own roles as well as that of their teacher. Indeed, a teacher might welcome many and varied questions about the mechanics of the operation in the initial stages of planning.

7. *Pupil choices are limited by their own experiences and knowledge.* In many areas pupils may be *willing* to contribute, but because of inadequate background may find themselves unable to make progress. After some preliminary reading, visual aids, class discussion, demonstration, and the like, almost any group will have a variety of questions with which it is vitally concerned. In areas of an especially technical nature, teacher-pupil planning may be far less elaborate than in other areas.

8. *Real choices are available to pupils in both content and method.* Selection of content *within a specified area* can afford the type of motivation necessary for active planning of presentation. Pupils frequently lose interest in the formulation of their own questions if they are told how the questions are to be solved. There are occasions when

---

[6] Goodwin Watson, "What Psychology Can We Feel Sure About?", *Teachers College Record*, 61: 253–257 (1960).

a teacher may find it desirable or expedient to select the specific content, but he can still allow pupils to determine the methods of investigation and reporting. In fact, the beginning teacher may want to involve himself in teacher-pupil planning gradually in this manner. There are times when we have real life problems thrust upon us. In the final analysis, the amount and type of pupil-directed activities will depend on the nature of the problem and the particular group involved. In most classes it is possible and desirable to involve pupils in selection of both content and methodology. It should be stressed, however, that teacher-pupil planning does *not* mean pupil planning.

Some teachers have sought to involve pupils only superficially in the teacher-pupil planning, telling pupils that they are to have an active part in the process and then proceeding to veto almost all suggestions offered. This is not only easily recognized but often deeply resented by children. If a teacher anticipates difficulties which the group has not realized he may feel compelled to make them known. The final decision is then left to the pupils. Of course, if certain actions are likely to clash with school policy the teacher *must* veto them. In such cases, however, pupils usually will respect him for doing so.

9. *In a democratic classroom pupils gradually assume more and more responsibility in directing their own learnings.* Democratic behavior develops through experience. As an individual learns to accept some responsibility he is given more responsibility. The same applies to the classroom situation. In any job or business responsibility is added gradually. The prudent teacher does not plunge himself and all his pupils into teacher-pupil planning at one time.[7] Usually it is desirable to begin such activities in one subject matter area while conducting the other areas of the curriculum in a different manner. Then, as both teacher and pupils gain confidence and skill, more and more responsibility can be shared with pupils.

10. *Active participation by all members is essential.* In most groups there are those who are shy and withdrawn while others are overly verbose. Both kinds of children must be helped to realize the need for cooperation and sharing. This can be accomplished by setting up a criterion demanding that each member contribute his share in research and reporting procedures.

11. *Situations are created in which each person is made to feel that he has a worthwhile contribution to make.* Some individuals are good at art work; others can meet and interview people easily; a few are especially adept at organizing materials; one person may have a hobby which

---

[7] G. G. Dawson, "Experiment in Teacher-Pupil Planning," *Social Education*, 24: 325–328 (November, 1960).

relates specifically to the problem. It is the responsibility of the chairman of each subgroup to direct its members in activities which seem most appropriate. At the same time the teacher must see that such arrangements are determined democratically. Also, he must see that pupils have opportunities to explore new areas of interest. For example, just because a pupil is particularly qualified in art work is no indication that he should do only art work in each of the committees in which he participates.

SUMMARY

The application of democratic (problem-solving) procedures to class-room teaching has been emphasized. The cooperative experience has been described as one in which the teacher acts as a joint participant in the clarification of needs and objectives, in the planning and direction of learning activities, and in the evaluation of pupil progress in terms of the goals established. Emphasis was on the function and place for democratic processes in today's elementary school. If children are to assume their proper roles in society, learning experiences should be consistent with these future expectations. "Pupils learn what they live" is a cliché which has been supported by research time and time again. In a democracy, cooperation is important, but individualism is needed too.

The second section of the chapter offered an illustrative model for the teacher who would employ teacher-pupil planning for the first time. The model is designed to render assistance to the teacher who must himself *create* his own approach. It should help him gain insight and work out important relationships for such an approach in his own classroom.

Finally, important principles and problems associated with teacher-pupil planning have been treated. Experienced teachers especially will want to know the relationship of the cooperative experience to findings from educational psychology. There are, of course, certain problems or difficulties associated with every teaching procedure; these have been discussed at some length.

QUESTIONS FOR STUDY AND DISCUSSION

1. What are some democratic foundations for the cooperative experience described in this chapter? What functions are served? What is the relationship between teacher-pupil planning procedures and those discussed in Chapter 7 (discussion activities)? Why is teacher-pupil planning con-

sidered more "democratic" than the approaches discussed thus far in this unit?

2. Study the model illustrated in the second section of this chapter. Illustrate how you would develop the approach in your prospective teaching. What changes would you introduce? Why? What areas of teacher-pupil planning do you anticipate would be most difficult to apply? Why? Observe a class involving teacher-pupil planning. Which area seems the most difficult to apply in practice? Why?

3. Certain critics have contended that teacher-pupil planning approaches to instruction lead to a de-emphasis on "content learning." Now that you have studied the instructional approach, what are your own views on the matter? What misconceptions are often associated with teacher-pupil planning? Would teacher-pupil planning be appropriate for teaching conceived as a process of knowledge acquisition? Why or why not?

SELECTED BIBLIOGRAPHY

Association for Supervision and Curriculum Development, *Perceiving, Behaving, Becoming*, Yearbook (Washington, D. C.: The Association, 1962).

Burton, William H., *The Guidance of Learning Activities*, 3rd Ed. (New York: Appleton-Century-Crofts, Inc., 1960).

Dewey, John, *Democracy and Education* (New York: The Macmillan Co., 1924).

Fantini, Mario D., "Open v. Closed Classrooms," *The Clearing House*, 37, No. 2: 67–71 (October, 1962).

Graham, Robert J., "How an 'Open' Class Works," *The Clearing House*, 37, No. 6: 331–333 (February, 1963).

Hoover, Kenneth H., "Learning Through Teacher-Pupil Planned Activities," *Journal of Teacher Education*, 11, No. 1: 50–54 (March, 1960).

McLean, Harvard W., "Models for Effective Groupwork," *The Elementary School Journal*, 67, No. 6: 271–275 (February, 1967).

Waskin, Yvonne, *Teacher-Pupil Planning for Better Classroom Learning* (New York: Pitman Publishing Corporation, 1967).

Watson, Goodwin, "What Psychology Can We Feel Sure About?", *Teachers College Record*, 61: 253–257 (1960).

Xavier, Sister Mary, "For Curriculum Improvement Involve Your Students," *Clearing House*, 41: 429–431 (March, 1967).

10

Personalizing Instruction:
The Challenge of
Individual Differences

As the pupils filed into her classroom for the first time, Miss Jones caught herself wondering about the differences among the individuals in this new class. Some were readily apparent, while other important differences would not become apparent even by the end of the year. As the boys and girls came into the room and found seats, Miss Jones noted differences in height, body build, health, grooming, clothing, and numerous other things. She knew also that some of the more important differences were not obvious. From past experience she was well aware of differences in general and special abilities, achievement, interest, personality, leadership qualities, attitudes, reading level, sex, and social class. The list was almost overwhelming! Yet Miss Jones knew that she was expected to meet the challenge of individual differences in her class. How was she to begin? Which of these differences should receive *first* consideration? And, finally, just how does one go about attacking the problem?

The foregoing illustration draws attention to the major problem associated with mass education. In keeping with the democratic tradition of schooling for all citizens, the American schoolteacher frequently will find all levels of ability represented in a single class. His entire approach to teaching must be adjusted to these differences. Perhaps due to the complexity of the problem, a great deal of controversy is associated with attempts to personalize instruction.

This chapter is divided into three parts. The first of these deals with the extent and nature of the problem. Special attention is given to various curriculum and instructional approaches designed to narrow the range of differences. The second section offers an instructional model for subgrouping within the classroom. The final section treats principles and problems associated with attempts to personalize instruction.

ASSESSING AND ANALYZING INDIVIDUAL DIFFERENCES

In grappling with the problem of individual differences, some attention must be devoted to the precise nature of those differences which bear directly upon school achievement. We often speak of the dull and the bright as if they represented clear-cut categories. Is the classification justifiable for instructional purposes? If so, what is the precise nature of these differences? What data are available to help the teacher provide for these differences? How effective have teachers been in their quest for techniques of providing for individual differences? These and other related problems are treated in the pages which follow.

How are dull and bright pupils characterized?

The term "normal" or "average" as applied to pupils is a high abtraction that relates to the degree of similarity or difference between individuals in a group setting. Each individual is unique. Some differences are insignificant while others, although great, are not particuarly important in terms of the usual classroom procedures. Some, however, are great enough to make a significant difference in the instructional process. One combination of these may be sufficient to make possible unusual contributions in intellectual pursuits; other combinations may severely limit one's potential contributions to society. In a democracy, however, the worth of *each* individual is cherished. The task of teaching, basically, is to assist each individual to develop his own potentialities. The teacher must first determine some of these potentialities, however.

Many teachers lay claim to their capacities for "spotting" the slow-learning child. "Is he not the individual who fails to respond to the moods of the class; the one who frequently fails to comprehend simple directions and explanations; the person who often 'loses' his books or papers; the one who bears the brunt of jokes and criticism? These, along with other traits, characterize such pupils," say teachers. They can just as readily "spot" characteristics of the bright. While some such traits *may*, and *frequently are*, associated with dullness and brightness, they are not as typical as one might think.

According to Johnson and Medinnus,[1] some of the slow learners will

---

[1] Ronald C. Johnson and Gene R. Medinnus, *Child Psychology: Behavior and Development* (New York: John Wiley and Sons, Inc., 1965), p. 166.

show considerable social competence and can benefit from training, whereas others may not. Many teachers have found that slow learners often become enthusiastic pupils when work is adjusted to their levels. Because these individuals tend to show little concern for the future, some teachers become disturbed—assuming this to be abnormal or somehow "bad." There is an urgent need for teachers to understand that such an individual appears to be different because *he thinks differently*. Rather than penalizing him for genetic factors, the resourceful teacher strives for an understanding of these differences. A slow learner remembers few details or isolated facts. Like all children, he responds readily to personal attention. This personal attention, however, frequently is not interpreted in the manner that may be expected. Remember, he thinks differently! Indeed, the rocky road of experience may have made him unusually self-conscious, subconsciously realizing that he somehow does not fit. A self-conscious person is usually a sensitive individual. The teacher who would be sympathetic and show added attention may only heighten his defensive feelings. At the same time he *wants* to be understood. In a sense, his feelings are like those of some minority groups. Those children who score between 75 and 90 in IQ tests are generally classed as slow learners.

The gifted child also differs significantly from the dull and the "average." He may appear to be happy and contented, or he, too, may be self-conscious, depending on the nature of his past school experiences. If he is able to tolerate what appears to him to be the "slow motion" of the rest of his class, leadership qualities may emerge. Sometimes, however, he may withdraw from reality. In general, the gifted child fares better than the dull. Not only can he receive recognition in academic school work, but his superior knowledge and understanding of his environment tend to cause others to turn to him for assistance. As a consequence, he is usually able to satsify his basic need structure.

There are other important factors of giftedness which have a direct bearing on methods of teaching. Among the mentally superior pupils, some are creative and some are not.[2] Psychologists have made a distinction between bright pupils who are "convergent thinkers" and those who are "divergent thinkers." [3] The convergent thinker tends to seek a single, predetermined "correct" answer to a problem. The divergent thinker, on the other hand, tends to be creative and constructive in seeking novel, experimental, and multiple solutions to a problem. The divergent thinker tends to become involved in "discovery" rather than the mere covering of material. Like the dull, he learns best through *doing*, but the type of

[2] Robert J. Havighurst, "Conditions Productive of Superior Children," *Teachers College Record*, 62 (April, 1961), pp. 524–531.
[3] *Ibid.*

doing is different. The teacher, *by utilizing appropriate teaching strategies,* may contribute substantially to the development of both divergent and convergent factors. If the school meets the needs of the extremes, along with the needs of the "average" pupils, the elementary school child today may *actually* experience *equal opportunity rather than equal exposure.* Although there are relatively few gifted pupils in terms of the total population, the types of procedures especially adapted to their needs are effective, to a lesser degree, for the above-average or bright pupils.

Bright pupils often differ considerably from the (relatively rare) gifted individual. This difference is one of degree, however. Recent studies on the relationship of IQ to creativity, for example, point to the ultimate importance of *predisposing* factors, especially the characteristic of *questing.* Getzels and Jackson [4] found that pupils who ranked in the top 20 percent on creativity measures were *below* the top 20 percent in IQ. Furthermore, they found that this group's scholastic *achievement* was equal to that of those who scored in the upper 20 percent on IQ tests. (It should be noted that IQ scores for *both* groups were "above average.") Thus it appears that any arbitrary separation of pupils on the basis of IQ alone would be inadequate.

What basic problems are associated with personalizing instruction?

At this point it seems appropriate to review the basic tenet of education in our democracy: Every child has a right to a free, public school education *commensurate with his abilities.* In most elementary school classrooms the teacher adapts instruction to the "average" pupil, and then supposedly meets the needs of the extremes through special help and various enrichment techniques. What actually happens in many large classes is that there is just not sufficient time to do much about those near the extremes. As a consequence, discipline problems become aggravated and the teacher becomes more and more frustrated.

The unusually dull pupil, like all other pupils, is entitled to assistance in becoming a useful citizen. He cannot meet standards for the average pupil, and there is no sound reason why such a standard should be imposed upon him. His parents pay taxes for the support of the school, just as do parents of the bright youngsters. He did not select his parents or decide that he would be dull! But he *is* dull and should not be penalized in school for it. Likewise, pupils at the other extreme need instruc-

[4] Jacob W. Getzels and Philip W. Jackson, *Creativity and Intelligence* (New York: John Wiley & Sons, Inc., 1962), p. 20.

tion suitable to their general levels of understanding. Instruction suitable for the average is all too often not sufficiently challenging for the above-average. Thus boredom and apathy follow.

Although there are a multitude of differences among the children in any group, as far as the school situation is concerned one's general scholastic aptitude (IQ) appears to be basic. That is to say, differences in interest, attitudes, personality, and the like are *basically* related to one's general ability to do school work. If this is true, then provisions for meeting this difference should lead to effectiveness in coping with other differences. A great deal of data is usually available through the school guidance counselor or the principal's office. One's general attitude toward school, personality, leadership qualities, and even general class achievement soon becomes apparent to the close observer. It is much more difficult, however, to estimate a pupil's general ability to do school work. As soon as class rolls are available the teacher should collect (for his own files) the general scholastic ability ratings (IQ scores) and the most recent reading test results for each of his pupils.

How does one assess an IQ score?

An IQ test may be given as soon as the first grade; some may be given sooner. Such factors as validity, reliability, and whether the test was one of power or speed must be considered in assessing IQ test results. Sometimes the teacher is so concerned with these variables that he becomes discouraged from using test results. At the risk of oversimplifying the task and because it is extremely important that test results be used to guide one in effective teaching, three basic considerations are suggested:

1. If one of the test scores is from a Stanford-Binet or Wechsler Intelligence Scale for Children, it should be selected as the best indication of ability.
2. Use IQ test scores as a guide only in determining if one has below-average, average, or above-average capacity to do school work. Do *not* record a test score. Although the differences between group IQ scores are somewhat related to the type of test involved, they are based on the normal curve of probability. This means that a score of 90–110 will be within the average range. Those below 90 can be classified as below average, and those above 110 can be classified as above average. Since IQ test scores are used only as a guide to teaching, exact scores are not of first importance here. In case of doubt the teacher should consult the school counselor.
3. Group IQ tests, such as the Otis Quick Scoring Mental Ability Test, California Test of Mental Maturity, or the SRA Tests of General Ability, are usually given by the teacher and are much less accurate than a Stanford-Binet or Wechsler Intelligence Scale for Children given by a psychometrist or psychologist to one child at a time.

Reading test results are usually recorded in terms of grade level. For example, a reading level of 4.3 indicates that when the test was taken the child was reading at a level comparable to that of the average child who has advanced 0.3 of the way through the fourth grade. If that child is now in the sixth grade a fraction would be computed as follows:

$$\frac{4.3}{4} \times 2 = 2.$$

The numerator of the fraction is the reading grade level and the denominator is the grade level at the time of testing. The number 2 in the fraction is the years that have passed since the reading test was given. The answer 2 would then be added to 4.3 to get the approximate level at which the child is reading at the present time. Thus the approximate *present* reading level of the pupil is 6.3. For an individual beginning his sixth year in elementary school this reading level would, therefore, be about 0.3 of a year above that of the average sixth grader.

In order to render the data readily accessible when needed, it is recommended that symbols which will indicate to the teacher relative IQ and reading levels be entered on a seating chart.

In the above square for Joe the "0" may indicate average IQ, while the "+" may suggest an above-average reading level.

What are some ways of providing for individual differences?

For the past 30 years various techniques and "plans" have been advanced for meeting the varying needs of pupils. As mass education has become more and more a reality, differences have become more and more pronounced. Many of the earlier practices involved a modification of the curriculum to facilitate special needs and interests. Although some of these innovations are still being used effectively in some schools, they usually need to be supplemented with corresponding modifications in instructional procedures. Among the more widely known modifications are:

Retention and acceleration. Retention was at one time quite common. Today, however, the practice is not used extensively. While "high" standards of competence are desirable, it is also recognized that "high" for one individual may be "low" for another. Being retained on the basis of limited capacity merely tends to aggravate the problem. Not only does it tend to neglect the social and emotional needs of the child, but it frequently does little to solve the problem asociated with intellectual progress. Indeed, most studies have clearly shown that deficient pupils who have been "passed" tend to achieve more than those who are retained. Arbitrary class standards of achievement, of course, *assume* equal or near-equal potential. This assumption was disproved some 50 years ago.

There are instances however when retention *is* recommended. Often retention is associated with immaturity, usually most evident in the lower elementary levels. This, of course, presupposes the adaptation of instruction to individual needs. Indeed, few children are willing to try to accomplish tasks above their ability levels. Acceleration, for similar reasons, is usually discouraged.

Homogeneous grouping between classes. For years now school after school has attempted some form of pupil selection for classes—often on the basis of scholastic aptitude (IQ) or reading achievement. While the idea initially had wide popular appeal, it frequently has been quite unsatisfactory in practice. One approach to this is selective placement in "high," "average," or "low" classes. For example, one group might be assigned to a high third grade class, another group would be placed in an average third grade class, while another would be put in a low third grade class.

Homogeneous grouping within the classroom. Pupil differences within any given class, despite efforts to make the group homogeneous, are exceedingly great. In discussing the heterogeneity of "homogeneous groups" Tyler [5] illustrates the difficulty in narrowing the range of human variability to any marked degree. The need for some system of classroom grouping within the classroom is emphasized, however. As Anderson [6] points out, "There appears to be widespread agreement that *flexibility* in grouping practices is desirable. Some types of organization fail of their purpose because of their rigidity." [7] Tyler and Brownell sug-

---

[5] Fred T. Tyler, "Individual Variability," in *Individualizing Instruction*, 61st Yearbook, Part I, National Society for the Study of Education (Chicago: University of Chicago Press, 1962), Ch. 10.

[6] Robert H. Anderson, "Organizing Groups for Instruction," in Fred T. Tyler and William A. Brownell, "The Ubiquity of Variability," in *Individualizing Instruction (Ibid.)*, Chs. 13 and 17.

[7] *Ibid.*, p. 253.

gest that grouping within the classroom on a flexible and variable basis may be helpful.[8]

Class enrichment. Ask any substantial number of elementary teachers how they provide for individual differences and the majority is likely to mention "enrichment." The term, as commonly used in teaching, refers to the provision of either or both *additional* and *different* activities for unusually capable pupils. Some teachers seem to associate *additional* work only with enrichment activities, however. Ask them how they meet the needs of slow pupils, and they are frequently less definite. What actually happens, in too many instances, is that the label acts as a "smoke screen" for doing very little in the area. With the mounting pressure of numbers, combined with more heterogeneous groups, the pressure of time may seriously curtail one's efforts, despite the best of intentions. It is the writers' contention that some systematic plan of enrichment is necessary before the task may be adequately accomplished in large classes.

It is quite common in the early grades of the elementary school for the children to be assigned to different reading groups. The most common plan seems to be three reading groups within a single class. The pupils in beginning reading are assigned to these groups on the basis of reading readiness. Dawson [9] points out, however, that the goal seems to be the achievement of a psychologically desirable balance between the personal growth needs of the child and the need to organize groups systematically for instructional purposes. He suggests that flexible grouping within the classroom often satisfies these needs. In order to achieve flexibility in the classroom, the teacher must be willing to move a child from group to group as his needs dictate.

What is the scope of the problem?

Despite efforts which may have been made to reduce individual differences between classes, differences within any given class can still be extreme. One pupil actually may read 50 or 60 pages while a classmate is struggling hard to read five or six pages! One pupil may solve 40 problems during the time it takes another to solve four problems. As long as classes were relatively small (20–25 in number) some form of enrichment for the extremes was reasonably satisfactory. Today, however, the

[8] *Ibid.*, p. 319.

[9] Dan T. Dawson, "Some Issues in Grouping for Reading," *The National Elementary Principal* (September, 1955), pp. 48–52. Copyright 1955, Department of Elementary School Principals, National Education Association. All rights reserved.

problem is complicated by larger classes. Having accepted individual differences in each class as an instructional reality, the teacher immediately is faced with the basic problem of coping with these differences. Clymer and Kearney,[10] while declining to prescribe any instructional formula, do suggest a number of needs that must be taken into account by every teacher in providing for individual differences:

1. The need to know the students

2. The need to recognize that not all teachers will adjust to individual differences in the same way

3. The need to provide generous time allotments

4. The need to plan carefully whatever is to be done in the classroom

5. The need to work effectively with the group as a whole

6. The need to move slowly into any type of adjustment to individual differences

7. The need to accept more noise and more confusion

8. The need to recognize failure and begin again

9. The need to accept less than 100 percent adjustment to individual differences

10. The need to recognize that adjusting to individual differences calls for plain, hard work.[11]

Thus, it is seen that provision for pupil variability can be a most perplexing problem. Sometimes instruction can be adjusted to the class as a whole; at other times the class can be effectively divided into two or three subgroups; occasionally small buzz groups of three or four members each are in order; on other occasions independent study is needed. The beginning teacher sometimes is inclined to view the problem simply as one of selecting the method appropriate at the time. Unfortunately, the problem is not that simple. Pupils learn at different rates and in different ways. For example, as illustrated later in this chapter, slow pupils often need a type of instruction quite different from that needed by bright pupils. Indeed pupils at the opposite extremes of ability, as a general rule, just do not think alike. Although it is known that a child *may* possess high potential in one area while displaying much less ability in another area, bright pupils *tend* to be bright in all areas of learning.

[10] Theodore Clymer and Nolan C. Kearney, "Curricular and Instructional Provisions for Individual Differences," in *Individualizing Instruction* (*op. cit.*), pp. 275–282.
[11] *Ibid.*

Likewise, slow children *tend* to be slow in all areas. As Burton points out, "It is probably safe to be suspicious of poor performance in one field coupled with obviously good results in most others." [12]

Perhaps the factor of similar levels of abilities within the individuals has led to more abuse in teaching than has any other single factor. Although *similarities* or *tendencies* do exist between one area of ability and another, there are numerous exceptions. Ability does not take into account such factors as interest, motivation, creativity, and perseverance; nor does it include special talents, general state of health, or the need for special remedial assistance.

A SUGGESTED MODEL FOR CLASSROOM GROUPING

The inadequacies of any one plan for grouping have been emphasized and, indeed, most current methods texts usually stop short of offering any such approach to teaching. The validity of such a position, however, is open to question. It has long been recognized, for example, that there is no one method of teaching that is appropriate for all occasions. Likewise, there is no one approach to evaluation or reporting that has an "edge" over other approaches. Yet a variety of these techniques are offered in practically all methods textbooks. Beginning teachers especially, want—and need—some specific guidance in adjusting instruction to the extreme individual differences found in most of today's elementary school classes. It is sheer quackery to disregard the fact of variation. Likewise, it is poor pedagogy to overstress either extreme. As a case in point, one is sometimes tempted to provide special activities for the bright while ignoring the dull—hoping he will not obstruct too seriously the learning activities of others. And some teachers are likely to spend a great deal of time with the dull, ignoring the bright, feeling that the latter can fend for himself.

This section of the chapter deals with *an* approach to grouping within the classroom. Just as any one teaching method is inadequate, the model which follows cannot be employed *per se* in all classes in all subject fields. In one important respect, however, it is more than just another teaching method. *Its purpose is to offer a useful framework for coping with the many individual differences to be encountered.* Indeed, certain aspects of the basic framework are highly controversial and will probably need some alteration in adjusting to the individual needs of pupils. It is

[12] William H. Burton, *The Guidance of Learning Activities*, 3rd Ed. (New York: Appleton-Century-Crofts, Inc., 1962), p. 236.

worth repeating that teaching is a *personal invention.* The grouping model which follows is designed to activate creative imagination among teachers.

Before any description of a systematic plan for class grouping can be given, a list of criteria must be established. Any plan which can satisfy these requirements is worthy of consideration.

1. Subgrouping within a given class must be flexible. Pupils must be permitted to shift from one group to another when the need arises. Furthermore, pupils from each group must have ample opportunity to work with members from other groups.

2. Class groups must be handled so as to minimize any feelings of stigma or superiority associated with different groupings.

3. Subgroups must *increase* the potential for *individualizing* instruction. As with homogeneously grouped classes, there is danger in assuming that a subgroup is homogeneous and that instructional materials and procedures can be adjusted to the needs of the group as a whole. Grouping elementary school pupils for instruction in reading, for example, has all too often resulted in a new type of "lock-step" teaching simply because the teacher has tended to treat the *groups* as homogeneous. Giving identical assignments to all pupils in a given group is little better than no grouping at all.

4. Subgroups must provide adequately for the social and emotional needs of children.

5. Group *and* individual cooperation and competition must be provided.

6. Each pupil must have an opportunity to meet the goals of instruction, commensurate with his capacities.

7. Grouping must be made in a given area. A child could belong to one group for reading, a different group for arithmetic, yet another group for science.

How does a teacher initiate grouping within the classroom?

During the first few weeks of the new school year it is proposed that the teacher organize the class along conventional lines. Instruction generally will be adapted to the needs of the "average" pupil. During this initial period pupils will be adjusting to each other, the teacher, and the new classroom. Then, *on the basis of achievement during this period,* three subgroups can be organized:

Group I. This group will be composed of those pupils who achieved considerably more than the average pupil during these few weeks. On the basis of past school records, present work, and standardized or informal tests, the pupils who are doing better than the average class member would be put into this group. This would normally consist of approximately the upper fourth of the class.

Group II. Members of this group will be those who made near average progress during the first few weeks of school. Their past school records and tests would indicate that they are average pupils. This group will be approximately the middle half of the class.

Group III. This group will consist of individuals who achieved considerably less than the average, as evidenced by slow or poor progress during the first few weeks of the school year. Their past school records and performances on informal and formal tests would place them well below grade level. This group normally would be the smallest of the three groups. They require more individual attention than the other groups.

In the first grade classroom, grouping will be initiated in a somewhat different way. In reading, for example, the grouping may develop this way. During the first few weeks (usually 3–6) the children will be working in the area of reading readiness. As soon as a few children are ready to begin formal reading instruction a group may be formed. Because of individual differences, all children in the class will not be ready to begin this instruction at the same time. After the first group is well launched into reading pre-primer or other reading materials, a second group may be formed. Finally, after an extended period of time the third group would be ready to begin regular reading activities. The use of formal and informal tests will assist the teacher in determining when grouping may be most effectively initiated.

How may pupils be prepared for groupings?

Since children tend to be fearful of the unknown, it is recommended that they understand and become actively involved in the group procedures. Many teachers have found that pupils generally are acutely aware of the injustices of expecting every individual to reach similar standards. A discussion of the problem can do much to clarify the issues. It should be kept in mind that grouping practices are merely expediency measures for meeting individual needs. If this goal is not maintained, grouping loses its usefulness.

It is desirable to clarify several important characteristics of the grouping model:

1. The recommended procedure for grouping is made wholly on the basis of achievement rather than on the basis of ability. (If the system operates

properly the eventual grouping *actually* will approach one based on ability, but this point need not be emphasized with pupils.)

2. An individual should be shifted from one group to another as his achievement warrants such a change. (This must be emphasized, because in practice, teachers tend to be reluctant to shift individuals from group to group.)

3. Even though the three groups will provide a *basis* for instructional purposes, the class will work as a single unit much of the time. Also, there will be the usual variety of other groupings and committee activities, which will function from time to time. These will often *cut across* achievement group lines. Special need groups, special interest groups, committee project groups are just a few of the many instructional groups which will be employed.

4. Although much movement will occur during the various class activities, it is obviously desirable to have each group together when subgroup instruction is needed.

5. Parents should be informed of the grouping plan, even though grouping in the elementary school is quite common.

How do goals vary from one group to the next?

The general class goals usually will be the same for each subgroup, but the expected behavioral outcomes may vary considerably. (See Chapter 4.) If the expected behavioral outcomes will be different it would then seem to follow that the pupil *experiences* necessary to achieve the goals (outcomes) also will vary.

This would indicate that *all* pupils will be expected to make some progress toward class goals. For the dull or otherwise low achievers, progress will be limited. The teacher must judge what essentials are necessary for at least nominal progress toward the lesson goals. The other two groups would be expected to achieve more.

What activities seem most appropriate for the low and high achievers?

It is appropriate at this point to turn to the findings from psychological research. Fortunately, there is an abundance of research readily available on the learning characteristics of the dull and the bright. Knowledge of these characteristics appears to be basic for any teacher who would provide adequately for individual differences.

A brief review of these characteristics dramatically indicates the folly of expecting all pupils to respond satisfactorily to the same type of instruction. Yet, this basically is what is expected when instruction is directed toward the "average" pupil.

Characteristics of Dull and Bright Children

Dull Children	Bright Children
1. Tend to have short attention span.	1. Tend to have a longer attention span and are usually more persistent in pursuit of goals.
2. Tend to have limited mental initiative and are imitative.	2. Tend to be highly initiative and are more creative.
3. Tend to have limited ability to work with abstractions and to generalize.	3. Tend to be capable of making logical associations and conceptualization.
4. Tend to be slow in forming associations between words and ideas.	4. Tend to be expressive with ideas and have an enriched vocabulary.
5. Tend to lack social intelligence, and outlook or point of view extremely local.	5. Tend to be socially sensitive to viewpoints of others and be socially adjusted.
6. Tend to have limited powers of assimilation and fail to recognize familiar elements in new situations.	6. Tend to have intellectual curiosity and powers of observation.
7. Tend to learn slowly and forget quickly.	7. Tend to have concentration and retention powers.
8. Tend to have limited powers of self-direction and be unable to set up and realize standards in workmanship.	8. Tend toward independence in work and study with the ability of self-criticism and self-checking.
9. Tend to have a slow reaction time.	9. Tend to be energetic, alert, and self-reliant.
10. Tend to have a narrow range of interests.	10. Tend toward diversity of interests and versatility.

How would the plan apply to a particular area of the curriculum?

Many beginning teachers are interested in some sort of ability grouping in their classes, but have difficulty applying the principles to their particular situations. Specific aspects of the problem as they have been applied in the area of reading will be reviewed.

One of the most critical, yet difficult, aspects of the problem is the task of varying depth and scope of instruction between the subgroups. In the Lyons and Carnahan Developmental Reading Series,[13] a program

[13] Guy L. Bond et al., *Just for Fun*, Teaching Guide, Unit One (Chicago: Lyons and Carnahan, 1962), pp. 2–19.

is developed for the three subgroups normally found in a class. Two editions of a reader are used in each class. At the time the two editions are presented, the children are told that the books look alike and they contain the same stories and illustrations; the only difference is that the authors have written the same stories in different ways. The child with a low reading score will read the Classmate Edition (simplified version of the selection) while the child who is reading at or near grade level will read the Regular Edition. The third group also will read the Regular Edition for the basic purposes and, in addition, should reread for creative and advanced purposes as illustrated for each story. The entire class is introduced to the story and the new words used at the same time. In teaching each unit, the pupils have whole-class activities and subgroup instruction.

Other specific plans for grouping in the area of reading are the Madison plan and the New Castle plan. These two plans have been reported to be quite successful.

The Madison, Wisconsin,schools challenged the practice of dividing the pupils in the classroom by the common three-group method.[14] The teacher introduced his single reading lesson in the basal reader each day to all the pupils in the classroom. Following the lesson presentation and work on the reading lesson, all the pupils who had mastered the lesson moved into more challenging reading materials. The children who had difficulties with a portion of the reading lesson were grouped according to the nature of the difficulty. The difficulties encountered by the children were resolved the same day that the basal reading lesson was given; thus, the groupings were temporary for those children who had difficulties. The following day, when a new reading lesson was given, there were new groupings for those children who had difficulties on that day's lesson.

Another successful innovation in the teaching of reading was made in New Castle, Pennsylvania.[15] In this reading program, all the children of the class were introduced to the story content of a basal reader by use of an enlarged film image projected on the blackboard while the textbook was used for practice and testing. The filmstrips were actual pictures of the pages in the basic reading textbook. All the children in the classroom got the same kind of introduction and were involved in the discussion concerning the reading materials with the teacher. After working together in this fashion the children worked individually in

[14] Duane Manning, *The Qualitative Elementary School* (New York: Harper & Row, Publishers, Inc., 1963), p. 74.

[15] Glenn McCracken, "The New Castle Reading Experiment: A Terminal Report," *Elementary English* (January, 1953), pp. 13–21.

their reading book for reading practice and to complete the lesson activities.

Other plans are also available to help the teacher meet the individual needs of his pupils. Individualized reading, individualized arithmetic, individualized spelling, and individually prescribed instruction (I.P.I.) are just a few of the innovations that are occuring in the educational field.

How can pupils be evaluated in ability grouping?

Marks or grades are merely symbols, which supposedly indicate a measure of progress. They are not the results of learning. At best they are only an indication of the quality or thoroughness of learning. However, as there is so much emphasis placed on them, particular attention must be given to the problem.

It follows that if the depth and scope of class activities vary from one group to another, pupils should not be expected to take the same tests. Each member of a given group, however, can be evaluated on the basis of his accomplishment in comparison with the other members of that group. This means, in effect, that any individual within the group may earn any mark from A to F or S to U. There still is competition, but the competition now is among those with approximately equal achievement and ability. Such a scheme seems to approximate closely competition evidenced in the larger society. For example, teachers do not compete *directly* with engineers, but they do compete with other teachers in their particular fields. Likewise, carpenters compete more directly with other carpenters than with electricians.

If, as is true in many schools, the teacher is required to base course and report card marks on the relative achievement of *all* pupils in a class he may be forced to limit those in Group III to a top mark of C, those in Group II to a top mark of B, and those in Group I to a top mark of A. This is inconsistent with what is here recommended, but if explained thoroughly to pupils and to parents most of them will readily accept the idea. The situation is different, however, if a grade of Satisfactory or Unsatisfactory is given. All children who are working at their achievement level would get an S with no relation to groups.

In some schools the teacher is permitted to indicate group differences on grade reports as follows:

Group   I—A_1, B_1, etc.

Group   II—A_2, B_2, etc.

Group III—A_3, B_3, etc.

An explanatory note can be entered directly on the school report to the effect that the subscripts are indicative of *class* level. For example, A_3 would represent top performance in the lower group of the class.

How does ability grouping affect other pupil differences?

The reader should bear in mind that there is some correlation between ability and achievement, interest, reading ability, and so on. Within limits, then, grouping may provide the initial impetus for meeting other needs. Very seldom will a slow reader be in the group of high achievers, for school achievement essentially is based on reading ability. There may be wider variations in the area of interests. It is a relatively simple task, however, to regroup pupils into committees or panels for interest projects. As pupils develop their own division of labor, the various tasks quite naturally are distributed somewhat according to ability. Seldom will one volunteer (or allow himself to be selected by his peers) for a job which he perceives as too difficult to accomplish. Many teachers, for example, have made wide use of panel groups in the upper grades. Frequently such an activity is initiated among the more capable pupils. As less capable pupils become more familiar with its application, however, they tend to volunteer on the basis of interest. Consequently, it is quite common to find members of all three groups on a single panel. This, of course, indicates the flexibility of such a grouping plan. *In many class activities individuals from each group will work together on projects and activities. Differences are made only in depth and scope of understanding expected, as reflected by evaluations.*

What effect does grouping have on the work load of the teacher?

One of the first inquiries usually made by an experienced teacher pertains to the amount of additional work such a technique would entail. This is a legitimate question, especially with today's generally crowded classrooms. For those who have had experience in the area, the answer depends on the length of time the program has been in operation. For the first year there seems to be little doubt that more work for the teacher will be necessary. After the first year, however, and after basic plans, procedures, and tests have been established, the system generally demands little more work than any other approach to teaching. After the first year the task is merely a matter of revising or changing those elements of the approach which need improvement. The overall effect is usually less work for the teacher. For example, with added pupil interest, problems seem to focus on the three degrees of learning activities and evaluation devices for each area of the curriculum. It might be well for the teacher to move into the system gradually. For example, he may want to try the system for reading only during the first year. Then, the second year, he may want to add arithmetic, and so on. A number of factors will determine how rapidly one will want to move into the system.

The success or failure of multigrouping within a classroom depends on the teacher's organizational skill, which tends to improve with experience. Even though the teacher may find the numerous-groups approach more work, if learning is enhanced and attitudes toward self and school are improved, it would seem to be a good investment of effort.

How serious is the danger of stigmas?

There is always the potential threat of stigmatization, regardless of the teaching method utilized. Much depends on techniques of handling details. It must be remembered that each child soon recognizes his own capacities and limitations. The peer group also is aware of each person's capacities and limitations. Some teachers feel that by assigning group names the threat of stigma is minimized. Such names as Bluebirds, Butterflies, Jet Pilots have been used; however, the children will soon know which is the top group and which group is the low group no matter what names are invented. To avoid the stigma of being in the low group, children must belong to non-ability groups for two or three other areas of the curriculum.

Will pupils tend to gravitate toward the "easier" groups?

This is one of the first objections raised by those contemplating such a scheme. Experience usually proves such fears to be groundless, however. By referring briefly back to the list of characteristics of the dull and the bright (page 217) one readily can determine why. One notes that the type of instruction which appeals to the dull tends to be very discouraging to the bright. For example, the dull pupil needs much repetition, whereas the bright child is usually bored by it. It is for this reason that the original *achievement* groups soon evolve into *ability* groups as well. Underachievers in Group III are almost compelled to work to get out of the group because of the type of instruction they experience. If the instructional groups *are* different and if instruction *is* adapted to the particular needs of the bright, the dull, and the average, as is supposed, there seems to be little danger of mass movement to the less difficult groups. Sometimes the average pupil who has been over-achieving meets some disappointment. He may find the work prescribed for Group I too difficult for him. It may be important, therefore, for such a pupil, with the teacher's help, to re-assess his strengths and limitations.

Are discipline problems reduced by group instruction?

People who are interested and who are receiving instruction at their approximate levels of operation tend to conduct themselves in an orderly manner. Some teachers have asserted that they would utilize the procedure if for no other reason than the improvement of class behavior. They contend that the difference usually is quite obvious. Undoubtedly, many factors bear upon such problems, and once again the question of cause and effect is a difficult one. Generally, however, pupils who are continually challenged tend to become more closely identified with their work. An interested pupil seldom creates a discipline problem.

CREATIVE DIFFERENCES IN CHILDREN

In personalizing instruction, a teacher must also accept the challenge of individual differences as far as creativity in children is concerned. For years creativity has been viewed as a fine arts activity. Music, art, drama, and literature seem to elicit the greatest creative output in our schools. Creativity is developed, however, in all aspects of living, and, consequently, in all areas of the elementary school curriculum.[16] Science is a highly technical and a highly creative discipline. Creativity is defined as "sinking down taps into our past experiences and putting these selected experiences together into new patterns, new ideas or new products." [17] In working with elementary children, creative differences must be planned in the activities of the clasroom.

How are creative children identified?

A creative child is one who is daring and courageous in his thinking. He is able to break away from conformity and is open to experience. He

[16] James A. Smith, *Setting Conditions for Creative Teaching In the Elementary School* (Boston: Allyn and Bacon, 1966), pp. 4–7.
[17] *Ibid.*, p. 4.

is ready to have one thing lead to another and can adjust quickly to new developments and changed situations. Creativity may be that successful step into the unknown; getting away from the obvious, the tested, and the safe. Creativity in a child may be the discovery of some new relationship in nature (new to the child) an ability to see things to which the average individual is blind. He is able to see, hear, and feel *more*. He has a real sensitivity to surroundings. A creative child is able to recombine ideas or see new relationships among ideas. Curiosity, imagination, discovery, innovation, and invention are all involved in creativity.[18]

Strang lists six characteristics [19] of a creative child: (1) imagination, the thrill of discovering; (2) purpose, doing something important to him; (3) whole-hearted awareness of beauty and wonder of the world, open to new experiences; (4) questioning mind, puzzled about many things; (5) power of concentration; and (6) the ability for spontaneous play with ideas and relationships of all kinds. Added to this list must be the characteristic of independence, which is exhibited by these children.

What are some ways of providing for creative differences?

The teacher and the classroom environment are the important elements in providing for the creative abilities of children. In providing for these differences, the teacher can encourage a degree of creativity by allowing freedom for energetic and unconventional exploration, but must set up clear protective limits to help children learn to control expressions of their urgent drives. He must allow the children to express their emotions, but help them express them in a positive, creative way. The teacher must provide a classroom environment which will allow the child to do independent, original thinking.

Some specific things each teacher may do to encourage creativity are:

1. Share enthusiasm with the child.

2. Give encouragement and praise for achievement.

3. Encourage the child to search for answers to questions.

---

[18] Paul E. Torrance, "Adventuring in Creativity," *Childhood Education* (October, 1963), p. 79.

[19] Ruth Strang, "The Creative Child," *National Parent-Teacher* (February, 1960), pp. 14–16.

The classroom teacher should help the child, first, to develop a sensitvity to the problem; then, he needs to help the child acquire the knowledge necessary to attack the problem; third, he needs to give the child an opportunity for productivity or action of some kind. A good teacher can encourage pupils to look at the familiar and see new aspects in it. One of the great blocks to creativity is the teacher who will not accept originality. For instance, a little child who has tried to express something original in his painting, or who has written an original bit of music or created a new dance but is forced by the teacher to follow a set pattern is likely to be very much discouraged. Sensitivity is largely encouraged and developed through the reactions of people in the environment to the child's attempts to see and do something different and new. The objective is to make the obvious meaningful.[20]

In providing for creative differences in the classroom, it must be remembered that creativity, as such, is not taught. A teacher must set the conditions for creativity. The teacher and the environment which he creates will aid in providing for the creative differences within children. The importance of ideation experiences (such as brainstorming) is treated in Chapter 6.

What basic problems are involved in developing creative activities in the classroom?

Most classrooms and school programs, hinder, stifle, and may eventually destroy creativity in pupils. Very few teachers prepare themselves to develop creative activities in the classroom. Taylor [21] suggests by his studies that only one out of 20 teachers is psychologically able to listen to an array of new ideas from pupils. Yet, this is a characteristic that is vital in developing creative thinking. First the teacher must be aware of what creativity *is* and then provide opportunities for the development of creativity in each child. One basic problem involved in developing creativity in children is associated with attitudes and direction in teaching. For example, the teacher may direct the children to make tulips from a model so that each tulip is exactly alike. By doing so he may feel he is directing a creative experience.

The crowded elementary school curriculum of today tends to minimize opportunities for development of creativity. So many pressures are placed upon already overcrowded curricula that very little time is avail-

[20] Ruth Strang, *Creativity of Gifted and Talented Children* (New York: Bureau of Publications, Teachers College, Columbia University, 1959), pp. 39–40.
[21] Calvin W. Taylor, "Clues to Creative Teaching: Evoking Creativity," *Instructor* (June, 1964), p. 54.

Harold M. Lambert

Individualizing instruction.

able for creative expression. The elementary teacher who feels his teaching schedule is already overburdened may slight creative ventures. This problem may be solved if the teacher will realize that creativity exists in all phases of human thought and endeavor, and that there is no single mode of creativity.[22] Creativity can readily be developed in the areas of social studies, language arts, science, as well as other areas of the curriculum. Creative ideas can result from the stimulation of a book, class discussion, or a film in any one of the areas.

[22] Regan Carpenter, "Creativity: Its Nature and Nurture," *Education* (March, 1962), pp. 391–395.

Restriction on research, inflexibility of the daily class schedule, discussions which produce tension and anxiety, and grading policies all may block creativity in the classroom. The lack of opportunities for pupils to follow their personal interests, few stimulating educational situations, lack of media, and a teacher who insists that all things must be done one way assures that the creativity of the children in the classroom will be stifled. These problems may be overcome in each classroom by an imaginative teacher and an inviting classroom atmosphere.

PROBLEMS AND PRINCIPLES IN MEETING INDIVIDUAL DIFFERENCES

In the preceding portion of this chapter, special attention was given to the nature and range of individual differences among elementary school children, how teachers generally have attempted to narrow this range for instructional purposes, and current problems associated with these differences. In view of the fact that a methods text should fulfill the criterion of "how to do," a systematized plan or model for classroom grouping was presented. The model presupposes a group of 25–35 unselected pupils. It has been noted that in such groups ability levels will often vary from dull-normal to gifted. Reading levels may vary from lower elementary to upper grade. Likewise, other differences tend to vary from one extreme to another. Some teachers may question the desirability of instructing such groups. *From a teacher's point of view* many would readily agree that the problem *is* difficult. But in a tremendous number of classrooms these conditions *are* representative of the reality of the situation.

There are many classroom situations, however, which do not approximate the conditions cited. The classes may be small; the dull and the bright pupils may be one or two only. This, in some respects, may simplify the problem; but in *any* class important differences exist—differences which need to be considered in teaching. The extent of these differences will, of course, determine what steps the teacher should take to cope with the difficulty. There are a number of general guidelines (made possible through the results of extended research) which bear upon the problem.

The purpose here is to offer general assistance to the teacher in (1) determining individual needs and capacities of pupils; (2) selecting techniques which may be most appropriate for *his* classes; and (3) making an acceptable application of teaching principles which bear upon the problem.

What are some inherent limitations in ability grouping?

In addition to the increased work for the teacher the first year, there are other variables which must be considered:

Classroom facilities. If there is not adequate room for pupils to separate themselves into subgroups the system may be ineffective. Such a problem would almost demand a more traditional approach to teaching.

Class size. Ideally, instruction is a personalized affair. Bringing pupils together in groups greatly facilitates this process. Flanders makes the point when he claims that individualization occurs as individuals fit into the cluster of group activities.[23] He emphasizes the group dimension of "social access" and shows how this factor influences possibilities for interaction among individuals. Subgrouping is desirable when classes become excessively large. Likewise, an upper limit for adequate subgroup functioning can be reached when opportunity for interaction is necessarily curtailed. Classes of more than 40 pupils may become unwieldy for such an operation.

Planning. Careful advance planning is essential. The teacher who is not able or willing to do careful planning should not embark on such a method of teaching.

Use of sociometrics. Some teachers desire to seat pupils sociometrically within the classroom. The type of grouping described may limit, but need not eliminate, such a practice. Instead of seating the entire class on the basis of sociometrics, *each group* may be so arranged.

What are some guiding principles?

There are a number of principles of teaching that may guide a classroom teacher in meeting differences among children. Such guidelines are based on the findings of experimental and applied research and are consistent with the classroom practices recommended in a democracy. They are general, so may need to be modified to meet specific situations.

[23] Ned A. Flanders, "Diagnosing and Utilizing Social Structure in Classroom Learning," in *The Dynamics of Instructional Groups*, 59th Yearbook, Part II, National Society for the Study of Education (Chicago: University of Chicago Press, 1960), Chapter 9.

1. Differences are wide and varied in *every* group of children.

2. For the purposes of class instruction, general scholastic aptitude (IQ) may be considered basic to other differences.

3. General classroom goals are attainable, in some measure, by every pupil.

4. Every pupil has a right to instruction at his level of comprehension.

5. If instruction is adapted to the individual, then pupil appraisal also must be individualized.

6. In large, unselected classes some form of grouping on the basis of achievement or ability is highly desirable.

7. Any grouping arrangement within a class should be flexible, involving many cross-group activities and movement from one group to another.

8. Each child has some degree of creative ability.

9. Competition with one's own progress is more desirable than the usual variety of class competition.

10. Instruction that is most appropriate for the dull generally is inappropriate for the bright, and vice versa.

11. Some *systematic* plan of meeting individual differences is essential, especially in large classes.

12. No one technique of adapting instruction to pupil differences may be considered superior to others. Rather, a combination of techniques is desirable.

SUMMARY

The foregoing chapter is concerned with the impact of human variability on instructional procedures. In the elementary schools of today, differences are extreme. Pressures created by excessively large classes recently have further complicated the problem. Homogeneous grouping has been introduced as a means of narrowing the range of differences. The very complexity of human variability, however, renders the most "homogeneous" group extremely heterogeneous.

In providing for individual differences, teachers have utilized a number of techniques. Enrichment activities, i.e., different learning experiences for certain pupils, have been used effectively, especially in relatively small classes. In large classes, however, the use of subgroups in a flexible arrangement is needed. The exact nature of such an arrangement depends on many factors, not the least of which is the teacher himself. As a means of introducing and clarifying some of the more obvious and still controversial problems associated with subgrouping, an instructional model was introduced. This model was recommended as a guideline for the teacher who would organize his own classes on a flexible, subgroup basis. The need for a systematized approach was emphasized. Creative differences within a group of children were also explored. Ways for providing for these creative differences and problems in developing creativity in the classroom were discussed.

Finally, the reader's attention was directed to general principles and problems associated with techniques of personalizing instruction. Specific characteristics of pupils at the extremes of ability were examined. Neither the gifted nor the dull think like "average" pupils. Accordingly, instructional procedures must vary considerably at different levels of comprehension. As a means of assisting the experienced teacher especially, who must maintain an overall picture of the problem of individual differences, a number of guiding principles were offered. It is hoped that such a list will be useful to those contemplating some systematized approach to the problem.

QUESTIONS FOR STUDY AND DISCUSSION

1. What is the extent and nature of individual differences among elementary school pupils? What problems are encountered when instructional activities are directed toward the "average" pupil? What recent changes in the schools have contributed to the seriousness of the problem?

2. Over the past 50 years numerous school systems have adopted some form of homogeneous grouping, i.e., grouping pupils by classes, usually on the basis of ability or achievement. Most of these school systems, however, have abandoned such plans. Why?

3. What advantages does the suggested model for classroom grouping have over homogeneous grouping? What are the basic features of this model? What problems seem to be associated with such an approach to teaching? Would you recommend such an approach for all teachers? Why or why not? What modifications would you consider appropriate for you? What basic aspects of the problem probably should not be altered? What factors usually prevent the more able pupil from being content with mediocre work in the easiest group?

4. Would some form of subgrouping within a class be appropriate in "homogeneously grouped" classes? Why or why not? What is the basic issue raised with respect to evaluation procedures? Why?

5. Why is it said that each child has a creative potential within him? What type of teacher would foster creativity within his pupils? What kind of classroom atmosphere would be necessary to develop creativity? Why?

SELECTED BIBLIOGRAPHY

Anastasi, Anne, *Individual Differences* (New York: John Wiley & Sons, 1965).

Bond, Guy L. et al., *Just for Fun*, Teaching Guide, Unit One (Chicago: Lyons and Carnahan, 1962).

Burton, William H., *The Guidance of Learning Activities*, 3rd Ed. (New York: Appleton-Century-Crofts, Inc., 1962).

Carpenter, Regan, "Creativity: Its Nature and Nurture," *Education*, 82: 391–395 (March, 1962).

Drews, Elizabeth, "Individual Differences," *The Instructor*, 75: 28+ (May, 1966).

Flanders, Ned A., "Diagnosing and Utilizing Social Structure in Classroom Learning," in *The Dynamics of Instructional Groups*, 59th Yearbook, Part II, National Society for the Study of Education (Chicago: University of Chicago Press, 1960), Chapter 9.

Getzels, Jacob W. and Philip W. Jackson, *Creativity and Intelligence* (New York: John Wiley & Sons, Inc., 1962).

Johnson, Ronald C. and Gene R. Medinnus, *Child Psychology: Behavior and Development* (New York: John Wiley & Sons, Inc., 1965).

Smith, James A., *Setting Conditions for Creative Teaching in the Elementary School* (Boston: Allyn and Bacon, 1966).

Strang, Ruth, "The Creative Child," *National Parent-Teacher*, 54: 14–16 (February, 1960).

Taylor, Calvin W., "Clues to Creative Teaching: Evoking Creativity," *Instructor*, 73: 54 (June, 1964).

Torrance, Paul E., "Adventuring in Creativity," *Childhood Education*, 40: 79–87 (October, 1963).

UNIT THREE

Some Emergent Instructional Patterns

MAN's environment has changed more in the last decade than in the entire preceding fifty years. Three forces have accounted for much of this change as it affects the schools: automation, a population "explosion," and increased federal and state financial obligations. As more and more pupils have flocked to the public schools, increased costs have added immeasurably to an already heavy tax burden. Sometimes, out of sheer desperation, traditionally accepted instructional practices have been modified to meet the needs of the moment. In other instances school systems have taken advantage of available research grants to conduct comprehensive investigation in ways of improving instructional practices. The results have been both encouraging and discouraging. On the one hand, vested interest groups have conducted studies *to prove* the feasibility of mass education at reduced costs. In some cases such groups would cheapen instruction with inadequately prepared teachers instructing groups of three to six hundred. For those who hold the traditional view of education as a process of acquiring knowledge, this type of "crash" program seems a reasonable solution to the dilemma. On the other hand, many interested groups have made the assumption that advances in the area of automation can be used to advantage in the schools. They believe technological advances can offset the pressures of accelerated numbers and spiraling school costs.

It appears likely that critical examination and reexamination of accepted instructional practices will continue indefinitely. Instructional patterns that are fully accepted today may be modified to meet changing conditions. Other instructional patterns will emerge as the fruits of extensive investigation accumulate. At the present time, at least three new instructional patterns seem to be emerging. Two are discussed in this unit: 1) programmed learning and self-instructional devices; and 2) the ungraded school. A third major development, teaching with the aid of television, seems to be a noteworthy extension of the use of audio-visual materials and resources. Accordingly, it is treated in Chapter 16. The reader may want to study the unique features of instructional television in connection with this unit.

All these new instructional patterns have a common characteristic: They are producing major changes in the traditional curricular pattern of our schools. Thus to many they pose a threat to an established order. Others will accept them as a challenge for better and more efficient instruction. In any event, one can safely predict that they are but prototypes of other drastic changes resulting from automation. The reader of this book, as no other teacher in history, will be charged with the responsibility of exercising initiative and creative effort in applying such devices. As a professionally trained person he must maintain a proper balance between those who would "let the machines do the teaching" and those who would rigidly resist innovations, preferring "the good old days." One thing is certain, however, the accelerated changes of our time will continue to influence instructional procedures.

Attempts to individualize certain aspects of instruction in large class groups have been made since the beginning of mass education. While some of the results have been most encouraging (see Unit II), the desirable one-to-one relationship often has been impossible to attain. Individual attention at certain times is essential for effective learning. This is especially evident in the large, heterogeneously grouped classes of today. It appears that a significant breakthrough has come from the very group most directly concerned with problems of behavior. Experimental psychologists have at last cooperated with educational psychologists to apply the principles of reinforcements to classroom instruction. The development of instructional programs has directed attention to instructional goals or purposes and the most efficient sequence for effective learning. Self-instructional devices have become popular in some schools as a means of individualizing instruction. These techniques seem to be most useful in the development of skills. As indicated in Chapter 11, programmed learning and self-instructional devices are not likely to *replace* existing teaching technology; rather, they appear to be useful devices for individualizing instruction when needed.

A second instructional breakthrough that has occurred is the ungraded school. At last the graded concept of the elementary school is being changed. The idea that all children progress at the same rate is not only being challenged, but a curriculum and school organization are now developed to enhance the individual rate of learning for each child. As noted in Chapter 12, many features of the ungraded school are compared with the regular elementary school.

Individualizing Instruction: Programmed Learning and Self-Instructional Devices

. . . . THE effect [of teaching machines] upon each student is surprisingly like that of a private tutor. The comparison holds in several respects: a) There is a constant interchange between program and student. Unlike lectures, textbooks, and the usual audio-visual aids, the machine induces sustained activity. The student is always alert and busy. b) Like a good tutor the machine insists that a given point be thoroughly understood . . . before the student moves on. Lectures, textbooks, and their mechanized equivalents, on the other hand, proceed without making sure that the student understands and easily leave him behind. c) Like a good tutor the machine presents just that material for which the student is ready. It asks him to take only that step which he is at the moment best equipped and most likely to take. d) Like a skillful tutor the machine helps the student to come up with the right answer. It does this in part through the orderly construction of the program and in part with techniques of hinting, prompting, suggesting, and so on. . . . e) Lastly, of course, the machine, like the private tutor, reinforces the student for every correct response, using this immediate feedback not only to shape his behavior most efficiently but to maintain it in strength in a manner which the layman would describe as "holding the student's interest."

B. F. Skinner

The preceding excerpt from Skinner's article appeared in *Science* (1958). It has been seized upon by many both inside and outside the profession as an answer to *all* educational problems. The phrase "teaching machine" is viewed by some as the vehicle by which a "crash" program for education can forge the United States ahead in the Cold War. Today many publishing houses are turning out these machines and others are getting into the act, often ahead of the programs in which they are to be used.

Why the sudden interest in teaching machines? The idea is not new by any means. Dr. Sidney L. Pressey, of Ohio State University, developed machines for instruction and testing in the 1920's. The U. S. Army developed and made widespread use of a self-instructional device before this time, during the first World War, for teaching recruits a proper trigger squeeze.[1] Perhaps more than ever before, the public is beginning to realize the full impact of the present crisis in education. The teacher and classroom shortage of today (along with increased costs) will be dwarfed by the impact of the so-called population explosion which is just now beginning to be felt. The inadequacies of mass instruction are becoming more and more apparent. Self-instructional devices apparently offer promise of "individualized" instruction at less cost than is possible under existing conditions.

Since the early decades of the present century, however, *individualized* instructional techniques have been sought. The Winnetka Plan and the Dalton Plan are two examples. Although they contained many merits, they were eclipsed by pressures brought about through mass education. The distinctive feature of self-instructional devices is that they offer the promise of individualized instruction to large numbers of pupils. Although the ultimate impact of automated teaching devices on the schools is as yet uncertain, they have contributed immensely to the systematization of an allied technique, programmed learning, which promises to render teaching procedures much more scientific than they have ever been before.

A program serves as a textbook for the teaching machine. Yet programming can exist independent of any machine. In fact, a number of textbooks are already appearing which utilize the principles of programming. *Programming* refers to a sequential arrangement of instructional materials in small, discrete units which provides the maximum rate of acquisition and retention. Basically, it is a technique for breaking content into appropriate units or steps for most efficient learning. Although most of the essential principles had been known for some time, it was the popularization of the teaching machine (since 1958) which gave the necessary boost to the instructional program. Most authorities predict that programmed learning will become much more important in the schools of the future.

This chapter is divided into three parts: Programmed Learning; Self-Instructional Devices; and Problems and Principles Involved.

[1] Charles I. Foltz, *The World of Teaching Machines* (Washington, D. C.: Electronic Teaching Laboratories, 1961), p. 3.

PROGRAMMED LEARNING

. . . "programmed learning" is . . . the application of the science of learning to the tasks of training and educating. . . .

At the heart of the method is the conception of human behavior as an orderly process that can be studied and understood in detail by the methods of natural science. . . . It soon became clear that . . . behavior could be brought to a desired final conclusion through a series of graduated stages. In each stage, the key process is the arrangement of a situation such that the behavior . . . produces consequences or effects that will bring the learner to the next stage. The design of these stages and effects is at the heart of all approaches to programmed instruction.[2]

The foregoing quotation from a recent book on programmed learning suggests the basis for a great deal of excitement in the field of education. The process of breaking down a body of content into its constituent elements or steps, asking the pupil to master one step before proceeding to the next, is as old as Plato. Modern research, however, coupled with the development of an effective teaching machine, has refined the procedure into a powerful and efficient teaching tool.

Programmed learning within the last five years has received enthusiastic support from a number of funding agencies. Among them are the United States Air Force, the Office of Naval Research, the Ford and Carnegie Foundations, and any number of schools and colleges throughout the country. According to Cook and Mechner,[3] in case after case significant gains in learning speed and effectiveness have been achieved by instructional programming. As techniques of more effective programming are being discovered and refined, a number of journals and newsletters have been established to assist in the dissemination of this information. Some of these sources have been listed in the latter part of this section.

What are the fundamental features of programmed learning?

Although there are still sharp differences within the profession as to what constitutes the most effective program, there is unanimous agree-

---

[2] Donald Cook and Francis Mechner, "Fundamentals of Programmed Instruction," from Stuart Margulies and Lewis D. Eigen, *Applied Programmed Instruction* (New York: John Wiley & Sons, Inc., 1962), p. 2.

[3] *Ibid.*, p. 3.

ment on a number of fundamental features. These are sound psychological principles which have been developed over several decades of intensive laboratory research.

First, the content is broken down into small steps, called *frames*. These frames may vary in size from two sentences to several small paragraphs.

The last part of each frame calls for a pupil response. This may be filling in a blank, writing out a response, or merely selecting from a number of alternatives.

Next, the pupil is provided with immediate feedback. Thus he is told the correctness of his response; if the response is incorrect he is told why and is ordered to try again. Immediate feedback of responses is called *reinforcement*. Many programs are written in a way that assures a pupil of being right most of the time.

The frames are arranged in a careful sequence, leading the learner toward the desired goal a bit at a time. The degree of difficulty between the frames is usually small, thus enabling the teacher to detect and correct problems along the way.

Programs are aimed at specific goals. This feature largely eliminates "busy work," where the learner is not sure of the basis of his assigned activity.

Program revision is based on pupil responses. The process of recording the pupil's behavior from each frame enables the teacher easily to detect areas of difficulty. Thus the pupil becomes the final authority on the value of a program.

The program is learner-centered. A pupil may vary his speed of learning as he desires. This is in sharp contrast to traditional methods of instruction, which tend to force all pupils into the same mold.[4]

What are the characteristic features of current programs?

At present there are two basic types of programs, depending on the type of response demanded of the pupil. The first of these and the most widely used, popularized by B. F. Skinner and his associates, is known as the *constructed-response* type. The second basic program, developed by Norman A. Crowder and his associates, is known as the *multiple-choice* type of program. Since each type is based on different assumptions with respect to learning, they will be discussed separately.

---

[4] This material is based on an analysis by Edward B. Fry, *Teaching Machines and Programmed Instruction* (New York: McGraw-Hill, Inc., 1963), pp. 2–3.

Constructed-response type. The constructed response type is broken into small steps to reduce pupil errors to a minimum. Pupil errors, according to Skinner's philosophy, may impede learning. Accordingly, the program consists of a *linear* program of overlapping frames. For each frame a pupil must make an *overt* (constructed) response, i.e., he must write out his answer. Skinner and his associates feel that the process of having the learner *construct* his response is a necessary learning process. While they do not deny subjective experience, they contend that only objective behavior can be measured. The pupil is reinforced or rewarded immediately for his response. This "knowledge of results" is assumed to be adequate reinforcement for continued learning. Here are examples from a reading program:

---

hair   My doll has long ___air.

---

hair   I have short h_____r.

By filling in the answers and immediately checking them with the correct response the pupil learns a little at a time until he finally understands the concept involved. Although the correct responses themselves are thought to be reinforcing, Skinner goes one step further and introduces in the questions a series of prompts, hints, or cues. At first these prompts lead the pupil to material from common knowledge that he presumably already possesses. These are called *thematic prompts*. Some thematic prompts are:

---

earns   He works and earn___ money.

---

school   Sue EARNS good grades in sch_____l.

Thematic prompts may make use of opposites and analogies:

Opposites:

---

not   When we are busy it is called work.
             When we are _____ working it is called play.

Analogies:

---

bark   Just as a bird will chirp, a dog will b____k.

Other types of thematic prompts include partial presentation of words, rhyming, matching, similarity of ideas or of grammatical construction, similarity of root words, obvious transpositions, and highly associative words. As the pupil progresses the number of prompts decreases until they *vanish*. In this manner Skinner weans the pupil from the problem, thereby almost forcing him to begin to think creatively for himself. As the pupil continues to progress, the steps may increase in size.

As an additional control over the pupil's response the Skinner group would minimize the effect of distracting stimuli. Thus they favor the use of the teaching machine over the programmed textbook, since it can isolate and present no more than a single item or frame at a time. They believe that through a series of successive approximations each frame should lead the pupil to the ultimate concept.

Multiple-choice type. As opposed to the constructed response type, we have the multiple-choice, "intrinsic" programming technique. This alternative approach was developed by Crowder to train Air Force technicians in problem solving activities. Crowder's group believes that programs should be presented in larger, logical units of a paragraph or more, each of which would *explain* some principle in its entirety. Thus a rule would be stated, followed by a number of examples of the rule. The learner then would be tested by a series of questions on the preceding materials. In essence the response is a choice between variables as in a multiple-choice test item. Incorrect answers suggested by the program are designed to correspond to popular misconceptions revealed by others who have taken the course. Instead of writing in his answers, recommended by the Skinner technique, the pupil merely selects a response.

TABLE 2.   *Contrast between the constructed-response and the multiple-choice type of instructional program.*

Constructed-response Type Program	Multiple-Choice Type Program
1. Pupil writes out (constructs) his response, as an aid in *learning.*	1. Pupil selects his response from among alternatives to *test* the extent of learning.
2. Pupil progresses in small, successive steps.	2. Pupil progresses in larger steps, making use of much larger frames.
3. Each response is reinforced immediately.	3. In case of incorrect responses, pupil is encouraged by explaining why he was incorrect.
4. Errors are reduced to a minimum (not more than 10 percent).	4. Errors used as a basis for digression into remedial programs (called branching).
5. A linear type program, aided by cues or prompts.	5. A complex program, emphasizing important relationships. Few cues or prompts used.

The Crowder group also believes that larger steps are necessary if the pupil is to get a good grounding in basic principles.

One of the most distinctive features of the Crowder technique is provision for continuous review. This is deemed essential to ensure mastery of points. To achieve this end, a technique known as *branching* is introduced. There are two types of branching.

Backward branching is employed when a pupil selects a series of incorrect answers. He is referred to a remedial sequence of steps designed to give him a fresh approach to the problem. When he has mastered that material he is led back to the main line of the problem.

Forward branching enables a pupil to skip steps of the material which he already knows. This, according to Crowder, is especially useful to the bright pupil who can grasp the material quickly.

The Crowder group uses only a few prompts, relying heavily on explanations of the material.

Analytically, the branching program is related to the multiple-choice examination, in contrast to the linear program technique where a response must be constructed. The pupil is faced with a *recognition* task (as opposed to a *recall* task in the constructed program), choosing between a number of alternatives. Unlike the multiple-choice test, however, the program provides immediate feedback by explaining why a particular item was correct (or incorrect).[5] Both program types lend themselves to publication in the form of books, discussed later in this section.

For clarification, the basic differences between the two types of programs are summarized in Table 2.

What are the essential steps in programming?

The task of developing adequate instructional programs must involve the individual classroom teacher. While the programming technique is rather complicated, the individual teacher is the person best qualified to judge the adequacy of a program. Many programs have been developed commercially and in some cases have proven quite effective. There *are* important differences from school to school, however, which must be considered. As someone once said, "It is easier to teach a physicist programming than it is to teach a programmer physics." There is a current trend toward the team approach to programming, involving both subject matter specialists and trained psychologists.

Essential steps in programming are outlined below.

Step 1. Determine the scope of the subject. How much detail does the programmer desire to include? Is the program to be used to the exclusion of other techniques and devices?

Step 2. Translate the concepts to be learned into behavioral terms. What verbal skills should the pupil have? What questions should he be able to answer? What discriminations should he be able to make?

Step 3. Determine if there is any logical sequence which seems to suggest an efficient way to organize the program.

Step 4. Select terms to be defined. State their relationships (RULEG system).

1. List the essential concepts (rules) on intersecting horizontal and vertical axes (ru matrix).

2. Collect examples of concepts in all their possible interrelationships.

3. Put in an ordered sequence.

4. Write examples which define the concepts, employing terms you want the pupil to learn.[6]

---

[5] Edward J. Green, *The Learning Process and Programmed Instruction* (New York: Holt, Rinehart & Winston, Inc., 1962), p. 144.

[6] Based on an analysis by Green, *ibid.*, pp. 148–151.

TABLE 3.   *Sample Ruleg Matrix*

Relationship	Ru 1	Ru 2	Ru 3
Ru 1	Definition of Ru 1	Ru 2 related to Ru 1	Ru 3 related to Ru 1
Ru 2	Ru 1 related to Ru 2	Definition of Ru 2	Ru 3 related to Ru 2
Ru 3	Ru 1 related to Ru 3	Ru 2 related to Ru 3	Definition of Ru 3

As Table 3 suggests, the concepts (rules) are supported with frames designed to bring out important relationships.[7]

Step 5. The program is tried on pupils and revised on the basis of data gained.

The outstanding advantage of programming, as seen from the foregoing description, is that it forces the teacher to concentrate on major concepts, their relationships, and a desirable sequence of presentation. Too often under traditional classroom situations the essential elements remain obscured by extraneous examples and relationships.

How does one assess an instructional program?

A most difficult task facing the user of instructional programs is that of evaluation. How is one to judge the merits or quality of a program? Although there are as yet no concrete rules to follow, a number of suggestions are possible.

In the first place, the final test of a program is its effectiveness with the pupils for whom it was designed. It might be desirable to try a new program on a small sample of a group before it is tried out with an entire class.

Since programming tends to begin with the simple and move toward the complex, the teacher can easily conclude that a program is too simple for his group. Thus he should inspect the entire program if he desires to judge for himself on the matter.

One definite indication of the appropriateness of the Skinner-type program is the error rate. This should usually be below 10 percent. A

---

[7] For a thorough analysis of the RULEG system, the reader is referred to Fry, *op. cit.,* pp. 53–58.

low error rate, however, is not a definite indication of an appropriate program, for it is entirely possible that the program is too easy.

Another important factor is pacing. If a training session continues too long without a break, a decided increase in error rate occurs. A high error rate soon after pupils begin a program, however, suggests that the program is too difficult.

A good program is characterized by frames which are precise and clearly stated. A common indication of poor programming is repeated demands for the same response. Furthermore, the number of prompts or cues can be examined. Too many prompts render error rate an unreliable index.

Each frame should contain one and only one idea. Review material, combined with a new idea, however, is an acceptable procedure. In any event, the frames should be arranged in order from simple to complex.

If the program is to be used along with other instructional techniques, the data must be explicitly stated in the program. Other features include such factors as vocabulary level, variety of examples, and adequacy of explanations. Again, the ultimate test of an instructional program rests with its effect on the pupils involved.

With the rapid increase in instructional programs and devices there is a very real danger of their misuse. Recognizing the danger, a set of interim guidelines was released in May, 1961, by a Joint Committee on Self-Instructional Materials and Devices, consisting of representatives of the American Educational Research Association, the American Psychological Association, and the Department of Audio-Visual Instruction of the National Education Association. This statement has been reproduced as follows:

The use of self-instructional programmed learning materials in teaching machines and similar devices represents a potential contribution of great importance to American education. But this contribution can be realized best only if users have information with which to evaluate self-instructional materials. Accordingly, the following interim guidelines have been prepared.

1. Teaching machines do not, in themselves, teach. Rather, the teaching is done by a program of instructional materials presented by the teaching machine. Any evaluation of a teaching machine thus requires an assessment of the availability and quality of programs for each type of machine, as well as its mechanical dependability.

2. A variety of programmed materials is becoming available, but not all programs will fit all machines. Thus only those programs compatible with a particular machine can be considered as available for use with it. A list of commercially available programs and devices may be obtained from the Department of Audio-Visual Instruction, National Education Association, 1201 Sixteenth Street, N.W., Washington 6, D. C. (Cost 50 cents.)

3. In evaluating the specific content which a self-instructional program purports to teach, the program can be examined to determine what the student is required to do and whether this reflects the kind of competence which the educator wishes to achieve. Like other educational materials, programs labeled with the name of a particular subject matter vary widely with respect to content and instructional objectives.

4. Just any set of question and answer material does not constitute a self-instructional program. One type of self-instructional material proceeds by small steps requiring frequent responses. These steps can be examined to see if they embody a careful, logical progression of the subject matter. Items in such a program are designed so that the student will respond to the critical aspects of each item or will perform the important operation which that item was meant to teach. Furthermore, such programs generally provide a wide range of examples illustrating each principle or concept.

5. Self-instructional materials are designed to adapt to individual differences by allowing each student to proceed at his own rate. Some types of self-instructional programs further adapt by "branching" to alternate material. For this purpose, questions are designed to diagnose the student's needs and to provide alternate material suited to these needs. The material is designed so that the choice of answer to a particular question determines which items will be presented next. Incorrect answers take the student to items containing information designed to correct the error before continuing through the sequence.

6. An important feature of almost all self-instructional materials is the record of the student's responses, which provides a basis for revising the program. The prospective purchaser should ask about the extent to which revision has been based on student response and how the preliminary tryout was conducted.

7. The effectiveness of a self-instructional program can be assessed by finding out what students actually learn and remember from the program. The prospective purchaser should find out whether such data are available and for what kinds of students and under what conditions the data were obtained.

8. Active experimentation with self-instructional materials and devices in school systems is to be encouraged prior to large scale adoption.*

How can the teacher use such a program?

Predictions that instructional programming foreshadows an important breakthrough in the science of teaching are coming from many sources, both within and outside the profession. Indeed, few teachers can offer many serious objections, for the technique provides a systematized approach to a number of problems that for years have impeded the effectiveness of teaching. A classic example is seen in the statement of purposes or goals, described in Chapter 4. While most teachers can

* Distributed by the Department of Audio-Visual Instruction, National Education Association, Washington, D.C.

intellectually accept the desirability of stating goals in behavioral terms, too often the task has been imperfectly understood as "just too much bother." Instructional programming cannot be used until such a task is achieved. Furthermore, the technique clearly defines the step-by-step process (in terms of overt behavior) essential to realization of the goal. The big question confronting the reader of this book, however, probably relates to the immediate use of such programs. When a teacher is introduced to any new technique he must in some way visualize how it can be used. The most popular use of programmed instruction, of course, has been with the automatic teaching machine. This device is treated in the section following. It seems appropriate at this time to suggest some practical uses of instructional programming that are independent of the teaching machine.

Within the past few years a great deal of attention has been directed to the use of programmed textbooks. Generally they have taken two rather distinct forms: *the horizontal levels* and the *scrambled text*. When using the horizontal levels text (patterned after the Skinner approach to programming) the reader begins with the top level of a section and proceeds through the text with that level only, turning pages until that section is completed. He then begins the second level, and so on, until he completes the text. Correct answers are presented on the page following the item or "frame."

The scrambled text is based on the Crowder approach to programming. The pupil is informed whether his response is incorrect or not, and why. Answers, of the multiple-choice type, are followed by a page number. The pupil chooses an answer and turns to the page indicated. If the response was correct a short explanation of the process involved is presented on the indicated page and the pupil is advanced to the next step. If the response was incorrect the process is reexplained on the indicated page. The pupil is directed to try again until the correct response is made and he is passed on to the next problem.

The effectiveness of each type of programmed textbook has been thoroughly demonstrated. In fact, a number of researchers have reported that learning proceeded as well with the programmed text or with other substitute devices as with mechanical teaching machines. Other research findings indicate that pupils learn about as much with a scrambled order text as with a tightly developed sequenced text. Concern for pupil "cheating" from programmed texts, by looking ahead for the answers, has been expressed frequently. On the basis of research findings, however, this does not seem to be a critical issue.[8]

The big issue today is how much of the teaching task is to be

[8] L. M. Stolurow, "Let's be Informed on Programmed Instruction," *Phi Delta Kappan*, 44: 255–257 (March, 1963).

relegated to programmed materials. While few of the most ardent enthusiasts would suggest that such a device could replace the teacher, many *talk* as if this very thing will happen. Furthermore, most of the commercially prepared programs are designed to cover the entire instructional content of given courses of study. In the field of beginning reading instruction, for example, complete programs have been developed. Thelen [9] seems to get to the heart of the matter when he identifies the basic issue as conditioning versus insightful learning. He points out that 80 percent of the current programs are based on a conditioning type of learning and that the other 20 percent are inadequately developed for the insightful type of learning. If, as Thelen suggests, insightful learning needs greater emphasis and if current programs are inadequate for such a task, it follows that today's programs might be legitimately restricted to the teaching of rote skills.

When learning is viewed as a basic process of inquiry, it seems likely that the program, in many cases at least, will need to be supplemented by class discussion or some other technique involving reflective thought. Such techniques would emphasize pupil speculations and conclusions and how pupils arrived at their conclusions.

A practical use of programmed materials is suggested by the multiple-choice (Crowder) type. The reader will recall that the pupil is presented with a number of alternatives from which to choose. If he is incorrect, he is informed of the basis of his error and instructed to try again. Now most teachers employ the multiple-choice test item. Furthermore, in many cases they go over such tests with their classes. While the process is deemed educationally desirable, a number of persistent problems arise. What is to be done with the pupil who answers most of the items correctly? How about the pupil who can answer few of the items? How is one to handle a situation in which the teacher is unable to explain (on the spur of the moment) why a particular foil is unacceptable? By using the Crowder technique as a basis a teacher can easily begin his own programming by writing out a reason for the correctness or incorrectness of *each foil*, and making copies available to each individual. Thus *tests* can be used as "programmed teaching devices" on an *individual basis*.

By trying out instructional programs for special purposes, a teacher should soon discover many applications for helping individual pupils. Sometimes these may take the form of remedial work, work to be made up as a result of excessive absences, and rote memorization of terms, definitions, and rules. As Ramsey [10] points out, one publisher has pro-

---

[9] Herbert A. Thelen, "Programmed Instruction: Insight Versus Conditioning," *Education*, 83, No. 7: 416–420 (March, 1963).

[10] Curtis P. Ramsey, "Curriculum Issues in Programmed Instruction," *Education*, 83, No. 7: 412–415 (March, 1963).

duced discrete units in social studies, designed as supplemental to the personal aspects of teaching.

SELF-INSTRUCTIONAL DEVICES

A self-instructional device (frequently referred to as a teaching machine) is merely a mechanical device for presenting to a pupil a succession of instructional items requiring some discriminative response and providing him with an immediate check on the accuracy of his response. Although a number of different designs have been developed, they all have common features.

1. A question or problem is presented to the pupil . . . [and] seen through a window. . . .

2. Some provision is made for the operator to record his answer. In some machines he indicates his selection from a number of alternative answers presented. In other machines he writes out an answer he has constructed.

3. As soon as his answer has been recorded, a pupil may obtain check on his accuracy. Some machines check the answer automatically. Others expose the correct answer for the pupil to evaluate his own work.

4. The sequence in which the items are presented is usually controlled by the machine.

5. The timing of the questions is usually under the control of the pupil. Since these machines are designed for individual use, each pupil may proceed at his own pace.[11]

The most commonly used device was designed by Dr. Skinner at Harvard University. A more complex machine, the talking typewriter, developed by Dr. Moore, is also available for classroom use today.

Dr. Skinner's machine employs questions that are shown one at a time. The correct answer is not exposed until the pupil has written an answer on an exposed frame of paper tape. When the pupil writes an answer with which he is satisfied he raises the lower lever at the left front of the machine. This exposes the correct answer and moves the pupil's answer under a transparent cover, where he can see it but can no longer change it. Thus the pupil can compare his answer with the correct answer. If he was correct he moves the lever to the right, thereby instructing the machine to mark his answer correct and reducing the number of times the question will appear again. (The number of corrections required

[11] John W. Blyth, "Teaching Machines and Human Beings," *The Educational Record*, 41: 116–125 (April, 1960).

for each question may be either one or two, depending on the way it is set.) The next question appears as soon as the lever is returned to the lower position. The talking typewriter responds audibly to the correct or incorrect responses made by the child and also tells the child what to do next. With the use of programmed tapes and electronics a child is able to type, and through typing learn to read.

How may these devices be used effectively?

Actually this question is at present unanswerable. Programmed learning and self-instructional devices are being tried now in a relatively few schools. Techniques which are most effective for the most part have not been tried, tested under experimental conditions, or reported. Yet there is every indication that many students who study this text will be using these devices. It seems appropriate, therefore, to direct attention to some of the techniques which are *likely* to be involved.

In the first place, it is highly unlikely that many classrooms will be equipped with teaching machines for *every* pupil in the immediate future. The cost of programming is difficult, time-consuming, and expensive. As Foltz points out, "a good program requires the services of a course specialist, a psychologist with knowledge of programming techniques and some knowledge of the course material, and often special technical personnel. Estimates for the original cost of a program for a single term run as high as $175,000." [12] Moreover, today good teaching machines are expensive, ranging from $20 to $250 each. This would suggest that, in many instances, a teacher might be confronted with a few machines in his classroom to be used to *supplement* regular class instruction. If a pupil is experiencing difficulty the teacher may use the machine as a diagnostic instrument—finding the learner's errors so that a specific type of practice can be given. In some cases the machine itself may be used to provide the remedial assistance, thus enabling the teacher to use his time more efficiently with the rest of the pupils. A child who is ahead of his classmates likewise may profit from the teaching machine if "programs in depth" are available. Pupils who enter the class late; those who transfer into the class; or those who have had extensive absences may similarly profit from self-instructional devices. If enough teaching machines are made available in the individual classroom, a group may be divided for purposes of instruction, thus enabling all pupils at some time to receive the benefits of this type of instruction.

The experimental evidence now available is generally concerned with

[12] Foltz, *op. cit.*, p. 26.

situations in which each pupil has had the benefit of a teaching machine. In a few cases elementary school classrooms already have been equipped in this manner and the number is rapidly increasing. How, then, will machines be used to augment class instruction when each pupil has access to one? Will they assume the role of total teaching, possibly replacing the teacher? This seems highly unlikely! Individual teachers will be needed where self-instruction ends. This point will be amplified further in the section devoted to limitations of self-instructional devices. After having completed a topic with the aid of programmed instruction, pupils will probably need the benefit of *group* analysis and discussion. There is a great deal of evidence to support the contention that the functioning of a group *as a group* can lead pupils to a higher degree of creativity and openness of experience than would ever be possible through purely individualized instruction. Moreover, it must be remembered that through self-instruction the pupil usually is informed that he is *either* correct or incorrect from a given context. It is essential that the teacher guide pupils into seeing the shades of gray between the two poles. Seldom will categorical "rights" and "wrongs" suffice. Many times it is necessary to help pupils visualize the different conditions and circumstances that may influence the "rightness" or "wrongness" of some fact, proposition, or event.

Why are these devices being so enthusiastically acclaimed?

Self-instructional devices are being enthusiastically endorsed by many because of the numerous (theoretical) values which may be derived from them. For the first time in the history of teaching there is the possibility of freeing the teacher from many necessary but monotonous activities. Programmed learning, for example, is particularly useful in certain well-defined areas: memory of facts, procedures, and the mastering of simple concepts and principles. It can also be used effectively as a testing device. Thus, by freeing teachers from such activities as drill, listening to recitation, and the marking of objective examinations, more time is available for the purely creative aspects of teaching.

The advocates of self-instructional devices are quick to point out the increased teaching efficiency made possible. Most teachers would readily admit that the average pupil is actively engaged or interested in class instruction *far less* than is theoretically possible. Foltz cites one survey which revealed that the average pupil was actively engaged or interested in classroom activity only 20 percent of the time. Preliminary studies with self-instructional devices indicate that learning time may be decreased as much as 50 percent over that needed in conventional classrooms. In 15 minutes on a good programmed instructional sequence, the average pupil probably devotes more active attention to instructional materials than he does in the course of one full class period in the conventional classroom.

Teaching machines are diagnostic. The teacher does not have to take valuable class or conference time in locating a pupil's area of difficulty. He knows precisely the basis for further work. In conventional situations a teacher may spend much time in merely locating an area of difficulty.

Perhaps the most important advantage of programmed learning is the reinforcement of responses provided. Skinner and his associates have accumulated evidence that a correct response needs to be reinforced in the shortest possible interval of time. It has been established that such reinforcement encourages the pupil to continue his efforts. Numerous studies indicate that maximum learning occurs when a correct response is reinforced one-third to one-half second after it is made. Conventional teaching cannot even approach this condition.

Teaching machines seem ideally suited to the problem of providing for individual differences, since a slow pupil may take as much time as he needs to master a problem. At the same time a bright pupil can also proceed at his own rate. He no longer need become bored or lose interest as a result of his superior ability to assimilate the material. Some enthusiasts even see this as a means of minimizing the emotional problems that inevitably arise from learning difficulties.

Finally, self-instructional techniques are a means of assuring greater mastery as a pupil advances from one grade to another. Under existing conditions the less able child often experiences tremendous emotional difficulty if he is retained in a grade. If, on the other hand, he is passed he is expected to master materials for which he has an inadequate foundation. Self-instructional devices, it is believed, can correct this problem through careful programming of fundamental concepts.

PROBLEMS AND PRINCIPLES INVOLVED IN PROGRAMMED LEARNING AND SELF-INSTRUCTIONAL DEVICES

In the preceding sections of this chapter an effort was made to acquaint the teacher with techniques of programming and some of the advantages of self-instructional devices. Let us now take a look at the problems and principles that govern their use. Programmed learning and self-instructional devices, perhaps more than any other techniques, represent the work of psychologists. For years there has been felt a need to place teaching on a more scientific footing. To many psychologists and educators alike, self-instructional devices represent a major step in this direction.

What are some basic problems associated with these methods?

Self-instructional devices represent a "new" development in the field of teaching. For all practical purposes their appearance did not begin until the late 1950's. The many problems associated with their use are in part related to their newness. Many of these problems will be corrected as experimentation moves forward. There are some problems, however, which seem to be more serious. They, too, will become more clearly delineated under the practical test of classroom experience. Nevertheless, we should now consider some of the more serious problems and hazards associated with self-instruction.

One of the greatest claims for programmed learning and self-instructional devices is that these techniques, in effect, serve as a private tutor. It is claimed that the machine is purely objective, "displaying more patience than is *humanly* possible." But, as Pressey [13] points out, ". . . a wise tutor does not all the time lean over a student's shoulder, continuously asking very easy questions." Rather, he sets the tasks, asks questions which stimulate critical thought, reassures the pupil when he is right, guides him aright when he is wrong, and tries to help him become progressively able to proceed on his own. Although Pressey concedes the possible value of self-instructional techniques for very difficult or special content material or for special groups of young children, he questions the desirability in many cases where the *older* child is already somewhat knowledgeable.

One of the most common criticisms of self-instructional techniques is the limited application possible. Critics contend that many of the more important outcomes of learning cannot be tapped in this manner. A critic asks, "How can a machine create a desire for reading? How can self-instruction develop social awareness? Can art appreciation be gained in this manner?" The point is made that probably most reading, listen-

[13] Sidney L. Pressey, "Some Perspectives and Major Problems Regarding 'Teaching Machines,'" from A. A. Lumsdaine and Robert Glaser, Eds., *Teaching Machines and Programmed Learning* (Washington, D. C.: Department of Audio-Visual Instruction, National Education Association, 1960).

ing, and viewing comprise a very complex experience, just as the values which are sought are also complex.

Even the *individualizing* feature of self-instructional devices which is so loudly acclaimed by its adherents is sharply criticized by critics. They wonder how such techniques will assist the socialization process of pupils. From kindergarten through the 8th grade the importance of living, working, and playing with others is emphasized. Some of the most brilliant minds of our time have been removed from society simply because they have demonstrated an inability to adjust to the rules established by that society. To claim the impersonal nature of such techniques as an asset is inconsistent with reality, say the critics. Social adjustment is an essential condition for effective learning.

One of the chief advantages seen from use of self-instructional devices is their unique manner of providing for individual differences of pupils. The child can work at his own rate, it is claimed. Again, the critics take issue, pointing out that since the early days of Binet testing it has been known that the mental age of a sixth grade class, for example, may range from age 7 to age 17. Reading level may vary as much as eight years! How can one program meet the needs of all? This problem, fortunately, has been studied somewhat even at this early date. Stolurow, after reviewing a number of research studies concerned with the problem, concluded that ". . . available research on the relationship between the learner's ability and his gains in learning do not justify the assumption that different programs have to be written for high and low ability groups." [14] He offers the hypothesis that a single program probably can be prepared for a wide range of abilities. Yet, if these findings are true, they contradict many other findings in the area of individual differences.

Perhaps the main concern relates to the psychological basis for programmed learning and self-instructional devices. The Skinner technique, presently the most popular, is based on an associational theory of learning. It is presumed that the learner must progress, one step at a time, until he finally gains the concept. Other psychologists, however, just as stoutly claim that the learner needs first to view the concept as an entity, filling in the necessary parts afterward. The Crowder group apparently favors such an approach. While each group admits the need for *both* approaches in certain situations, they do *not* agree on when and where one approach may be preferable to the other. Likewise, the problem of reinforcement of responses is a source of controversy. Al-

[14] Lawrence M. Stolurow, *Teaching by Machine* (Washington, D. C.: U. S. Department of Health, Education and Welfare, Cooperative Research Monograph No. 6, 1961), p. 59.

though both groups recognize the need for reinforcement, they do *not* agree as to the nature or frequency of this reinforcement.

Another source of contention among the "experts" is the nature of "stepping" and the use of prompts. The fact remains that the size of steps needed and the use and frequency of prompts has not been experimentally established. It seems logical that size of the steps and nature of prompts should vary with the nature of the material, the grade level of the pupil, and possibly his ability level. As yet no one is certain how critical these problems are.

A similar problem is associated with backward and forward branching. One who fails to respond correctly to a series of questions is taken backward for "remedial" work. Similarly, one skips certain schedules if he responds correctly. It is possible that "skipping" may leave so many gaps in any close-woven program that it leaves the pupil with a series of disconnected questions. If so, how can one be assured that he will grasp the overall concept effectively?

A more practical consideration concerns development of programs. For years it has been assumed that the educational needs of children in one community may be substantially different from those of children in another community. Can a program for arithmetic in school A, for example, be used in an arithmetic class in school B? Can two teachers in the *same* school who teach the *same* subject use identical programs? If not, who is going to write the programs? How much time, energy, and expense will be involved?

At the present time the most challenging problem is that of defining, in behavioral terms, what responses are needed. As indicated in Chapter 3, teachers have been prone to state their goals as complex generalizations, e.g., "to understand . . . , to appreciate. . . ." For the most part teachers lack training in techniques of reducing learning to the overt responses which would be indicative of progress or goal fulfillment. While such inadequacies are not being defended as professionally sound, they do represent realities which must be met. If the classroom teacher is unable to accomplish a task, who can do it for him? After all, an outside individual usually cannot understand the particular needs of a group as well as the classroom teacher.

Finally, programmed learning and self-instructional devices are expensive. As indicated earlier, the cost of a program for a single term may run as high as $175,000. Today machines costs $20–$250 each. If one is to be provided for every pupil the total cost may be prohibitive. One talking typewriter costs approximately $40,000. There is also the problem of adjusting the size of classrooms. It has been suggested that to provide adequate space for a teaching machine for every pupil the number of square feet of floor space in the conventional classroom would have to be at least doubled.

What are some of the basic principles in construction?

The principles which follow, for the most part, have been derived from carefully controlled research. Although many have been known for some time, they apply especially to programmed learning and to some extent indicate why many psychologists are enthusiastic about the prospects offered through programmed learning and self-instructional devices. The principles which follow are based on programming techniques developed by B. F. Skinner and his associates.

1. Learning occurs (behavior is learned) as a pupil responds or reacts. Such responses should be overt so that appropriate feedback can be applied by the teaching machine.

2. The learner is led to become progressively more independent of previously learned behavior. Prompts which are numerous in the early stages of a program are gradually eliminated as learning progresses.

3. Learning is enhanced when it is systematically reinforced. This simply means that once a desired behavior has been performed the learner should be made aware of his progress immediately following the response.

4. A high proportion of correct responses is necessary. This is simply another way of stating that the accumulation of errors serves as punishment. It has been noted that programs which are difficult enough to result in many errors are extremely frustrating to the learner.

5. Learning progresses from simple to more complex relationships.

6. Learning is an individual experience.

7. Learning proceeds (transfers) from the known to the unknown. Programmed learning begins by evoking responses which are already known. Then the sequence leads to responses to new stimuli.

8. Programmed learning is based on a detailed analysis of the pupil behaviors deemed necessary for learning.

9. A pupil works and learns at his own rate.

10. Steps between each item are small. Although this principle has been subject to some controversy, most psychologists concede that size of the step is somewhat dependent on the situation.

What principles govern their use?

As with all instructional techniques, the effectiveness of self-instructional devices depends on their appropriate *use*. In the final analysis, it is the classroom teacher who is the controlling factor in determining how effective these devices may be. A number of principles apply:

1. At present, programmed learning and teaching machines will *supplement* other instructional techniques only.

2. Pupils can "loaf on the job" when using a self-instructional device. The teacher needs to check their progress from time to time.

3. Sometimes a program may be too difficult. If not corrected the experience may be extremely frustrating and demoralizing to the child.

4. Self-instructional devices cannot supply *all* the data needed in many areas of instruction. Planned discussion periods at intervals are essential.

5. Self-instruction is not equally effective in all areas. For example, it has so far been most effective in the areas of mental skills, procedures, and the formulation of simple concepts and principles.

6. Automated teaching devices are as yet incapable of coping with the so-called intangibles of instruction, such as values, creativity, and group processes.

7. The teacher must determine how well a program meets the instructional objectives of his particular class.

8. Various personal factors (e.g., health, age, interests, and vitality) influence the length of sustained effort a child can tolerate for a program.

What implications do programmed and self-instructional devices have for teaching?

It seems evident at this time that programmed learning is here to stay. The increased pressure of mass education, the individualized instructional features involved, and the sound psychological basis for such a technique is almost overwhelming. Mechanical self-instructional devices may represent a major break-through in education at a time of crisis. Nevertheless, it is still too early to predict how much influence they will have on the profession as a whole.

More important than the role of the devices and the programs themselves, however, is the fact that these means of instruction force the teacher to become explicit about both his instructional goals and the processes employed in attaining them. Explicit identification of variables and functional relationships which influence modification of behavior through instruction will undoubtedly continue as a basis for attempts to improve education.

Another significant feature of the programmed learning movement is its source. For years experimental psychologists have been content to restrict their activities to the study of rats, cats, and other laboratory animals. Sometimes they have looked disdainfully at professional educators who were attempting to work with complex human beings. For the first time in years there is real hope that these behavior specialists will be able to work with practitioners in the field. The reciprocal interaction between laboratory research and practical tryout is essential.

It seems likely, then, that programmed learning is destined to have a positive, beneficial effect on the profession of teaching. This effect will be achieved, however, only if reasonable prudence and caution are used. All too frequently educators (and others) have permitted the pendulum to swing too far, too fast. It is evident, even today, that self-instructional devices cannot do everything. They will not replace the teacher as some enthusiasts predict. What they may do, however, is free him from many unnecessary routines, thereby enabling him to bring into play forces of creativity and inspiration so urgently needed.

SUMMARY

The foregoing chapter represents an attempt to acquaint the teacher with the whole problem of programmed learning and self-instructional devices. Attempts have been made to acquaint the teacher with some of the complex problems of programming instruction. The construction of a program, for example, necessitates a sequential arrangement of instructional materials which will provide optimum learning and retention. Questions must be stated and answers provided which will continuously reinforce or encourage the learner. In addition, necessary *prompts* must be included, especially in the early phases of programming.

The self-instructional device, frequently known as a teaching machine, is a mechanism which is designed to accommodate programming. It must be self-operating, enabling the learner to indicate his response before it moves on to the next item.

Relatively little emphasis has been given to classroom techniques. In the first place, programming and teaching machines are *self*-instructional! Furthermore, their recency of development does not allow enough time for any systematic analysis. It is felt, however, that self-instructional techniques can be used to *supplement* other techniques.

Among the many potential values of these devices is their individualized nature. At last there is some promise of private instruction, somewhat akin to tutorial techniques, which can be used with large numbers of children.

A great deal of emphasis was given to principles. These were divided into purely psychological principles, which provide a *basis* for the use of self-instructional devices, and teaching principles, which serve as instructional guidelines.

Finally, attention was directed toward some of the many problems and hazards associated with programmed learning and self-instructional devices. Many of the problems relate to the newness of the movement. Others are more basic, going back to the theoretical bases involved. Many of these problems may be identified and resolved in the near future. Until that time the teacher is urged to beware of bandwagon approaches to the problems of instruction.

QUESTIONS FOR STUDY AND DISCUSSION

1. What is the essential relationship between teaching machines and programmed learning? Why did the popularization of the automatic teaching machine contribute to programmed learning?

2. What are the basic contributions of programmed learning? What novel ideas, if any, are employed?

3. What factors could render programmed learning ineffective for the basic processes of inquiry? Can you suggest allied techniques which might overcome some of these problems?

4. What are the essential differences between the Skinner-type and the Crowder-type programs? Which one seems more versatile in coping with the processes of inquiry? (You might want to refer to Chapter 3 again before you attempt to answer this question.)

5. What practical advantages do you see in self-instructional devices and programmed learning? What limitations are evident? It has been said that self-instructional devices tend to focus attention on an aspect of instruction (conditioning processes) which is already overemphasized. Do you agree or disagree? Why or why not?

SELECTED BIBLIOGRAPHY

Arnstine, Donald G., "The Language and Values of Programmed Instruction," *Educational Forum*, 28, No. 2: 219–226; 337–346 (January,

March, 1964). Reply by Paul Komisar and James E. McCellan, "Professor Arnstine and Programmed Instruction," *Educational Forum*, 29, No. 4: 416–475 (May, 1965).

Briggs, Leslie J., "The Teacher and Programmed Instruction; Roles and Potentials," *Audio Visual Instruction*, 9, No. 5: 273–276 (May, 1964).

Fry, Edward B., *Teaching Machines and Programmed Instruction* (New York: McGraw-Hill, Inc., 1963).

Garner, Wayne L., *Programmed Instruction* (New York: Center for Applied Research in Education, 1966).

Green, Edward J., *The Learning Process and Programmed Instruction* (New York: Holt, Rinehart & Winston, Inc., 1962).

Lumsdaine, Robert, *Teaching Machines and Programmed Learning, II* (Washir~ton, D. C.: Department of Audio-Visual Instruction, National Education Association, 1965).

National Education Association, *Selection and Use of Programmed Materials: A Handbook for 'i eachers* (Washington, D. C.: Department of Audio-Visual Instruction, National Education Association, 1965).

National Society for the Study of Education, *Programmed Teaching*. 66th Yearbook, Part 2 (Chicago: University of Chicago Press, 1967).

Ramsey, Curtis P., "Curriculum Issues in Programmed Instruction," *Education*, 83, No. 7: 412–415 (March, 1963).

Raphael, Sister M., "The Teaching Machine: Monster or Miracle?", *The Catholic School Journal*, 65, No. 5: 25–28 (May, 1965).

Skinner, B. F., "Teaching Machines," *Science*, 128: 967–977 (October 24, 1958).

Changing School Organization:
The Ungraded School

"Poor Kenny White," exclaimed Mrs. Sandon, "he just doesn't fit into my middle reading group but he does read better than the children who are in my low reading group." "What can I do?" she asked herself.

What can Mrs. Sandon do? Should Kenny be frustrated in his reading program by being placed in the middle reading group? Or should Kenny be assigned to the low reading group perhaps to become unchallenged and bored? How often do such problems arise? It is quite likely that each elementary school child will at some time "stand out" from his class subgroups, which have almost become a tradition in today's school. Even if he should "fit" into a reading group, he also varies in spelling, arithmetic, social studies, science, language arts, music, art, physical and health education. Not only are curriculum problems to be considered, but also the difficulty of timing and pacing pupils in the schools.

Mr. Wilson complained, "Merilee always finishes ahead of the class in her assignments. I'm tired of thinking up things to keep her busy while she is waiting for the other pupils in her class to complete their work. I *can not* give her material that will be covered next year in school. What can I do for her?"

This incident is also a common problem for the traditional elementary school teacher.

In short, increased enrollment in the elementary school has again focused attention upon a basic educational concept: *Each pupil progresses at his own rate.* Since mastery of the basic skills is not completed in any one year, the traditional grade-a-year plan has been recently reexamined. It is recognized that some pupils can complete the elementary

259

curriculum in *less* time than is normally allotted; others need *more* time for the basic essentials. The obvious solution is the *ungraded school.* This new curriculum plan is built upon the fundamental principle that each child is different and that he must be free to progress at his own rate of development through the elementary school's curriculum.

This chapter is divided into three parts. The first of these is designed to acquaint the reader with the ungraded school. By establishing purposes and techniques in the ungraded school, it is hoped that the reader will be able to view the impact the ungraded school may have upon pupils, teachers, and the community. The second section of this chapter illustrates an approach for establishing an ungraded primary school. It is not intended as the *only* approach to the ungraded school; rather, it is designed to bring into focus information pertinent to the teacher who is contemplating the approach for the first time. The final section of the chapter introduces basic principles and problems which function in an ungraded school.

UNGRADED SCHOOL

Many school facilities today are experimenting with the ungraded school at all levels; the *ungraded primary school,* however, seems to be past the experimental stage. In fact, some form of the ungraded primary can be found in all sections of the country. The ungraded plan has many different labels such as the nongraded school, flexible primary unit, levels system, ungraded primary, primary unit, nongraded primary, primary block, and primary system.

Some schools are operating on a kindergarten-primary ungraded sequence, a primary sequence only, or basically six year nongraded program. Many of these schools have used this approach for more than a decade.

What are the purposes for organizing an ungraded elementary school?

One of the purposes in organizing an ungraded elementary school is to provide for a longitudinal, sequential program in the curriculum. The aim is to provide for the continuous progress of each child, without skipping or repeating any part of the program. Children of approximately equal academic, social, emotional, and physical development are placed together in subgroups. They then advance at their own individual rates without regard to chronological age.

The possibility of providing for individual differences within the classroom seems to be the main purpose for organizing an ungraded school. Inasmuch as the differences between children are great, the school structure is designed to meet these needs without the usual restrictions imposed by the graded school. It has long been recognized that some pupils need longer than the traditional four years for mastering the basic skills of kindergarten-primary education; others of course need much less time than is normally provided. The ungraded program, in effect, replaces grade levels with *developmental levels* and facilitates the completion of each level according to the developmental rate of each child.

What curriculum changes are involved for an ungraded school?

The curriculum is at the center of a school's program. Some curriculum considerations for an ungraded school are: [1]

1. A longitudinal view of the curriculum.

2. The content of instruction.

3. The timing and pacing of learning.

Each of the curriculum considerations will be discussed separately.

A longitudinal view of the curriculum. The nongraded curriculum must give attention to the continuity and sequence of materials. Skills taught at the first level must be built upon in the second, and so on in the nongraded program. Goodlad and Anderson state:

The substance of the desired longitudinal view is a set of threads or *organizing elements* running vertically through the curriculum and around which learning activities should be organized. There are two sources for determining organizing elements: the learner *behavior* sought and the areas of *content* to be used in developing such behavior.[2]

It is the teacher's job to organize those elements that run vertically in the curriculum along the lines of pupil behavior and subject matter

[1] John I. Goodlad and Robert H. Anderson, *The Nongraded Elementary School* (New York: Harcourt, Brace & World, Inc., 1959), pp. 79–89.
[2] *Ibid.*, p. 80.

content. The curriculum change involved is one of viewing the curriculum as a series of interrelated parts, each dependent upon the other. These organizing threads, once identified, become the relatively fixed or constant components of the curriculum.

Skills and concepts taught in our traditionally graded elementary schools do not lend themselves to grades very well because children do not enter each grade all alike. Skills and concepts that are designated for the third grade, for example, may be well beyond some third grade youngsters and yet these same skills and concepts often have been already mastered by other third grade children. In the ungraded school, skills and concepts are developed on sequential, longitudinal bases corresponding to growth and developmental patterns of children. For example, Betty Lines and Mary Wash have been in the ungraded school two years. Mary is working on skills and concepts that are quite different from the skills and concepts Betty is working on. Mary is developing faster than Betty in school so she is pushing ahead of Betty in her school work and thus working on more advanced skills and concepts.

The content of instruction. In the ungraded school the curriculum is viewed over a span of several years. Instructional content is viewed as a series of concepts, skills, and values essential for future learning.

. . . . whether or not the wet lands are taught in the fifth grade becomes less important than the extent to which each child is deepening his insight into certain effects of environment on patterns of plant, animal, and human life. Whether or not levers are taught in the sixth grade becomes less important than the extent to which each child is developing understanding of principles of force. Whether or not Susan is reading the third book in a given series becomes less important than the extent to which her word analysis skills and eyemovements are developing at a steady pace. What is taught then becomes less important than what concepts, skills, and values are being learned and how well.[3]

The time to teach a particular body of content then becomes less important than steady growth and progress in particular developmental skills.

The timing and pacing of learning. In both the nongraded and graded schools, teachers must cope with problems of pacing and timing. For the teacher in a nongraded school, however, this task is somewhat simplified. For years, child development specialists have been advocating

---

[3] *Ibid.*, p. 84.

the importance of adjusting instructional activities to the developmental level of each child and proceeding upward on this basis. The ungraded school's curriculum is developed exactly in this style. The teacher of a graded school also adheres to this principle, but he must, in addition, hold an allegiance to the grade level concept. He must begin where the child is but must also cover certain materials expected at a given grade level so the child may be promoted to the next grade level.

The teacher of a nongraded school is free to guide the timing and pacing for each child without the pressure of covering a certain amount of materials in a given amount of time. In effect then, the teacher in a nongraded school will time and pace the child in accordance with what he knows about the *learning process*, the *learner*, and the *materials to be learned*. The actual work of timing and pacing in an ungraded school involves starting the child at his own particular level and then helping him develop the skills, concepts, and values necessary in this area before he is advanced to the next level.

Curriculum changes in an ungraded school are not as tremendous as one may think. Both the graded and the ungraded school should be built upon many of the same principles. Essentially the curriculum considerations of any elementary school should include a longitudinal view of the curriculum, instructional content, and the art of timing and pacing for optimum benefit of each child. The main advantage of the ungraded school seems to be the removal of traditional grade impediments to facilitate this process.

What is the impact on the pupil?

The pupil in an ungraded school program is assured of individual attention throughout his elementary school life. Children are not held back or "flunked" nor are they accelerated in the usual sense of the graded school. Fewer children experience failure and frustration in the ungraded school because the child is not expected to work on a level at which he cannot succeed. Children are not made to repeat first, second, third, or any other grade. *They merely begin in September where they stopped in May.* Those who are able to progress more rapidly than others are not required to slow down and possibly develop poor study habits while they wait for the slower pupils to catch up. Immature and slower learning children may work in smaller groups and individually and thereby receive more individual attention from the teacher. In addition to this, the sequence of learning experiences is more consecutive and continuous, allowing for lags and spurts which normally accompany a child's development.

Anderson and Goodlad [4] conducted a survey in 1960 to determine the practices in 89 communities involving about 550 nongraded schools. In terms of pupil achievement it was reported that:

Wherever statistical data permitted statements on the significance of the differences, a significant difference was rarely reported that was not in favor of the nongraded groups.[5]

In view of the various studies reported on the probable impact upon the pupils, it is important to discuss the results of the various studies. In a nongraded school, the child's attitude toward the teacher was a positive contribution listed in many of the studies. Better achievement and personal adjustment were matters of conjecture; however, the more extensive studies seemed to favor the child in the nongraded school in both achievement and personal adjustment.

What is the impact on the teacher?

The greatest impact upon the teacher seems to be a renewed emphasis on meeting the needs of each child in the ungraded group. More careful teacher evaluation of pupils is possible because of the new focus on the individual needs of each child. Indeed the teacher must constantly see each child as an individual.

A second teacher "adjustment" involves the necessity of ascertaining the actual developmental level of each child rather than expecting him to conform to a given grade level. The teacher must not only adhere to the principle of individual differences, but he must adapt instructional activities accordingly so that the learner may reach each next higher level at his own pace.

The third area that affects the teacher is the matter of increased teacher cooperation and team work. Individual capacities and capabilities of each teacher can be utilized better when teachers are willing to cooperate and work in teams. In the ungraded program close cooperation is essential. This factor was emphasized in a recent survey.

At first there is considerable apprehension and/or tension among some teachers, especially traditionally-oriented teachers. This anxiety, most respondents seemed to feel, gives way to satisfaction within a short time. Teachers in

---

[4] Robert H. Anderson and John I. Goodlad, "Self-Appraisal in Nongraded Schools: A Survey of Findings and Perceptions," *Elementary School Journal*, 62: 261–269 (February, 1962).

[5] *Ibid.*, p. 263.

nongraded classes engage in more planning and more cooperative study than they did in graded schools.[6]

It was also reported that teachers in nongraded schools seemed more relaxed in their work. Furthermore, there was more positive emotional involvement by those teachers who participated in the development of the nongraded plan in their schools.

Even though the teacher's workload of thirty children in the classroom is similar to the teacher in a graded school, it is seen that teachers of ungraded schools tend to become more cognizant of children's needs; they teach from level to level instead of from grade to grade; and they tend to become more cooperative and relaxed in their teaching responsibilities.

SUGGESTED MODEL FOR AN UNGRADED PRIMARY

An important fact to keep in mind is that the ungraded primary is *not a method of teaching*, but merely an administrative tool designed to encourage and promote instruction which places emphasis on individual growth and developmental patterns of children. New and/or improved methods of instruction, however, often become an outgrowth of this flexible organization.

As one looks at the ungraded primary model, goals need to be set at various levels, and they should be considered as only desirable minimum requirements rather than maximums of attainment. Quality teaching incorporates both a program of minimum essentials and experimentation which encourages the individual learner to explore his specialized interests to a point of self-satisfaction.

An outstanding feature of the ungraded primary is that it permits a child to work at his own instructional level and to progress accordingly without the stigma of failure. Even though Sally is moving ahead of Susan in her class assignments there is no stigma of failure placed upon Susan. Susan is working at her capacity level and is achieving success at this level. It is important for the teacher to constantly stress individual differences to the children as well as adapting them in his instructional program.

This section of the chapter deals with the development of an ungraded primary model. Prior to any description of the ungraded primary

[6] *Ibid.*, p. 265.

plan, one must keep in mind that it may vary somewhat and still be a well-organized nongraded school program in theory and in actual practice.

How does a teacher work within the ungraded classroom?

The teacher in an ungraded classroom will have a teacher-pupil ratio very similar to the graded classroom teacher. The ungraded concept does not bring about a net "saving of teachers." Teacher aides and team teaching can be just as helpful in the ungraded classroom as they are in the graded elementary school.

In working in the ungraded classroom especially, constant pupil observation is essential. The teacher will need to observe carefully the pupil's performance at work and at play. In observing and evaluating various behaviors a variety of techniques have been used effectively.

1. Pupil interview.
2. Teacher-made tests.
3. Standardized tests.
4. Pupil self-evaluation.
5. Behavioral Journal entries.
6. Daily assignments and work by the pupils.
7. Questionnaire.
8. Sociometric techniques.

The *pupil interview* will give the teacher an opportunity to discuss with the child his aspirations and goals. The first step that must be considered in the pupil interview is establishing rapport with the child. The teacher should help the child feel at ease by sitting closely together, talking about something of interest to the child, and establishing an atmosphere of congeniality and friendliness. In recording the interview, very little writing should be done; however, enough must be written to aid the teacher's memory for writing a complete record following the interview. During this interview it could be determined if the child feels he is ready to move on to the next level of work. It is also appropriate for the teacher to discuss with the child his future plans and what he may be studying next.

Standardized tests may be used by the classroom teacher as a tool for diagnosing particular weaknesses a child may have as well as a tool for comparison with the norms established on tests. Because of the individualized nature of the ungraded classroom, standardized tests are extremely useful for determining the difficulties a particular child may be having in specific skills and concepts. For instance, the teacher may give a child an achievement battery of tests such as the *California Achievement Tests*, Complete Battery. The teacher would then be able to determine how well the youngster is doing in reading, arithmetic, English, spelling, and handwriting as compared to standardized norms. For example, Tom was given this test by Miss Greenly. The tests indicated that Tom's weaknesses were in word forms in reading, meanings in arithmetic reasoning, and word usage in English. Miss Greenly then set up an approach for Tom so he could master the needed skills in these three areas. It was not necessary for Miss Greenly to have Tom repeat the three entire units but to work only in the three areas of weaknesses within the reading, arithmetic, and English units. In other areas Tom was working up to his capacity.

Pupil self-evaluation is a helpful device for the child as well as the teacher. This self-evaluation may be used in conjunction with the interview or as a separate device. However it is used, the child gains insight into his own problems and so will the teacher. Billy, for instance, had very poor study habits and Mrs. Burns pointed them out repeatedly to him, but very little change took place. Mrs. Burns had Billy take a self-evaluation study habits inventory. In responding to the instrument Billy became more aware of his poor study techniques and what he was doing inappropriately. The self-evaluation study was beneficial for Billy because he gained insight into his own problems and correction became easier.

Behavioral Journals have been used for years by teachers of both the graded and the ungraded schools. The Behavioral Journal also has been called the *Anecdotal Record*. Journal entries are used as aids for understanding each child and the problems he has had and still may have. A typical entry in the Behavioral Journal could be:

Tuesday, Feb. 4. I walked down the aisle and asked Johnny for the paper on which he was drawing. He was drawing during social studies study period. He said, "I wasn't drawing anything." Finally after my insistence he handed the drawing to me. Why did he deny drawing?

From these entries in the Journal it is possible for a teacher to understand children better. This one entry may not disclose very much but many different entries over a period of years will help the teacher gain increased understanding of each child.

Constant teacher evaluation of the child's day-to-day work is another essential evaluation tool. Correcting papers and daily assignments provide a means for the teacher to diagnose particular concept and skill errors.

Questionnaires are useful devices for getting additional information about a particular area of the curriculum or problems the children may be having. These devices will give the teacher an immediate reaction on certain problems.

Sociometric techniques are important in the ungraded school. The ungraded school teacher can use these techniques for determining social acceptance of each child. They were treated in Chapter 8.

The foregoing observational tools and techniques are useful to help the child with specific problems and to aid in determining his assignment to developmental levels. Assignment to the next higher developmental level may be made whenever the teacher believes the assignment will be in the best interest of the child's growth and developmental pattern. Each child will be studied through observation, testing, and past school records to determine proper placement.

The teacher in the nongraded school must organize his classroom for maximum effectiveness. Goodlad and Anderson have this to say on grouping within the classroom:

Such flexibility should be planned with both pupil welfare and maximum teacher effectiveness in mind. We recommend, first, that each nongraded classroom be organized around achievement groups, interest groups, and work-study skill groups simultaneously.[7]

By organizing his classroom into small groups, the teacher will then be able to better provide for individual differences and make better use of his time. Grouping procedures are utilized for the sole purpose of *enhancing individual instruction*.

The teacher's work within the ungraded classroom then will consist of observing children, determining their individual needs, diagnosing particular problems, and offering special assistance in areas of strengths and weaknesses. He will be constantly aware of the need for reassignment of children to new levels and will group the class for maximum efficiency and pupil needs. He will be using all the effective methods and techniques that the teacher in the graded school has been using for years but in all probability he will be using them more effectively.

How do pupils move through the classroom assignments and units of work?

There seems to be as many different ways a child may progress through classroom assignments and units of work as there are schools

[7] John I. Goodlad and Robert H. Anderson, *op. cit.*, p. 99.

using the ungraded approach. Many of the ungraded schools do have several things in common, however.

Goals, concepts, and skills are determined for each level of development in the various curriculum areas. Assignment to these levels are made on the basis of individual achievement as determined by teacher observation and standardized testing. There is no time limit for completing a given level and assignment to the next higher level is made when a child has satisfactorily completed his present level of instruction. When the child has mastered the skills and concepts of a particular level, an evaluation of his achievement is made. Evaluating pupil progress in the ungraded school is much more than recording test scores. An adequate and effective program of evaluation incorporates objectivity, provides continual assessment and serves as the key to continuous curriculum improvement. When an instructional level appears to be too difficult for a child, he should be reassigned to a level where he can meet success and work without frustration. Progress records are kept on each pupil. As he accomplishes various skills in a particular level, it is desirable to check them off on his progress record. This, too, serves as a guide as the child progresses through his classroom assignments and units of work.

A school in Milwaukee [8] used this approach in reading levels of the ungraded school. The pupil's progress in reading was recorded on a series of levels, 1 through 12. Level 1 was pre-reading, level 2 was chart reading, level 3 was pre-primer, levels 4 and 5 were primers, levels 6 and 7 were first readers, levels 8 and 9 were second readers, levels 10 and 11 were third readers, and level 12 was independent reading. In this program, the child progressed from one level to the next only when the teacher felt he had gained the skills necessary for that level. The shift from one level to the next occurred at any time during the year. In this particular school program instructors tried to keep the child near his age group. It was felt that normally a child should not be advanced more than one year beyond that of his chronological age-mates and vice versa. It was reported that, as a general rule, a period of six semesters was necessary for completion of the primary program.

An important aspect of the developmental levels is that each child may progress through the levels at his own rate. In the graded school, children are placed in reading groups, but the faster developing child is usually held back by the slower developing child in his particular reading group. In looking at the twelve reading levels, they are very similar to a graded school reading program. The children will follow the same developmental, sequential program in both the graded and nongraded school, but in the nongraded school each child is on his own to progress up

[8] Alan T. Wilson, "The Ungraded Primary School," *The American Teacher*, 43: 5–6+ (February, 1959).

through these levels as fast as he can without being held back for another child in his class.

Normally the teacher will handle only three or four levels within his classroom, so a child may be moved to another closely cooperating teacher during the school year because he progressed through all the levels within his classroom in which he was placed at the beginning of the school year. Usually no more than one move to another classroom is necessary during the school year.

How do goals vary in an ungraded primary?

In discussing the goals of the ungraded primary, a comparison of the graded school with the nongraded program would be in order. (See page 271.) This comparison was taken from "The Continuous Progress Plan of Primary Grouping," Reno, Nevada.[9]

In comparing the two programs the differences in goals are quite evident. A goal of the ungraded school is to allow each child to develop at his own growth and rate. The stigma of failure is not present in the ungraded school because another goal of this plan is to adjust the program to fit each child's needs. A third goal of the program is that he need not repeat. He may progress slowly and irregularly but he need not repeat an entire sequence. Where the child stops in his work in May, that will be the place he will begin the following September.

Flexibility is a fourth goal of the ungraded school. Group placement or level placement is characterized by individual attention according to physical, mental, social, and emotional maturity. Development of good mental health is a fifth goal for the ungraded program. Pressures and threat of failure are minimized. Frustration is reduced, thus enhancing mental health. The sixth goal of the ungraded school is derived from the longitudinal nature of the program. Curriculum materials and activities are viewed over a span of several years. Learning is viewed vertically and the curriculum is built upon these vertical levels.

Goals which are similar to those of the graded school are to assist each pupil in developing to the limit of his ability in the basic skills, to provide every child an opportunity to develop a healthy body and mind through physical education, and to develop an appreciation for the fine arts. Additional goals for each type of school organization include responsibility for making democratic decisions and for preparing for democratic citizenship. The goal of providing instructional materials, facilities, and staff needed for maintaining a good school program is also present in both plans.

[9] Marie Kingdon, "Grades or Levels?" *Michigan Education Journal*, 39: 514–17 (April, 1962), p. 516.

GRADED AND NONGRADED COMPARISONS

Graded	*Nongraded*
1. It is assumed that all children of the same chronological age will develop to the same extent in a given period of time.	1. It is assumed that each child has his own pattern and rate of growth, and that children of the same age will vary greatly in their ability and rate of maturation.
2. A child who does not measure up to adult standards of what should be accomplished in nine months is called a "failure."	2. No child is ever considered a "failure." If he does not achieve in proportion to his ability, the cause is studied and the program adjusted to fit his needs and problems.
3. If a child "fails" he is required to repeat the grade in which he does not meet the standards.	3. A child never repeats. He may progress more slowly than others in the group, but individual records of progress make it possible to keep his growth continuous.
4. A decision as to grade placement must be made after each nine months.	4. Decisions as to group placement can be made at any time during the three-year period (a fourth year may be necessary for social, emotional, or maturative adjustment).
5. Grade placements are based too largely upon academic achievement.	5. Group placement is flexible, based upon physical, mental, social, and emotional maturity.
6. Fixed standards of achievement within a set time put pressures upon teachers and children which cause emotional tensions and inhibit learning.	6. Elimination of pressures produces a relaxed learning situation conducive to good mental health.

How can pupils be evaluated in this particular school?

As has been pointed out, the ungraded plan follows a flexible time schedule in developing learning experiences for each child. The main feature in pupil evaluation then is *to compare a child's own past activities with what he is doing at the present time.* It is valuable to know how the child's present performance compares with his past performance because this will give the teacher an idea of the direction and the rate at which the child is developing in mastering tasks in various areas of the curriculum. A folder should be kept for each child. Periodically, papers should be collected from each child and these papers should be placed in his folder. These papers should be *representative of his daily work,* not just his best papers! Frequently, these materials should be compared in the presence of the child so he may know his progress from one level of achievement to the next. This folder becomes an excellent device for use in parent-teacher conferences as well. In this type of evaluation, the child is praised for his efforts from one level to the next.

Standardized tests also may be helpful in comparing the child with established test norms. They may be especially useful in identifying strengths and weaknesses. An effective evaluation program will incorporate objectivity in the assessment of the child's progress.

How does the ungraded school affect the work load of the teacher?

In the beginning stages of planning and organizing an ungraded program, the teacher's work load is greater. Like any change or new venture, additional time is necessary in understanding and developing the program. Attending in-service programs, reading professional materials, and attending teacher meetings are all necessary when implementing a new program. After the ungraded program has been launched, the teacher's work in the classroom need not be more demanding than that which is normally expected of the teacher in a graded school. The teacher-pupil ratio is similar in both the graded and nongraded school. The use of teacher aides and team teaching techniques is as effective in the ungraded school as it has been found in the graded school.

This program has the big advantage of focusing attention on the individual child, rather than on the class as a whole. The teacher's work load will consist of instruction in small groups, large groups, and individual guidance as needed. The desirable methods and techniques used by the teacher in the graded classroom are also used by the teacher in the ungraded classroom. The good teacher in either the graded or ungraded school will have approximately the same work load. In either program, the teacher should be keenly aware of individual differences and the need for individualizing instruction.

Are discipline problems greater in an ungraded primary?

Discipline problems are no greater in the ungraded school than one would find in the graded school. In fact, the ungraded school plan should result in a decrease of discipline problems.

According to Woodruff [10] discipline is a concept which involves many different ramifications. Among some of his suggestions were:

[10] A. D. Woodruff, "Discipline," *Encyclopedia of Educational Research*, 3rd Ed. (New York: Macmillan Co., 1960), pp. 381–385.

1. Discipline should be preventive rather than corrective.

2. Overprotection of the child should be avoided.

3. Pupils should see the goals of their school activities.

4. Overall goal should be to increase individual responsibility and self-control.

The ungraded school's organization is structured along vertical lines or threads which the child follows in his progress in school. This individualized approach requires of the child individual responsibility and thereby fosters the development of self-control. Each pupil is quite aware of his goals in school activities along this vertical sequence; as he progresses from one sequence to another he assumes increasing responsibility for his own learning. In this type approach discipline is preventive; the need for correction is less frequently needed.

PROBLEMS AND PRINCIPLES IN AN UNGRADED SCHOOL

In the preceding section of this chapter, many comments and explanations have been given concerning the ungraded school plan. By following these procedures a teacher may effectively make a break from the procedures of the graded school. Although the ungraded program has progressed beyond the experimental stage in many schools, there are many problems yet to be resolved. Even the principles concerning the ungraded school are still being revised in this relatively new area. By becoming thoroughly acquainted with the principles and problems of the ungraded school, the teacher may become more effective in the manipulation of the many variables involved.

What are some of the problems?

In the ungraded school plan there are several problems that should be faced. At the conclusion of a year in the nongraded school plan, Haas suggested several problem areas that demanded constant attention.

1. There is a need for careful selection of staff members.

2. There is a need for continuous in-service program to assist staff members in implementing a nongraded team teaching program that promotes continuous progress for each pupil.

3. There is a need to keep members of the community informed about the educational program.[11]

A fourth problem area seems to be the provision of adequate materials that reflect a sequential approach rather than a graded approach.

The need for careful selection of staff for an ungraded school program must not be overlooked. Staff members must be *committed* to the ungraded school plan. A directive from the principal or superintendent to the staff of an elementary school indicating that they will be in an ungraded plan next year may be doomed to failure. Staff members need to be convinced of the excellent possibilities involved in reorganizing the school into the ungraded scheme. Even after staff members accept the idea, group planning is essential.

In-service activity is another area of concern in the ungraded school. In-service workshops, meetings, and planning sessions are indeed an important phase of any educational program, but this is especially true when a staff starts a new program. An in-service program will help all staff members in becoming better acquainted with the ungraded school and will also aid teachers in implementing the ungraded concept.

The school community needs to be continually informed about the school. This is very important when a major change is being made in school organization. The use of parent-teacher conferences as well as Parent-Teachers' Associations and other community meetings are useful avenues for informing the public.

The fourth problem area for the ungraded school is the lack of adequate and ungraded materials. Teachers in the ungraded school do not want textbooks and other materials which have grade level designations. They need materials that are developed on a sequential, vertical sequence. There is presently a shortage of textbooks planned along the lines of developmental levels. Publishers, however, have accepted the challenge and are rapidly correcting the situation.

What are some of the principles?

The following principles, paramount in the ungraded school, were adapted from "The Primary Cycle Reading Guide," which was made by the Flint Community Schools.[12]

1. Places pupils in achievement groups based on readiness for and growth in particular threads of curriculum development.

[11] Arthur Haas, "First-Year Organization of Elmcrest Elementary School: A Nongraded Team-Teaching School," *American School Board Journal*, 151: 22+ (October, 1965), p. 70.
[12] Kingdon, *op. cit.*, p. 517.

2. Permits each child to progress continuously through these curriculum threads according to his individual growth.

3. Maintains the best accepted teaching techniques.

4. Emphasizes the natural growth and development of each child rather than comparing his achievement with that of other children.

5. Provides for flexibility in the movement of children to groups in which they can achieve satisfactorily.

6. Allows for extending the program for the slow learner over a longer period and provides greater challenge for the superior learner as well.

7. Offers the following advantages for pupils and staff:

   a. Gives all children the satisfaction of progressing.

   b. Leaves no gaps in the child's learning experiences.

   c. Eliminates repetition of materials.

   d. Helps with early diagnosis and adjustment of slow learners and gifted children.

   e. Lessens retardation.

   f. Reduces blocking and frustrations.

   g. Removes pressure from pupils and teachers by emphasizing total growth rather than subject matter.

   h. Minimizes artificial standards and traditional marking.

   i. Helps make better adjusted and happier children.

8. Allows each child to pace himself in the learning process.

The above principles may serve as guidelines in organizing, planning, and operating a successful ungraded school plan.

SUMMARY

The ungraded school concept is built upon the principle that each child is different and that he progresses at his own rate. No child is penalized by waiting for slower pupils; nor is one pushed ahead to keep up with the faster maturing children. One of the purposes of an ungraded elementary school is to provide for a longitudinal, sequential program in the curriculum for each child. Thus the ungraded school has an organizational structure that accommodates the sequential and longitudinal development of boys and girls.

In the ungraded school, the curriculum is planned over a period of years rather than from year to year. The time to teach a learning concept becomes less important because the steady growth and progress within a particular learning concept is the important task of instruction. Teachers begin instruction at that point where each child is ready for instruction. The child then progresses from level to level. No repeating of a sequence is necessary. Pupils in an ungraded school have fewer failures and frustrations because each child is taught at his level of development. The child works where he has an opportunity for success.

There are several problems to be found in the ungraded school organization. These problems, however, are being solved by careful staff selection, in-service training, community information, and adequate ungraded teaching materials.

Several principles are involved in the ungraded concept; a few will be summarized here. Each child is allowed to progress continually because he is placed at his own learning level, based on his readiness for and growth in the curriculum. The pupil is compared to his own previous achievement, not with other children. Flexibility is maintained throughout the ungraded school; thus, the slow, average, or fast maturing child maintains his own pace in learning.

QUESTIONS FOR STUDY AND DISCUSSION

1. In the ungraded school, organizational reform is but a beginning. Why should attention be given to school function, curriculum design, teaching, and evaluation? What essential element would be left out if the ungraded school was an ungraded school in name only?

2. Why is the ungraded school curricula organized on a longitudinal, sequential basis? Is not the graded school program organized the same way? Why? What differences are there between the graded and nongraded curricula? What differences would this make with the pupils?

3. Skills and concepts taught in the elementary schools do not readily lend themselves to grades. Why is this so? How does the graded school take this into account? How does this affect the child in the elementary school?

4. What problems are involved in both the nongraded and graded school as it relates to timing and pacing of learning? What is the probable impact on the pupils? Who should time and pace the children? Why?

5. The ungraded school should change the mental attitude of the pupils. Why would this change take place? Do failure and frustrations aid learning? When does a child learn from his mistakes?

6. What problems do teachers have in teaching in the ungraded school? How

is the mental health of teachers affected in the nongraded program? Why is the teacher's work load considered no greater than in a graded school?

7. Does it seem possible that pupils in the classroom could move through units of work on an individual basis? Could a teacher direct thirty different children as recommended?

8. Small children are responsible for their actions in the ungraded school. Why are not discipline problems greater? How may a teacher insure that the discipline practices in his classroom are preventive rather than corrective?

SELECTED BIBLIOGRAPHY

Anderson, Richard C., "The Case for Non-Graded, Homogeneous Grouping," *Elementary School Journal*, 62: 193–197 (January, 1962).

Anderson, Robert H. and John I. Goodlad, "Self-Appraisal in Nongraded Schools: A Survey of Findings and Perceptions," *Elementary School Journal*, 62: 261–269 (February, 1962).

Carbone, Robert F., "A Comparison of Graded and Non-Graded Elementary Schools," *Elementary School Journal*, 62: 82–88 (November, 1961).

Goodlad, John I. and Robert H. Anderson, "Educational Practices in Nongraded Schools: A Survey of Perceptions," *Elementary School Journal*, 63: 33–40 (October, 1962).

————, *The Nongraded Elementary School* (New York: Harcourt, Brace & World, Inc., 1959).

Haas, Arthur, "First-Year Organization of Elmcrest Elementary School: A Nongraded Team-Teaching School," *American School Board Journal*, 151: 22+ (October, 1965).

Hunter, Madeline C., "Teachers in the Nongraded School," *NEA Journal*, 55, No. 2: 12–15 (February, 1966).

Kingdon, Marie, "Grades or Levels?" *Michigan Education Journal*, 39: 514–517 (April, 1962).

Skapski, Mary King, "Ungraded Primary Reading Program: An Objective Evaluation," *Elementary School Journal*, 61: 41–45 (October, 1960).

Woodruff, A. D., "Discipline," *Encyclopedia of Educational Research*, 3rd Ed. (New York: Macmillan Co., 1960).

UNIT FOUR

Coping with Persistent Instructional Problems

MANY times the learning experience is adversely affected by persistent problems associated with instruction. Although such problems are inextricably interwoven with instructional practices, frequently they must be isolated for analysis. Four such problems have persisted over the span of several decades. Therefore the problems of evaluation, maintaining classroom discipline, directing study activities, and utilizing instructional materials and resources have been selected for intensive exploration and analysis.

Measurement, evaluation, and reporting procedures remain major functions of instructional practice. Although most educators are aware of the unnecessary and often detrimental emphasis associated with these procedures, they remain a major function of classroom instruction. Indeed, an essential function of the learning experience is self-evaluation. Pupils must constantly evaluate the worth of their own learning experiences. Likewise, the teacher, if he is to be effective in guiding learning, must evaluate and assist pupils in their own evaluations. Accordingly, Chapter 13 offers several illustrations of measurement, evaluation, and reporting procedures. Teacher-made tests, observational procedures, and various reporting techniques are treated. In the final analysis, the quality of measurement and evaluation determines the quality of the learning experience.

Discipline problems, for many years, have been and still remain one of the most serious limitations of effective instruction. Inabilities in human relations account for at least eighty percent of all people who lose their jobs in industry. Likewise, most teachers who lose their jobs are unable to cope with the interpersonal relationships of pupils.

Problems of maintaining effective class control are even more acute today than they were two or three decades ago. A number of factors have contributed to this state of affairs, among them: (1) greater emphasis on compulsory education, (2) social promotion policies, (3) emphasis on an education for everyone, and (4) larger classes.

Beginning teachers especially are prone to seek quick solutions to discipline problems. They reason that if this one problem—discipline—can be worked out their chances of survival are assured. While the reasoning process is valid, the problem is considerably more complex. Discipline problems may be symptoms of more serious difficulties. They frequently are closely related to lack of pupil interest in school. Some teachers, for example, are unable to provide adequately for the individual differences of pupils. It is the rare child indeed who will *not* create class disturbances when class expectations are too high or too low for his capacities. Yet some teachers typically expect all pupils to read the same books, to do the same problems, and to keep up with all other members of the class. As might be expected, these teachers often find they are devoting about ninety percent of their energies to problems of class control.

In a "how-to-do" book, however, one expects to find useful guidelines for coping with such a problem after it develops. Therefore, a general plan of action is offered in Chapter 14. It is recognized that once discipline problems arise they must be disposed of effectively if an atmosphere conducive to effective learning is to be maintained.

Directing study activities, treated in Chapter 15, is another persistent instructional problem. When, where, and how to study is an issue which changes as the philosophical basis for American education changes. The last few decades have seen a shift of study activities from the home, to the classroom, and back again. The impact of public school criticism is reflected in variations of homework requirements.

Basic to effective study activities is the class assignment. Inadequate assignments often render study activities inadequate. Nevertheless, the nature of assignments reflects a teacher's theory of learning. Learning as a process of knowledge acquisition suggests memoriter type assignments, while learning as a problem-solving experience suggests assignments requiring reflective thought.

Chapter 16 deals with still another persistent instructional problem: the use of audio-visual materials and resources. Although these resources will be used in all phases of the instructional process, they deserve special treatment. Today's teacher has at his disposal an increasing number of different materials and resources. As the chapter title suggests, they are tools for enhancing learning. They do *not* replace the teacher. A motion picture, for example, is not used as a substitute for instruction; rather, it is used to supplement instructional activities. Likewise, educational television cannot replace the face-to-face contact of teacher and pupils. The emphasis in Chapter 16 is on the integration of audio-visual materials and resources in the instructional process. Appropriate use of a number of specific materials and resources are discussed: motion pictures, television, demonstrations, the chalkboard, opaque projection, the overhead projector, resource visitors, and field trips. Some attention also is given to general sources of audio-visual materials.

Assessing Learning Experiences: Measuring Instruments, Evaluation and Reporting Procedures

THE evening was hot and the hour was late. Mrs. Williams heaved a sigh of relief as the last parent left her third grade classroom. "These teacher-parent conferences are always quite a strain," she thought as she filed the last of the pupil folders. Each parent had in effect asked the same question: "How is my Johnny doing in school?" As Mrs. Williams reflected on her responses she heard herself saying:

"He's doing fine. In fact, he made one of the highest grades in the class."

"The boy is experiencing a little difficulty in concentration. You will notice from his responses on this test that his answers are often vague and sometimes a bit far-fetched."

"Johnny appears to be confusing some of the important facts. You will notice here that he was not sure what took place in the science experiment."

"Mary is a quiet girl, but she does well on her spelling tests. I would say she is doing outstanding work."

Mrs. Williams' experience is repeated in much the same manner in thousands of schools throughout this country. Parents want to know "how Johnny is doing." The teacher reports he is "doing fine" or "not doing so well" on the basis of a test or tests. Both parties may feel a bit dissatisfied with the experience, but they lack the ability to analyze the situation. Most of the assumption implied in Mrs. Williams' responses indicate sources of error which can render measurement and evaluation much less effective than expected:

1. Mrs. Williams seemed to be confusing measurement with evaluation. Although the two processes are related, evaluation includes much more than assessment of test performance.

2. By alluding to facts, such as a science experiment, Mrs. Williams appeared to equate factual retention with learning. Although facts are indeed essen-

tial in the learning process, they more appropriately serve as means to ends rather than as ends in themselves.

3. Neither the parents nor Mrs. Williams displayed evidence of understanding the meaning of specific, observable outcomes of learning. While test performance is considered *one* important observable outcome of learning, other behavioral evidences of goal fulfillment also are important.

4. Mrs. Williams seemed to be measuring a pupil's progress wholly on the basis of the progress of other pupils in the class. Most teachers are aware of the extremely wide variation in abilities among children. Yet, these same teachers often will measure and evaluate pupil progress on the assumption that all have an equal chance. A score of 80 by one child might represent "high" performance while the same score by another might represent "low" performance.

5. Mrs. Williams, in her concept of evaluation, seemed to be neglecting certain important intangible factors, such as attitudes and opinions, critical thinking ability, mental health, work and study habits, and social skills. Such intangibles can be measured by translating goals into expected behavioral outcomes.

This chapter is divided into three major sections: Techniques of Measurement and Evaluation; Use of Report Cards; and Functions and Principles of an Effective Program. This chapter is concerned with measurement, evaluation and reporting procedures. The very close, often indistinct and overlapping, relationship of these areas is emphasized.

TECHNIQUES OF MEASUREMENT AND EVALUATION

Human beings are constantly involved in the process of making judgments and reaching decisions about the value of an experience. This is usually called *evaluation*. The process can be general or it can be specific. The young child, for example, sometimes decides he dislikes an adult because that person has thwarted an immediate desire. Sometimes an adult evaluates in a similar fashion, as in the case of disliking all redheads. More appropriately, however, evaluations are of a specific sort. That is to say, one usually evaluates for a specific purpose. He may, for example, want to buy a house for a permanent or summer residence, for a relative or friend, or for rental purposes.

In the process of making evaluations one often relies on *measurement*. The house-buyer measures cost in terms of income, distance from a shopping center, floor space available, and so on. Likewise, the teacher uses a variety of measuring instruments to assist him in evaluating a pupil's progress. For some purposes, tests afford reliable data, as in the case of understandings related to academic achievement. For other purposes, as in the case of attitudes and appreciations, observation will produce the most reliable results. Through measurement, a *quantitative amount* of some experience is assembled, as in the case of a test score. Evaluation, on the other hand, attempts to assess the *value* of the quantity to be measured. Measurement in and of itself is meaningless; it can do no more than facilitate the ends of evaluation. To cite a previous example, a score of 80 on a test must be *evaluated* in terms of the goal or purpose involved. Evaluations made with inadequate or improper measuring instruments serve no useful purpose and lead to erroneous conclusions.

How does one judge measurement and evaluation tools?

Two teachers administered a standardized achievement test to their children in their classroom. One group indicated considerably higher achievement than the other.

Is it safe to conclude that the one group had, in fact, achieved more than the other one? Even if the groups had been equated prior to the instructional program, the test does not necessarily indicate greater achievement by one group, for the test may lack *reliability* and/or *validity*.

Score differences should be due to factors other than chance. There are three primary sources of chance variation in test scores that can be minimized or avoided.[1] When these sources are present they may render the measuring instrument *unreliable*. A measuring instrument is said to be *reliable* when it measures some particular aspect of learning consistently. Under such conditions the instruments will produce similar results at different times. In other words, scores can be trusted—they will be *consistent*. Three primary sources of unreliability are:

Scoring unreliability. A test score may be unreliable when dependent on the person doing the scoring. Essay tests, discussed in a later section of this chapter, are particularly susceptible to such an error. Seldom will

---

[1] For an excellent analysis of these factors, the reader is referred to Dorothy Adkins, *Test Construction* (Columbus, Charles E. Merrill Publishing Co., 1960), pp. 11–16.

two individuals assign identical scores to an essay test. Even a single scorer may assign quite different scores to the same paper after a time lapse. Objective test items usually are much less susceptible to scoring unreliability than are essay tests, rating scales, and check lists.

A teacher can substantially reduce scoring unreliability by making use of the qualified essay item described in this chapter. He can also minimize the hazard by reading responses to a single question before going to subsequent items. Sometimes greater objectivity can be attained merely by having pupils put their names on the back of their test papers. Such precautions minimize the "halo effect" or the tendency to be influenced by general personality factors. The individual dimensions of a rating scale can be reversed for the purpose of minimizing response set biases.

Content or sampling unreliability. A test seldom includes more than a sampling of learnings acquired. While a vast number of test items is desirable, the tester usually is limited to a relatively few items. If the sampling is too small, resulting scores will be affected by the accidental inclusion or exclusion of certain items. By chance an individual may be confronted with items which represent areas of high achievement, or by chance the items may be taken largely from areas of little achievement. In either case the results will be misleading. The essay test is especially vulnerable, due to the limited number of items possible. Sampling unreliability also can be present in objective tests, especially if the teacher finds it easier to construct items in one area than another.

Content unreliability can be minimized substantially by giving due consideration to the major objectives established prior to the learning experience. If, for instance, five major goals have been formulated for a particular unit of work, at least one essay item should be designed to determine progress toward each goal. This may necessitate a longer period of time, or two different days, for testing. Likewise, objective items should be included in approximate proportion to the degree of emphasis given each major goal.

Observational techniques, especially rating scales, are susceptible to sampling unreliability. The teacher may omit an important factor simply because of his own inability to visualize its importance prior to the experience. The difficulty is resolved somewhat by the inclusion of an *anchor item* (scale). This is an item which is sometimes called a *catchall* or *general impression rating*.

Chance unreliability. Even after a test has been checked for scoring and sampling error, scores will vary. This provokes the question, "Just how much test score variation can one expect to result from pure chance factors related to test performance?" If a pupil could take a test 100 times or more and the results averaged each time, one could readily predict the amount of chance error involved. It is possible, however, to make a reasonable prediction on the basis of *one* performance. This can be accomplished by forming a separate test of the even-numbered items and another test of the odd-numbered items of the original test and comparing results. This is commonly called the *split-half* method of determining reliability. According to Diederich, ". . . it is usually safe to say that the standard error of a 'short' teacher-made test of up to 50 items will be three raw-score points, while the standard error of a 'long' test of 100 items will be five raw-score points." [2] The *standard error* represents differences expected from pure chance.

Sometimes a teacher will desire to make comparable test forms for parts of his group. By having each subgroup take *each* form, it is relatively easy to determine the comparability of the two tests in the manner described above.

The trustworthiness or consistency of test scores (reliability) is one aspect of the *validity* of a measuring instrument. *An instrument is valid if it measures what it is designed to measure.* If test scores are not trustworthy (consistent), then a test cannot be valid. Nevertheless, test scores can be highly consistent without serving the purposes for which they were intended. In other words, a test score can be reliable but not valid. If it is valid, however, it must be reliable. The following illustration should further clarify the concept:

Mr. Meek administered a test covering a unit in history to his pupils and found the scores to be reliable on the basis of the "split-half" method. His test emphasized the customs of the pioneers, whereas the original learning experiences dealt with the westward movement of the pioneers.

The test could have easily produced consistent (reliable) results, but it obviously did not serve appropriate (valid) purposes. Sometimes classes taught by different teachers are all measured by the same standardized achievement tests. Unless the groups involved have emphasized identical or very similar purposes, the results are neither comparable nor valid.

The *validity* of a test score ultimately rests with the relation of responses on the test to a measure of behavior in situations that will be

[2] Educational Testing Service, *Short-Cut Statistics for Teacher-made Tests*, Bulletin No. 5 (Princeton, New Jersey, 1960), p. 14.

encountered by the student later.[3] This frequently is known as *empirical* or *statistical validity*. Unfortunately, such a condition is extremely difficult to determine. Hence, the independent criterion measure often must be substituted with another criterion which provides reasonable assurance that the test will serve its purpose. Thus the term *logical* or *content validity* is often used. The basic test of content validity involves a direct comparison of the actual behaviors involved in the stated goals of instruction with the behaviors needed for success on the test.[4] Test items of a *situational nature* approach a true measure of the behavioral outcomes anticipated in the original goals or objectives. All other kinds of evaluative devices, likewise, should be based on the behaviors defined in the instructional outcomes.

Another criterion for assessing the value of a measuring instrument is *objectivity*. This concept relates to clearness of meaning and procedures. Most words have several meanings. Therefore, it is important for a teacher to clarify intended meaning so that pupils will understand the question in the same way. Both essay- and objective-type items run the risk of being misunderstood. The qualified essay item described later in this chapter may greatly increase objectivity. Likewise, modified multiple-choice and true-false items enable the pupil to indicate his particular frame of reference when responding to the item. Rating scales which call for such ratings as "excellent," "good," and "poor" tend to lack objectivity. Unless specific behavioral descriptions of such terms are supplied, different raters, and even the same rater at different times, will use different interpretations of the terms.

Another aspect of objectivity is associated with scoring procedure. Use of a scoring key reduces the effect of personal bias. A scoring key usually consists of a copy of the test with an indication of the acceptable responses and the various weights to be assigned to each.

What constitutes an appropriate level of test item difficulty?

For many years one of the leading controversies in the area of test construction has focused on the level of item difficulty needed to determine progress toward goals. Some teachers have assumed that a knowledge of the essential facts in given areas should be sufficient evidence of goal achievement. Others, pointing out the wide gap between theory and

[3] Adkins, *op. cit.*, p. 17.
[4] Alfred Schwartz and Stuarte Tiedeman, *Evaluating Student Progress* (New York: David McKay Co., Inc., 1957), p. 77.

practice, have suggested that more than retention is needed. Thomas [5] offers an excellent analysis of the controversy when he describes three levels of behavior, planning, and understanding which seem to bear upon the issue:

Behavioral or performance level. Whenever feasible, a teacher judges a pupil's behavior directly. The following outcomes can be judged through direct observation:

After these units the pupil

adds fractions correctly;

prepares and delivers oral reports effectively;

recognizes birds in the local area;

summarizes effectively.

In many such situations in which some sort of skill is involved, it is relatively easy to provide test situations in which the *actual* behavior may be involved. This is the best way of measuring pupil progress, for it is a record of *actual behavioral change* desired in the lives of those involved. Test items which involve direct behavior frequently are known as *performance items*.

Planning or situational level. Unfortunately, it is not always possible to measure behavioral changes directly. In the first place, the teacher may not have an opportunity to see each pupil in a realistic situation which demands a direct application of the learning involved. Frequently the outcome will not be applied to any real life situation for several weeks or even months, simply because the learner will not find himself in a situation demanding such application. The teacher, in an effort to determine degree of understanding, will be obliged to resort to less direct measures. In such instances he can do no better than *simulate* an experience involving an appropriate application. In other words, he builds a realistic situation which demands an application of that which has been learned. For example, in a unit on first aid one evidence of understanding the principles involved would probably be: "He administers proper first aid when one is bleeding." It is impractical to cut someone to test the child; it is possible, however, to simulate or act out the experience. Since it is impossible to objectively evaluate such an experi-

[5] R. Murray Thomas, *Judging Student Progress*, Rev. Ed. (New York: David McKay Co., Inc., 1962), pp. 33–37.

ence for all 35–40 pupils in a class, a written description of a realistic situation may be as close to reality as is possible. Thus one is measured on the basis of what he would *plan* to do in the situation rather than his *actions* in the situation. Such a procedure obviously is a compromise with what is desired, because people do not always behave the way they plan to behave. For instance, in the foregoing illustration one might describe a fully adequate plan of action, whereas in the actual situation he might become hysterical and do nothing. Despite the exceptions, however, an indication of what one *thinks* he would do in a lifelike situation is a reasonably sound prediction of what he actually would do. Therefore most people plan ahead.

Factual or recall level. Sometimes teachers assume that if a person can recall the important facts in an area he will make actual applications when needed. Using the preceding illustration, one could assume that a pupil who could describe what to do for bleeding could be reasonably expected to apply that knowledge. It is assumed that the pupil will use such information to *plan* his actions and that he will *behave* according to his plans. There is considerable evidence, however, indicating a considerable gap between *verbal* understanding and actual behavior. Behavior expected in a recall situation is very similar to the behavior experienced in the original learning situation. Thus the pupil is expected to store in his mind certain information, and the behavior expected later consists of remembering this information. Experience in transfer of learning afforded by the test is slight.

The levels of behavior described in the foregoing, to be sure, are somewhat arbitrary. There will be occasions which are borderline cases, but it is believed that such an hierarchy (crude as it is) serves a useful purpose. Some writers, in forming tests, have developed as many as six or seven categories or levels of item difficulty.[6] As it is quite evident that the behavioral or performance level of testing is preferred, this type of item should be employed whenever possible. Lacking the opportunity for performance test items, a teacher should emphasize the planning or situational item. By so doing he usually will find that some of his test items, in reality, demand behavior at the performance level, some at the planning or situational level, and some at the factual level. It should be noted that actual performance is impossible without the employment of facts. Likewise, one's *plan* of action in a simulated situation demands the use of pertinent facts. Thus both the behavioral and the situational test item indirectly measure factual retention, but they do more! The pupil is

[6] Benjamin S. Bloom, Ed., *Taxonomy of Educational Objectives, Handbook I* (New York: David McKay Co., Inc., 1956), pp. 62–200.

required to take another step(s) in the direction of life applications. Therefore, the description of test items which follows emphasizes the planning or situational level assuming that performance tests frequently are not possible. Test items of this nature are difficult to construct, but they are, nevertheless, worthwhile. When used as teaching devices they materially increase the degree of transfer of training from the schoolroom to related life experiences.

What testing and observational tools assist the teacher in evaluating pupil progress?

The process of evaluation begins with a statement of goals or purposes. As illustrated in Chapter 4, the goals of each unit (and lesson) are described in terms of actual behaviors the teacher hopes will result from the instructional process. Once anticipated pupil outcomes are stated, it is relatively easy to select class activities (methods) which seem reasonably certain of developing the learner in the direction of the anticipated outcomes. Finally it becomes necessary to determine how effective the learning experiences have been in helping the pupil accomplish the goals (evaluation). Thus the teacher is faced with the problem of determining what pupil behaviors should indicate goal accomplishment. During the regular class activities many outcomes can be evaluated. Additional evidence of goal achievement, however, usually is desired through the medium of written tests. To illustrate the close relationship between goals, method, and evaluation, an example is given below:

After this unit in reading, the pupil should further *understand* the "tall tale" stories, as evidenced by:

1. His response in a class discussion comparing tall tale stories with other fictional materials;

2. His ability to write his own tall tale story;

3. His skill in discriminating between tall tale paragraphs and real life situation paragraphs.

The teacher, on the basis of the three behavioral outcomes, could plan a class discussion, a writing exercise, and a situation or some situations requiring discrimination between tall tales and real life situations. The experiences do lend themselves to measurement and evaluation, but they will be *learning* situations. Some pupils will show little achievement simply because they are *in the process* of achieving the goal. A test can indicate what has been achieved *as a result of* the learning experiences. Tests also serve as learning experiences in themselves.

It is suggested that the teacher make a copy of each of the unit goals, listing the major concepts which pertain to each. He then can make a brief note of the type of test question(s) which seems most appropriate for each concept. A resourceful teacher will jot down ideas as he goes along—while the goals and concepts are fresh in his mind.

Although a multitude of test types have been described most of them can be classified as multiple-choice, true-false, matching, completion, and essay. Except for the essay-type item, test questions are said to be objective. This does not mean that the test item itself is objective, but that the scoring of the item is more or less objective. For example, five different people scoring the item independently should assign the same score. Essay items, conversely, are said to be of a subjective nature. Thus the score assigned to an item would be somewhat dependent on the scorer and his values. Emphasis here has been placed on those test types which generally have proven most effective in practice.

Multiple-choice test items. Learning has been described as, basically, that of resolving issues—both great and small. Accordingly, many teaching methods are merely systematized approaches to the resolution of issues. Testing, then, ideally would become an additional experience in the resolution of issues. The multiple-choice item seems to lend itself to the problem-solving situation better than other objective-type test items. Many of man's most difficult problems involve the making of choices between known alternatives. The choices made in relatively simple problem situations often materially affect his degree of success and/or happiness in life. This, according to Harris,[7] is not greatly different from the problem of a pupil choosing between alternatives on a multiple-choice test item. The long test of time has convinced test constructors of the generally superior versatility and convenience of multiple-choice items. While other forms can be used effectively in special situations, the multiple-choice is more widely applicable and generally effective.[8]

The multiple-choice question consists of an item stem and four or five responses, one of which is the best answer. The other answers are usually referred to as foils or distractors. The item stem can be in the form of a direct question or an incomplete sentence. In essence, the item stem poses the problem situation and the possible answers represent the alternative solutions. The pupil "solves" the problem by making a choice. All the foils or distractors should be plausible to those who lack the

---

[7] Chester W. Harris, Ed., *Encyclopedia of Educational Research*, 3rd Ed. (New York: The Macmillan Co., 1960), p. 1507.
[8] *Ibid.*

necessary understanding of the concept application involved. Some teachers include distractors which on the surface are all quite acceptable, i.e., they represent accurate statements. Only one of the five possible answers is best, however, *in terms of the situation posed.* As a general frame of reference the possible answers should include one *preferred* answer; one distractor will represent a near miss; another will indicate a crude error; while the remaining distractors will tend to fall some place between those two extremes. Teachers sometimes make use of the distractors "all of these" or "none of these." These responses can be used effectively only when the question calls for a highly specific answer which is either completely correct or incorrect.

As indicated above, many teachers have constructed test items in such a manner as to merely elicit responses which have been memorized. Items which require the learner to demonstrate an *application* of learning to new and practical situations are much superior to factual, recall items. An application-type item requires that one understand an abstraction, *in addition to* making an appropriate application to a new situation. According to Bloom, the problem may be ". . . a) posed in a situation which is fictional, b) one which is drawn from material with which the student is not likely to have yet had contact, or c) on a problem known to the student, but a new slant that he is unlikely to have thought of previously." [9] He concludes that the new slant on common situations probably represents the most suitable source of new, yet realistic, items. Such items, however, are most difficult to construct.

As in any type of test item, there are likely to be a number of reasons for a pupil failing to make the appropriate applications to a multiple-choice test item. He could misunderstand the item stem or any one of the distractors; he could interpret the question in a unique way; or he simply may not possess an adequate understanding of the concepts necessary for the application. If the first two reasons are involved the item is not valid *for that particular individual.* Sometimes a teacher desires to achieve greater validity by giving the pupil an opportunity to qualify or otherwise justify his answer. This enables the teacher to give credit for a choice which might have been justifiably selected *from the pupil's point of view,* even though it ordinarily would have been considered incorrect. Ultimately, however, the teacher must decide whether or not the reason given is sufficient to warrant full credit for the response.

To further illustrate the modified, situational form of the multiple-choice item, an example follows:

[9] Bloom, *op. cit.*, p. 125.

The following illustration is taken from the unit concerning "tall tale" stories. One of the unit goals could be stated as follows: "After this unit the pupil should be able to understand the characteristics of a "tall tale story." One of his test questions has been reproduced:

_____ A. What is one characteristic of a tall tale story?

    1. A rumor or piece of gossip.

    2. Exaggerated narrative about some event.

    3. A written legend about some event.

    4. A true narrative about some event.

  B. Indicate a reason for your choice.

If it can be assumed that, during the instructional process, the teacher did not use the specific situation employed in the test item, the test question involved a knowledge of the facts or concepts employed, *in addition to applications of these learnings to new situations.* Thus the pupil must "go the second mile" to respond properly to the question. The preferred response to the example A was 2. It is possible that an individual will select the appropriate response on the basis of some purely extraneous element which has little relationship to his understanding of the concept involved, or it may be that a pupil has developed a partial understanding of the concept involved. In either case, B should serve to probe, still further, one's depth of understanding. As indicated previously, it is always possible that the reason for an inappropriate choice will be quite acceptable when seen *from the respondent's point of view.* Thus the *modified* forms enable the teacher to give credit in such conditions as seem warranted.

Sometimes the question arises as to whether or not some credit should be allowed for a "near miss." Let us suppose that distractor 3 in Item A is a near miss and that distractor 1 happens to be a "crude error." Is it not reasonable to assume that the individual who selects 3 has a better understanding of the issue than the individual who selects 1? Davis and Fifer [10] found that the practice of allowing some credit for such item distractors increased test reliability without reducing test validity. Sometimes one wonders if credit should be extended for the respondent's qualification (reason) when the original response is inappropriate. In some instances such a practice will be quite appropriate,

[10] Frederick B. Davis and Gordon Fifer, "The Effect on Test Reliability and Validity of Scoring Attitude and Achievement Tests with Weights for Every Choice," *Educational and Psychological Measurement,* 19: 159–170 (1959).

especially if the preferred response and the near miss are nearly alike. Thus one *may* select the near miss for the same general reason that another would select the preferred response.

True-false test items. True-false test items have lost much of their original popularity within recent years. There are many serious limitations associated with their use. Among the most serious is a tendency for the user to emphasize isolated facts which often hold slight validity in relation to the class objectives. Contrary to popular belief, the true-false item is so difficult to construct that it has little usefulness.

> The basic weakness of the true-false item is not its susceptibility to guessing, as is often suggested, but its tendency to ambiguity. Writing a collection of statements which are categorically true or false is a difficult task.[11]

This type of question tends to penalize the brighter pupil, as he is more likely to think of the exception which can alter the intended meaning. Furthermore, test makers tend to make more items true than false, to use specific determiners (all, never, entirely, and so on), to use textbook language, and the like.

It is possible, however, to substantially improve the true-false item so that it can serve a useful function. Even if one desires to emphasize broad concepts and selection among alternatives on a test, it is quite likely that he also will desire to test for certain specific data. In such a case the true-false test item becomes quite useful. The item can be substantially improved by *encouraging pupils to apply what they have learned.* For example, a teacher constructed the following true-false item for such a purpose:

OY is a diphthong in boy.

The item demands at least some understanding in relation to application. It also is desirable to write questions which emphasize main points rather than minute details. One of the most important means of improving the item is to use the *modified* form. Such items are designed to permit a pupil to justify or to improve an answer so that it will become a correct answer. The pupil is asked to correct all incorrect items. In order to guard against the addition or deletion of something like the word "not" as a means of correcting an item, it usually is necessary to underline certain key clauses or phrases. The pupil is asked to change

[11] Harris, *op. cit.*, p. 1508.

the underlined portion in such a manner as to make the statement correct. Illustrating with the previous example:

OY is a diphthong in boy.

If change is necessary the pupil should alter the underlined portion only. Pupils may be allowed some credit for the mere recognition of a true or false statement and additional credit for their ability to make appropriate corrections.

Completion test items. For a time, when objective tests were in vogue the completion item was overemphasized. Like the true-false item, its answer was easy to defend by merely referring the pupil to a particular page in his textbook. As a consequence, specific details and, all too often, meaningless verbalism were emphasized. The objectives of the subject area often were forgotten when tests were being constructed. The inevitable result was a tendency to gear the entire instructional process to memorizations. Pupils, likewise, realizing they would be tested in such a manner, tended to emphasize the recall of specific details and terminology.

Despite the inherent weaknesses involved, there are occasions when the meaning of a term and the like is important enough for the inclusion of some recall items. In fact, most tests will contain a limited number of such items. As its name implies, the item is answered by the completion of a statement. There is an ever-present danger, however, of a statement so mutilated that the respondent is unable to understand the meaning intended. For this reason, some teachers have changed the uncompleted statement to a question form. The following example was taken from an arithmetic test:

A numerator is _____.

What is a numerator? _____

Although both forms elicit the same information, the second one is probably easier to answer because it is worded as a complete thought. Furthermore, the answers can be placed in a column to facilitate marking.

Matching test items. Like the completion item, the matching question is of relatively minor importance. It is used when teachers desire pupils to relate such things as dates and events, terms and definitions, persons and places, or causes and events. Its chief disadvantage is that it is not very well adapted to the measurement of real understandings as opposed to rote memory. Because the separate items in the exercise should be homogeneous in nature, there is the likelihood of test clues which reduce validity. Multiple-choice items should be used whenever possible to replace the matching test item.

Appropriate use of the item is facilitated by (1) having at least five and not more than twelve responses, (2) including at least three extra choices from which responses must be chosen, and (3) using only homongeneous items or related materials in any one exercise.

Essay test items. One of the most controversial test items is the essay question. Prior to the advent of the objective test in the early decades of the present century, the essay item was the basic tool for testing. In most of the countries of Europe this is still the case. The weaknesses of this type of item are many. Yet, for certain purposes, it is invaluable. The item, unlike objective items, measures a pupil's ability to compose an answer to a question in prose.

The essay test item is particularly vulnerable to unreliability, discussed earlier. Unlike objective items, however, it is also subject to scorer unreliability. To some extent, a pupil's mark on such an item is dependent on the reader rather than on the actual quality of a response. Such weaknesses, however, can be minimized with due precautions. The item is probably here to stay for four main reasons:

1. The use of objective tests only would tend to adversely affect teaching methods and the curriculum generally.

2. It is relatively easy to construct valid and reliable essay tests, as compared to the difficulty experienced in constructing objective tests.

3. The essay item demands a demonstration of writing ability not required by objective items.

4. The essay test apparently has uniquely beneficial effects on pupil learning.

As with other test items, the essay question can be substantially improved if it is so constructed as to elicit an application of learnings to new or different situations. Test reliability can be improved by giving hints concerning the structure of the answer expected. Sometimes this is called the *qualified* essay question. An illustration of the *situational* essay, in which the answer is somewhat *qualified*, follows:

The teacher who wrote this question was teaching a unit on the use of the library. Her purpose was: "After this unit the pupil should have developed skill in finding library resources."

1. You want to find information about gopher snakes. There are no books that treat gopher snakes only. Discuss how you would find the information, beginning with the card catalog and what you would do when you locate a book.

Scoring reliability is substantially improved by formulating an answer in advance of attempting to mark the questions. Sometimes it is desirable to underline or otherwise call attention to key points. Pupils, likewise, may be asked to underline key phrases to call the reader's attention to important points.

With the variety of different test items available, a teacher may wonder which ones to use. For most tests at least a few of most of the foregoing types of items might be included. Generally there will be more multiple-choice items than any other single type, but the fact remains that only a certain type of test item may be preferable for determining achievement toward a particular class objective.

Although the problematic test item has proved to be a most versatile measuring instrument, there are numerous classroom evidences of progress toward goals which cannot be readily tested. Direct observation of pupil behavior is of utmost importance. Unfortunately, observation is subject to gross error. In fact, the reliability and validity of observation can be so low sometimes as to make the evaluation utterly useless.

Miss Duncan was marking report cards. In the space allotted for "citizenship" she was instructed to put a + (good), √ (fair), or − (poor). As she came to each report card she attempted to assess the quality of the factor on the basis of general impressions.

The foregoing type of evaluation is all too common in the public schools. This practice not only lacks reliability and validity, but it tends to endanger rapport between teacher and pupil. The child tends to resent such a haphazard approach to evaluation. Some teachers, feeling dissatisfied with such a practice, have given up all attempts to evaluate performance in this way. Others, realizing its potential value, have sought to devise instruments which minimize some of the more apparent difficulties encountered. Generally, they have made use of rating scales, check lists, and Behavioral Journal entries.

Rating scales. Although rating scales have been developed and used as effective *measuring* instruments, they are usually most effective as *gross guides to evaluation.* Rating scales are used for evaluating situations or charactics that are present in varying degrees. The word *scale* indicates a graduated scaling instrument. They seem to work best for judging behavior or products which are easily observable. Due to their subjective nature, they are usually used as supplementary evaluations or in areas where more objective instruments are not available.

As in the case of other instruments used for evaluative purposes, the teacher first must decide what is to be judged. If he has already stated goals in terms of behavorial outcomes, the task is relatively easy. The specific outcomes often form the main points on the scale. Each trait or dimension to be evaluated is then broken down into three or more descriptions, representing qualities of performance. These are usually arranged systematically below a horizontal line. When completed the evaluater checks any point along the line from an indication of a very strong to a very weak performance. By writing out somewhat detailed descriptions greater validity may be assured. The illustration which follows was one teacher's attempt to devise a scale for evaluating oral reading:

Pauses appropriately at punctuation marks.	Pauses properly for periods, but overlooks other punctuation marks.	Runs together words; punctuation marks avoided.

The number of categories for each trait or dimension being scaled has been a subject of some discussion. Generally, the greater the number of categories available the greater the accuracy of observation will be. Due to the difficulty of constructing and using instruments of several categories, many teachers prefer scales with three to five categories.

Reliability of a rating scale can be improved if the rater is permitted to disregard any dimension(s) which does not seem to be present in sufficient quantity for an evaluation. Somewhat related to this is the problem of agreement between observations or observers. For many purposes at least three observations should be obtained. By pooling the judgment of a number of persons, greater reliability can be achieved.

As indicated in the foregoing discussion, validity is increased by establishing somewhat detailed descriptions of the factor being evaluated. Another technique for increasing validity is use of an *anchor item,* enabling the observer to make a general appraisal of the effectiveness displayed. An anchor item may be necessary for several reasons. In the first place, construction of a rating scale makes it necessary for the user to predict all dimensions of importance in the performance. Seldom is this possible, especially when one considers the wide variability of pupil personalities represented in a heterogeneous group of children. Furthermore, there is some evidence that a general impression dimension, although woefully inadequate as the *only* criterion, may effectively serve as *one* criterion. An example of an anchor item on a rating scale is: What is your general impression of the child's use of punctuation marks?

The fallacy of using a rating scale as a *measuring* instrument becomes evident when one realizes that the units or categories are arbitrary, and that the comparative interval sizes are not equal at all points along the continuum. For example, small differences at the extreme "desirable" or "undesirable" end of the scale indicate a greater variation than an equal difference at the middle of the scale. Thus one child may earn an "average" score on the basis of "average" ratings on all dimensions. On a similar scale, another pupil may receive a better than average score even though one or two dimensions are extremely weak. The scores may not be indicative of the relative worth of the performances, as indicated in the following illustrations:

Mary was awarded a numerical score near the average category on the basis of the following dimensions deemed important in oral reading: Enunciaton; Audience Contact; Words Not Able to Pronounce; Punctuation; Expression. She was rated near average on *all* dimensions.

Susie was awarded an above-average score on the basis of the same dimensions. Although she was especially strong in most traits, she received very low ratings on Expression. These low ratings, however, still enabled Susie to earn more points than Mary.

It should be obvious, therefore, that extremely low (or high) ratings on one or more dimensions can, in effect, render all other dimensions almost valueless. A *numerical score* sometimes fails to reveal special weaknesses or strengths. Many teachers, instead of attempting to use the rating scale to *measure* dimensions of a performance, use the ratings as mere *guidelines* in *evaluating* the performance.

In addition to the foregoing problems associated with the use of rating scales, the user should be aware of certain other factors which can limit their usefulness:

1. *"Halo" effect.* This factor seems to be associated with a response set of the person or object being rated. While there is some basis for the belief that it helps to reverse some of the dimensions being evaluated, some teachers find the practice a bit confusing.

2. *Tendency to avoid extremes.*

3. *Personal bias.* This factor can cause a rater to exaggerate certain dimensions, while minimizing others in terms of preconceived notions.

Despite the many sources of error commonly associated with rating scales, they can serve a very useful purpose and should find a place in every classroom instructional program. There are numerous traits which are measurable only through observational procedures. A number of personality traits are amenable to rating. These are: efficiency, originality, perseverance, quickness, judgment, energy, scholarship, leadership, and intelligence. As more precise trait definitions are developed other personality traits may soon become amenable to reliable rating.

Check lists. A check list differs from a rating scale in that no effort is made to evaluate the dimensions. It consists of items or dimensions, such as activities or characteristics, which are checked if present. Its chief function is to call attention to the items themselves rather than to their relative importance. The instrument has many uses. It often is used when some standardized sequence of operation is involved, such as a science experiment. Sometimes it is used as an aid in checking off certain characteristics, such as the readiness for a particular task, for example, reading readiness.

Behavioral Journal. A Behavioral Journal is a factual, observational record of specific incidents in the life of a pupil. Each entry should be *significant* of the trait or dimension under consideration. Such observations are recorded often enough to indicate *direction* of growth. Although the Behavioral Journal has many obvious limitations, it is useful when one must evaluate progress toward goals which cannot be judged in any other way. After surveying the existing research in the area, Harris [12] found that social adjustment and growth, personal and emotional adjustment, and related factors could be effectively evaluated on the basis of cumulative entries in the Behavioral Journal.

The instrument consists of (1) identifying data, such as date, time, and place of the incident; (2) a description of the situation in which the incident occurred; and (3) a *factual* description of the incident.

The user must continuously guard against mixing his personal evaluations with his report of the incident. It has been found that evaluations should be withheld until a number of incidents are recorded. Teachers tend to make their recordings too general for effective use. By quoting what was said, one is much more likely to make an accurate record of the actual event than by merely interpreting what happened. An example of an entry in the Behavioral Journal follows:

April 4, 1968. The boys from my classroom were on the basketball court. Jimmy was standing near the basket. The ball bounced toward him. Jimmy reached out to get the ball and ran off the court with the ball. The boys ran after Jimmy and grabbed the ball from Jimmy. He lowered his head and walked away. Later he told me, "The boys don't like me and I hate them!"

[12] *Ibid.*, p. 931.

The number of entries needed for a reasonably accurate evaluation has long been a subject of discussion. Obviously, the more entries one has on file the more likely he is to obtain an accurate picture of the dimension under investigation. By averaging just one entry per week for a child, a teacher usually can present a defensible case if necessary. It is extremely important that the user avoid the collection of data only for the purpose of confirming a preconceived point of view. As in all other aspects of teaching, the teacher must be as objective as possible—recording both positive and negative data which seem significant. In an attempt to attain maximum objectivity, some teachers have established a time-sampling system. For example, one may decide that an entry of Johnny's behavior on Thursday of each week will be made. The actual entry will consist of the first significant incident which occurs on the prescribed day. A few entries on pupils with problems, when combined with those of other teachers, are extremely valuable in helping the guidance counselor develop a program of remedial treatment.

USE OF REPORT CARDS

Reports to parents have been and still are the major means of communication between teacher and parents. They have been criticized as professionally unsound; they have created misunderstandings between teacher and parent and teacher and pupil; they have been altered repeatedly. Yet the basic problems remain virtually unchanged. Although few people are completely satisfied with this technique of reporting, report cards are here to stay—at least for the foreseeable future.

What are the basic problems associated with report cards?

The basic premise underlying the use of report cards is sound. Parents do need periodic reports on the progress of their children; they need guidance in cooperating with the school. Indeed, report cards have become traditional. Efforts to replace them with other techniques of reporting have usually met with strong parental resistance.

The most common report card is the A-B-C-D-F form, representing a range from exceptional to unacceptable work. The marks are usually based on where a pupil stands in relation to the rest of his class. Another common type of report card is the S-U form, which is used mainly in the lower elementary grades. The marks represent "Satisfactory" or "Unsatisfactory" work based on the pupil's own effort rather than comparison with other children in the classroom.

While the two systems of reporting appear simple enough, they have proven most unsatisfactory in practice. Marks of this kind are extremely abstract. What does a "C" or "S" mean, for example? Does it mean that Johnny has been content with mediocre work? What elements of the educational process were included in the mark? What can his parents do to help him improve his class achievement? The traditional report card tells none of this. Furthermore, a "C" or "S" in one curriculum area may not be equivalent to a "C" or "S" in another area.

Many parents and teachers alike object to report card grades based on total class achievement only as in the A-B-C-D-F system. It is recognized that, under such a system, some pupils can make "A's" with a minimum of effort, while others are destined to fail because of their limited abilities; however, the S-U marking system has faults, too. Lumping together excellent, good, and fair achievement tends to decrease pupil effort. Furthermore, marking pupils according to their capacities to achieve is no simple matter. Parents still want to know how their children stand in relation to the rest of the class.

In the elementary school, report cards have been supplemented and sometimes replaced by letters and/or parent-teacher conferences. Parent-teacher conferences are extremely helpful in the elementary schools because a teacher may receive information concerning the child that may be difficult to receive from any other source. The parents attending these conferences also feel that they are cooperating in their child's educative process. Communication is not directed "one-way" like a report card, because at a conference the parents and the teacher may discuss in a frank, understandable way the difficulties or achievements made by the child. Reporting at parent-teacher conferences, then, becomes an excellent means of supplementing the report card.

Other reporting innovations have included separate marks for a variety of characteristics associated with learning. Some of these factors included initiative, cooperation, attitude, social habits, work habits, and so on. In addition, spaces have sometimes been provided on the report card for teacher and parent comments. These too have often been disappointing in practice. How does one measure such factors as initiative and attitude? Does lack of initiative always reflect on the learner? Is it not likely that, in some cases, the difficulty might be more closely associated with the teacher than with the pupil?

What are some trends in school reports?

In an effort to correct at least *some* of the inherent weaknesses of report cards, a number of changes are becoming fairly common. Today
many school systems have adopted a dual marking system. Such reports
contain one mark for achievement in relation to the entire class and
another mark for the pupil's estimated individual ability to achieve. One
pupil, for example, may receive an "A" or "S" grade based on the progress of the rest of his class, but may receive only a "C" or "√" for effort.
This simply means that he has not been working very hard for his "A"
or "S." On the other hand, another pupil may receive a "C" or "S"
grade, but an "A" or *no* check for effort. This indicates to the parents
that the child has been working very hard for his "C" or "S." Thus, no
further encouragement from his parents is in order. Today's report card
frequently contains a few spaces for comments. A teacher may or may
not elect to further clarify a report by making written comments. In
addition, parent-teacher conferences are being urged in some school
systems whenever they seem necessary.

Recently a number of comprehensive studies have been made with
respect to school reports. One of the most intensive of these was conducted by Langdon and Stout. In this study 865 families from eight
different states were interviewed. The investigators, among other things,
wanted to know what the parents would like in a school report. The
parents wanted report cards consistent with the above, but they wanted
more:

*One thing parents always want to know: Will we be told if our child is hav-
ing difficulty, even if it is not regular report time?* They say that they want
to feel sure that if there is any difficulty, they will be notified at once; that
they do not want poor work to come as a shock at report time when they
have supposed all was well; that they want to know in time to be of help
before it is too late. Many feel that a quarterly or even a six-weeks' report is
not enough; that they would like to know more often how their child is getting along. If the school is one where parents are encouraged to ask about
their youngster's work and are welcome to come to school, the teacher makes
this clear.[13]

It is seen from the above that these parents wanted to know immediately when a child encountered difficulty. This group of parents appropriately conceived themselves as being active participants in the edu-

---

[13] Grace Langdon and Irving W. Stout, *Helping Parents Understand Their
Child's School* (Englewood Cliffs, N. J.: Prentice-Hall, Inc., 1957), p. 379.

cative process. They wanted to know of the difficulty *in time,* so that appropriate remedial action could be taken.

While it seems highly unlikely that *all* parents would be able and willing to cooperate as much as desired, Langdon and Stout's study does indicate a healthy trend: *Parents are coming to recognize their role in the educative process.* The report card is a form of communication. While it still leaves much to be desired, it is often the *only* direct form of communication, and, as such, is an extremely important aspect of teaching. As indicated in a report by the Texas Association for Supervision and Curriculum Development, ". . . reporting methods and understandings need to be developed with a view of getting away from teachers' reporting *to* parents except as a temporary station on the way toward reporting as communication between teachers, parents, and pupils." [14]

The psychological impact of report card grades is tremendous. In teacher education so much time has been devoted to studying content, along with instructional methods and techniques, that the central position of grades and reporting often comes as a shock to the new teacher. Yet the report card is sometimes the only remaining link which connects parents and teacher—both of whom have a vital interest in the education of children. Both parties can and *ought* to be cooperating participants in the educative process. It is the responsibility of the school to initiate and encourage such a relationship.

FUNCTIONS AND PRINCIPLES OF AN EFFECTIVE PROGRAM

The foregoing techniques and procedures of measurement, evaluation, and reporting should be useful to the teacher who desires to improve the teaching-learning process. They deal with some of the most critical problems in teaching and suggest practical applications. Emphasis has been on construction and use of measurement and evaluation instruments. Emphasis also has been on the use of raw data in the evaluation of pupil progress. This chapter would not be complete, however, without some treatment of general functions and principles of a measurement and evaluation program. For the teacher who has developed some skill in technique, these general guidelines may serve well.

---

[14] Texas Association for Supervision and Curriculum Development, *Reporting is Communication* (Washington, D. C.: Association for Supervision and Curriculum Development, 1956), p. 57.

What functions do measurement and evaluation serve?

Unfortunately, some teachers have thought of measurement and evaluation devices as little more than tools for determining degree of factual retention. It has been established that the practice of testing for detailed facts creates learning situations which likewise emphasize the memorization of facts. Facts are *important*. Most tests, however, should also go beyond factual retention to generalization and use. Regardless of how broad or worthy one's objectives may be, the type of measurement and evaluation expected, to a marked degree, determines the nature of that which is learned. Therefore, this aspect of the instructional program is more than just a check on progress; it permeates the entire instructional program. Some of the more important functions are listed below.

1. *Measurement and evaluation serve to determine progress toward major class goals.* Goals which are stated vaguely are extremely difficult to measure. Throughout this book emphasis has been placed on goals in terms of actual behavioral outcomes expected.

2. *Measurement and evaluation may serve a diagnostic purpose.* By discovering weaknesses in the instructional program, the teacher may reteach for the purpose of correcting deficiencies.

3. *Tests may serve as a review of important concepts.*

4. *Tests may help the learner make applications to life experiences.* This may be especially true when the teacher employs *application* or *situational* test items as recommended in this chapter.

5. *Through measurement and evaluation (rating scales and check lists especially), the learner may become more adept at self-evaluation.* The ultimate purpose of any instructional program or aspect thereof should be to make the learner better qualified to direct his own affairs.

6. *The processes of measurement and evaluation enable both the teacher and the child to compare achievement with other members of the peer group and the learner to make self-comparison.*

7. *Measurement and evaluation often motivate pupils to greater effort.* Although there are many other sources of motivation, few doubt the value of measurement and evaluation as one primary source.

What principles govern these procedures?

Many of the specific guidelines which have been established in this chapter may be summarized as general guiding principles. Even though an individual may have acquired a great deal of skill in developing and applying sound measurement and evaluation techniques, repeated review of the principles which follow may be most helpful.

1. Measurement and evaluation include tests of all types, rating scales, check lists, Behavioral Journals, and any other instrument which can be applied effectively to pupil behavior.

2. Measurement, evaluation, and reporting are continuous processes.

3. Measurement, evaluation, and reporting are usually more effective when pupils understand and become active participants in the experiences.

In constructing tests the guidelines which follow may be applicable to all types of items.

1. Avoid ambiguity.

2. Be sure to test in terms of class goals.

3. Avoid specific determiners.

4. Make keys for all tests.

5. Avoid textbook and figurative language.

6. Make questions brief and concise.

7. Do not include an item several times unless it is a diagnostic test.

8. Avoid tricky questions.

9. Determine length of test by maturity of children and time available.

10. Group similar types of questions together.

11. Acquaint pupils with all types of examinations.

12. Make provisions for easy scoring of the test.

A number of guidelines apply to each test type.

A. Completion items

    1. Avoid over-mutilated questions (statements).

    2. Do not indicate answer by length of blank.

B. True-false items

    1. Avoid double negatives.

    2. Avoid statements partly true and partly false.

3. Include at least 15 items.

C. Multiple-choice items

1. Avoid making best choice consistently short or consistently long.

2. Use complete rather than incomplete statements.

3. Make every possible response plausible to some pupils.

D. Matching items

1. Use not less than five items nor more than twelve.

2. Keep all responses and statements in the same category.

3. Keep each matching test on one page.

4. Make the number of choices greater than the number of blanks.

E. Essay items

1. Use this type largely to see if pupil understands functional relationships.

2. Always indicate clearly the type of discussion desired; call for brevity.

3. Weigh questions only on basis of indicated responses.

SUMMARY

In this chapter techniques of measurement, evaluation, and reporting have been emphasized. The functional importance of reliability, validity, and objectivity has been stressed, as they apply to the process of measuring and evaluating pupil progress. Emphasis was placed on the improved versions of multiple-choice, true-false, and essay items. Such improvements are designed to help the pupil relate classroom learnings to real life applications. Included among the guides to observation were rating scales, check lists, and Behavioral Journals.

Reporting procedures were discussed. The basic problems associated with the report card were emphasized. Parent-teacher conferences were briefly mentioned as a supplement to the report card. Finally, some basic trends in reporting procedures were given.

The last portion of this chapter represented an attempt to review and summarize some general functions and principles of an effective measurement, evaluation, and reporting program.

QUESTIONS FOR STUDY AND DISCUSSION

1. What functions are served through classroom measurement? How do measurement and evaluation differ? What criteria are most useful in assessing the value of a measuring instrument? Measurement and evaluation have been described as the weakest aspect of the instructional process. Why?

2. Describe the different levels of item difficulty. Why is the "behavioral level of difficulty" considered preferable? Now construct some sample multiple-choice test items at the behavorial level. What problems do you encounter?

3. "The nature of test item expected determines the nature of the learning experience." Defend or refute this statement.

4. Which test type is preferable? Why? Question a group of teachers as to the type of test item most often utilized. What discrepancies do you find? Why?

5. What are the limitations of traditional report cards? How are reporting techniques being improved? What curriculum problems complicate the situation? It has been said that measurement and evaluation represent the weakest dimension of the instructional process. Why? What "solutions" seem most promising?

SELECTED BIBLIOGRAPHY

Adams, Georgia S., *Measurement and Evaluation in Education* (New York: Holt, Rinehart and Winston, Inc., 1964).

Adkins, Dorothy, *Test Construction* (Columbus, Ohio: Charles E. Merrill Books, Inc., 1960).

Ahmann, J. Stanley, *Evaluating Pupil Growth*, 2nd Ed. (Boston: Allyn and Bacon, Inc., 1963).

Association for Supervision and Curriculum Development, Sixty-Seventh Yearbook, *Evaluation as Feedback and Guide*. Edited by Fred T. Wilhelms (Washington, D. C.: The Association, 1967).

Chandler, Theodore A., "Improving Your Testing," *The Instructor*, 75, No. 2: 46–48 (October, 1965).

National Council for the Social Studies, Thirty-Fifth Yearbook, *Evaluation in Social Studies*. Edited by Harry D. Berg (Washington, D. C.: The Council, 1965).

Bloom, Benjamin S., Ed., *Taxonomy of Educational Objectives, Handbook I: The Cognitive Domain* (New York: David McKay Co., 1956).

Ebel, Robert L., *Measuring Educational Achievement* (Englewood Cliffs, N. J.: Prentice-Hall, Inc., 1965).

Eisner, Elliot W., "Critical Thinking; Some Cognitive Components," *Teachers College Record*, 66, No. 7: 624–634 (April, 1965).

Gorow, Frank F., *Better Classroom Testing* (San Francisco: Chandler Publishing Co., 1966).

Hammel, John A., "Report Cards: A Rationale," *National Elementary Principal*, 43: 50–52 (May, 1964).

Kooker, Earl W., "Evaluation, Vital Element in Teaching," *The Instructor*, 74: 3+ (June, 1965).

Krathwohl, David R., Benjamin S. Bloom, and Bertrand B. Masia, *Taxonomy of Educational Objectives, Handbook II: Affective Domain* (New York: David McKay Co., Inc., 1964).

Smith, Fred M. and Sam Adams, *Educational Measurement for the Classroom* (New York: Harper & Row, Publishers, 1966).

Thelen, Herbert A., "The Triumph of 'Achievement' Over Inquiry in Education," *The Elementary School Journal*, 60, No. 4: 190–197 (January, 1960).

Thomas, R. Murray, *Judging Student Progress*, Rev. Ed. (New York: David McKay Co., Inc., 1962).

Thorndike, Robert L., "Educational Decisions and Human Assessment," *Teachers College Record*, 66, No. 2: 103–112 (November, 1964).

Trow, William C., "On Marks, Norms, and Proficiency Scores," *Phi Delta Kappan*, 48, No. 4: 171–173 (December, 1966).

Weinberg, Carl, "The Price of Competition," *Teachers College Record*, 67, No. 2: 106–114 (November, 1965).

Maintaining Effective
Class Control:
Discipline Problems

ONE of the most difficult tasks of teaching is that of establishing and maintaining order in the classroom. Few hours go by without some behavior incident—be it large or small—which needs a teacher's attention. All teachers of children have discipline problems. Some teachers, however, have more than their share of classroom disturbances. Why is the problem of such magnitude?

The children were planning a class party. Mrs. Brady had turned the class over to the president of the class and left the room. Although most of the group were anxious to become involved in the planning process, Johnny proved to be a disturbing element. After being warned once or twice, he was literally ejected from the room—not by the president, but by those near enough to be disturbed by his unsolicited remarks.

Pupils in the foregoing situation were: (1) highly *motivated* to plan a problem of immediate concern; (2) they participated; (3) in essence, they established their own rules of conduct; and (4) individuals not willing to abide by the rules were subject to removal from the group. Although the classroom teacher cannot always provide these four ingredients, they might serve as useful guidelines. Indeed, if all pupils possessed a *consistent desire to learn* (motivation) there would be little difficulty in maintaining order. A number of specific techniques of motivation were described in Chapter 6. This chapter deals with methods of coping with problems which *result from ineffective motivational techniques*. It is recognized that even the best teacher at times will be forced to deal with such *symptoms* before he can remove the *causes* of the problem.

The chapter is divided into two parts: Discipline Problems; and

Principles and Problems in Handling Discipline. The reader is urged to study Chapter 6, Motivation Activities, along with this chapter. *It is recognized that most discipline problems arise as a consequence of ineffective motivation.*

DISCIPLINE PROBLEMS

A group of college students recently asked a number of experienced teachers to describe their most serious discipline problems. The responses which follow were repeated many times:

"I have difficulty in persuading pupils to conform to the rules."

"In my class children insist on talking with their neighbors."

"Today's youth often resist reading and drill lessons."

"I am bothered with the few who continually attempt to attract attention."

"Some pupils have given up. They defy anyone who would put them to work."

"Most disturbing is a wide variety of 'little things,' such as tardiness, requests to leave the room, locating books or pencils."

"I am disturbed by the inability of some pupils to control their own behavior in an acceptable manner."

The foregoing anecdotes suggest much of the current problem. Teachers themselves seem to expect different standards of conduct. Indeed, one's concept of discipline reflects his views on the nature of man. If, for instance, one thinks of children as being inherently "mean" or "bad," he is likely to think of discipline as enforced conformity. At the other end of the continuum are those who think of discipline as guided growth in self-control. This premise leads one to view the problem as an aspect of *teaching.*

What is discipline?

The word *discipline* is apparently derived from the root word *disciple* —meaning to follow or study under an accepted leader. In early civilization discipline implied teaching or helping one to grow or achieve. Later it became associated with blind conformity. Today it means many things to many people. It is probably the most talked about but least understood of all problems of teaching. As a matter of fact, there is practically no research on the subject.[1] Perhaps this condition is due to the fact that it was originally a very comprehensive and amorphous concept which has become smaller and smaller as different parts are crystallized and separated into different categories. For example, such problems as delinquency, emotional disturbances, and problems resulting from mental and educational retardation now tend to be handled as separate problems, as contrasted with the situation a few years ago. Today discipline tends to be confined largely "to the thoughtless and irresponsible acts of young people who are not maladjusted but are just uneducated and unsocialized." [2] The aim of good discipline is to help the individual adjust to the personal and social *forces* of his experiences.

First, the child must learn to adjust to himself as a growing and developing individual. He must achieve certain developmental tasks of the elementary school period if happiness and success in later tasks are to be achieved. These tasks include: (1) learning physical skills, (2) building wholesome attitudes, (3) learning to get along with age-mates, (4) learning an appropriate social role, (5) developing fundamental skills of communication, (6) developing concepts necessary for living, (7) developing conscience, morality, and scale of values, (8) achieving personal independence, and (9) developing attitudes toward social groups and institutions.[3]

Second, the child must adjust to the existing culture and institutions within which he participates. A reasonable degree of cooperativeness, conformity, and consistency of behavior is expected. Above all, he will have to accept certain basic cultural contradictions, such as race and religious minorities and nationality conflicts. Finally, he often will have to adjust standards of his home environment to those of the school.

Thus, the problem of discipline today consists mainly of helping the child develop disciplined and acceptable inner controls. The concept has shifted from uniform demands on everyone to the acceptance of variations in behavior by individuals and even the toleration of variations for a single individual as he is faced with changing conditions.

What variables tend to provoke discipline problems?

The room was hot and "stuffy." It was Friday and the last thirty minutes of the day. Everyone was excited about going to Jane's birthday party after school.

---

[1] Asahel D. Woodruff, "Discipline," in *Encyclopedia of Educational Research* (1960), p. 381.

[2] *Ibid.*

[3] Robert J. Havighurst, *Developmental Tasks and Education* (New York: David McKay Co., Inc., 1962), pp. 15–28.

Miss Bantz was more than a little disturbed. She had planned her lesson well, but after a few minutes most pretenses of interest had disappeared. Finally, Billy blurted out, "Why do we have to study this arithmetic anyway?"

At this point, Miss Bantz could contain her emotions no longer. She assured the class that the study of arithmetic was important so they could handle their financial problems when they were grown up.

About this time, Mark dropped a book. A few children giggled and began talking among themselves. Miss Bantz, visibly shaken, rapped for attention and said, "All right, if you can't discuss this problem you can open your arithmetic book to page 218 and do all the arithmetic problems on that page. If you don't finish the assignment in the remaining time, you will have to do it as homework."

A few pupils grumbled cautiously, but most of them made at least some pretense of doing the problems.

What caused Miss Bantz's problem? Was it the coming birthday party? The pupils? The arithmetic lesson? Or was it caused by Miss Bantz herself? An examination of the situation discloses a number of contributing factors. In the *first* place, there was the coming party. Such circumstances are numerous in the public schools of today. A typical elementary school may have all kinds of activities which disrupt the school day! A number of school situations which tend to contribute to disorder in the classroom are:

The last few minutes of the day.

The last few minutes prior to lunch.

The last few minutes of the day on Friday.

The first part of the class following recess or fire drill.

Before a holiday or classroom party.

The first few days of school.

Appearance of a substitute teacher.

The last few days of school.

Another variable contributing to Miss Bantz's discipline problems was *teacher-caused.* She was unable to develop an important purpose for studying arithmetic and tended to put the blame on pupils. Few people are able to make effective progress when they are uncertain as to why they are working at a task. Elementary school children need constant reminders of purpose, interpreted in language which they can readily understand. This means that it must be near their operational level of behavior. Would it have been possible to relate the study of arithmetic to their immediate interests or needs? The resourceful teacher would likely say "yes."

Furthermore, Miss Bantz permitted her emotions to interfere with sound teaching techniques. In the first place, it is not psychologically sound to assign school work as punishment. Neither is it appropriate to discipline a group for the transgressions of a few. Many discipline problems are, in fact, teacher-caused. Some of these are:

Inappropriate activity for the time of day or circumstances

Sarcasm

Inconsistency

Being impolite and inconsiderate

Having favorites

Gossiping about pupils in public places

Failure to make class and lesson purposes clear to pupils

Using the same method day after day.

Failure to provide for individual differences

Talking "over" noise

A classroom which is either too hot or too cold

Taking time out for calling roll, taking lunch money, and the like

Confusion resulting from disruption of class routines

Vague assignments

Emphasizing factual-type tests

A *third variable* contributing to disorder within Miss Bantz's classroom was *pupil-caused*. Pupils are usually quick to exploit an unfortunate situation. Some of them dislike school and most teachers associated with it. Others, just like all human beings, react in terms of health, emotions, and passing interests. More will be said of pupil-caused problems later.

While there is no "quick" solution to Miss Bantz's problem, the resourceful teacher might have openly acknowledged the pupils' preoccupation with the party by comparing arithmetic with arithmetic activities needed for a party, such as, how many cupcakes, balloons, or chairs are necessary for a party? Fractions could be taught through dividing a birthday cake, and so forth.

What is the nature of discipline problems?

You are working with . . . American children. This is not the same as training animals: a dog, a horse, a rat, or a cow or a team of oxen. Animals are never supposed to rebel . . . burn the lessons . . . into their brains, and into every pore of their bodies.

. . . Only the leaders think in dictator countries. The people obey. Your job is different. Your children must think *and* obey. They must fit in *and* break out. They must follow accepted paths *and* break out on their own.[4]

The elementary school child may be tasting independence as he goes off to school. This independence in a democratic society is most important. Yet without some conformity chaos follows. Hymes [5] makes a most useful distinction between *children with problems and problem children*. He contends that the vast majority of children are "well children" who need no more than "straight" teaching. Like all human beings, they have problems from time to time. With these children the teacher discusses, explains, interprets, and talks. This he calls the logical approach. With a few pupils, however, one must do "remedial teaching." These are the individuals whose past experiences have "hurt" them. They tend to be suspicious, resentful, and overly egocentric. By every act they "cry out" for attention, for success, for love, for security. With these few individuals (the "problem children") the teacher must do "remedial teaching," i.e., he must say "no" and mean it. These are the pupils who will hurt others and create an undesirable learning situation. Although they need and demand attention, they must be "stopped"—compelled to conform to class rules—*and then treated with all manner of kindness possible*. In Chapter 5 specific instructional techniques were offered for dealing with the less able and less interested pupil. These are frequently the persons who need the so-called remedial approach to discipline.

How can discipline be developed within stable children?

Discipline is hard for children to learn because it is made up of innumerable specifics. Truth, honesty, dependability, respect for property, privacy, personality, helpfulness to others, and protection of smaller people are just a few of the rules of society that each new generation must

---

[4] James L. Hymes, Jr., *Behavior and Misbehavior: A Teacher's Guide to Action* (Englewood Cliffs, N. J.: Prentice-Hall, Inc., © 1955), pp. 8–9. By permission.
[5] *Ibid.*

learn to uphold. Some children learn such lessons at home and need only *apply* them at school. Others must *learn* the rules of the game. The acquisition and alteration of attitudes and values take time. Patience is essential. One's teaching task in discipline is similar to his task in any other field. Children learn some things by listening, but they are more likely to remember and act on their *own words and ideas*. They need to solve their own problems: to make proposals, seek out and analyze the available data, test their own hypotheses, and examine their own results.

Placing emphasis on group and individual problem-solving techniques demands that one have a lot of faith in the capacity of a child to develop and uphold high standards of conduct. Pupils want, and have a right to expect, reasonable limits on their actions. Indeed, they often will impose unnecessarily high standards on themselves if given a free hand. In the final analysis, the boys and girls must do most of the thinking and most of the talking. The children must do their own learning.

Children will learn more quickly if they are permitted to assist in setting up their own rules of conduct. The teacher, however, must retain the right to determine what action is necessary when rules are broken. This is made necessary because behavior results from many *different* causes. The action to be taken must be determined by the cause(s) and the individual involved. For instance, a class may decide that late assignments should not count as much as those turned in on time. There are times, however, when such action would be most inappropriate (sickness, special emergencies, etc.). The teacher must weigh each case separately.

How does one respond to misbehavior of stable children? First he must determine the cause(s). If the teacher decides that the individual does not yet know or understand what is expected, he should *talk, discuss, and explain*. Sometimes difficulties result from the immediate environment, in which case it will be important to move the individual or otherwise *alter the environment*.

Occasionally a behavior problem demands more extreme action than that suggested in the preceding paragraph. Should the teacher then punish? Psychologists often refer to punishment as that action which blocks a given behavior. For example, the warning, "Don't talk while Mary is giving her report," is a punishment. This is the negative approach. Reward also can be used to control misbehavior. The teacher can say, "Now if we pay very close attention to Mary we should determind just how the _____ process works." Both reward and punishment are effective—both are appropriate techniques to use. Whenever possible, however, reward (the positive approach) should be used. Punishment causes one to remember because of pain, discomfort, or fear, whereas reward gives pleasure or satisfaction.

According to Hymes,[6] punishment should be used with caution. The resulting learning tends to be of a transitory nature, e.g., until the teacher has to leave the room. He offers some helpful guidelines in the appropriate use of punishment:

1. *Use it with stable children only.*

2. *Use it when youngsters are "ignorant of the law."* One must sometimes say, "Do not touch this machine"; "Do not move this microscope"; "Do not tamper with the chemicals in this cabinet."

3. *Use it only when they must learn the law quickly.* The pressure for quick results, however, does not often originate with what the child is doing. It is more often associated with the way the teacher is feeling!

4. *Use it only when the law is a specific one, applicable to a definite situation.*

The use of physical or corporal punishment is not mentioned in the preceding discussion, because it is usually considered an inappropriate technique to use with school-age children.

How can discipline be developed within disturbed children?

The thirsty man knows his trouble. He can tell you: "I want water." The hungry man can verbalize his emptiness: "Food. Give me food." The sleepy one can say to you: "I'm so tired I cannot keep my eyes open." These . . . youngsters do not know their trouble. They have no words to explain how they feel. They cannot say: "This is where it hurts." . . . They hurt, but they cannot tell you where or why or how.

. . . These psychological hungers are not nicely located—in the belly, in the throat, in the eyelids. They are all through the body . . . everywhere . . . in every pore, muscle, and nerve.[7]

A few children—probably not more than three or four in an average classroom—have not had their basic psychological needs adequately fulfilled. The result is a "gnawing emptiness" which tends to dominate their behavior patterns. They are the problem children. They are the ones whose problems seem to obscure the individuals behind them! Identification is easy—just look for the individuals who are always getting into trouble; the ones with negative school reputations.

Instead of proceeding with a straightforward approach to *teaching*,

[6] *Ibid.*, pp. 71–72.
[7] *Ibid.*, pp. 83–84.

a reverse order of procedure is in order for these children. They first must be stopped. They will hit others, make wisecracks, talk back, or do anything to attract attention. These children may be trying to satisfy nagging hungers. They seek—*they demand*—recognition, success, love and affection, a sense of personal worth. These behaviors represent their attempts to adjust. Although they realize that such behaviors often get them into difficulty, they know of no other alternatives. Some recognition, transitory as it is, is better than no recognition. The teacher must be firm with these children; otherwise, they will take over. Without firmness, without limits, the learning environment of up to thirty-five other pupils will be seriously jeopardized. One must be firm—say *no* and mean it—but he must also be *gentle*. As Hymes says in his book, *Behavior and Misbehavior*, the teacher must be firm but not severe. He will stop the child but not try to hurt him. *He* understands. The feeling is inside. It will not let him look with angry eyes—sympathy will show through. The misunderstood child "feels" the difference, simply because he has had ample experience with the other kind of treatment—when the correction was cold and hard. As a professionally trained person, he puts himself inside their skins, thinks with their brains, sees with their eyes. Then, and only then, can he understand that in spite of all the deviltry "inside" these children they are not at fault.

Teachers know what these children want. They will say with assurance: "He wants attention, to have his own way, to be boss." The analysis is easy because the clues are obvious. The next step also would be simple, except for the fact that one sometimes allows emotions to blur his vision. The classroom is a miniature society. Some people will lead, get the headlines, receive the glory. In many situations the teacher has the power to determine who receives these rewards. Who needs them the most? At this point the "starved" child for the first time may be able to satisfy his hungers in a socially acceptable manner. But what about the stable child? Do they deserve such rewards, too? Yes, but they can wait, for their basic needs are not nearly as demanding as are those of problem children. Furthermore, they have developed acceptable techniques of achieving such rewards on their own initiative. *Good behavior for stable children is an avenue to rewards. With problem children the rewards must come first so that they can develop good behavior.*

The problem is by no means solved, however, when such children are given opportunities to lead or otherwise gain recognition. They tend to overact or overrespond. The *new* experience for them is almost more than they can handle. Sometimes they may identify the reward as an excuse to disturb even more. This is a natural consequence, for such children have been accustomed to gaining attention in such a manner. In other words, they may get worse before they get better. As indicated in Chapter 8, when children are grouped sociometrically those who need the added security of close proximity with their mutual choices tend to overact. Even so, this is a sign of progress. The teacher "looks the other way" or, if necessary, channels the behavior into more constructive areas. A doctor does not expect a severely wounded patient to recover overnight. He has faith in himself, the patient, and the treatment being prescribed. These children are also sick—not just for a day, a week, or a year. Their "sickness" may extend over a period of one to fifteen years. Time and patience are essential. Cooperation with other teachers, with administrators, and with parents is needed. Indeed, a school-planned program of treatment is vitally needed.

There is one group of disturbed children which is not easily recognized as needing help. These children are the quiet ones—those who are not causing anyone else trouble but are nevertheless in trouble themselves. They are specialists at covering up. The trouble is there, but is bottled up inside. They are the ones who seek perfection, hide their emotions, or daydream. They are often fearful of social interaction, sometimes refusing to recite in class. "Pushing" is not the answer, nor is exacting high demands from them a satisfactory approach. They lack confidence in themselves, but clues to the causes are not readily apparent from their behavior. Thus, it often becomes necessary to turn to their pasts for answers to the problem. Parents, earlier teachers, and friends can often provide useful sources of data. In the meantime one can establish situations which provide a release for these "tightly sealed" feelings. Opportunities for composing stories or plays will help. Role playing may also provide the needed release. Although they may cause little or no trouble within the classroom, they are actually in greater trouble than those who overtly misbehave. It is a serious mistake to ignore them. They are the ones who can suddenly explode someday and literally destroy those with whom they associate.

How does one detect typical behavior problems?

Although symptoms of children with difficulty sometimes are revealed when least expected, there are certain activities which are especially likely to provide clues. Reference is here made to fairly stable children who, like all human beings, need help from time to time. As indicated in the foregoing section, seriously disturbed boys and girls are readily detected. The teacher is in an ideal position to prevent common problems from seriously undermining one's mental health. Certain activities tend to reveal valuable clues to personal-social adjustment.[8]

1. *Any time when controversial issues are discussed.* Significant clues to adjustment are indicated by the individual who rigidly defends his own ideas just because they are his own. He sometimes rejects opposing views because he dislikes the individuals proposing them. In all probability, such a pupil is experiencing some difficulty in satisfying his need for security.

2. *Self-directed activities.* Among the many advantages of the self-contained classroom is the opportunity it provides for the teacher to observe the work habits of children. Pupils who display over-dependence on others, those who are easily distracted, and those who "give up" easily can undoubtedly profit from immediate attention. Some of these individuals may lack a sense of personal worth; others may be bothered with home or other out-of-class problems; while still others may merely need goals clarified or re-emphasized.

3. *Group activities.* Even casual observation during group activities will disclose those who have difficulty in cooperative behavior, those who dominate, and those who tend to react negatively when their ideas are rejected. It is in such activities that a teacher can partially determine why certain individuals are always on the fringe of the group. While the behavior pattern may not be serious enough to result in total rejection, it can seriously impede one in reaching his maximum potential.

4. *Role-playing activities.* The type of role which one chooses to play may offer valuable clues to personality adjustment. Even more revealing are those roles assigned or suggested for certain individuals. During the unrehearsed free time play, clues are derived from those who show unusual hostility, tenseness, and so on.

5. *Pupil-led committee activities.* In these situations it is easy to spot those who have difficulty in accepting responsibilities from members of the peer group. Sometimes a pupil who usually displays high initiative in teacher-directed activities will show very little progress in pupil-led activities. This type of behavior indicates difficulty—perhaps too much parental domination.

6. *Recess activities.* Here the teacher notes the spontaneous groupings which prevail. Sometimes pupils who seem at ease in the formal classroom situation will show quite different reactions in play at recess. They may withdraw, display shyness, or even become aggressive when classroom inhibitions are released.

---

[8] Georgia Sachs Adams and Theodore L. Torgerson, *Measurement and Evaluation* (New York: Holt, Rinehart & Winston, Inc., 1956), pp. 183–184.

All children have problems or difficulties. Many such problems are of a transitory nature. The reasonably well-adjusted child can cope with most problems. Sometimes, however, problems persist or one's adjustment to them is inadequate for healthful living. Clues are available to guide the close observer in isolating the difficulty. The remedial action necessary will, of course, depend on the unique circumstances associated with each case.

What guidelines are useful in dealing with class disturbances?

Although it is essential that the teacher distinguish between "normal" and "disturbed" pupils, there are a number of general guidelines which many teachers have found to be effective. The reader, however, is cautioned against assuming any fixed procedure in class disturbances.

Disturbing conversation. Sometimes such a disturbance can be ignored. If it threatens to spread, the teacher can move to the area of disturbance. He may offer to help the pupils get started on an assignment. If the teacher is talking to the entire group, a pause or a question to one of the disturbing pupils can effectively solve the problem. Although some teachers are quick to separate pupils who disturb, this is often an inadvisable procedure. The practice may create resentment and serve to spread the problem to other parts of the room.

Passing notes. Such activities are symptomatic of a boring experience or lack of appropriate challenge. Frequently a change of pace takes care of the situation. It is not appropriate to read notes aloud to the class.

Over-dependence of one child on another. This is a problem which will usually work itself out. The pupils sometimes need each other until wider social acceptance is possible. Wider social acceptance is encouraged through emphasis on group work in which pupils are grouped sociometrically.

Hostility between individuals and/or groups. Talk with each of the participants individually. Try to find the cause prior to any drastic attempts at reformation.

Cheating. Cheating may occur as a result of overemphasis on grades or the establishment of unrealistic standards. In the chapter treating individual differences, the importance of making assignments and tests commensurate with pupils' abilities was emphasized. If the task is too hard for the person he will be forced to cheat in order to meet the requirement.

Tattletales. Children should be taught the difference between tattletales and reporting. A tattletale is one who tells *personal* things, whereas a child who *reports* about another child has been given the responsibility to do so because the child being reported is breaking a *school or classroom rule*.[9]

Temper tantrum. When a child in the classroom has a temper tantrum everyone in the classroom should avoid giving the child an audience. "No one ever throws a tantrum or has a fit of hysterics by himself." [10] The teacher must call him to his desk or the teacher may need to remove him from the room so other children will not give him an audience. The teacher may find out what caused the child to be upset and then present the lesson in a different way. This may prevent it from happening again.

Refusal to comply with a teacher request. Sometimes a teacher makes a simple request, only to discover that the child refuses to obey. What should be done under the circumstances? Should the refusal be ignored? Should the teacher meet the conflict with force? The action to be taken will, of course, depend on the nature of the request. Refusal to comply with simple requests usually is associated with high emotional tension. Usually the teacher can take the child by the hand and direct him toward that which was requested; however, it may be necessary to take the child from the room and discuss the problem with the child. It is very important, however, that teacher requests be followed. Failure to comply should be subject to certain consequences. Unreasonable requests should be avoided. A reasonable request for one pupil may be unreasonable for another.

What are some questionable practices of classroom discipline?

"You forget about the things they taught you in college. I have discovered some things which really work."

---

[9] Blanche McDonald and Leslie Nelson, *Successful Classroom Control* (Dubuque, Iowa: Wm. C. Brown Company Publishers, 1959), p. 156.
[10] *Ibid.*, p. 114.

Miss Brown was perplexed. "Why," she asked herself, was there such a discrepancy between college instruction and classroom practice in the area of discipline?"

The dilemma is a real one. Many teachers discover and adopt some "pet" technique that "works" in maintaining order in the classroom. By "works" they usually mean "keeps pupils quiet or orderly," and "here and now." Many classroom teachers tend to look beyond surface and temporary conformity. It has been established that forced conformity does not equip children to become progressively more able to cope with their own affairs. The overwhelming majority of lawbreakers who serve time in penal institutions continue their criminal records when they are released. Forced conformity in the classroom may cause the child to "boil over" at any time. In such cases the teacher eventually finds himself devoting about ninety percent of his energies to maintaining order, while only ten percent go toward the primary purpose of his job.

One of the most important functions of education in a democracy is to help boys and girls develop skills in working and playing together. Socialization with those who differ in so many respects is not an easy goal to attain. Application of democratic principles as a way of life can hardly be cultivated by authoritarian disciplinary techniques. Learning to apply the rules of democracy is a slower and more difficult procedure than forced conformity, but as pupils develop these techniques they need progressively less assistance from the teacher. The disciplinary techniques which follow generally are considered inappropriate or at least of questionable value:

Corporal punishment. The term refers to discipline by bodily contact. Not only is this a dangerous technique for the teacher (the pupil may strike back!) but it can be both physically and psychologically damaging to the child. Recent studies of parents and administrators indicate that more than half of those polled favored granting teachers the right to give a child a "licking." [11, 12] Students in psychology, however, generally do not regard corporal punishment as desirable.[13] Furthermore, there have been a number of court actions against teachers who have used corporal punishment.[14] Pupils themselves tend to resent

[11] William W. Brickman, "Leadership, the Rod and Education," *School and Society*, 81: 43–44 (1955).

[12] A. H. Rice, Ed., "Most Superintendents Favor the Use of Corporal Punishment," *Nations School*, 58: 57–58 (1956).

[13] Reprinted with the permission of the publisher from Percival M. Symonds, *What Education Has to Learn from Psychology* (New York: Teachers College Press), copyright 1958, Teachers College, Columbia University.

[14] Lee O. Garber, "The Teacher's Right to Administer Corporal Punishment," *Nations School*, 53: 83–84 (1954).

this sort of punishment, claiming that adults seldom if ever know all the facts in the situation.

Isolation. Separating a child from his peers tends to reinforce the craving which induced the behavior in the first place. It may be necessary to isolate a pupil *temporarily* as a stopgap measure, but continued use of the technique can only lead to greater frustration, deeper feelings of guilt, and resentment.

Imposition of school tasks for punitive purposes. Such a technique, in essence, punishes a child by making him do school work. Thus, he tends to associate *misbehavior* with school work.

Forced apologies. Forcing a child to verbalize an apology that he does not feel is a way of forcing him to lie. It solves nothing!

Sarcastic remarks. This creates resentment and lowers the esteem of the teacher in the eyes of the children.

Removal from the situation. While there will be times when a child must be removed from the classroom, it should be used only as a last resort. In such instances the teacher is admitting his inability to handle the situation. When it becomes necessary the offender should be sent to a specific member of the teaching or administrative staff. In other words, he should not be sent from the room without adequate provisions for supervision.

Demerits. One's conduct within the classroom should not be associated with academic marks. The two are important yet distinct aspects of learning. The act of penalizing a child in one area for transgressions in another area tends to establish an undesirable association. To illustrate: a child penalized academically for misbehavior may develop an attitude of "What's the use" toward his school work. Likewise, a child who is rewarded academically for "good" behavior may substitute "being nice" for academic achievement.

What action can be useful in coping with defiant pupils?

It has long been established that individuals do not act rationally while under extreme emotional stress. Due to changes of the internal body chemistry, the person involved tends to act first and think later. This is normally a valuable protective mechanism essential to man's survival. In a highly industrialized society, however, one's emotional reactions can be quite detrimental to his survival at times. This is especially true of the classroom teacher. We expect children to experience difficulty in controlling their emotions from time to time. Teachers, however, are expected to control their emotional reactions. Nevertheless, there are times when any adult is subject to lose some control over his emotions. It is at such times that a teacher may impose some form of discipline which later seems quite inappropriate. In order to avoid more loss of face or obvious inconsistencies, he usually finds it desirable to let the punishment or impositions stand.

In times of extreme emotional stress many persons tend to revert to a form of infantile behavior. And, of course, discipline for a very young child, because of his limited reasoning ability, tends to be more authoritarian than discipline for an older child. What action can be useful in coping with the well-known tendency to revert to infantile behavior under extreme emotional stress? It is easy to admonish one not to lose control over his emotions, but the danger is ever-present, even with the best of us.

In as kind a manner as possible, Miss Jones asked Johnny to stop talking with his neighbor, but the conversation continued. After three or four other reminders she decided that the boy should be moved from his friend. Johnny refused, saying, "You can't make me move."

What is to be done under the circumstances? The infantile tendency is to apply force. Yet our rational senses tell us that such action is inappropriate. Johnny needs to know *why* he must quit talking to his neighbor—because it is preventing work from being completed.

It is proposed that teachers (especially those who tend to become upset easily) determine *in advance* a general plan of action designed to cope with the defiant child. This plan of action might well be memorized —"burned" into the brain cells—so that it will be remembered at times when emotional responses tend to dominate rational thinking. While it is recognized that any such plan must have its limitations (the discipline should fit the individual), it *may* prevent one from applying even more inappropriate measures. The plan of action which follows is designed to serve as alternate ways of handling the situation; however, each teacher should develop his own approach to the problem in terms of school policy.

Situation: Bill is conversing with his neighbor while the teacher is explaining an important point.

1. Stop and look directly at the offender.
2. Call his name.

3. Politely ask for his attention.

4. Request that he move to another seat.

5. Isolate him from the rest of the class.

6. Remove him from the situation.

Occasionally a pupil will defy the teacher by refusing to change seats or leave the room. Because of the high emotional tension this engenders the teacher needs to plan in advance a course of action. As indicated in an earlier section, he may take Bill by the hand, or the teacher may say, "Perhaps we had better discuss this after class." The offender then usually follows through with the requested action. If he does not and the disturbance continues, the teacher might be forced to resolve the situation by removing the child from his group.

Group and individual problem solving requires discipline.

While the suggested plan of action may not be fully appropriate for any given pupil, it is at least preferable to the incidents described below:

When Bill refused to move Mr. Jones grabbed him and shoved—hard. Bill fell and broke his arm.

When Tom refused to move, Miss Mika assigned him an hour with the principal. The boy said, "I don't care. Why don't you make it three hours?" Miss Mika made it three hours; whereupon Bill dared her to make it more.

One should not infer from the foregoing that such defiance is likely. Indeed, it never will be experienced by some teachers. Usually when it does occur the teacher is somehow at fault. So what? When the situation arises it cannot be wished away. The problem must be dealt with immediately! Furthermore, a child should not be permitted to get by with such behavior without some corrective action. This can only encourage others to react in a similar manner. An appropriate learning environment must be provided for all children!

PROBLEMS AND PRINCIPLES IN HANDLING DISCIPLINE

In the foregoing portion of this chapter emphasis was placed on *techniques* of discipline. Teachers must help pupils develop a desire to learn. Learning in today's schools, however, occurs in a social setting. Classrooms are crowded; individuals from all walks of life are thrown together; interests, abilities, and achievement vary tremendously within each class group. Such factors necessarily create problems of classroom order. Thus, the desire to learn must be carefully guided in such a way as to create optimum conditions for all. It is not too difficult to discover and evolve discipline techniques which work for the moment. It is more difficult to develop techniques which will eventuate into *self-*discipline. Nevertheless, this is the aim of effective teaching. Individuals who lack self-discipline tend to become a menace and liability to society.

This portion of the chapter offers a number of psychological principles which have been established through extensive experimentation. They should be especially useful to experienced teachers who wish to check their own techniques against pertinent research findings.

What are some problems in handling discipline?

Individuals are different. Some differences can be readily detected; others are subtle but have been established through scientific investigation. Discipline problems are probably the most subtle and least understood of all aspects of teaching. Teachers assume that disciplinary measures which seem reasonable to them should appear reasonable to children. It must be remembered that behavior is caused; it reflects the values which one holds. Children from middle class homes, for instance, tend to accept the teacher and approve of formal education as an instrument for "getting ahead." Children from lower class homes, however, tend to want to break away from school as soon as possible; they frequently desire to avoid being "taken-in" by the teacher; teacher approval may even pose a threat to acceptance by members of their own social class group.

Discipline must be interpreted in terms of the individuals involved. Some children live by one set of standards at home and are expected to live by another set at school. Some children may already know the social expectations of the school society; others must learn them. Furthermore, some individuals are emotionally equipped to *learn* appropriate rules of conduct, while others need remedial assistance.

While there is a natural tendency to look for a set of rules which work, techniques of discipline must be as variable as the individuals who occupy the classroom. Discipline problems are but symptoms of numerous factors which make a person what he is. The mere process of keeping pupils busy and orderly is not enough. Ultimately they will be expected to operate under their own initiative and direction. An important function of the school is to *build* these essential ingredients of good citizenship.

In the preceding paragraphs emphasis has been placed on the *individual* nature of discipline. Yet some consistency is essential. A teacher who would normally accept or at least tolerate a given act must not suddenly start punishing pupils for such behavior. Both teacher and children need clearly defined guidelines to follow.

What are some principles in handling discipline?

For several years teachers have attempted to follow acceptable disciplinary practices. Often recommendations have been derived largely from tradition or nonverified experiences of outstanding teachers.

Most educators accept the well established proposition that disciplinary problems are caused; that the school experience must be adjusted to fit the child. The school is viewed as the primary institution through which democracy as a way of life can be practiced. The principles which follow are basic to the problem of discipline. It is interesting to note that the guiding principles for effective motivation are essentially the same for effective discipline. Again, a close relationship between the two areas is evident. The principles which follow are treated more extensively in Chapter 6. They are listed again briefly for emphasis.

1. Reward is more effective than punishment.

2. Motivation which originates with the individual is more effective than that which is imposed from without.

3. Immediate reinforcement of a desirable response is needed.

4. Motivation is contagious, i.e., a highly interested and motivated teacher tends to produce highly interested and motivated pupils.

5. A clear understanding of purpose enhances motivation.

6. All children have certain psychological needs which must be met.

7. Self-imposed tasks tend to create more interest than do teacher-imposed tasks.

8. "External" rewards sometimes are necessary and effective in stimulating initial interest.

9. Varied teaching techniques and procedures are effective in maintaining interest.

10. It is economical to capitalize on existing interests.

11. Activities which stimulate interest for the less able may be inappropriate for the more able, and vice versa.

12. High anxiety makes learning difficult or impossible.

13. Anxiety and frustration in mild form can be beneficial to learning.

14. If the task is too difficult and if assistance is not readily available, frustration quickly leads to demoralization.

15. Each pupil has a different level of frustration tolerance.

16. Peer group pressure is much more effective in discipline than adult-imposed pressures.

17. All human beings need and expect the imposition of reasonable limits to guide their conduct.

SUMMARY

In this chapter and in Chapter 6 emphasis has been placed on motivation and discipline as overlapping and interrelated problems of teaching. When all pupils are highly motivated to learn there can be no serious discipline problems. Motivation springs from certain basic physical and psychological urges. The psychological urges (needs) include acceptance, approval, self-esteem, achievement, and independence.

Discipline was discussed in terms of achieving the ultimate end of self-discipline. Among the important variables considered was the necessity of distinguishing between stable children and those needing remedial help. Pupils whose physical and psychological needs have been neglected tend to cause more than their share of trouble. They must be corrected, but also must have their needs fulfilled. As with motivation, a reverse order of teaching is needed, i.e., they must first *do*, then *discuss*, and finally *read*. All children must *learn* appropriate behavior patterns. This demands time and patience, just as might be expected in any area of the instructional process. It was suggested that some general *planned* approach be utilized in the event of highly charged emotional reactions. One such approach was offered as a guideline.

Finally, a number of general principles and problems were developed. Although many of these principles apply equally well to the problem of motivation, discussed in Chapter 6, they were listed again briefly for emphasis. Motivation and discipline are thus seen as aspects of the same basic problem.

QUESTIONS FOR STUDY AND DISCUSSION

1. How is discipline related to motivation, discussed in Chapter 6? Why are discipline problems, like problems of motivation, considered symptomatic of other more basic problems?

2. In this chapter different approaches were suggested for stable and "disturbed" children. How do the groups differ? Why are different approaches considered necessary?

3. On what basis might discipline problems be considered as a method of teaching? Some teachers claim they devote 90 percent of their time to problems associated with pupil control. What underlying instructional problems probably contribute to the situation? Consistency is an important aspect of class control. Does this mean that all children should be treated alike? Why or why not?

4. Why is corporal punishment considered an inappropriate form of discipline? Survey the questionable practices of classroom discipline, visit one or more elementary classes, and then discuss discipline problems with the teachers. What differences between theory and practice do you find? How do you account for this?

5. What advantages do you see in developing some plan of action prior to

the development of discipline problems? Would you permit children to assist you in developing such a plan? Why or why not? How would you alter the plan offered in this chapter to meet your own needs? Why would you do this?

SELECTED BIBLIOGRAPHY

Brown, Edwin J., "So You Have Discipline Problems . . . . ," *The Catholic School Journal*, 63, No. 2: 23–25 (November, 1963).

Dreikeurs, Rudolf, and Vicki Soltz, "Your Child and Discipline," *NEA Journal*, 54, No. 1: 34–47 (January, 1965).

Fantini, Mario D., "Reward and Punishment," *The Clearing House*, 41, No. 4: 252–254 (February, 1966).

Frances, Sister Mary, "Discipline Is. . . . . ," *NEA Journal*, 54: 26–28 (September, 1965).

Gnagey, William J., *Controlling Classroom Misbehavior. What Research Says to the Teacher*, No. 32 (Washington, D. C.: National Education Association, 1965).

Holliday, Frances, "A Positive Approach to Elementary School Discipline," *NEA Journal*, 50, No. 4: 25–26 (April, 1961).

Hollister, William G., "The Behavior-Guidance Tools of the Classroom Teacher," *Virginia Journal of Education*, 59, No. 8: 11–13 (May, 1966).

Hymes, James L., Jr., *Behavior and Misbehavior* (Englewood Cliffs, N. J.: Prentice-Hall, Inc., 1955).

Jones, Morris V., "The Legal Status of Corporal Punishment in the Public Schools," *California Journal of Educational Research*, 15, No. 3: 142–149 (May, 1964).

Marie, Sister Jeanne, "The Trouble with Discipline," *The Catholic School Journal*, 67, No. 4: 50–51 (April, 1967).

Ornstein, Allan C., "Techniques and Fundamentals for Teaching the Disadvantaged," *Journal of Negro Education*, 36, No. 2: 136–145 (Spring, 1967).

Robinson, Donald W., "Police in the Schools," *Phi Delta Kappan*, 48, No. 6: 278–280 (February, 1967).

Rosenberg, Shirley Sivota, "Should Teachers Wield the Rod?" *Parents' Magazine*, 39: 74–75+ (February, 1964).

Directing Study:
Assignments, Guided Study,
and Homework

THE direction of study activities is one of the most important responsibilities of teaching. It has been established that the average pupil spends seventy percent of his time in reading activities alone. Study activities are not treated as a separate approach to problem solving. Yet much of the reflective thinking activities of pupils are based on these activities. Many elementary school pupils, instead of becoming less dependent on the teacher, may be becoming more dependent on him. Why is this? It certainly is not because of the lack of opportunity for independent study. For many years teachers relied almost exclusively on the assign-study-recite procedure. The assignment was the key to teaching under this type of organization. In its simplest form this technique consisted of the following:

1. The teacher assigns a certain number of pages to be studied.

2. Pupils study the assigned material, either at home or at school.

3. During the next day the teacher asks questions on the content of the assigned material.

4. The process is repeated over and over again.

This procedure persisted for many years beyond the time of its rejection by experimentally derived principles of learning. Today it is not in harmony with the modern concept of learning as the modification of behavior through the formulation of relationships and insight. Even prior to the rejection of learning as merely the mastery of facts, educators were questioning the practice of assigning several hours of homework every day. Enthusiasts were quick to point out the inadequacies of home study. Some even advocated the elimination of homework.

The assign-study-recite approach to teaching, however, persisted, simply because the teacher's concept of learning was unaltered. The objective testing movement of the thirties merely reinforced the notion of learning as a process of memorization and recall.

The scientific movement in education, given emphasis by John Dewey and his followers, today is being felt even in the most traditionally-oriented school systems. Learning as a process of continuous problem solving is bringing about a closer scrutiny of study activities. Homework is no longer considered a "dirty" word, even though school study is still emphasized. Attempts to prove the superiority of one over the other have been disappointing, perhaps because of the many uncontrollable variables involved.

Today teachers generally realize that problem-solving activities (reflective thinking) are important both as assigned homework and as school study activities. Children do need guidance in semi-independent study at school. They also need opportunities to work independently of the teacher. The key type of study activity, of course, is the assignment. In fact, the assignment is a key factor in all phases of instruction. The processes of panel discussion, reports, and almost any other teaching method depend on the quality of assignments. As previously noted, the assignment is a vital part of lesson planning. Nevertheless, the importance of this teaching technique in connection with study activities makes a thorough analysis of the problem essential. Without effective assignments there can be little effective school study or homework.

THE ASSIGNMENT

Illustration   I: As the bell sounded ending the school day Mrs. Smith held up her hand for attention. "Oh, I almost forgot to make the assignment," she shouted. "For tomorrow study Chapter 7 and answer the questions at the end of the chapter."

One child started to ask a question, but changed his mind as he scrambled out after the rest of the pupils.

Illustration   II: Mr. Dalle reminded the pupils that they were to copy the assignment from the board as he checked the cafeteria money. The assignment read: "Bring to class three clippings which relate to our study of colonialism. Be prepared to share your findings with the class."

Illustration III: About halfway through the discussion about the farm, Mrs. Holmes summed up the discussion about milk by asking, "How does the milk get from the farm to our door?"

After a few minutes Mrs. Holmes observed that "we apparently need more information about this question. How might we find the information needed?"

A variety of sources and ideas were mentioned.

Mrs. Holmes then said, "As an assignment let's get the information we need to determine how the milk gets from the farm to our homes. You may want to ask your parents, or go to the library for a book on milk, or use one of the other sources we mentioned. We will discuss what we have learned about the milk tomorrow."

The three assignments illustrated were recently recorded by a group of student observers. They reflect three different philosophies of education. The first rests squarely on the notion of education as a process of memorizing facts and principles. This often is known as "textbook teaching." The assignment as given can lead only to boredom and frustration.

The second assignment is somewhat more acceptable than the first. Attempts are made to relate class study to real life problems. Nevertheless, it does place the teacher in the role of a taskmaster. Children are given little indication of the assignment purpose. It has the advantage of being a bit more definite than the first assignment and, since it is presented at the beginning of the day, some of the vagueness can be eliminated through pupil questions or supplementary instructions.

The third assignment is consistent with today's concept of education as a process of problem solving. Through skillful guidance the children were able to recognize the problem and to see the need for more data. The assignment was clearly an attempt to secure data needed for further reflection on a problem. Pupils were motivated and given a certain amount of leeway to pursue the problem in their own way. Yet the assignment was reasonably definite.

Further reference will be made to the three illustrated assignments in the discussion which is to follow.

What are some important purposes of assignments?

In the first place, the assignment is necessary as a basis for classroom activities. Without some preparation for the class experience, the child must rely on his own repertoire of experience, along with the opinions, beliefs, and ideas of others. As such, he is in no position to analyze problems objectively. If the assignment is similar to the first illustration cited, pupils can do little more than recite factual answers provided by the textbook. If the assignment is to provide a basis for class discussion it should be made with this end in mind, as indicated in Illustration III. Sometimes a list of thought-provoking questions is sufficient. Such questions, however, should lead the child *beyond* the material presented in the textbook.

A second purpose of the assignment is to provide additional practice in applying material studied in class. This is especially necessary in the mastering of certain so-called skill subjects. Reading, arithmetic, and English teachers very often find it necessary to assign enough practice work to insure mastery. It is important, however, that the basic principles be thoroughly understood before practice is attempted.

A third function of the assignment is to provide for individual differences among children. The extremely wide range of interests and abilities found in most elementary school classes today poses a continuous challenge. The teacher, through careful observation, can recognize some of the special needs of pupils and adjust assignments accordingly. Not all children, for example, will need an equal amount of practice in the area of skills. In the area of social studies, especially, children will be interested in different problems or different phases of the same problem, as indicated in Illustration III.

Still another function of the assignment is the opportunity for supplementing material studied in class. Many of the issues studied today are of a controversial nature, necessitating a number of approaches to a problem. Furthermore, the wider the study the greater the number of associations possible. This is an important factor in the retention and transfer of learning to other life problems.

Finally, assignments may be valuable in helping pupils become progressively more able to direct their own learning activities. The basic function of formal education is to render individuals capable of assuming the responsibilities of democratic living. This simply means that children should be prepared to learn independently of the teacher by the time they have completed public school education. As Goldstein [1] points out, the main objectives of homework in the elementary grades should be good study habits, independent work skills, and self-discipline. He feels that these objectives are of vital importance in advance education and that they are best taught by good homework in the elementary grades.

[1] A. Goldstein, "Does Homework Help?" *Elementary School Journal*, 60: 212–224 (January, 1960).

What characterizes an effective assignment?

It must be apparent to the prospective teacher that assignment making is no easy task. On this key factor rest much pupil motivation, personal growth, and transfer value of the school experience. Burton has presented a thorough analysis of good assignments in the 49th Yearbook of the National Society for the Study of Education:

1. The objective, the thing to be done, should be stated in clear, simple language. . . .

2. A provocative and convincing connection should be made between the subject matter of the assignment and the typical activities, interests, and needs of the pupils' current lives.

3. Assignments . . . must also serve desirable social purposes of education, that is, lead to the development of outcomes useful in the organized society of democratic life. . . .

4. Study guides, questions, and other aids should be included. . . . Co-operatively arranged questions and guides are of value.

5. Assignments must provide for different levels of achievement and for greatly varied study of learning activities, in accord with the range of differences in ability, interest, and needs within the group. . . .

6. Assignments should be directed to matters for which pupils and teachers see a need for study. . . .

7. Assignments should initiate and motivate substantial units of work, . . . Day-by-day assignments of truly fragmentary type should be avoided rigorously, since, if these are to be used, the benefits of the large unit are lost. . . . The small number of assignments using greater time indicates the use of large units. . . .

8. Assignments should use all the time necessary for explanations, for answering pupil questions, for development an adequate plan of action, for arranging subsidiary individual and committee assignments, and for making sure all know what is to be done.

9. Assignments may be made at any stage of the lesson in such way as to take advantage of or to develop need or interest and at the same time preserve continuity.

10. Assignments should be such that evidence of progress and achievement can be derived each day with reasonable ease. . . .

11. Pupil participation in selecting and developing assignments and methods of procedure is definitely desirable.

12. The expenditure of considerable time and energy on the part of the teacher and pupils and careful, detailed planning are fully justified by the importance of assignments.[2]

After studying these 12 characteristics of a good assignment, the reader is urged to reread the three illustrations cited in the preceding section. Do any of these illustrations satisfy the criteria established? If not, what changes might be made to correct noted deficiencies? How often has the reader experienced fully adequate assignments? It is apparent that the 12 characteristics of a good assignment are somewhat idealistic. Nevertheless, they do offer a valuable framework toward which a teacher should strive. *Without adequate assignments, adequate learning is impossible.*

What important teaching techniques are associated with effective assignments?

As indicated earlier, assignments are designed to direct the learning activities of children. Dallmann[3] states that worthwhile assignments will help the child realize that school isn't the only place for formal study. These learning activities are performed both in the classroom and at home. Many teachers provide the learner with assistance in the initial stages of problem solving; it enables him to clarify instructions which prove inadequate after the task is begun; finally, the teacher is in a position to observe and to correct any deficiencies which may become apparent, and then unfinished work may be taken home, if necessary.

There are occasions, of course, when routine practice assignments may be necessary. In any event, however, a wise teacher should make a check to determine how well directions have been understood. Invariably some points which seem perfectly clear to the teacher appear vague and confusing to children.

For many years the most appropriate time for making assignments was debated. So long as the assign-study-recite technique was used this was indeed a critical issue. Even much later, and as long as *daily* lesson plans were in vogue, the issue was considered a critical one. Today, however, with the unit structure and with lesson plans encompassing topics of work within a unit (as opposed to individual periods of time), it is

[2] William A. Burton, "Implications for Organization of Instruction and Instructional Adjuncts," *49th Yearbook, Part I,* National Society for the Study of Education (Chicago: University of Chicago Press, 1950), pp. 231–233.

[3] Martha Dallmann, "Homework," *Grade Teacher,* 79: 36 (November, 1961).

recognized that the best time to make an assignment should be that point in the lesson which leads up to it effectively. In the third illustrated assignment cited earlier in this chapter, Mrs. Holmes made an assignment when it became obvious that further data were necessary about milk delivery from the farm to the home. The children were interested in the problem and immediately recognized the need for more data prior to further discussion. As Burton points out, time needed for making an assignment may vary. The time taken for a worthwhile explanation is time well spent.

Some teachers prefer to dictate or have pupils copy assignments from the board. (See Illustration II.) Reference can then be made to the assignment when the day's activities make it appropriate. This technique has the advantage of providing adequate time for reference and discussion. All too often pupils and teacher alike become so engrossed with class activities that the assignment is either forgotten or presented hurriedly at the close of the day. This type has the potential disadvantage of being imposed by the teacher. Perhaps the "best" technique rests with the competencies and preferences of each teacher. The important point is that the assignment should be an integral part of teaching and should fulfill a felt need on the part of the learner.

How detailed should an assignment be? Some teachers prefer to spell out in every detail steps to be taken. Others like sketchy assignments, thereby enabling the child to bring his own originality and creativity into play. It must be recognized that a lot depends on the particular conditions involved. Assuming other conditions are equal, however, it is recognized that less capable pupils need more specific directions than the more able ones. Also, the more immature child will need specific directions, too. When it seems desirable to emphasize originality and creativity, the point should be made in the assignment. A teacher should remember that vagueness in an assignment can quickly frustrate and demoralize even the most able learner.

How are assignments evaluated?

Evaluation of pupil work has long been a problem with teachers. The amount of time and energy necessary for a reasonable evaluation can become excessive, thus robbing the teacher of time needed for some of the more creative aspects of teaching. Children, on the other hand, usually feel that if they do an assignment the teacher should evaluate their efforts. Although both positions are logical and defensible, the problem need not be as complicated as it often appears to be.

Reference is made to those chapters which deal with the formulation of unit and lesson goals or objectives. The reader will recall that a general objective should be followed with specific behavioral outcomes. These outcomes are designed to indicate progress toward goals. The illustration which follows is reproduced from Chapter III.

After this unit in reading the pupil should further *understand* the "tall tale" stories, as evidenced by:

1. His response in a class discussion comparing tall tale stories with other fictional materials.

2. His ability to write his own tall tale story.

3. His skill in discriminating between tall tale paragraphs and real life situation paragraphs.

The specific behaviors indicated suggest a variety of activities—activities, of course, must be *assigned*. Thus, by giving some thought to how assignments will be *used*, both pupil and teacher are in a position to determine the most appropriate technique of evaluation. If, for example, the purpose of the assignment is to obtain data needed for class discussion (See Illustration III cited earlier in this chapter), evaluation may consist of an informal evaluation of pupil contributions to the class discussion. (For techniques of evaluating class discussion, the reader is referred to Chapter 7.) The number of contributions possible are limited, however, in a discussion involving 25–35 pupils. The teacher then may ask that the papers be turned in to the teacher. It should be a relatively simple matter to check papers of those who had little or no opportunity to share their findings with the class. Frequently assignments will be associated with committee or project work which will be evaluated as a part of the finished project.

There are times, of course, when assignments must be evaluated very carefully. By determining the nature and extent of evaluation *in advance of the assignment* and then informing pupils of this when the assignment is made, the problem is minimized. A little time devoted to the construction of a few key rating scales and check lists may mean a tremendous saving of time and energy in the long run.

GUIDED STUDY ACTIVITIES

In a sense, the school's first and last task is to help the child learn how to learn. As we have seen, human learning, as distinguished from animal learning, is essentially a process of inquiry. The method of inquiry has both an experimental and a social dimension. In its experimental aspects, learning as inquiry is a matter of trying out, testing, experiencing the world first-hand, playing with ideas. In its social aspects, learning or inquiring is a matter of comparing notes, checking one's response against that of others, communicating and sharing experiences, trying to see an event through the eyes of others.

E. V. Sayers and Ward Madden [4]

The concept of learning as involving the processes of critical thought and analysis has directed attention to supervised study as an essential aspect of teaching. Teachers are beginning to realize the inadequacies of the "keeping order" notion of supervised study. Children must share and reflect; they need the careful guidance of teachers to help them overcome major and minor difficulties. Too often children have been allowed to persist in trial-and-error techniques of solving problems.

Why have guided study activities?

The acceptance of democracy as a way of life has placed renewed emphasis on the *processes* of instruction. No longer is the teacher considered the final authority whose job is to supply pupils with answers. Rather, democratic processes must be *experienced*. This involves the analysis of critical problems in give-and-take situations. Committee planning, cooperative endeavor, and group analysis are deemed essential. This demands time and space, along with adequate supervision. The teacher serves as a guide as well as a resource person.

Another advantage of guided study is the motivation provided. Assignments, when conceived as an integral part of teaching, often need to be implemented immediately. Thus, pupils are able to "strike while the iron is hot." Study activities are at least started while the teacher is present to give added encouragement and direction in the early stages of learning.

One of the most important advantages of guided study is the availability of school resources and materials. The library is a must when real life, critical problems are being weighed. Today the use of films, recordings, maps, and pictures is encouraged. Most school systems maintain an ample supply of these for pupil use. It usually is impossible for children to complete certain craft activities, for example, while at home.

[4] E. V. Sayers and Ward Madden, *Education and the Democratic Faith* (New York: Appleton-Century-Crofts, Inc., 1959), p. 437.

What problems are associated with guided school study?

The activity classroom is not without its limitations. First and foremost, there is the difficulty in providing ample time for study. It is extremely easy to let class explanations extend a few minutes longer than intended; pupil questions about any assignment frequently take longer than anticipated. The result may be inadequate time to get started before it is time to go to recess or move into some other area of the curriculum.

There is also the problem of space and general classroom organization. Differentiated assignments often demand that different pupils and subgroups engage in different activities at the same time. Certainly reading activities cannot be performed effectively when children a few feet away are discussing a group problem. With the formation of six or seven groups it is often difficult to render assistance when needed. At the same time, guided study activities enable some pupils to "get lost in the herd." These children may digress from the problem without the teacher's knowledge.

A problem that is becoming more and more apparent as children of all ability and interest levels continue throughout their school years is the challenge of individual differences. A few pupils have become discouraged and, for all practical purposes, have ceased to achieve. They are in school primarily because they are required to be there. Realizing the trend toward automatic promotion, such children sometimes permit certain members of their group to do all the work. This creates feelings of unfairness and frustration among those who might otherwise be highly motivated. In such cases democratic processes can become a farce.

Guided study poses the problem of the nature and amount of assistance needed. Sometimes teachers want to give children answers. They are themselves frustrated with the seemingly slow and uneven deliberative processes. In such cases pupils may learn to wait for answers which they know will be forthcoming. However, sometimes teachers *should* give children answers. Especially is this true when the child has reached an impasse. Then an answer or some guidance from the teacher will assist the child along his deliberating process. Other teachers are inclined to mark papers or take care of some of the routines of teaching while children work. This is based on the false assumption that pupils just naturally know how to study and solve problems. The mere presence of the teacher, as he passes from one part of the room to another, can have a stimulating effect on children engaged in study activities.

What group forces influence guided study?

The effectiveness of guided study is influenced by a number of group forces. Class committees, for example, make up *socio* groups. A *socio* group, according to Coffey,[5] is usually composed of both voluntary and involuntary members. The "voluntary" members have a keen interest in the goals of the committee, while the "involuntary" members see the activity as merely a "job to be done." The socio group (or committee, as it is usually called) is bound together by a visualized goal of the group. Such groups are emphasized constantly in instructional procedures.

The basic group force (and one which is frequently overlooked) is the *psyche* group. This group is an informal structure which exists among all individuals at all levels. Rules and regulations (if they exist at all) will be transient. The psyche group is necessary to fulfill the emotional needs of individuals. It is small, usually ranging from two to six members. In this group one can say what he pleases without any fear of rejection. At its highest level it takes the form of the husband-wife relationship. In the school situation it is often known as the *clique*. Teachers do not form psyche groups. They can split them by changing the environment, but they have no control over the new group(s) which will be formed. The group is nonsecret. One need only observe, for example, "who pals around with whom," or "who plays together during recess."

The psyche group sets the pattern for class achievement. If the group limit is set below an individual's capacity he will not exceed it—not by vote but by "common consent." The standard which the leader sets usually determines the limits. This explains in part why progress of some committees is disappointing. The dominant psyche group *within the committee* sets the limits of achievement.

In guiding study activities involving "individual" or committee assignments, the informal psyche group must be taken into account. For an objective appraisal of the existing psyche groups within a given class, the reader should employ techniques of sociometry, described in Chapter 8. It must be remembered, however, that achievement limits *may* be set by children who are *not* in the particular class group involved. Keen interest by the leader (whether he is a member of the particular class group or not) will set the stage for high achievement. Psyche and socio group forces cannot be separated. Efforts to improve the processes of group problem solving by employing the socio group are appropriate. It is important, however, to utilize the values and strengths of the psyche

[5] Hubert Stanley Coffey, "Socio and Psyche Group Process: Integrative Concepts," in *Perspectives on the Group Process* (Boston: Houghton Mifflin Company, 1964), pp. 46–54.

group for maximum social and intellectual achievement. Although there are other group forces, the interaction of socio and psyche group forces is basic to effective study activities.

What are some recommended techniques of effective study?

The importance of guided study has been stressed, but up to this point little attention has been given to specific techniques. This is an extremely complicated task, for the simple reason that the modern school identifies study with learning; and this is a key problem of this entire book. As Burton contends, "Teaching should aim to develop in the child independent study habits." [6] How this is to be accomplished is a problem that varies with each individual. Many books have been written and many pupil surveys have been made in an effort to analyze the problem. As might be expected, the findings have been varied and sometimes contradictory. Nevertheless, pupils' reports on their study methods show that certain methods are designated more often by good pupils than by poor pupils. One of the most extensive of these surveys, according to Strang, included students from Grades 4 to 12. Ten significant methods of study were characteristic of the high-scholarship, most intelligent, and underage groups:

1. Have a clear notion of the task before beginning the work of a particular study period.

2. Make complete sentences while writing.

3. Seek to master all the material as progress is made from lesson to lesson.

4. Grasp the meaning of the chart or table without difficulty.

5. Try to interrupt work at a natural break in the printed material, such as the end of a chapter.

6. Do not take notes while reading.

7. Work out complete examples to illustrate general rules and principles.

8. Have on hand the materials required.

9. Use facts learned in one class in preparation for another.

10. Read each topic in a lesson until it is clearly understood.[7]

[6] William H. Burton, *The Guidance of Learning Activities*, 3rd Ed. (New York: Appleton-Century-Crofts, Inc., 1962), p. 301.

[7] Ruth Strang, *Guided Study and Homework*—"What Research Says to the Teacher," pamphlet No. 8 (Washington, D. C.: National Education Association, 1955), p. 6.

While there is no guarantee that these statements by students coincide with their actual habits, they do offer some assistance in coping with the problem.

Listed below are some specific instances in which active guidance of study activities is warranted. These are merely illustrative of the countless study problems which may be encountered and that there is no one way of handling them.

1. *Lack of interest.* This may be due to lack of drive, in which case the preparation of provocative and interesting questions may be useful.

2. *Inability to see the problem clearly.* If this problem does not reflect a poor assignment it is possible that the child is unaccustomed to accepting responsibility and initiative. Often it reflects an undesirable home situation. Individual, careful assistance over a long period of time is usually needed.

3. *Lack of knowledge of sources and how to use them.*

4. *Inability to judge the worth of facts.* Probably the most useful approach to this problem is through questioning, helping the learner disclose for himself the inconsistencies of his thinking.

5. *Difficulties with analysis.*

6. *Need for special practice in specific habits.* Numerous studies show that guided practice on complex skills is beneficial. A guide for improving reading comprehension often entails the following points: a) Make a brief, rapid survey of the chapter for the purpose of getting an over-all view of the topic. Pay particular attention to main divisions, side headings, italicized words, and pictorial illustrations. b) Read the chapter carefully for more precise meaning. Look for theme or summary statements, usually to be found at the beginning or the end of each paragraph. c) Re-read the main ideas expressed in the chapter. d) Try to recall the main points and review those which are still unclear.

HOMEWORK

Issues of teaching associated with homework probably have aroused some of the most heated controversy in the field of teaching. The homework issue has been debated for several decades by those within as well as those outside of the profession. Yet the end is not in sight! What factors contribute to this controversy? What are some of the aggravating conditions which "keep the fire burning"? These and other problems will now be considered.

What purposes are served by homework?

As has been emphasized in different contexts of this chapter, the aim of formal education is to prepare the child to cope with his own problems effectively. Guided study at school, while providing some independence from the teacher, cannot compare with the independence afforded through home study. This is the one instance in which the pupil exercises completely individual initiative and self-direction. Although he is guided somewhat by the assignment, he is left to his own resources for the procedure in solving the problem. The proponents of homework point out that these are the conditions which foster a self-actualizing person.

Another important function of home study is the transfer value involved. The appropriate kind of homework provides a pupil with the opportunity to relate selected problems of school to real-life experience. This enables him to "see" the connections, to reinforce school learnings, and to test such experiences for himself under natural conditions.

Homework also is viewed as an avenue through which desirable home-school relations can be fostered. It is relatively easy to make assignments which will involve parents. They may not only bring the child and his parents closer together, but can also keep the adult abreast of the child's learning experiences. The proponents of homework ask: "What can be more complimentary to the parent than to have his son or daughter ask his opinion on some school problem?" "What father can object to discussing with his child the occasions he finds for arithmetic in his work?" He is, however, likely to be resentful of trying to explain new math!

Finally, the value of homework in establishing habits of work or endeavor cannot be overlooked. Children who do not form the habit of pursuing intellectual activities after school hours, it is claimed, tend to follow the same pattern in adult living. They tend to be satisfied with mediocre performance on the job; they often fail to keep abreast of national and international developments. Homework advocates point out the difficulty of revising habits which have been fixed for a period of years.

What are some problems associated with home study?

The opponents of home assignments are quick to refute the claims of those who favor homework. They point out that the learner's so-called independence while studying at home is a two-edged sword. One's independent work actually amounts to little more than following directions which are too often vague and confusing. Often he finds himself doing mere "busy work," i.e., work with no greater purpose than to keep him busy.

As for the transfer value of homework, the opposition asks only that the record be checked. Proof can be found that the vast majority of home assignments still consists of reading chapters in textbooks, writing out answers to factual questions, or practicing some skill. This type of assignment does not transfer, regardless of the place and time it is completed.

The claim that home study builds parent-child and parent-teacher relations is highly unlikely. The opponents of homework suggest that the opposite extreme is much more likely. Home assignments, as typically given, can only interfere with normal family living. The child often cannot participate in normal family activities when he is saddled with homework each evening. Parents who are tired from the day's work often do not feel like answering questions related to home assignments; many parents, of course, are not qualified to render such assistance.

The opponents of homework question the habit-forming value of independent study, pointing out that children especially tend to rebel against required study activities. They may see home study as a nuisance to be tolerated until they can find a way out. Homework opponents once again direct attention to the evidence. Homework has been assigned for many years. Yet a surprisingly small percentage of the American people ever read a weekly news magazine or subscribe to a daily newspaper. Barely half of them ever bother to vote.

In addition to refuting the asserted values of homework, the opposition makes a big point of the health factor. Why, they ask, must a child spend four to six hours in school and then an additional one or two hours with home study? Should a growing child be asked to put in hours similar to his parents, who are normally on a 40-hour work week? What are the conditions for study? While some may have an adequate place and adequate lighting facilities, too many children must work in front of the television set with the rest of the family.

Perhaps most important of all the objections to homework is the claim that it is unfair to expect an equal amount of progress from each child. Some children have chores to do after school. One couple out of every three or four family groups is divorced. Other children have lost one or both of their parents for other reasons. Some parents who do live together are constantly fighting and quarreling. Some pupils are more capable than others; some get help and cooperation from their parents or older siblings, while other parents are openly opposed to home study.

What are some recent trends in homework?

It is seen from the foregoing arguments that homework *can* be beneficial or it *can* be quite harmful and undesirable. Can the benefits be realized while the hazards are minimized? Many school authorities believe so! The reader will recognize that most of the advantages claimed for home study are based on the premise that learning is a process of problem solving; whereas the opposition seems to assume an assign-study-recite approach to learning based on knowledge acquisition. The guidelines which follow have been used effectively by many outstanding teachers.

1. There is a trend toward the project type of assignment which requires several hours of preparation. This is a natural outgrowth of the unit structure of organization. Individuals or small groups have different assignments. These usually are started at school and then continued at home and at school until completed. In such cases one assignment may continue for a week or more.

2. There is a trend toward leaving the week-ends free from assigned school study.

3. Efforts are being made to give the child greater leeway in preparation of homework. This often is accomplished by making an assignment three or four days in advance of the due date.

4. It is recognized that a pupil should have at least one evening each week free of homework.

5. Assigned home study is becoming more activity-centered. Fewer and fewer teachers are assigning chapters to be read or factual questions to be answered for the next day.

6. Arising from a problem-solving approach to teaching, there is a trend toward greater reliance on the cooperative assignment between pupil and teacher.

7. With younger children homework is being minimized and in some cases eliminated entirely.

GENERAL PRINCIPLES ASSOCIATED WITH STUDY ACTIVITIES

In the foregoing analysis attempts have been made to acquaint the student with some of the more important problems and conditions associated with study activities. The techniques and suggestions offered should be especially useful for the beginning teacher. As one moves along, however, bringing his own techniques and innovations into play, he will from time to time find it necessary to check up on himself. Not only are conditions changing at an alarmingly rapid rate, but continuous improvement is essential. The best teacher is always in the process of "becoming." He is never completely satisfied with past performance. Therefore, the principles listed here should serve as a useful framework for guiding the learning process.

1. The key factor in the direction of study activities is the assignment.

2. Assignments are coming to be recognized as an integral part of teaching.

3. As an integral part of the classroom experience, they are made whenever class activities clearly indicate their need. There is no best time for making an assignment.

4. Assignment making, based on learning as a problem-solving experience, is a joint experience between pupil and teacher.

5. Assignments which are cooperatively given are frequently cooperatively completed, involving pupil teams and committees.

6. Assignments often are differentiated on the basis of pupil needs, interests, and abilities.

7. The evaluation of an assignment depends on the purposes served.

8. Assignments apply to both school and home study. Assignments begun at school often are completed at home.

9. School study is useful in providing needed direction in the early phases of assignment activities.

10. Guided class study provides opportunities for diagnostic and remedial work associated with study activities.

11. All children (and especially slow pupils) profit from specific guidance in "how to study."

12. The informal psyche group (clique) in part sets the limits of achievement.

13. Homework which is an outgrowth of class activities is both essential and desirable.

14. As home conditions vary widely, no equality of homework performed can be expected.

15. Whenever possible parents and teacher work together in providing for home study.

16. Competing activities demand that the student have some evenings free from study responsibilities. It has been recommended that a maximum of two homework assignments be given per week.

17. Whenever possible, assignments must foster creativity and originality.

18. The ultimate end of study activities is to prepare the child to direct his own learning.

SUMMARY

The foregoing chapter has been concerned with the major study activities of teaching. Emphasis was placed on the assignment as the vehicle for guiding and directing the problem-solving activities of children. It was noted that this represented a marked transition from a few decades ago, when the assignment was based on the acquisition of knowledge almost exclusively. This was reflected in the then popular assign-study-recite formula for teaching.

Fallacies of extensive home study were soon recognized. Children were receiving assistance in study activities from parents, neighbors, older siblings, or anyone who happened to be available. This, in effect, took most instructional responsibility from the hands of professionally trained teachers. Thus, the supervised study movement gained momentum. Homework was de-emphasized and denounced on all sides. Some school systems even succeeded in eliminating home study. Scientific investigation, however, has failed to establish the superiority of one over the other.

As the concept of the educational task shifted from that of mere acquisition of knowledge to education as a process of coping with real-life problems, the relative merits of homework also changed. It was realized that education as a process of doing and interacting with others demanded *both* school and home study. Today the nature and quality of homework has changed. Functional understandings, and the formation of relationships and associations are now considered to be worthy purposes for study activities.

Finally, a list of principles was presented for the purpose of offering continued guidance to the teacher. These principles were based on a sound psychology of learning.

QUESTIONS FOR STUDY AND DISCUSSION

1. What factors have contributed to recent criticism of class assignments? Why are common assignments for all pupils not recommended? What basic functions do assignments serve? How may effective assignments contribute to retention of that which is learned?

2. What basic assumptions are associated with guided study activities? What are some emerging trends with respect to study activities?

3. What factors tend to mitigate against homework for elementary school pupils? How can such factors be corrected? A few schools have an established policy discouraging assigned homework except on special occasions. Why? What are some recent trends associated with homework?

SELECTED BIBLIOGRAPHY

Augelita, Sister M., "Homework in the Primary Grades," *Catholic School Journal*, 60: 41 (October, 1960).

Bond, George W. and George J. Smith, "Establishing a Homework Program," *The Elementary School Journal*, 66: 139–142 (December, 1965).

Burton, William H., *The Guidance of Learning Activities*, 3rd Ed. (New York: Appleton-Century-Crofts, Inc., 1962).

Carlton, Lilyn, "Let's Do 'Our' Homework," *The Clearing House*, 36, No. 8: 492–493 (April, 1962).

Congreave, Willard, "Learning Center . . . Catalyst for Change," *Education Leadership*, 21, No. 4: 211–213+ (January, 1964).

Cutler, Marilyn H., "How Much Homework? Schoolmen Aren't Sure," *Nation's Schools*, 77: 64–67+ (February, 1966).

Dallmann, Martha, "Homework," *Grade Teacher*, 79: 36 (November, 1963).

Goldstein, A., "Does Homework Help?" *Elementary School Journal*, 60: 212–224 (January, 1960).

Van Til, William, "How Not to Make an Assignment," *NEA Journal*, 53: 49–51 (October, 1964).

Enhancing Learning:
Audio-Visual Materials and Resources

EFFECTIVE communication can no longer be considered possible with words alone. The very nature of our language, coupled with the limited experiences of most people, often makes it difficult to convey ideas and information efficiently without resources beyond words.[1]

The preceding excerpt from Jerrold E. Kemp's *Planning and Producing Audiovisual Materials* pinpoints the importance of instructional materials in the elementary school classroom. Young children with limited experience need materials and devices which will enhance their learning opportunities. Audio-visual materials, when used appropriately, are uniquely suited to the task.

THE NEED FOR AUDIO-VISUAL MATERIALS AND RESOURCES

Although some instructional materials have been used by enterprising teachers for hundreds of years, the full impact of their value is just beginning to dawn on the great majority of teachers. Certainly the unbelievably rapid progress in the direction of automation has been felt. In some instances instructional materials have appeared prior to a felt need. The use of educational television, for example, was being urged by the public prior to its acceptance by teachers generally. In some cases increased use of instructional materials has become a fad. Thus, films may be used from time to time because "it is the thing to do," "other

[1] Jerrold E. Kemp, *Planning and Producing Audiovisual Materials* (San Francisco: Chandler Publishing Company, 1963), p. 3.

teachers are using them," or "this is a mark of a modern teacher." The major impact of audio-visual materials, however, can be attributed to a new concept of the final goal of education. Teachers are beginning to realize that "The final goal of education is not memorized information; it is a changed individual, who lives differently because he has learned." [2]

There is a vast difference between facts and meanings. When learning was viewed as a process of assimilating facts for future use, audio-visual materials were of relatively minor importance. They were time-consuming, reducing the amount of factual material which could be presented. The assumption that behavior is a function of knowing the facts, however, is a fallacious one. Pupils have persisted in behaving contrary to facts. They have continued to cheat on examinations after memorizing the rule that "honesty is the best policy." They have continued to use the wrong pronoun after memorizing the rules of grammar. Despite much current public pressure to pour on even more facts, teachers are coming to realize that something is wrong. They realize that an educational system which hopes to change behavior must do much more than provide facts. It must deal with personal perceptions—with individual meaning. Meanings exist within each individual and cannot be manipulated or controlled. Thus, the teacher's role becomes one of helping children explore and discover personal meaning of events for themselves. The teacher's task, basically, is one of creating a favorable climate for learning. Bridging the gap of time and space for *personal meaning* often demands the use of a film, picture, chart, or diagram.

How is the "Cone of Experience" related to teaching for meaning?

The "Cone of Experience" (see diagram) is used by Edgar Dale, a leader in the field of audio-visual materials, to illustrate graphically the relationship of audio-visual materials as one proceeds from direct experiences to highly abstract (verbal) symbols.[3] The base of the cone represents direct, purposeful reality as we live and learn. As one proceeds up the cone, the experiences become progressively more abstract and less direct. From the level of doing or experiencing, the pupil passes to the level of observing others. Finally, at the apex of the cone, he must rely

[2] From *Audio-Visual Methods in Teaching*, Rev. Ed. by Edgar Dale, p. 11. Copyright 1946, 1954 by Holt, Rinehart and Winston, Inc. Reprinted by permission of Holt, Rinehart and Winston, Inc. For a comprehensive and practical treatment of audio-visual materials, the reader will find Dale's book most helpful.
[3] *Ibid.*, p. 42.

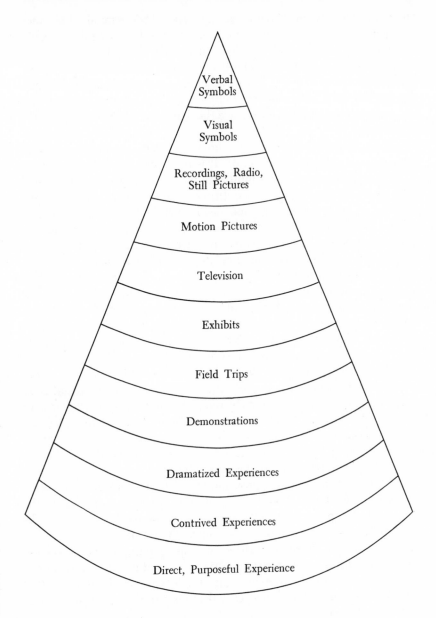

FIGURE 2. *The "Cone of Experience"*

(From *Audio-Visual Methods in Teaching*, Revised Edition, by Edgar Dale. Copyright 1946, 1954 by Holt, Rinehart and Winston, Inc. Reprinted by permission of Holt, Rinehart and Winston, Inc., p. 43.)

wholly on symbols which *represent* experience. Dale reminds the reader that the bands of the cone should not be regarded as rigid, inflexible divisions. He also reminds us that "increasing abstractness" does not mean "increasing difficulty." The bands of the cone merely help us see the experiences of learning and living in an order of increasing abstractness as one moves from direct reality. It is true, however, that as one moves further from direct experience the danger of misconceptions tends to increase.

Direct, purposeful experience is life itself. Dale refers to it as "something you can sink your teeth into." It is the "bedrock of all education."

Teachers, however, often must deal with a replica of reality. Sometimes they simulate reality by *contrived* or *dramatized* events. Perhaps the real situation is too large, too small, or too dangerous to approach directly. The Army and Air Force have made wide use of mock-ups for training purposes. Before a trainee is entrusted with an expensive airplane, he is "checked out" in simulated flights. Astronauts experience weightlessness and many other anticipated hazards of space flight before they are launched. Likewise, a model of an oil refinery plant is a contrived experience. The actual plant may be so large and complicated as to render direct experience of minimum value to the novice. A contrived experience differs from the original in size, in complexity, or both. As Dale says, it is an "editing" of reality and often is preferable to the direct experience itself. Frequently in the area of social relationships a simulated learning experience is preferable to the real thing. Mistakes in social situations can be extremely traumatic and costly in the area of human relationships. Since simulated situations are just make-believe, analysis without the usual emotional involvement is possible. Direct, contrived, and dramatized experiences are similar, in that the child copes with reality personally. He is the *actor—*the *doer.*

Demonstrations are visual presentations of things, processes, or events to be learned. They differ from contrived experiences insofar as the learner at this point becomes a spectator. A model, of course, can be used for demonstration purposes so long as the learner is an onlooker. A large model of a flower is realistic in helping pupils comprehend the space relationships of the various parts to each other. It is not the real thing, however, and this type of teaching does possess limitations. It is obvious that for certain purposes a demonstration may be superior to direct experience.

Field trips provide the learner opportunities to observe other people doing things. The learner does not have a real stake in what happens. He merely watches the scene unfold. Frequently, however, he can ask questions, ascertain facts, or otherwise participate in the chain of events.

If so, the trip provides both abstract and direct experience.

Exhibits are placed on the next higher band of the cone because they tend to relegate the learner to the role of a mere spectator. He usually has less opportunity to become directly involved in exhibits than when on a field trip. The exhibit, although a representation of reality, is usually simplified to emphasize certain aspects of the thing, process, or event.

Through *television* and *motion pictures* the learner may live an experience vicariously. People of all ages are devoting an increasing amount of time to television and films. Television can supply a dimension beyond the range of motion pictures. It can give us on-the-spot coverage of an event. Thus, the subject matter of life itself can be observed. Congressional investigations, live news broadcasts, political nominating conventions, important news, and scientific events represent but a few of the events which can now be observed directly via television. Nevertheless, such events are abstracted by the cameraman. It is he—not we—who determines what "shots" will be taken. In captivating the human interest angle *as he sees it* erroneous concepts may be formed. Important details may be omitted entirely. As so often happens, the real-life drama (as in the case of political conventions) may become dull and boring at times.

Motion pictures are considered more abstract than television because they usually omit more of the "unimportant" details. Important events may be "spotlighted," covering tremendous time and space within a short class period. Television, of course, makes heavy use of films also.

Still pictures, radio, and *recordings* are considered more abstract than the aforementioned materials simply because they represent specific aspects of a visual or an auditory experience. As Dale points out, they ". . . have been roughly classified as 'one sense' despite the fact that no experience can be so named in terms of the central nervous system." [4] The author can dramatize certain events by visual or auditory emphasis, eliminating many common distractions.

Symbols are placed at the apex of the cone because they represent the most abstract of all experiences. We have now passed from the realm of vicarious experience to abstract representations of the experience. Charts, graphs, diagrams, written and spoken words are *substituted* for the experience. They merely designate things, processes, or events. All physical resemblances to the objects or ideas have been removed—only meaning has been left. Although symbols are indeed necessary to make any form of complex communication possible, there is the ever-present

[4] *Ibid.*, p. 52.

danger of misunderstanding. "Good child," for example, will mean different things to different people. As indicated in the preceding section of this chapter, verbalization can be mistaken for meaningful learning. Symbols, of course, are normally used with every other audio-visual material represented on the cone.

How are audio-visual materials most effectively used?

The children in Miss Black's fourth grade class were making a study of the state in which they lived. Just before lunch, she announced that they were to see a movie on "The Navajo Indians," adding that "some knowledge of an Indian culture should be useful." The movie ended just in time to walk to the cafeteria. Some of the children made the following comments as they passed through the hall:

"The movie was interesting, but I wonder what it has to do with our state."

"The things the Indians did were certainly funny."

"Did you notice how they planted corn?"

"Gee, the people are poor!"

After the noon recess, the children were looking forward to a discussion of the film. Instead, Miss Black decided that "we had better do our arithmetic now." She added, "I am glad you enjoyed the film, however. We will be studying Indians later on and, since the film was available, I thought we should see it."

The foregoing anecdote is an all too common occurrence in the public schools. This is not to suggest that the film was a waste of time. On the contrary, there is evidence of a great deal of worth in the experience as it was used. Perhaps it would be beneficial to the reader if he were to stop at this point and analyze the situation, pointing out specific values, as well as the limitations, of such an experience. There is evidence that showing the film apparently aroused a great deal of interest in specific aspects of an Indian culture. It seemed to set the stage for a spirited discussion or analysis of Indian life.

Unfortunately, the audio-visual experience was based on three or four false premises. First and foremost, the teacher apparently assumed that showing the film was valuable in and of itself. She apparently assumed that the film could "stand alone." Audio-visual materials often are called *aids*, suggesting that they can only *support* (and cannot replace) instruction. Furthermore, the children were not prepared for the experience. They failed to see clearly the purposes involved. Miss Black's vague expression that "some knowledge of an Indian culture should be useful" does not indicate the *why of this particular experience at this particular time.* Moreover, pupils not only need to know *why* they are looking and listening, but they should know *what* they are looking and listening for. A few questions would have been useful. For example: "What probably accounts for the Indian contrast in clothing with that of people in our state? Why don't they farm the way we do in our state?" Perhaps the most serious erroneous assumption made was that the audio-visual experience was complete with the mere showing of the film. Pupils were stimulated to ask questions. They were *ready* for a critical analysis of the experience! The tendency to "cover a predetermined amount of material" or to hold to a rigid predetermined time schedule can stifle learning.

There are no fixed procedures for use of audio-visual materials and resources. As an aid or support for class instruction, they must be *integrated* with instructional methods and procedures. There are, however, a few useful guidelines for the use of any audio-visual experience. They include preparation, administration, and follow-through. Each of these will be discussed in turn.

What preparation is needed? The use of any audio-visual material demands preparation and planning. The teacher must ask himself if a specific audio-visual device is better than any other experience for *this* particular time. He, as well as his pupils, must clearly understand how it is to be used. A film, television program, or filmstrip should be previewed and guide questions prepared. The same principle applies to other audio-visual materials. For example, the teacher must know and prepare children for what to look for on the field trip, with a resource speaker, exhibit, or demonstration.

What administrative procedure should be followed? Unfortunately, there is no clear-cut answer to this question. In the use of any material which requires a darkened room written notes should be minimized or eliminated entirely. Frequently a film can be stopped for emphasis and discussion, or can be rerun. Likewise, the steps of a demonstration must be clearly delineated. High points of a field trip or resource presentation should be pinpointed during the experience.

What follow-through procedures are necessary? Many audio-visual materials, like other teaching methods, need a follow-through. Many times in the case of a film, demonstration, field trip, exhibit, or resource speaker the real problem-solving experience follows the presentation. "What conclusions can be drawn from this demonstration? What experiences have we had which would support or contradict the points made in the film?" The follow-through often involves critical analysis or reflective thinking. It takes time but is usually time well spent. A movie which takes 20 or 30 minutes may prompt a discussion lasting ten minutes to several hours. The example cited at the beginning of this section illustrating a use of a film might well have prompted a worthwhile discussion extending for more than one school day.

USES AND PROBLEMS ASSOCIATED WITH CERTAIN AUDIO-VISUAL MATERIALS AND RESOURCES

It is extremely hazardous to state specifically what type of experience goes with any particular audio-visual device. Many times the specific purpose will dictate the device needed. At other times the age and nature of the children will suggest what resource is needed. In some instances the particular competencies and/or preferences of the teacher will be the determining factor. Within these limits, however, specific guidelines and suggested uses may be helpful.

What functions do motion pictures serve?

Through the film we can see and hear recorded experiences from anywhere and everywhere in the world. We cannot accompany the raft "Kon-Tiki" as it drifts from Peru to Polynesia, but we can view the motion picture of that name and "live" the adventures of the journey. We may not be able to climb the Himalayas or visit the interior of Africa or the pyramids of Egypt or Mexico, but motion pictures will show us many of the significant things that the men who made them saw. Nor can all of us visit steel mills or peer through a telescope at the moon, or look into a microscope that shows the circulation of the blood. . . . But we can see all these things through motion pictures.[5]

Almost every teacher makes some use of motion pictures. Too often, however, educational films have been misused. When are they appropriate? It must be remembered that, when using a film, the pupils are spectators; they are not overtly engaged in the experience. Consequently, the experience is more abstract than direct. It has a place:

1. *As a means of creating interest* in a unit, lesson, or topic.
2. *As a review or recapitulation* of a unit, lesson, or topic.
3. *As a vicarious field trip.* Sometimes it is not feasible to take a

[5] *Ibid.*, p. 213.

school journey at the time needed. The film can provide a desirable substitute, especially if it highlights points which are consistent with the class objectives.

4. *As an accessory experiment.* The film may be especially useful in situations where the necessary facilities for the experiment are not available. Furthermore, there are areas in which otherwise competent teachers may not be qualified to conduct certain experiments.

5. *As an accessory microscope or microprojector.* Especially in the area of science, there are phenomena which cannot be readily viewed at the appropriate time through ordinary microscopes or microprojectors. Such events as the process of fertilization, cell division, and the like often fall into this category.

6. *As a problem-solving experience.* Occasionally a film may be stopped before it is completed, allowing pupils to form their own conclusions. If learning, for the most part, involves a process of continuous problem solving (as assumed in this book), the teacher will need to adjust his use of a film accordingly.

As a general guideline for the use of motion pictures, the 12 values listed by Dale [6] should be helpful. A motion picture can:

1. Present certain meanings involving motion

2. Compel attention

3. Heighten reality

4. Speed up or slow down time

5. Bring the distant past and the present into the classroom

6. Provide an easily reproduced record of an event

7. Enlarge or reduce the actual size of objects

8. Present physical processes invisible to the naked eye

9. Build a common denominator of experience

10. Influence and even change attitudes

11. Promote an understanding of abstract relationships

12. Offer a satisfactory esthetic experience.

Films as instructional devices are also subject to a number of hazards, some of which are not readily apparent. For instance, a teacher should always have a substitute lesson prepared just in case the film does not arrive as scheduled or in case of mechanical failure. He also

[6] *Ibid.*, pp. 214–221.

must select only those films which are within the comprehension range of his children.

What is the place for educational television?

"But there is in mankind an unaccountable prejudice in favor of ancient customs and habitudes, which inclines to a continuance of them after the circumstances, which formerly made them useful, cease to exit."

Benjamin Franklin

In certain respects, the uses and problems of educational television are similar to those of motion pictures. The resemblance quickly diminishes, however, when one considers television from a distance and visualizes its potential contribution to an entire school.

In summarizing ten years of research into television (sponsored by the National Educational Television and Radio Center), Kumata [7] offers the following conclusions:

1. On the basis of subject matter and short-term retention tests, no significant differences between TV and conventionally taught students were noted.

2. Motivation was seen as an important factor in ascertaining instructional television effects.

3. Superiority of television was reported more often in lower education than in higher education.

4. Increasing the size of classes, having proctors in the TV room, providing for feed-back facilities did not have any significant effect on amount learned for television students. It was noted, however, that talk-back facilities or two-way TV was not a substitute for the interaction situation. Such facilities did give students reassurance.

5. The mode of presentation, TV or face-to-face, had no differential effect upon retention of subject matter.

6. Not enough evidence had been obtained to make conclusions about the so-called "intangibles" of education, such as attitude change and gain in critical thinking ability.

On the basis of the foregoing findings, it appears that television is having a tremendous effect on the profession of teaching. Although some

[7] Hideya Kumata, "A Decade of Teaching by Television," from *The Impact of Educational Television,* edited by Wilbur Schramm (Urbana, Ill.: University of Illinois, 1960), pp. 176–185.

educators are justifiably concerned that TV may become the "tail that wags the dog," teachers must be willing to change their concepts of teaching continually as new inventions and discoveries are made. Educational television will not *replace* the classroom teacher, nor is it the most desirable tool in many situations. There is clear-cut evidence, however, that it is destined to revolutionize present-day concepts of teaching in some areas. Really *great* teachers, impossible for many school systems to acquire, can be made available to many through such a medium.

What are the most promising uses of educational television?

There are three main potential uses for televised instruction: enrichment, supportive teaching, and full teaching.

1. *Enrichment.* When used to enrich class instruction TV is similar to any other audio-visual device. It may be used to clarify obscure material, provide special illusrtations of points made in class, or amplify ideas presented. As the broadcast progresses it is wise for the teacher to place on the blackboard an outline of the concepts, points, or illustrations presented. It is desirable to use the chalkboard *during* the viewing session rather than prior to the session. Otherwise pupils, knowing what is coming, may lose interest.

2. *Supportive teaching.* The use of TV in supportive teaching is similar to that in enrichment teaching. The basic difference is in the demand made upon television in the receiving classroom. When used to *enrich* a course of study it is conceived as an auxiliary to the curriculum; when used in *supportive* teaching it may provide the bulk of classroom instruction. Under these conditions, the teacher's task is to *augment* as best he can the instruction on TV. Supportive teaching usually requires cooperative planning between the television instructor and classroom teachers.

3. *Full teaching.* Contrary to the contention made earlier in this chapter that audio-visual materials can only *support* (but not replace) regular classroom instruction, TV as a device may, under certain circumstances, assume the entire burden of instructing children in school or at home. In such cases pupils must be supervised. This responsibility, however, may be assumed by teachers' aides. Since every facet of the instructional process is in the hands of the television teacher, assignment materials, texts, and the like must be distributed well in advance of the lessons. Likewise, a guide for the classroom supervisor (instructions for distributing maps, paper, and tests, collecting homework, and so on) must be prepared in advance.

Provision also must be made for the supervisor to handle routine classroom tasks. This would include such tasks as roll-taking and handling pupils' academic problems.

Some type of "talk-back" system may be useful in closed-circuit * full teaching. Telephones, letters, written printed forms, and two-way sound systems are a few of the devices which have been used for this purpose. Again, the classroom supervisor must be thoroughly acquainted with the mechanics of the system.

In many situations it seems desirable to alternate live instruction with televised teaching. The relative amounts of each type of instruction would vary, depending on specific needs of the group.

It seems obvious from the foregoing that, if TV is to be used in *supportive* or *full* teaching, present-day concepts of the curriculum must be revised. Much resistance is to be expected, but changes have been and are being made to accommodate this revolutionary teaching device.

What are the limits of instruction via television?

Every teacher should be thoroughly familiar with the limits imposed by TV. Their seriousness will depend on such factors as facilities available, the resourcefulness of those involved, and the nature of the classes and children.

1. *Face-to-face contacts.* As previously indicated, a number of devices have been employed to overcome partially this limitation. Pupil participation can be handled indirectly through some feed-back device. For example, participation may be effected by using ideas in assignments, projects, and tests; by *discussing* with fellow *pupils;* or by following up a lesson with *individual research.*

2. *Abstract ideas.* There are times when the interaction of pupil and teacher provides about the only avenue now known to "get across" high abstractions. Furthermore, certain kinds of abstractions can become dull in the hands of a television teacher.

3. *Limitations commonly associated with other audio-visual devices.* The reader should bear in mind that television is rather "high" on the "Cone of Experience." This simply means that the medium is much more abstract than direct experience. The greater that reality is abstracted, the greater is the *possibility* of misunderstanding.

---

* Here televised instruction is fed from camera to classroom, usually by coaxial cable. Closed-circuit setups are "private" installations.

How are demonstrations used?

The demonstration is essentially a group experiment in which selected children actually do the experiment. Those who watch may suggest procedures, controls, and safeguards. Demonstrations are used in many ways:

1. As a motivation device.
2. As a technique for extending work out of class.
3. As a means of clarifying points during a lesson.
4. As a device for adding emphasis.
5. As a tool for skill development.

The problems associated with demonstrations are normally associated with all audio-visual materials. They have been treated earlier in the chapter.

How is the chalkboard used?

In essence, the chalkboard is used as a means of demonstration. It is probably the teacher's most valuable tool. When used properly it may add immeasurably to the quality of a lesson. Yet most of us have seen this common visual device woefully misused. Some teachers tend to rely heavily on verbal instruction because of actual or assumed inadequacies in the use of the chalkboard. One may feel that he is "not artistic" or "can't write or print legibly on the chalkboard." All teachers, with little conscientious effort, can use the chalkboard effectively.

Most teachers use the chalkboard to outline informal lectures and reports, clarify word meanings, spelling, and so on. Some teachers, however, fail to make full use of this teaching tool because they lack imagination or foresight as to the versatility of the instrument. A number of practical uses follow.[8]

1. *The template method.* The template is a device for drawing diagrams, symbols, and designs on the blackboard which must be accurate or drawn repeatedly. In arithmetic, for example, the teacher frequently must draw various angles; in science, he often needs to illustrate by sketching some experiment; in social studies, the teacher repeatedly needs to draw an accurate geographical boundary. Chalkboard templates

[8] Walter A. Wittich and Charles F. Schuller, *Audio-Visual Materials*, 3rd Ed. (New York: Harper & Row, Publishers, 1962), pp. 53–58.

can be made of any thin, stiff, lightweight material. Heavy cardboard, Masonite, or plywood have been used. By providing some sort of handle, the template may be held securely to the chalkboard while the outline is being traced. When not in use, templates may be hung from hooks attached to the underside of chalkboard rails.

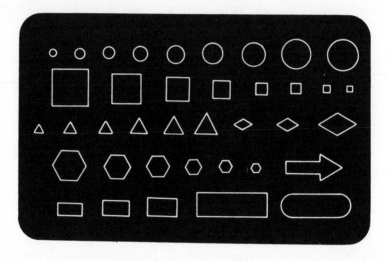

FIGURE 3. *One type of template.*

2. *The grid method.* The grid technique is amazingly simple, consisting merely of marking off the desired sketch into squares. Then the sketch is transferred to the chalkboard by duplicating the original, one square at a time. If detail is desired the original sketch is marked off in smaller squares; if relatively little detail is needed the squares can be larger. The grid technique is surprisingly rapid.

3. *The pattern method.* For basic visualizations which must be used repeatedly, the pattern method probably has no equal. In social studies, the teacher who often needs an outline sketch of the United States, or in arithmetic, the teacher who needs to illustrate line graphs repeatedly will find the technique worthy of consideration.

As a first step, an outline is drawn carefully on a heavy piece of tracing paper. Then, using a leather punch ⅛ or 3/16 inch in diameter, the outline is perforated at approximately one-inch intervals. When completed the pattern is held against the blackboard and rubbed with a dusty eraser. (The eraser should be rubbed back and forth across the perforations rather than patted.) The dots are then connected with chalk. Patterns which are used repeatedly can be mounted on windowshade rollers and filed or suspended from hooks along the chalkboard rail. Commercial

FIGURE 4. *Stick figures showing movement.*

patterns are now available for such subject areas as mathematics and geography.[9]

4. *The hidden chalkboard method.* By stretching a wire along the top of the chalkboard and hanging inexpensive cloth from the wire, a drawing can be hidden until needed. Some teachers frequently find this technique most useful when sequential material must be shown.

5. *The stick figure method.* Any teacher can make line drawings with a minimum amount of practice. As the illustrations suggest, motion can be "captured" with ease.

6. *The projection method.* By focusing an opaque projection on the chalkboard a complex diagram can be traced with ease. Different colored chalk can be used to capture detail. By varying the distance from projector to chalkboard the images are made larger or smaller. This is a technique which pupils can perform readily.

Some teachers who experience difficulty in writing legibly on the chalkboard have found printing relatively easy to master. With a little practice most teachers find that they can print on the chalkboard almost as rapidly as they can do cursive writing. Caution should be taken to attain appropriate spacing and size.

When should opaque projection be emphasized?

Many times a teacher desires to show a flat picture to an entire class. Unfortunately, this poses problems of communication. Pictures held at the front of the room seldom can be seen by children at the back of the room. When pictures are passed from one child to the next there is seldom adequate time for each pupil to study them. Furthermore, unless there are several pictures one child will be occupied while 35 other children wait.

Today the opaque projector seems to be ideally suited to the showing of flat pictures. Any picture, sketch, diagram, or even a printed page can be projected on a wall or screen directly from an open book or magazine. Most schools now have opaque projectors which can take illustrations up to 10″ x 10″ and provide 1000-watt illumination. Although some darkening of the room is necessary, it does not have to be complete.

When is the overhead projector appropriate?

Within the past few years the overhead projector has become modified into one of the most valuable instructional aids. In fact, it is one of the most versatile tools on the market. Unlike the older models, today's

[9] Corbett Blackboard Stencils, 548 Third Avenue, North Pelham, N. Y.

overhead projector is light enough to be carried from classroom to classroom. It enables the teacher to face his pupils at all times while projecting material on a screen to the back or side of him. Furthermore, the transparency overhead projector can be used in a completely lighted room.

The teacher can supplement the transparency with a number of devices and techniques to enhance interest and attention. For example, it can be used in place of a chalkboard. The grease pencil and a clean, unexposed sheet of transparency film is used in place of the chalkboard. As the teacher writes, the image is cast upon the screen. Another unique feature of the transparency overhead projector is the *revelation technique*. This technique enables a teacher to reveal projected material bit by bit. By using an opaque piece of paper as a mask, areas can be readily blocked out.

The overhead projector is not only versatile but is extremely simple to maintain. Other than cleaning the glass and replacing the bulb no part need concern the user. The bulb has a life expectancy of about 75 hours and can be changed by merely flipping it from its springboard socket.

How can resource visitors be used effectively?

Any school teacher should make full use of community resources. Perhaps the most practical and useful resource readily available is the resource visitor. Many times a class visitor is "heard" when a teacher is not. The resource visitor represents the "real thing" to children. He may be the avenue needed to help the learner visualize important practical applications of the topic under investigation. A resource visitor, however, can be an utter failure unless adequate preparation is made in advance of his visit. In the first place, the visitor must know in advance precisely what is expected of him. Also, he may need assistance in putting his message across to pupils. Many potential school visitors are not skilled in techniques of communication. Some are even fearful of speaking responsibilities. Some knowledge of the strengths and weaknesses an individual feels along these lines might, through careful class preplanning, substantially affect the outcome. As Kinder [10] points out, a resource person may lecture, talk informally, answer questions, show how to do or make something, draw or show prepared pictures, or bring to the classroom something for examination.

A few pertinent guidelines and suggestions may be beneficial in mak-

[10] James S. Kinder, *Audio-Visual Materials and Techniques*, 2nd Ed. (New York: American Book Company, 1959), p. 494.

ing the visit of the resource person pleasant and profitable to all concerned.

1. *Brief the visitor ahead of time.* A list of pupil questions is usually most helpful. Not only does such a list guide the visitor in deciding what is wanted and expected, but it prepares children with a guide for listening.

2. *Prepare the introduction.* The person responsible for introducing the visitor (this need not necessarily be the teacher) should state briefly and concisely the qualifications of the individual for the occasion. If a definite time period is desired for questions, it is wise to state it just prior to the presentation.

3. *List key questions on the board.* Even though both speaker and pupils may have a list of questions in advance, this serves to pinpoint the major problems with which the group is concerned. It also may serve to keep the speaker on the subject.

4. *Write a letter of appreciation.* Individuals who have taken time from their work to visit school should be accorded at least the consideration of an expression of appreciation. A pupil committee can assume this responsibility.

5. *Follow-through.* It is important to review with the class the important ideas or points presented. Frequently these may be compared with data from other sources.

A resource visitor *can* be a waste of time for a class, even though he is well qualified in the area for which he has been invited. Here the teacher must carefully evaluate the person on the basis of his potential to project himself to the children's level. Can he talk "in their language"? Is he likely to be understood? Does he have a tendency to stray from his topic? Does he hold any obvious biases or prejudices? Are pupil questions likely to offend or confuse him? These and other questions should be answered satisfactorily before inviting him. This sometimes necessitates a visit by the teacher. It may be that another teacher or the administrator can offer the desired reassurances.

It is important to remember that a resource visitor is nearly always a parent, relative, or friend of somebody in the class. If an experience is not very rewarding a great deal of tact may be necessary.

How are field trips made meaningful?

While few teachers would deny the tremendous potential of field trips, many seldom if ever avail themselves of this valuable teaching tool. Why is this? For many trips transportation, permissions, and a variety of other details must be arranged. Yet the field trip offers opportunities for learning which can hardly be acquired in any other way. The reader will note that the field trip has been placed near the middle of the "Cone of Experience." In many situations, however, the field trip represents direct, purposeful experience—the very bottom band of the cone. The children who are studying plant and animal identification; the class who in social studies is studying about the baker; the children who are concerned about cotton farming—all these may participate *directly* through the opportunities afforded by the field trip. In short, the field trip brings the somewhat artificial setting of formal education in direct contact with "life as it is."

There *are* problems in arranging for field trips. The nature of these problems places limits on the number of trips that can be taken. Nevertheless, most of the obstacles can be minimized through careful forethought and planning. The suggestions which follow have been useful to many school teachers.

1. *Whenever possible, let the idea for the school journey evolve from the children themselves.* Pupils who are given some freedom in directing their own learning activities often establish for themselves the need for a school trip.

2. *Whenever possible, utilize pupil committees to obtain field trip data.* In many instances the entire class need not take the trip. Groups of children living within the same general vicinity may be asked to interview certain local residents; teams can visit downtown stores; sometimes an individual child may collect the data needed.

A class wanted first-hand information on the legislature. As one child's father was a member of the state legislature, he arranged for the class to visit while the state legislature was in session. With a minimum amount of effort, different committees of pupils were excused on successive days, thus assuring adequate coverage of the special legislative session.

3. *Guide pupils in preparing a list of questions in advance of the trip.* A copy of this list should be placed in the hands of each child. If the excursion calls for the services of a guide, he too should be afforded a copy. For smalll children a list of questions should be prepared in advance, too; however, the teacher may need to review these questions with the children frequently rather than the children carrying a copy of the questions.

4. *Arrange for transportation and parents' permission and the necessary expenses.* These are details which may be worked out through general school policy.

5. *Take adequate safety precautions.* It is often advisable to organize the class into committees, making each responsible for some facet of the

journey. A teacher also takes along a first-aid kit and instructs children as to the appropriate clothing to be worn.

6. *Provide for a follow-through.* The school trip is not an entity within itself. The discussion, analysis, and/or report which follows such an experience may be more beneficial than the trip itself.

As a culmination of the trip, pupils and teacher might well *evaluate* the experience. "Did it serve our purposes? What factors did we like most? If we were to take the trip again, what suggestions would we have for improvement?"

It is evident that field trips *can* be effectively planned and executed. For best results they require careful and cooperative planning. Perhaps most important of all, they may show that classroom learning is closely related to the everyday activities of people.

In what ways may a tape recorder aid learning?

There are many ways in which a tape recorder may be used to save effort and energy as well as adding interest to the class. A tape recorder could be used in the elementary school classroom within the curriculum areas of reading, language arts, creative dramatics, speech, music, social studies, current events, arithmetic, and foreign languages. Other events in conjunction with school life could also involve a tape recorder such as PTA meetings, conventions and the like. For example, in reading readiness a tape recorder could aid the child in helping him to become aware of the variety of sounds about him, thus training him in auditory discrimination which is essential for phonics in reading. After familiar sounds, the next step would involve recording words that sound similar, such as "candy-dandy." Even in the upper grades, a tape recorder could be used to develop and evaluate good oral reading. A pupil could read the story and make a tape recording. Later, at a listening station he could replay the recording and check his own errors in the oral reading activity.

Over the past few years the tape recorder has become economical in both cost and operation; therefore, it is quite possible for each classroom in the elementary schools to have a tape recorder available at any time throughout the school day. The operation procedures are so simplified that an elementary school child is able to record and replay the tapes.

SOME SOURCES OF AUDIO-VISUAL MATERIALS

A discussion of the values and uses of instructional materials and resources would not be complete without some indication of how they may be made available to the classroom teacher. The amount of materials and resources presently available to the schools is staggering to the imagination. The problem usually is one of sifting through the multitudinous sources and selecting the most appropriate. Basically, there are two main sources of audio-visual materials: those which exist *within* the local school and community, and those which are *outside* the school and community.

Imago Photograph

Pupil participation with the tape recorder.

Utilization of the audio-visual materials and resources *within* the school and community primarily is one of initiative and imagination. The first step is to become thoroughly familiar with the audio-visual materials made available through the school. This is usually accomplished through the audio-visual department of most public elementary schools. The community itself, however, is probably one of the best single sources available for making classroom instruction realistic. Pupils generally have lived most of their school lives within a single community. Usually they can offer the first clue to worthwhile field trips and resource persons. By inquiring, investigating, and then maintaining an up-to-date file of community resources, one may be able to take the trip or invite the resource person at the appropriate time. Some system of recording an *evaluation* of community resources utilized enables one to take full advantage of experience. There are valuable community resources for *every* teacher. When his teaching begins to "drag"; when pupils become restless or bored; when the learning experiences seem to lack meaning—then it may be time to look to the community for help. Children live in a community, and they will live in a community when their formal school experiences are completed or terminated. By keeping formal education close to community living, a teacher is more likely to accomplish the basic educational goal: *to help the child do better those desirable things he will do anyhow.*

Sources of learning materials *outside* the school and community are many and varied. Perhaps the first and most important source is through professional organizations of teachers. The National Education Association, for example, serves as a clearing house for free and inexpensive materials. There are departments and commissions which serve almost all specialized areas of instruction. Through professional organizations one not only learns of audio-visual sources, but he may discover many imaginative ways of using them, based on the experiences of other teachers.

There also are many nonprofessional organizations which make materials available to teachers. Such materials were once somewhat slanted toward a particular point of view or product, and this is still true in some cases. Perhaps due to increased competition, there is much less of this sort of thing than formerly. Colleges and universities, in some cases, are extending their services in this direction. The Bureau of Educational Research at Ohio State University, Columbus, Ohio, is an example. It publishes one of the best *Sources of Teaching Materials* available, for a nominal fee. Information is provided about films, filmstrips, recordings, slides, radio and television programs, and free and inexpensive teaching aids. The National Educational Television Center at Bloomington, Indiana, is a good source for TV tapes. Another basic source is the United States Office of Education. Teachers can obtain many publications by writing the U. S. Government Printing Office. The Yearbook of Agriculture, maps from the Department of Interior, and the like are usually made available to teachers free of charge.

Sources for many flat pictures are the commercial magazines and pamphlets that are available. After the magazines are read, they are usually discarded. The teacher could request the school children's parents to send to the school these discarded magazines. The pictures could then be cut out and stored for future use. A file of flat pictures and printed materials related to units of work in the classroom could be developed from this inexpensive source.

GENERAL PRINCIPLES AND FUNCTIONS IN USING AUDIO-VISUAL MATERIALS AND RESOURCES

The foregoing treatment of audio-visual materials and resources is designed to help the teacher make full use of instructional resources. By first conceptualizing the place for audio-visual materials and then following the guidelines proposed for the use of specific materials and resources, most teachers can enhance learning. Teaching techniques, however, to be most effective, must be consistent with basic psychological principles. This section is concerned with basic principles and functions associated with the use of audio-visual materials and resources.

What basic principles apply?

The basic dimensions of all teaching are principles of learning. If an instructional tool (whether it be a teaching method or an audio-visual device) is ineffective, the basic cause(s) can be traced to misapplication of these basic principles. Therefore, let us clarify general principles which govern the use of audio-visual materials and resources.

1. No one type of material should be used to the exclusion of others.

2. Certain materials are more appropriate than others for certain types of understanding, or in connection with certain objectives.

3. Audio-visual materials and resources should be used as an integral part of teaching.

4. Careful teacher-pupil preparation of audio-visual materials and resources is essential.

5. Children must be keenly aware of the purpose(s) of an audio-visual device and must be held responsible for the data provided.

6. A follow-through is essential.

7. Audio-visual materials and resources basically are used as a substitute for direct experience.

8. Audio-visual materials and resources are used to increase powers of communication.

9. Instructional materials and resources sometimes are preferable to direct experience by modifying time and space dimensions.

10. Instructional materials and resources enhance learning to the extent that they enable the learner to increase associations and relationships.

11. The use of an audio-visual device is justifiable only when it serves one's purposes as well as any other material.

What are some of their proven contributions?

Thus far in this chapter the values of audio-visual materials have been assumed, primarily on the basis that they enable a teacher to approximate more direct, purposeful experience than would otherwise be possible. What does the evidence indicate? Does use of a film, for example, have instructional values over and above instruction *without* the use of the film? Evidence has been accumulating over a period of years. Although the greatest research interest has been shown in the area of motion pictures (and recently educational TV), it is apparent that the use of audio-visual materials may contribute to effective learning in many ways.

1. *Reduces verbalism.* Instructional devices supply a concrete basis for the conceptualization of ideas. In essence, their use appears to make wide association of ideas possible, thus contributing to the formulation of complex relationships.

2. *Increases the permanence of learning.* The basic function of all education is to prepare the learner for more effective living. It is assumed that one will be able to *apply* what he has learned to the multitudinous problems of living. Yet one cannot apply what he does not remember. It has been established that the rate of forgetting often is exceedingly rapid. How may the use of audio-visual materials minimize this factor? By building a broad repertoire of associations and relationships *at the time of learning,* retention is increased. The vividness of the experience alone frequently intensifies memory.

3. *Adds interest and involvement.* It is clear that a high degree of interest or motivation to learn is one of the best guarantees that learning will occur. Audio-visual materials and resources are ideally suited to this task.

4. *Stimulates self-activity.* By dramatizing things, processes, and events the learner is inclined to act on his own initiative. Multisensory devices may "give him the idea."

5. *Provides a uniformity of percepts.* In many situations teachers are never certain that the child sees what he is supposed to see. In science, for example, one can assume only that each pupil actually is studying what he is supposed to be studying under the microscope. Audio-visual materials can eliminate this sort of guesswork.

6. *Provides continuity of thought.* Due to the ability of some audio-visual materials to narrow time and space concepts, pupils may much more readily understand involved processes than would otherwise be possible.

7. *Provides experiences not easily obtained through other means.* What can be better than to hear an actual address of a past President of the United States? The dramatic impact adds depth, variety, and efficiency to learning.

It is seen from the foregoing that audio-visual materials, when used effectively, can contribute in many ways to the learning process. Once again, they cannot do the job alone; their usefulness rests, basically, as tools for enhancing learning.

SUMMARY

In the foregoing chapter the use of audio-visual materials and resources for enhancing learning has been emphasized. The recent emphasis on audio-visual devices was attributed to a "new" concept of learning through a process of continuous problem solving. Audio-visual materials were seen as useful in making instruction more concrete and purposeful. The "Cone of Experience" was used to illustrate the abstraction properties of different audio-visual devices. To illustrate: audio-visual materials can bring the learner in direct contact with reality—the so-called doing level; they may enable him to experience reality vicariously, through the use of his senses alone; or they may rely wholly on the process of visual and/or verbal symbols. Although these three levels of abstraction rarely operate singly, they help the teacher conceptualize audio-visual materials and resources along a continuum from least abstract to most abstract. It was emphasized that the "Cone of Experience" indicated abstraction properties only, and did not suggest that any one device was superior to any other. The worth of an instructional device was seen as a property of specific situations and purposes.

Next, three basic steps for the use of all audio-visual materials and resources were treated: preparation, administration, and follow-through.

Recognizing the diverse properties of audio-visual materials and resources, the uses and unique contributions of some of them were treated extensively. Treated specifically were: motion pictures, television, demonstrations, the chalkboard, opaque projection, overhead projection, resource visitors, field trips, and tape recorder. Television was seen as a tool which is destined to revolutionize many present-day concepts of the curriculum.

Some of the many proven contributions of audio-visual materials and resources were treated. Among the most important of these was the ability of audio-visual materials to reduce verbalism and to provide a uniform basis for percepts. Finally, some general sources of audio-visual materials and resources were indicated. Emphasis was placed on the initiative and imagination of the teacher in discovering and evaluating two general types of sources: those existing within the community, and those outside the community.

The last section of the chapter reviewed some general principles and problems associated with audio-visual materials and resources. These principles were considered basic to the use of all audio-visual materials and resources. They, in essence, sum up the case for such devices.

QUESTIONS FOR STUDY AND DISCUSSION

1. What functions are served through the use of audio-visual aids and resources? What limitations are involved? How does the "Cone of Experience" concept relate to basic reality? What limitations do you see in the concept?

2. Select and show a film. What problems did you encounter? What functions does a follow-through discussion serve? Should a follow-through discussion ever be omitted? Why or why not?

3. Educational television has been lauded as a possible replacement for the classroom teacher. Why is this highly unlikely? What major problems are associated with instruction via TV? What beneficial results seem likely?

4. What advantages are associated with such instructional resources as resource speakers and field trips? What disadvantages? What advance prep-

aration is essential for such experiences? What follow-through activities are necessary?

SELECTED BIBLIOGRAPHY

Brown, James W., Richard P. Lewis, and Fred F. Harcleroad, *A-V Instruction; Materials and Methods.* (New York: McGraw-Hill, 1964).

Dale, Edgar, *Audio-Visual Methods in Teaching*, Rev. Ed. (New York: Holt, Rinehart and Winston, Inc., 1954).

DeKieffer, Robert E., *Audiovisual Instruction* (New York: Center for Applied Research in Education, 1965).

Delaney, Arthur A., "Guidelines for Selecting, Planning, Conducting, and Evaluating Field Trips," *Teachers College Journal*, 36, No. 3: 102–104 (December, 1964).

Goldman, Edward, "A Giant in Knee Pants: Educational Television," *The Clearing House*, 39, No. 1: 45–47 (September, 1964).

Gordon, George N., *Educational Television* (New York: The Center for Applied Research in Education, Inc., 1965).

Hamm, Mabel L., "Pains and Pitfalls in TV Utilization," *Teachers College Journal*, 34, No. 6: 192–196 (May, 1963).

Kemp, Jerrold E., *Planning and Producing Audiovisual Materials* (San Francisco: Chandler Publishing Company, 1963).

Schultz, Morton J., *From the Teacher and Overhead Projection* (Englewood Cliffs, N. J.: Prentice-Hall, Inc., 1965).

Solway, Clifford, "Film, Television and Reality," *Teachers College Record*, 68, No. 3: 197–199 (December, 1966).

Taylor, I. Keith, "Educational Implications of the TV Medium," *AV Communication Review*, 12, No. 1: 61-74 (Spring, 1964).

Thompson, Frank A. and Joseph R. Koszela, "The Opaque Projector Still a Valuable Tool," *Chicago Schools Journal*, 46: 211–213 (February, 1965).

Wagner, Guy, "What Schools Are Doing—Preparing Attractive Bulletin Boards," *Education*, 83, No. 2: 124–125 (October, 1962).

Index

A

Ability grouping (*see* Individual differences)
Acceleration, 209–10
Aims of instruction, 51 (*see also* Goals)
Aims of education, 51–53
Analytical thought (*see* Concept formation)
Assignment, 333
  characteristics of, 336–37
  evaluation, 338–39
  principles, 347–48
  purposes, 334–35
  techniques, 337–38
Audio-visual aids, 351
Audio-visual principles, 372–74
Audio-visual problems, 358–70
Audio-visual sources, 370–72
Audio-visual aids, use of, 356–58

B

Behavioral Journal, 267; 300–01
Brainstorming, 108–10
  afterthoughts, 110

Brainstorming (*Cont.*)
  leadership role, 109

C

Chalkboard utilization, 363–66
Check lists, 300
Child, Elementary School, 1–8
Class control (*see* Discipline)
Class discussion (*see* Discussion, class)
Concept, 32
  attainment, 37–39
  formation, 33–39
  functions of, 35–36
  impeding factors, 38–39
  properties of, 34–35
"Cone of Experience," 352–56
Corporal punishment (*see* Discipline, questionable practices)
Creative thinking, 108–11 (*see also* Intuitive thought)
Creativity in children, 222
  identified, 222–23
  problems, 224–25
  providing for, 223–24
Curriculum guide, 75

D

Democratic procedures (*see* Teacher-pupil planning; Group processes)
Developmental tasks, 11–12
Discipline, 310
 and defiant pupils, 324–26
 and disturbed children, 317–19
 guidelines, 321–22
 nature of, 315
 problems, 312–14
 problems and principles, 326–29
 questionable practices, 322–24
 and stable children, 315–17
Discussion, 121
 class, 122–23
 class versus panel, 137
 defined, 121–23
 evaluation, 133–34
 panel, 134–46
  audience, 146
  leader, 141–42
  organization, 140–41
  participation, 141–44
 questions, mechanics of, 133
 plan, 128–29
 principles, 131–33
 problem analysis, 125–26
 problem identification, 125; 138
 problem solution, 126–27
 problem types, 123–25
 problem and principles, 147–48
Dramatic play, 160–171
 appropriate, 163–64
 problem, 165–66
 problems and principles, 171–79

E

Enrichment, 211
Ethics, affective goals, 68–70

Evaluation, 282
 functions and principles, 304–07
 standards, 283–301
Extrinsic motivation, 101–02

F

Field trips, 368–70

G

Goals
 affective, 55–57
 broad and specific, 62
 and concepts, 62–63
 cognitive, 53–55
 construction of, 63–67
 and instructional method, 60–61
 problems and principles, 67–71
 and pupil behaviors, 65–67
 psychomotor, 57–58
 relationships, 58–61
 and test items, 288–90
Grouping
 evaluation, 219–20
 goals, 216
 prepared, 215–16
 within class, 214–15
Growth patterns, 2–8
 later, 6–8
 middle, 3–6
 preschool, 2–3

H

Halo effect, 299
Homework, 344
 problems, 345–46
 purposes, 345
 trends, 347
Homogeneous grouping, 210–11
Hypothesis, 40–41

I

Individual differences, 204
  dull versus bright, 205–07; 217
  evaluation, 219–20
  flexible class grouping, 214–15
  model for class grouping, 213–22
  problems and principles, 226–28
  teacher role, 220–21
Individual interests, 100
Instructional innovations, 231
Instructional method (defined),
  28
Intuitive thought, 43–45
I.Q., 208–09

L

Learning
  and instructional methods, 28–
  30
  nature of, 17
Learning processes, 18–20
  knowledge of results, 25–26
  readiness, 20–22
  retention, 27–28
  repetition, 26–27
  reward or reinforcement, 23–24
  transfer, 24–25
  whole versus parts, 25
Lesson plan (illustrations), 128–
  29; 169–71; 195–97
Lesson planning, 90–92

M

Matrix table, 156
Measurement, 282
  evaluation of, 283–87
  functions and principles, 304–07
Motion pictures, 358–60
Motivation, 96

Motivation (*Cont.*)
  bases of, 97
  high, 107–08
  incentives, 101–02
  and leadership patterns, 104–06
  low, 106–07
  pupil, 107–08
Motives, nature of, 99–102

N

Needs
  basic, 8–11
  psychological, 8–9
  teacher aid, 9–11

O

Opaque projection, 366
Overhead projection, 366–67

P

Parent-teacher conferences, 302
Planning, 74
  lesson (*see* Lesson planning)
  levels of, 75
  problems and principles, 92–93
  unit (*see* Unit planning)
Problems
  of advocacy, 124
  fact, 124
  value, 124
  policy, 124–25
Problem solving (*see* Learning,
  nature of)
Programmed learning, 234
  constructed response type, 238–
  39
  evaluation of, 242–44
  features of, 236–40
  multiple-choice type, 239–40

Programmed learning (*Cont.*)
  problems and principles, 250–56
  steps, 240–42
Purposes (*see* Aims)

Q

Question techniques, 130–33 (*see also* Problems)
Questionnaire, 268

R

Rating scale, 297–300
Reading programs, 217–19
Reliability, 284
Report cards, 301–04
Retention, 209–10
Resource visitors, 367–68
Role playing (*see* Dramatic play)

S

Self-instructional devices, 247
  functions, 249–50
  problems and principles, 250–56
  use, 248–49
Sociogram, 158
Sociometry, 152–53
  criterion question, 153–54
  data, 154–55
  data analysis, 155–58
  data utilization, 158–60
  problems and principles, 171–79
  stability of choices, 176–77
  and teacher judgment, 173–74
Study, 332
Study, guided, 339–42
Study techniques, 343–44
Subject area layout, 80–81

T

Tape recorders, 370
Tattle-tale, 322
Teacher-pupil planning, 181
  data collection, 192–93
  defined, 183–86
  democratic bases, 182–83
  developing learning activities, 191–92
  evaluation, 193–94
  functions, 186–88
  illustrated model, 190
  misconceptions of, 188–89
  plan, 195–97
  problem clarification, 191
  problem identification, 190–91
  problems and principles, 197–202
  reporting techniques, 193
Teaching method (*see* Instructional method)
Televised instruction, 360–62
Temper tantrum, 322
Test items, 287–97
  difficulty of, 287–90
  essay, 296–97
  matching, 295–96
  multiple-choice, 291–94
  true-false, 294–95
Transfer (*see* Learning processes)

U

Ungraded school, 259–60
  assignments, 268–70
  curriculum, 261–63
  discipline, 272–73
  evaluation, 271–72
  goals, 270–71
  impact on pupils, 263–64
  impact on teachers, 264–65

Ungraded school (*Cont.*)
  model, 265–73
  problems and principles, 273–75
  purposes, 260–61
  teacher work, 266–68; 272
Unit (defined), 76–78
Unit plan (illustrated), 84–89

Unit planning, 78–79; 81–83
Unit, resource, 75
Unit, teaching, 76

V

Validity, 286–87